THE LOST PROMISE
OF PROGRESSIVISM

AMERICAN POLITICAL THOUGHT

Edited by
Wilson Carey McWilliams & Lance Banning

THE LOST PROMISE
OF PROGRESSIVISM

ELDON J. EISENACH

UNIVERSITY PRESS OF KANSAS

Published by the University Press of Kansas (Lawrence, Kansas 66049), which was
organized by the Kansas Board of Regents and is operated and funded by Emporia State
University, Fort Hays State University, Kansas State University, Pittsburg State
University, the University of Kansas, and Wichita State University

Library of Congress Cataloging-in-Publication Data

Eisenach, Eldon. J.
The lost promise of progressivism / Eldon J. Eisenach.
p.   cm. — (American political thought)
Includes bibliographical references (p.   ) and index.
ISBN 0-7006-0625-4 (cloth)
1. Progressivism (United States politics)   2. United States—
Politics and government—1865–1933.   3. United States—Politics and
government—20th century.   I. Title.   II. Series.
E743.E26   1994
973.8—dc20   93-44712

British Library Cataloguing in Publication Data is available.

Printed in the United States of America
10 9 8 7 6 5 4 3 2 1

To Emlyn and Gretchen

CONTENTS

ACKNOWLEDGMENTS

This book is the result of a long-standing dialogue between my own reading of our country and the understandings of countless fellow students of American political theory, history, and culture. In courses, conferences, and correspondence, I have been privileged to be in the company of interlocutors who have, without their knowing it, helped me to conceive and write this book.

The Progressives taught us that we owe much more to institutions—and those who found and run them—than we usually acknowledge. Those associated with *Studies in American Political Development*, especially the founding editors, Karen Orren and Stephen Skowronek, have provided fertile soil for studies like mine that seek to combine political history, theory, and institutions. The conference that they and Joyce Appleby organized at UCLA in May of 1990 was a condensed and face-to-face version of what *Studies* has done for eight years. Another conference was also noteworthy in this regard. In April 1991, under the auspices of the Conference for the Study of Political Thought and the Yale Social Thought and Ethics Program, Rogers Smith valiantly tried to bring good order to a meeting of students of American history, literature, politics, religion, and philosophy as we agonized over American identity. It was there I discovered how much I could learn from James Kloppenberg.

I owe a special debt to Telluride House at Cornell University. While serving as a visiting professor in the Government Department in 1991–92, I was one of three faculty guests at this unique student residence. Thanks to the living amenities at Telluride, I devoted the academic year to doing most of the detailed research and all of the writing of the first draft for this study. With the added inducements of students to teach, darts to play, and popcorn to eat, the setting for sustained and enjoyable work could not have been improved. To these pleasures must be added my experiences with the office staff of the Government Department, whose friendly and cooperative ways made my readjustment to Cornell so easy. Lastly, the institution that merits acknowledgment most is my family. Their wonderfully mixed response to my year away—encouragement, skepticism, and acceptance—helped me maintain both my morale and my perspective.

INTRODUCTION

Within the past generation the United States has witnessed an incredible increase in theoretical reflection about its foundations and purposes. Historians have sought to redefine our theoretical and ideological origins. Political theorists and constitutional scholars have refined these redefinitions to forge new understandings of the history of our political and legal thought. Political scientists and historians have charted new understandings of the relationship between political ideas and the mobilizing ideologies of social and political movements. Philosophers have reworked ideas of rights and revalued ideas of human agency and freedom. Reconstruction has vied with deconstruction in the discovery of alternative ways of reading our history and our theory. Feminist and multicultural scholars have exploited these redescriptions to provide new pasts and therefore new futures for women and minorities.

While much of this scholarship and reflection is tied quite directly to contemporary events and movements in our political culture, it has arisen in equal measure from deeper causes and discontents. The young John Stuart Mill perfectly characterized our society in describing his own: having "found itself out in a grievous error," it "has not yet satisfied itself of the truth" (Mill, 1986, 233). Today, the gap between the grip of public doctrines dominating our political life and the reach of theoretical reflection informing our intellectual life is so great that their respective articulators might inhabit separate worlds. From the standpoint of higher intellectual culture in America today, our reigning political ideas lack both truth and meaning—they do not explain how our society functions, they cannot provide coherent policy direction, and they are incapable of mobilizing the moral energies of the citizenry.

For Mill, the crisis of collective truth was also a crisis of personal meaning; personal identity, he thought, must be anchored in some larger system of social meaning if one is to lead a self-directed life. For us this mutual dependency is even more direct. Our *only* source of a common American identity is political; our fundamental political ideas are largely constitutive of our personal identities as Americans. If the moral and intellectual integrity of our most basic political ideas is in doubt, so, too, are its ideological products and the authority of political groupings organized around those ideologies. Disconnected from our individual, group, and common identities, the reigning public discourse appears manipulative, ritualistic, and hollow.

Such is not necessarily the case, however, in our intellectual and moral discourse in the larger intellectual culture. Everywhere in American universities and in higher journalism one finds passionate philosophical engagement and serious political reflection even as the participants and their audiences have largely removed themselves from active political participation. In an earlier period, beginning in the mid-1880s, America also experienced a period of intense creativity in our political, social, and economic theory, one also initially removed from prevailing political institutions and practices. The rise and growth of the academic social sciences and the modern university in America is the most obvious proof.[1] Other evidence is the way these new ideas were given credence and power through the simultaneous rise of a national periodical press and a nationally oriented readership. A third sign is the rapid rise of dynamic national organizations and institutions of every shape and kind—governmental, religious, educational, professional, trade, labor, women's, industrial, financial—which both embodied and enforced the ideas that gave these new institutions legitimacy, purpose, and power. When seen in combination, the new intellectual, journalistic, and organizational worlds constituted something like an alternative political order growing inside, but in deep opposition to, the prevailing one. For those in and of this new world, it constituted an alternative personal and national identity as well, one which challenged identities defined by the party system, localism, and a rights-based and legalistic constitutional vocabulary. Even as this period witnessed "the most profound and rapid alteration in the material conditions of life that human society has ever experienced" (Haskell, 1977, 1), it also underwent a comparable intellectual and even spiritual transformation. These transformations soon began to carry over into the larger political world, destroying many of its intellectual and institutional foundations. A new regime in thought began to become a new regime in power; new personal identities began to become publicly recognized and even definitive of citizenship.

The purpose of this study is to restore intellectual, moral, and institutional coherence to the new ideas and new identities called into being by Progressive intellectuals and reformers. I want to show how and why, by the eve of World War I, Progressive political ideas came to dominate pub-

---

1. See Haskell, 1977, 1–23, on ways American scholars have described this transformation.

lic discourse in America. This enterprise demands an initial focus on the *origins* of these ideas as *theory* and not on their party-political and programmatic use as ideology. A new "regime in thought" requires specialized settings and a specialized audience before it can attempt to become a new regime in a political or "constitutional" sense. Progressive political ideas had an initial intellectual and moral coherence, I argue, because it spoke first and gave voice to a culturally coherent audience, one increasingly estranged from prevailing political ideas, institutions, and practices.

In the first chapter I seek to recover this initial coherence by locating the authors of Progressive political theory, their institutional locations, and their wider audiences and connections. In the next two chapters I trace the ways in which Progressivism redefined American identity in nationalist and historicist terms and thereby devalued prevailing constitutionalist, legalistic, and party-electoral expressions of citizenship. Their historicist readings of American nationality were also "spiritualist" readings because they stressed the importance of inner belief, shared values, and active virtue in civic life. Deeply held opinions were more important than legal conformity; the informal influence of shared commitment was greater than the formal power of external rules.

In the three following chapters, I explore the content of Progressive political theory in three areas, constitutional theory and practice, the economy, and ideas about democracy and personal freedom. In each case, Progressive theorists' critique of prevailing ideas and practices and their reform alternatives are grounded in their new view of American nationality. And in all cases, a rights-based language of constitutional law, economic freedom, and political democracy is firmly rejected.

The final chapter explores a central paradox in the career of Progressive political thought in America: at the very moment of its political triumph it disintegrated as a coherent political theory and soon thereafter as a viable public doctrine. It is a central contention of this study that many of the key values, interests, and hopes of the most profound and creative of the Progressive intellectuals were *lost* with the election of Woodrow Wilson. This requires some initial clarification. From its intellectual origins in the 1880s until the victory of Wilson and the Democratic party, Progressive ways of thinking seemed to have conquered almost every major cultural and intellectual bastion in America except constitutional law and dominated every major national institution (many of its own creation) except the courts and the party system. And by the election of 1912, even the two major parties deferred to its intellectual hegemony by adopting much of the rhetoric and style of the newly formed Progressive party. Moreover, the ways in which the United States mobilized militarily and prosecuted the war in Europe seemed to confirm the victory of Progressive visions of citizenship, national destiny, and the new industrial economy. Immediately after the war, however, Progressivism suddenly seemed to have become incoherent as a political theory and demoralized as a political movement. Its leading programmatic ideas mutually subverted and destroyed each other; its earlier core constituency suddenly divided and then disintegrated; its ethnocultural message seemed to exclude more people than it included.

My attempt to explain the later incoherence of Progressivism assumes an initial coherence and a partly realized political viability. It also suggests that the ideology of liberalism (and its mirror image, conservatism) defining public doctrine after World War I originated in the incoherence of Wilsonian progressivism and has never quite recovered. This may also help to explain why the period from the 1920s to the recent past was one of stagnation in the creation of articulate political and social theory.[2] American academics and intellectuals in this period treated many of the public doctrines of the Progressives as inevitable or as self-evident and eternal. Having banished these ideas to the netherworld of "liberal consensus," they proceeded to ignore and then forget many others. And what is worse, following World War II, they attached to this consensus a traditional and abstract rights-based and constitutionalist discourse. This discourse was not only inappropriate clothing for our policies and practices, it had previously served as the mantle of the enemies of Progressivism and the organizational, cultural, economic, and social world it brought into being and which we now inhabit. The passage from Progressivism to liberalism, then, was a kind of euthanasia of articulate and contestable ideas, an implicit denial that America either needed or had them—even as America as a superpower was projecting its way of life in every corner of the world. The conservatism that developed in opposition to the New Deal was equally devoid of intellectual interest or coherence—and equally feeding on fragments of Wilsonian progressivism without knowing it.

My hope is that my analysis of Progressivism will help to clarify the "liberal-conservative" ideas that dominate our public discourse today and explain why both appear to thoughtful people as "grievous error." A further hope is that a recovery of Progressive political theory as a coherent public doctrine will provide both perspective and direction to the current historical and theoretical scholarship among academics and intellectuals who have "not yet satisfied [themselves] of the truth." Reversing John

---

2. The one major exception was in law. In the major law schools and among prominent jurists in the period from World War I to the mid-1930s there was launched a critique of American law and legal practice ranging from technical treatises on law and the economy to the constitutional role of the courts, from the psychoanalysis of the craving for legal certainty to new logic of jurisprudence. Horwitz, 1992, 145–92, and Stevens, 1983, 131–71, discuss the major legal writings and movements in this period. These are briefly discussed in my conclusion.

Stuart Mill's own search, one might say that the beginning of wisdom for today's creative social and political theorists is to rediscover "truths which [liberals] have forgotten, and which the prevailing schools of [conservatism] never knew" (Mill, 1969, 163).

To some extent this rediscovery is already taking place, albeit without much historical self-consciousness or perspective. Prominent among the new theoretical productions is the unwitting reproduction of many ideas first propounded by progressive intellectuals and academics at the turn of the century. The Progressives were nationalist to the core, and they often put forward this national viewpoint in direct opposition to an abstract "rights-based" discourse, whether expressed as individual rights, as states rights, or as constitutional formalism. On one level, this move could be read as a restriction, an emphasis on substantive national goods against universal and "value-neutral" ideas of rights. On another reading, however, their nationalism was deeply cosmopolitan precisely because the prevailing language of rights prevented the formation of common purpose and sanctioned the most narrow kinds of localism and civic irresponsibility. Read in the former mode, Progressive nationalism is a conservative contraction of the American ideal because of its emphasis on the historic community, the power of the past, and the collective disciplines and responsibilities required to achieve a common future. Read in the latter mode, Progressive nationalism is a liberating call to a larger life, an escape from an illusory individualism trapped in a polity that thwarts civic capacity and democratic purposes.

Contemporary discourse raises many of these same themes and confronts this same duality. Everywhere, it seems, one hears the words "community," "family," and "responsibility." Calls for the assertion of individual rights are increasingly replaced by calls to collective service. The Progressives raised their temple of social justice on the razed temples of "abstract rights" and "constitutional formalism." Many social and political theorists today speak a language of reconstruction in such phrases as "pragmatic liberalism" or "liberal virtues" or "liberal purposes" as the precondition for the achievement of individual rights. Naked "rights talk" is "the impoverishment of political discourse" (Anderson, 1990; Macedo, 1990; Galston, 1991; Glendon, 1991). Is this new and critical literature a contraction or an expansion of freedom? Are these calls for substantive purpose and responsible citizenship a retreat from liberalism or an extension of it? Conversely, are calls for individual rights inherently progressive, or can they, too, be ways of protecting extant privileges, prevailing practices, and hidden hierarchies? How does one distinguish a political right from a social entitlement? However these issues are formulated and resolved, it is quite clear that political claims voiced in the language of rights will increasingly need to meet substantive tests of public good before they are accorded a serious hearing. Chanting the mantra "moral pluralism" is no longer sufficient to stop discussion— even in our law schools, today's seminaries of yesterday's orthodoxies.[3]

Contemporary conservatives are even more ignorant of their Progressive legacy than are liberals, if only because so few of them have their primary home in major American universities. But political intellectuals of all persuasions today seem hesitant to claim Progressivism as a worthy inheritance. Liberals might applaud Progressives' turn-of-the-century efforts to create the welfare state but are mystified and even angered by all their talk of social justice as the collective achievement of an American "Christ ideal." Another unfamiliar (and uncomfortable) context is nationalism. A strident American patriotism verging on the worst forms of triumphalism seems an inseparable part of the democratic vision of Progressive academics and intellectuals. This national patriotism is found in the background of every Progressive critique of the prevailing political and economic system, sometimes standing alone, sometimes tied to Anglo-Saxonism, sometimes as a code word for the triumph of the kingdom of justice or of scientific sociology. Democracy, nationalism, religion, social knowledge, and the march of social justice all get mixed together in ways that equally amaze and offend the modern liberal.

Finally, there is the context of "race" or "people" conceived within a social evolutionary theory of history. There can be no American nationality without an American people. We have been wrongly taught that "social Darwinism" is inherently conservative, just as "rights talk" is inherently liberal. Progressives, from the most scientific-technocratic to the most radical-socialist, conceived of their projects as having coherence and meaning because they were located within a social evolutionary framework of history. This framework is what legitimated Progressivism's scientific status and freed it from the localism, religious sectarianism, and provincialism of competing forms of social knowledge and political guidance. And this same framework connected American scholarship to British and German thinking, providing both the ideals and the fact of a world-historical enterprise (Kloppenberg, 1986, 95–114; Mann, 1955; Stokes, 1983). Wherever one turns—feminist theory, the theology of the social gospel, theories of economic competition, consumption, and distribution, or theories of personality development and pedagogy—one confronts a social evolutionary framework within which a coherent "people" or "race" is the primary subject and agent.

Until the intellectual, moral, and institutional projects of the Progres-

3. Recent revisionary works include Glendon, 1991; Horwitz, 1992; Levinson, 1988; and Perry, 1988. Only Horwitz locates his discussion within the framework of the earlier Progressive attack on abstract rights.

sives are more fully understood, however, we can hardly begin to understand our own responses to them. This dependency flows from the simple fact that they created the institutional locations and much of the language through which liberal and conservative academics and social critics now speak. No matter how unfamiliar many of their names are today, Progressives wrote the textbooks that dominated and disseminated social knowledge for the college-educated and their auditors for over forty years. They trained the next two generations of academics—those who taught us.

To understand what Progressive academics and intellectuals taught us, then, is to understand features of ourselves and our vocations that are often unacknowledged or suppressed. The first lesson they taught is that all social knowledge deserving a hearing must be cosmopolitan in origin and national in import. A related teaching is that specialized knowledge and training is at once a call to examine critically the institutions and practices of our society, a privileged receipt of a valuable national resource, and a pledge to national service. Progressive intellectuals and academics invented a conception of citizenship that stipulated that the possession of social knowledge entailed the duty of reflecting on and articulating ideas of national public good unmediated by party, interest, region, or sectarian religion. And because there can be no democracy without the dominance of democratic citizens of this type, the only viable democracy is national democracy. And because national democracy is a substantive goal rather than a constitutional fact, universities, professional associations, and other powerful "private governments" have a special responsibility to further its attainment. All of these lessons of Progressive social science and social theory are explicit in their scholarly research, their textbooks, their popular writings, and their own political activities. They saw the university as something like a national "church"—the main repository and protector of common American values, common American meanings, and common American identities.

In recovering from his "mental crisis," Mill tells us in his *Autobiography*, he began to rediscover ideas he had previously ignored or rejected. But for Mill this rediscovery was in fact "a discovery, giving [him] possession of truths not as traditional platitudes but fresh from their source" (Mill, 1963, 175). The Progressive intellectuals examined in this study were, in this respect, something like Mill. Many of their most fruitful ideas were reformulations and reworkings of American traditions and ideas which the America of their day had ignored, rejected, or forgotten. Their journey of rediscovery/discovery often meant leaving America in order to find it. My own rediscovery of what they found has, in turn, been something of a discovery. What I found was not lost truths so much as forgotten ways of constructing social knowledge that integrates meaning and truth.

1

PROGRESSIVISM
AS NATIONAL REGIME

Between the last decades of the nineteenth century and the start of
the First World War, the United States underwent a profound series of
changes. Political institutions witnessed the most obvious forms of
change. Up to the beginning of the 1890s, political parties ruled almost
without challenge, dominating political communication and policy
agendas, organizing the electorate, and dictating to office holders, both
elective and appointive, the public policies to initiate, legislate, administer, and adjudicate. By the eve of World War I the system of nationally
competitive political parties dominating our political culture lay in ru-
ins. The effects of hostile regulation, changing voter values, alternative
means of political expression, and centers of public power outside the
system of electoral politics combined to transform the relationship of
the citizen to government. (Bledstein, 1976; Burnham, 1970; Kelly,
Harbison, and Belz, 1983, chaps. 19 and 21; McCormick, 1986, chaps.
5 and 9; McGerr, 1986; Skowronek, 1982; and Wiebe, 1967, chaps. 5
and 6). Although this story has been told often and well as originating
in the electoral realignment of 1896, perhaps the most cogent description of the momentous shift in regime norms and practices is given by
Martin Shefter:

> For each of the major institutional reforms of the Jacksonian era,
> the Progressives sponsored an equal and opposite reform. The Jack-
> sonians had increased the number of executive offices subject to
> popular election; the Progressives sought to reduce that number
> and to create the position of chief executive through such reforms
> as the short ballot and the strong mayor plan of municipal govern-
> ment. The most extreme version of this strand of reformism—the
> city manager plan of government—removed even the position of
> chief executive from direct popular election. The Jacksonians ex-
> tended the franchise; the Progressives contracted it through regis-
> tration, literacy, and citizenship requirements. The Jacksonians
> established party conventions to nominate candidates for elective

office; the Progressives replaced them with primary elections. The Jacksonians created a hierarchical structure of party committees to manage the electorate; the Progressives sought to destroy these party organizations or at least to render their tasks more difficult through such reforms as nonpartisan municipal government, and the separation of local, state, and national elections. Finally, the Jacksonians established a party press and accorded influence to the political editor; the Progressive movement was linked with the emergence of a self-consciously independent press (magazines as well as newspapers) and with muckraking journalists.[1]

WOMEN

As the male electorate was being demobilized and their party leaders stripped of power and prestige, women were being rapidly mobilized, at first and necessarily outside the party-electoral system, in the Prohibition movement beginning in the 1880s, and, as parties became weaker and other forms of political power became stronger, increasingly inside the political system as organizers and activists for family-oriented issues. But whether possessed of the vote or not, beginning in the 1890s, politically active women and their male allies became leaders, publicists, and sponsors of an avalanche of local, state, and national legislation regarding child and female labor, compulsory school attendance, the age of female consent for sex and for marriage, food safety, housing conditions, and prostitution.

That women played these roles before they could vote (woman suffrage did not exist east of the Mississippi River until 1915) attested to the increasing effectiveness of "nonparty" or "antiparty" politics and to the responsiveness of elected officials to pressures from outside the party-electoral framework. The clearest symbol of the strength of this new system of "postparty" politics (Silbey, 1991, 237–54) is prohibition. Having its origins and first successes in the pre–Civil War North, the issue was revived in the 1880s and 1890s. The victories were dramatic: by 1900, thirty-seven states had local option laws; by 1906, 40 percent of the population lived in dry areas; in 1913, Congress had enough votes to override Taft's veto and banned interstate shipments of

1. Shefter, 1978, 232. An excellent recent summary of writings on the stalemate party regime period of the late 1870s through the mid-1890s is Skocpol, 1992, 67–88.

liquor into dry states.[2] Taft's stand was dictated more by his concern for the Republican vote in the Midwest than by a commitment to laissez-faire: three years earlier, he had signed the Mann Act prohibiting the interstate shipment of prostitutes.

Most of these Progressive reforms were the direct result of legislation, altering the power relationships between political institutions, organized interests, and the electorate and regulating the behavior of individuals, business organizations, and public officials. As important as these directly mandated changes were—many were only symbolic and others were weakly enforced—there were equally important innovations in the voluntary institutional expression of new values and new collective purposes projected on a national scale. Women, for example, not only organized nationally as issue-oriented pressure groups (Women's Christian Temperance Union [WCTU], 1879; National American Woman Suffrage Association, 1890; College Equal Suffrage League, 1908; National Woman's Party, 1916), they also created national institutions that expressed and anchored their particular identities as women. The General Federation of Women's Clubs (1892) and its black counterpart, the National Association of Colored Women (1896); the National Consumers' League (1899); the National Women's Trade Union League (1903); and the Young Women's Christian Association (1906) all gave national focus to previously local activities and provided the base from which to organize and expand throughout the country. When one adds the Settlement House and Charity Organization Society movements, both well established and thriving in the early 1900s, it is apparent that a national infrastructure of leadership, communication, and organization for political issues of interest to women was coming into place at the turn of the century.[3]

2. Kelly, Harbison, and Belz, 1983, 475–77; Greene, 1984, ''Temperance and Prohibition''; Clark, 1976, 101–13; and see Timberlake, 1963. On the place of prohibition in the Progressive movement, Boyer, 1978, 195–98. Congress sent the amendment to the states in late December 1917 and it was ratified by January 1919 by an aggregate state legislative majority of over 80 percent—hardly an expression of either postwar bitterness or the revenge of the rurals. As early as 1887, twenty-seven state Republican platforms urged some form of prohibition and only one platform opposed any form (Buenker, 1978, 172).

3. Cott, 1987, 23, 33, and 53; Bliss, 1908, 1308, for statistics on women's clubs; and see Skocpol, 1992, 323–40, 350–54. See Davis, 1984, 194–217; Skocpol, 1992, 343–50; and Trolander, 1987, 3–21, on settlement house movements and Progressivism; and Boyer, 1978, 143–61, on charity organizations. Although all of these organizations transmitted political ideas to their members and most supplied leaders for Progressive political reform activities and, later, the Progressive party, other new women's organizations formed at this time expressed less directly concerns of identity and self-expression. Within a four-year period beginning in 1900, the

CHURCHES

If women as political actors symbolized a new kind of national politics, so, too, did churches, clergymen, and active Christian laymen. Like women, throughout the nineteenth century, churches and "parachurch" organizations (e.g., charities, home and foreign mission societies, tract and Sunday school movements) were outside the party-political system, even though denominational affiliation and religious style had a marked effect on nineteenth-century partisan loyalties.[4] Although the abolitionist movement and the Whig, Liberty, and American party origins of the Republican party were clearly expressions of northern evangelical Protestant values, this inclusion was weakly institutionalized and quickly became subordinated in the Republican party, first to military victory and then to electoral victories based on coalitions of local and sectional interests (Frederickson, 1965; Gienapp, 1987; Keller, 1977, 1-121; Kelley, 1979, 187-261; Kleppner, 1970; and Walters, 1977). Prior to the Civil War, Protestant churches had even developed large national networks of ecumenical organizations and publications—later termed "the evangelical united front" (Foster, 1960)— but, again, only with the demise of party and with their own huge expansion in resources, did the churches become national political forces in their own right. Spurred on by the New Theology and the social gospel, evangelical Protestantism rapidly expanded its power and reach through its thriving system of universities, colleges, divinity schools, and its newly formed city and state federations, culminating in 1908 in the founding of the Federal Council of Churches of Christ in America. New parachurch organizations were also created or expanded at this time: Christian youth and student movements, settlement houses, mission training societies, and a host of social action organizations are the most prominent. One such set of institutions, southern Negro colleges and secondary schools established by northern mission societies, simply replaced the federal government in the South in the function of training freedmen for leadership in their communities. By

---

Daughters of the American Revolution (DAR), the Colonial Dames, the National Society of U.S. Daughters of 1812, and the United Daughters of the Confederacy were organized (Grimes, 1980, 91).

    4. Jensen, 1971, and Kleppner, 1970, show this electoral relationship up to the election of 1896. The point made here is that with the decisive victory of the Republican party, the decline in turnout, and the demise of party competition in the East and Midwest, the religiously based institutions of evangelical Protestantism came to play direct roles in political life quite outside the party-electoral framework. See Clubb, 1978, 61-79, for post-1896 effects on party organizations and strength.

1914–15, eighty-five schools and thirty colleges served more than 30,000 students (2,500 in college and professional programs) with a combined faculty of more than 2,000, of whom 60 percent were black.[5] Many clergymen and Christian laymen began working outside and even against the organized churches as evangelists for urban reform, Christian Socialism, and cooperative movements.[6]

UNIVERSITIES

Parallel to the growing institutional power of women and evangelical Protestantism and the reform issues they espoused was the organization of specialized knowledge as a political force outside of the party and electoral system. Symbolized by the founding of Cornell in 1867, of Johns Hopkins in 1876, and of the University of Chicago in 1891 and by the rapid growth of the state universities in the Midwest, specialized graduate instruction quickly became a major component of higher education, setting the standards for both the organization of disciplines and how they were taught. With the addition of Ph.D.-granting graduate schools at the older universities (Columbia, 1880, Harvard, 1890, Wisconsin, 1892, Princeton, 1901, Illinois, 1906, California, 1909, Michigan, 1915) the numbers of graduate students expanded from fewer than 900 in 1885 to 2,382 in 1890, 5,832 in 1900, and 9,370 in 1910. Undergraduate enrollment growth was also rapid, from just over 150,000 in 1890 to 237,000 at the turn of the century to 600,000 shortly after World War I.[7] Fueled by generous state legislators in California and the Midwest and by vast infusions of money and logistical support from private philanthropy, major national universities were

5. McPherson, 1975, Appendix B, 409–16. For purposes of comparison, in 1903 the state university of Alabama had 396 students, Louisiana, 400, Mississippi, 260, North Carolina, 651, and South Carolina, 215 (Bliss, 1908, 426–27).

6. Kuklick, 1985, chaps. 13–17, on the theological underpinnings of social action; Handy, 1984, chaps. 4 and 6, on the social gospel and Progressivism, and 147–51 on the creation of ecumenical federations of "cooperative Christianity" in the period 1890–1908. Hopkins, 1940, on the theology and organizational structure of the social gospel movement. Dombrowski, 1936; and Dorfman, 1949, vol. 3, chap. 5, on the relationship among popular radicalism, the social gospel, and Christian Socialism. Boyer, 1978, chap. 11, on the downplaying of churches and clergymen in the urban reform revival of the 1890s—even by clergymen—in favor of laymen-led organizations that would cut across denominations and avoid sectarianism.

7. Mills, 1964, 69; Oleson and Voss, 1979, xii. The contrast to Germany is striking. Germany rapidly expanded social welfare programs in this period, but kept access to higher education strictly limited (Heidenheimer, 1981).

created in this period.[8] In 1900, five universities (Harvard, Columbia, Johns Hopkins, Chicago, and California) conferred more than half of all doctorates; almost 90 percent of doctorates were awarded by the fourteen charter institutions of the American Association of Universities founded that same year. At the end of World War I, five private universities (Chicago, Columbia, Cornell, Harvard, and Yale) accounted for almost half of the national total, while three public ones (California, Illinois, and Wisconsin) accounted for about one-sixth. Along with university expansion and reorganization was the foundation of professional associations and journals, especially in the newly created social sciences. These associations and their allied journals were powerful engines for political critiques and reforms, providing ideas, organizational resources, and networks. Following the founding of the American Economic Association in 1885 and the American Academy of Political and Social Science in 1890, the philosophers (1901), the sociologists (1905), and the political scientists (1906) quickly established professional groups. Both the professionalization of disciplines and the reorganization of universities were supported through new private foundations that supported research projects, created research bureaus, and funded organizations that linked these new universities together.[9]

JOURNALISM

All of this institutionalization would not have had the decisive political effects it did unless it created strong bonds of loyalty and purpose within and between these new national organizations. Moreover, even granting the consolidation and élan of these institutions, their internal energies and external ends could not have been successfully projected into the larger social and political world without extensive networks of communication and publicity independent of and often in opposition to existing centers of authority and power. To some extent, abolition-

8. In 1899 alone, the thirty-four largest gifts for public causes totaled $80 million, of which $55 million was pledged to higher education. Oleson and Voss, 1979, xi. Between the late 1890s and the mid-1920s, the endowments of the national universities increased dramatically: Johns Hopkins, from $3 to $24 million; Yale, $4 to $58 million; Columbia, $9 to $63 million; Harvard, $10 to $86 million (Mills, 1964, 45).

9. Bledstein, 1976; Barrow, 1990, 122, on production of Ph.D.'s, and chap. 3, on the role of Carnegie and Rockefeller funds in university reorganization through the creation of the Carnegie Foundation for the Advancement of Teaching and the General Education Board; and Mills, 1964, 67–73, on numbers of Ph.D.'s and the founding of graduate schools and professional organizations, and 43 on expansion of endowments.

ism, mugwumpery, and the standing ecumenical establishment had bequeathed a sizable post–Civil War literary and journalistic legacy, but its New England religious and political provincialism required a massive overhaul and the infusion of much new intellectual and financial capital to meet new national conditions and serve new national purposes. The specialized journals and reviews are too diverse to warrant mention here, but some of the older denominational organs such as the *Independent* and *Outlook* are noteworthy because in the 1880s and 1890s they became general-purpose weeklies with large advertising revenues and circulations. Thanks to the generosity of the McCormick and Armour fortunes, Chicago began to challenge New York and Boston as an intellectual center with two successful weeklies on these same lines.[10] When one adds the readers of the venerable *Chautauquan* of the Methodists and of the Disciples' *Christian Century* to this list, a huge portion of a national reform constituency was created and consolidated. These weeklies were supplemented by a rash of popular and inspirational novels connecting personal piety, social ethics, and national reform. Edward Bellamy's *Looking Backward* of 1888 and Mrs. Humphrey Ward's *Robert Elsmere* of that same year were best sellers. The urban moral awakening of the 1890s was expressed in a series of popular novels. The social gospel theologian Washington Gladden (*The Cosmopolis City Club*) and the radical editor and journalist Benjamin Flower (*Civilization's Inferno*) each had their novels published in 1893, setting the stage for William Stead's *If Christ Came to Chicago*, published two years later. This best seller spawned many imitations, including one in 1896 by Charles Sheldon, a Congregational minister from Kansas. *In His Steps* sold over two million copies.[11]

The major journalistic innovation of this period was the formation of mass circulation monthly magazines. These new monthlies created a voracious demand for material and provided new opportunities for ambitious reform-minded poets, fiction writers, and intellectuals to spread their ideas, gain a certain measure of celebrity, and in the process, even get rich. Beginning with the *Century* in 1881, and followed by *Cosmopolitan* (1886), *Scribner's Magazine* (1887), and *McClure's*

10. Mott, 1957, 367–79 on the history of and contributors to the *Independent*; 1957a, 422–35, on *Outlook*; and 1957a, 292–94, on Armour- and McCormick-funded publications. Jacob Riis, Booker T. Washington, Theodore Roosevelt, and Edward Everett Hale all published their autobiographies in *Outlook* before publishing them as books. The Progressive economists Richard T. Ely and Franklin H. Giddings both wrote for the *Independent*, with Giddings serving on its board.

11. Mott, 1957b, 280–81; Boyer, 1978, 169–87, passim, for discussion of the novels by Gladden, Flower, Stead, and Sheldon in the context of urban reform movements.

(1893), these magazines soon battened on ever-increasing circulation and advertising. *Century* and *Scribner's* each had more than a hundred pages of advertising per issue by the late 1890s; both *Cosmopolitan* and *McClure's* had equivalent advertising and even larger circulations, with the latter approaching half a million and the former passing a million in 1906.[12] Whereas these magazines appealed to both men and women, two other late-nineteenth-century magazines, *Ladies Home Journal* and *Woman's Home Companion*, were aimed especially at women and regularly featured the leaders of Progressive causes in their articles and columns. The *Ladies Home Journal* sold over two million copies each month by the end of World War I, becoming the most lucrative magazine in the world.[13]

ECONOMY

These national networks of communication and these new ways of organizing politically active publics would not have been possible without changes in the organization of the economy. National railroad transportation, national advertising, rapidly rising personal income for the increasingly urbanized middle classes, and the consolidation of both finance and production made possible the creation of economic organizations, markets, and constituencies to challenge locally based political parties and economic activities as the source of power and direction. Indeed, the huge business, financial, and labor organizations were themselves autonomous sources of political power and loyalty.

When the newly formed labor federations and trade associations and the interlocking connections between investment banking and industrial sectors are taken into account, it is apparent that locally oriented political and economic systems could neither accede to the demands of the large organizations nor wholly withstand their blandishments. Given decentralized political authority and locally based but transjurisdictional political parties, the stage was set for a self-sustaining and mutually beneficial system of corruption. National business corporations and railroads were systematically blackmailed and fleeced by state and local governments exercising their police powers to protect

12. Mott, 1957b, 457–80, for history of and contributors to *Century*; 480–505, for *Cosmopolitan*; 589–607, for *McClure's*; 717–32, for *Scribner's*. In 1904, *McClure's* boasted to its readers that its authors of investigative articles engaged in extensive research to back their findings and that they were paid a minimum of more than $1,000 and often up to $2,500 per story.

13. Mott, 1957b, 536–55, for history of and contributors to *Ladies Home Journal*; 756–72 for *Woman's Home Companion*. The editor in this period was paid more than $100,000 per year.

small-producer capitalists and local realty interests. The party organizations would, however, for the right price, arrange favorable environments across these jurisdictional boundaries to create economies of scale in production and marketing.[14]

At the national level, accommodating all of these competing interests was of such an order of complexity—simply bargaining over tariffs became more than Congress could handle by the early twentieth century—that major financial and industrial policies were by default set in the federal courts. Indeed, at the beginning of this period, the power of the president and the administrative capacity of the executive branch were so deficient (and deliberately so, given the power of political parties) that even the generation and diffusion of social and economic statistics were often beyond its level of competence. Thus, to coordinate and regulate transport, business and finance, foreign trade policy, and labor-management relations at the national level required much more than the political will to respond to powerfully voiced demands: it required the reconstitution of the national state, a reconstitution that could be created only in opposition to the prevailing system of parties and lawyers and courts.[15]

Exceptions to this description of the national political system can be produced—for example, the Civil Service Act of 1883, the Interstate Commerce Act of 1887, and the Sherman Antitrust Act of 1890—but close examination of their provisions and enforcement only confirms the power of party, section, and locality. That federal appellate courts regularly intervened in national regulation was less a testimony to their autonomous power than to the incapacity of Congress to agree on clear standards. Only in the decade preceding our entry into World War I and in the bureaucratic legacy of that war can one discern "the creation of the American state" as permanent and quasi-autonomous institutions (Skowronek, 1982).

14. Keller, 1977, 319–42, 384–94, and 409–38; and McCormick, 1986, 311–55. Charles Evans Hughes, governor of New York and, later, justice of the Supreme Court, remarked somewhat ruefully that while "apology is sometimes made for these methods as necessary for the protection of enterprises against reckless and blackmailing assault . . . the security of business in this country cannot depend upon the debauching of legislators and the perverting of administration." Hughes, 1910, 105; see also Croly, 1909, 353, on corporations preferring state to central regulation because this was "the cheapest form of blackmail they could pay to the professional politicians."

15. Skowronek, 1982, part 2; Keller, 1977, 289–438; Orloff, 1988; and Orloff and Skocpol, 1984, on the lack of administrative integrity and capacity to explain the late arrival of the welfare state and national social spending generally when compared to developments in Britain and other major European countries.

INTERNATIONALISM

A more convincing exception lies in the area of foreign policy—the one area constitutionally reserved to the national government and reposed largely in the federal executive. Although subject to the pressures of party and congressional patronage, foreign policy provided the one area where "state building" could proceed earlier and faster than in domestic areas. War, in particular, contributes to "the health of the state," and, in the American context, the clear beneficiary was the presidency. The executive was able to wrest power from Congress and professionalize the foreign policy and trade bureaucracies (Becker, 1982; Rosenberg, 1982, 52–54). A dramatic symbol of this rapid expansion of executive authority is the budget for the United States Navy. Expenditures rose from $13 to $22 to $55 million in the years 1880, 1890, and 1900—and then doubled again by 1906. In this same period exports increased much faster than either population or gross national product (GNP), from $13.50 to $20.41 per capita between 1890 and 1906 (Bliss, 1908, 969). In short, the governmental units that most rapidly began to institutionalize "state" norms and transcendent national values were those that were already somewhat removed from party control because they did not directly impinge on the network of local and regional interests.

Running parallel to and even preceding these "nationalized" governmental institutions was the rapid expansion abroad of American financial, business, and religious organizations. By the early 1890s, more than five thousand American and Canadian missionaries (60 percent women) were serving overseas. The Student Volunteer Movement (SVM) for Foreign Missions, begun in 1888 by a young Cornell graduate as a recruiting and support group, signed up in one year six thousand college students who pledged to become foreign missionaries. At this same time investment banks actively began seeking foreign outlets for U.S. capital. As soon as the gold standard issue was resolved at home, direct investment abroad quadrupled between 1897 and 1914, reaching an annual rate of $2.6 billion. Technologically advanced and vertically integrated industries shared in this overseas expansion, often quite independently of government support or sponsorship.[16] A prescient article, "The American Invasion of Europe," appeared in a 1901 publication of the American Academy of Political and Social Science,

16. Rosenberg, 1982, 29, on SVM; Handy (1984, 115) estimates that the Student Volunteer Movement placed a total of more than 20,000 foreign mission workers by the early 1940s. Rosenberg, 1982, 25–26, on investment banks; and see Becker, 1982, for the general relationships of business to U.S. foreign policy in the period 1893–1921.

recounting the attempted expansion of American urban transit and railroad companies into Paris, St. Petersburg, and southeast England.

Both organizationally and culturally, the institutions that consciously articulated and enforced claims of a national public good were established largely outside of formal governing institutions and in direct opposition to the most powerful informal governing institution of them all—the mass-based political party. Put in a slightly different way, many of these nongovernmental organizations, like the political parties they were beginning to supplant, took on the characteristics of ''parastate'' institutions; that is, they claimed to speak for and to establish on a voluntary basis what they claimed to be the collective ends of the national community. Their leaders, spokesmen, and supporters often saw themselves as the ''authentic nation'' exercising higher forms of citizenship. Whether expressed in the religious language of ''Christianizing America,'' the moral language of ''the new social ethics,'' the social science language of ''the evolution of industrial society,'' or the corporatist language of ''economy and efficiency,'' a new and national public doctrine was coming into being in and through these parastate institutions. And as this new public doctrine gained credence and power, it both weakened and transformed the roles of parties and elections and their allied governing institutions, especially legislatures. In short, the cultural, intellectual, and institutional basis for a new political regime was being created.

AN INSTITUTIONAL UNDERSTANDING OF REGIME CHANGE

New political regimes do not just happen any more than old regimes quietly fade away. Regime changes are born of conflicts of power, of ideas, and of institutions. In America, two regime changes issued from the wars of 1776 and 1860, both of which could legitimately be called revolutionary wars. But even ''electoral revolutions'' in the form of massive voter realignments bear revolutionary features insofar as they are followed by dramatic shifts in institutional power and public policy. Every regime change has clear winners and losers, both at the level of power and policy and at the level of regime-legitimating ideas. From an institutional and regime-change perspective, then, the issue of whether there ''really was'' a Progressive movement and whether that movement had coherence is really misplaced. We would literally be incapable of a coherent description of twentieth-century American society—its political, cultural, and economic institutions and practices—without already utilizing the new discourse and doctrines that brought it into being.

Therefore, rather than add another voice to an increasingly convoluted and often frustrating conversation regarding the meaning of Progressivism,[17] I proceed in this study from quite another standpoint. My primary operating assumption is that institutional relationships, practices, and purposes define political orders and distinguish one political regime from another. A second assumption is that the period beginning roughly in the 1890s and continuing until World War I witnessed the establishment of a new regime in the sense that these new institutions and practices overcame and displaced many of the institutions and practices of an earlier regime. Both the institutions defended by the old regime—local democracy, local economy, national courts, and coalitional political parties—and the attacking institutions of what became the new regime represented distinct sets of social and economic interests and cultural, moral, and religious values.

These opposing interests and values were not merely *represented* by institutional conflict, however, as if institutions are external to those interests and values. On both sides of this conflict competing interests and values had to legitimate the power and purposes of their respective institutions and practices. But the only way justification or legitimation of these institutions and practices can take place in a democratic political forum is in the form of a coherent "discourse" that mobilizes followers and empowers the leaders through their respective institutions. The creation and articulation of this institution-legitimating discourse (most clearly evident in the case of new institutions and values challenging the existing ones) also serves to constitute or "found" these institutions and, insofar as its creators and adherents are loyal to them, to constitute or at least transform the identities and actions of the people in them. To understand the political meaning of this period from an institutional perspective, then, requires an exploration of that political language—or discourse—which came to constitute the institutions, personal identities, and practices of what we now call Progressivism. And insofar as Progressivism weakened, demoralized, and even destroyed key institutions of the previous regime, it subordinated and devalued the ways of life or "practices" constituted in those older institutions. Therefore, to understand the language of Progressivism also requires an exploration of its opponents' discourse: When and how was the previous regime constituted both as institutions and practices and as a legitimating discourse, an authoritative public doctrine?

---

17. Two recent summaries of the literature framing this discussion are Rodgers, 1982, 113–32, and Sarasohn, 1989, vii–xvii.

This task is both inherently difficult and additionally complex for reasons that are unique to America. There is a tacit assumption in our culture that we have always had only "one" political order, most assuredly since the Civil War, quite certainly since the Constitution, probably since the Revolution, and possibly since the earliest colonial period. Because our identity as Americans is grounded almost exclusively in political values and political institutions—what else do we have in common?—to speak in regime terms is risky if it impeaches our core identity as Americans. Thus, there is a sort of cultural and psychological imperative to see our history as "seamless"—one political era merging into another, foreshadowed and even destined to become what each becomes—precisely to give coherence and continuity to our own identities and futures as Americans. We each have a very personal stake in our political "founders"—whoever they may be—and in the ideas we see them as embodying. We each also have a very personal stake in particular political and social institutions and practices that these people "founded," and for the same reason.

This identity imperative remains true even when we read our history as seamless in another sense, as a recurring cycle of redemption and declension, a constant battle between the forces pulling us into old world (or capitalist or advanced capitalist) corruption and those seeking to reclaim our original promise. Thus, whether history is read as ritual (the ongoing march of free institutions and democracy) or as jeremiad (the recurring battle of democracy against its enemies) a present identity is created and sustained, and simultaneously, a standpoint for political values is provided. And from either direction, the onward march as ritual or the dialectical progression as jeremiad, every act of opposition to or denial of present institutions and practices is a reaffirmation of some *other* set of institutions and practices as the grounds of our identity and the guide to our practices.

Our identities as Americans are therefore located primarily in political *narratives*—in histories and prophecies—and not in abstract theories. Because each of us exists in time, we experience ourselves as coherent because we envision a past, a present, and a future. But if our *shared* identities as Americans, our tickets of entry as equal members into a "people," are largely constructs of political narrative, then an attack on *some* identity-constituting institutions is an attack on some members' identities, and therefore on their claims to self-respect and equal membership. This attack is a necessary part of the struggle for the public recognition of new values, new institutions, new practices, and new identities. It is no wonder, then, that under the guise of agreeing with each other because we have always belonged to "one" common political order, Americans can engage in such deep political conflicts over the meaning of that order and that our politics is so often a thinly disguised *Kulturkampf*.[18]

Every attack on a given political discourse, a given horizon of meanings, a "prevailing ideology," is also a call to ground identity and personal meaning in another discourse, another horizon, another "ideology." Thus, to take a contemporary example, even when the most radical of feminists take to task the American revolutionaries, the abolitionists, or the New Dealers because of their lack of concern for gender equality, the "us" betrayed by "them" is, for all that, still an American us, an identity grounded in a political founding, a particular narrative of identity and meaning.[19] Now it is possible, at least for some intellectuals, to avoid all this Americanist entrapment and step "outside" the problem by grounding their identities in objective social science, or in Kantian philosophy, or in Western culture, or in Marxist revolution, but the cost of this move is an effective loss of citizenship, a

---

18. Buenker, 1978, uses this term in a chapter title to describe urban moral reform efforts. The ethnocultural explanations of party conflict, Jensen, 1971, and Kleppner, 1970, and the larger attempt to write our political history from a cultural perspective, Kelley, 1979, make this feature central to their arguments.

19. The recent historiographical struggle over retroactive inclusion in "the Progressive Era" is most germane here. The strategy is first to deny that such a thing as "a progressive movement" with a clear identity actually exists. This assertion dilutes or reads out the foundational role of northern WASPs. "The Progressive Era seems to have been characterized by shifting coalitions around different issues, with the specific nature of those coalitions varying on federal, state, and local levels, from region to region, and from the first to the second decade of the century" (Filene, 1970, 33). This many-sidedness in action is mirrored by a lack of programmatic coherence and even consciousness: "Urban liberalism [in the Progressive era] was not the result of a systematic program . . . [it was] the sum of countless positions taken by thousands of legislators . . . shaped by the cross pressures of social change, partisan politics, and legislative in fighting" (Buenker, 1978, 206, and see vii-ix; see also Sarasohn, 1989, vii-ix, and note 21 below on Rodgers). Then, having foreclosed the possibility of a victory of one particular way of life against other ways of life, the next step is inclusion of everyone into this now nonexistent Progressivism. "Fifty years of intensive investigation have failed to establish any consensus on the precise meaning of that elusive word." "Until recently most accounts of the Progressive Era, either explicitly or by implication, have excluded the urban, immigrant-descended working class from participation" (Buenker, 1978, vii and 198). "Twenty-five years ago . . . the concept of a progressive movement was first beginning to dissolve under scrutiny." "The Democrats have come to be regarded as a more effective, clearly motivated element in Progressive Era politics. . . . The Progressive Era Democrats have been resurrected. . . . Many southern Democratic congressmen [are] 'unsuspected progressives.' . . . The South has risen again in its reputation as a breeding ground for reformists" (Sarasohn, 1989, ix). It is no wonder that Daniel Rodgers warns us that the concept of "hegemony" will not prove very useful in understanding Progressivism—especially if it is understood in a way as muddled as this (Rodgers, 1982, 121). See also chapter 4 below on Woodrow Wilson as a Progressive.

sort of internal emigration out of the country as a historical community.[20]

A REGIME UNDERSTANDING
OF POLITICAL IDEAS

To understand Progressivism as a distinct regime that contested and
displaced another regime requires that we be particularly attentive to
this special American problem of a politically established personal
identity. Those who created and shaped the ideas that transformed our
politics in this period neither created them out of whole cloth nor simply registered the altered material and social conditions—as if everyone
else were only a bit behind them in their recognition. (This latter view
is often encouraged by victors and later historians in a display of democratic inclusion and as a way to make their victory more bearable by
the vanquished.) Because Progressives wrote quite consciously as
Americans and because they were attacking ideas and institutions on
which many of their fellow Americans—and even they themselves—located their identities, we must explore how they came to find alternative resources, alternative institutions, and alternative selves by which
and through which to create an alternative public doctrine. In this way,
an institutional understanding of American political regimes impels us
to articulate an institutional understanding of American political
ideas.

Accompanying all regime-changing ideas are newly constituted or,
more exactly, reconstituted, political identities contending first for recognition and then for dominance. To study the texts containing these
ideas, therefore, also requires us to study the texts' authors—who they
were, how they saw themselves, with whom they identified in the past.
In short, we must explore both the writers and their writings to see
their "horizons" if we are to understand the meaning and power of
their political ideas. Here, however, a caveat is in order. The decentralized and pluralistic nature of formal political powers in America—the
lack of a coherent and centralized state—necessarily distorts and disag-
gregates coherent political ideas. This fact suggests that we must never
start by asking what ideas Progressive political activists *used* at any
given time to get elected or to further a reform agenda. Rather, we must
focus on what ideas Progressive thinkers *created* or, better, reconsti-

20. This is never quite an either-or situation: the America of this "internal immigrant" may simply be relocated in a history that the historical political communities in America have never imagined or shared, e.g., America as international
working class or as secular enlightenment vanguard.

tuted from the past, if we are to understand Progressivism at its intellectual origins.[21] Very often, in fact, this creation of ideas is more a major *relocation* into politics of ideas previously subordinated or even "outside" of politics—a process of transporting sources of local personal identity (e.g., New Englander, mother, Methodist) into the larger society by "politicizing" issues not previously thought to be (or permitted to be) "political" at the national level.[22] The examples of both abolitionism and turn-of-the-century feminism need no elaboration in this context.

This relocation of ideas and identities from nonpolitical (e.g., family) or regional-political (e.g., New England) locations into national political space should not be taken as suggesting that the study of political ideas from a regime perspective is simply a study of political culture. Two factors stand in the way. The first is that most "cultural politics" takes place within a given regime, so the battles are fought within a stable framework of political language and political institutions.[23] Second, to reduce political ideas and political identities to political culture and then to political behavior begs the questions of where these culturally constituting ideas came from and, most important, of

21. Daniel Rodgers's very influential essay "In Search of Progressivism" (1982) reasons backward precisely from use and not creation: "If we imagine the progressives, like most of the rest of us, largely as users rather than shapers of ideas" (127), we can then see them employing "three distinct social languages . . . full of mutual contradictions" (123). "Only by discarding the mistaken assumption of a coherent reform movement" can we see this period for what it was: "an era of shifting, ideologically fluid, issue-focussed coalitions, all competing for the reshaping of American society" (114). By begging both the question of change in basic institutions of power and of original and systematic political ideas (perhaps Americans do not need them), the vanquished of the old regime simply disappear without a trace in Rodgers's analysis while the remaining conflict is only *among* the Progressives *who now seem to be almost everyone.* It is no wonder, then, that the beginning of Rodgers's search (and that of most historians of Progressivism) begins at the turn of the century, that is, after most of the larger theoretical and cultural battles had already been long fought and on their way to being won in the dynamic and creative reaches of American society.

22. This issue is made more complex because of federalism, which itself "localizes" all sorts of political values and identities and preserves their locality under the doctrines of states' rights and strict constitutional construction. Simply to place previously local political issues into the national agenda radically changes national politics. The so-called rise of the religious right in America during the 1970s is a result of this kind of relocation—the sudden "appearance" of previously localized identities and practices. Theodore Lowi, "Before Conservatism and Beyond," unpublished ms. 12–19, explains the rise of contemporary American conservatism in just this way.

23. The textbook example of this phenomenon is the period of political party hyper-competition and stalemate, 1876–1896. See Keller, 1977, 544–87; Kleppner, 1978; and Silbey, 1991.

why only some of these become constitutive of political identities, political movements, and political conquests. The cultural dimension of political struggle is most valuable in explaining the depth of nineteenth-century party loyalties and in connecting personal values to public policies. And it was of almost infinite value insofar as it displaced the crude and unconvincing explanations of that period based on economic interest. But without understanding more articulate and systematically formulated political ideas, the cultural dimension in itself cannot explain significant changes in the contexts of these power struggles and how and why different political institutions and practices favor different forms of "cultural politics."[24] Only in this way can we avoid the illusion that we can or have reached some "end of ideology" in our politics, some end state where neutrality regarding ways and ends of life can be an operating political principle.

There is one last feature to a regime understanding of political ideas that bears early mention. Political ideas and the identities they carry become quite altered when they become institutionalized. Most obviously, when institutionalized governmentally and enforced, these ideas become literally authoritative. This is often hard to see in America with our weak, decentralized, and pluralistic structures of authority. And, in fact, these structures do serve to distort and diffuse the attempts to translate coherent social theories into coherent policies and practices. Nevertheless, the use of coercion in our political system is certainly in plain view, and the legally enforced boundaries of authority between governing institutions following a political struggle (e.g., between courts and legislatures, or between the president and Congress) are also obvious. But even powerful "voluntary" or "quasipublic" institutions that exercise significant power over their own members and in the larger society (universities, professions, churches, corporations, the national media) are constituted from ideas that have all the markings of politically authoritative ones; each and every one of these institutions encode particular American political identities and values, include and honor some ways of life, exclude and even dishonor others. And as the boundaries between public-coercive and private-voluntary have become increasingly blurred—this in itself was an achievement of Progressive public doctrine—the coercive institutions of the national government have become the silent or not-so-silent partner in the ac-

24. This is another way of saying that because powerful institutions themselves embody particular cultural, ethnic, religious and political values, the relative power of one or another set tends to determine the grounds of which cultural-political battles are fought in the larger society. This may be why, for example, so much heated political battle now take place in universities—the assumption being that these institutions are strategic for larger conquests.

tivities of every powerful institution in our society.[25] Because of these features of political ideas in an institutional setting, it is best to see successful regime-founding political ideas as *public doctrines*. "Public" ideas are those that establish and legitimate institutions that exercise public power and therefore frame the language in which our common life is understood, discussed, and conducted. These public ideas are also "doctrines" in the quasi-religious sense of constituting personal and collective meanings that become the standard for full inclusion and equal respect in the political order and, *therefore*, the psychic or "spiritual" bonds holding the nation America together.

> Were you looking to be held together by lawyers?
> Or by an agreement on a paper? or by arms?
> Nay, nor the world, nor any living thing, will so cohere.

> —Walt Whitman (1926, 265),
> "Over the Carnage Rose Prophetic a Voice"

THE PROBLEM OF HEGEMONY
AND SOCIAL CONTROL

Because the concept of hegemony and prescriptions for its use have been introduced into American scholarship largely from neo-Marxian and feminist perspectives, it is often thought that its employment carries with it those same political postures. This is unfortunate, because the concept is particularly useful for the study of Progressive public doctrine from the institutional perspectives urged here. From this perspective and from the perspective of groups contesting for power, hegemony is not *a* problem but *the* solution. This is as true for reformers claiming to extend freedom as it is for those trying to protect advantages sustained by the prevailing order. Hegemonic control is another way of indicating that a regime is truly established and legitimate because even the vanquished accept its terms—better yet, if the vanquished have so accepted the terms that they think they were part of

---

25. Although it is most obvious during periods of war and war mobilization, this blending of public and private has been most fully seen as part of the working constitution of contemporary political life in Lowi, 1969.

the victorious forces.[26] And in the American political context, where formal political power is so fragmented, where democratic norms are so valued, and therefore, where the opportunities to subvert the coherent exercise of authority are so manifold and so acceptable, the overthrow of one regime and the institution of another one requires victories across many contested terrains before the political prize is truly won.

Victory that lasts cannot be a superficial one, on the order of winning some elections and passing some laws. Indeed, such is the fugitive nature of political authority in America that the passage of laws (even laws that are actually enforced) is often more the symbolic crown of victories achieved earlier and elsewhere (e.g., the Eighteenth Amendment). In the apt words of Theodore Roosevelt regarding international political competition, mere external "political conquests" are as nothing compared to internal "ethnic" ones, by which he meant the flourishing of the "American Way of Life" in the world (Ninkovitch, 1986, 226). Whereas in the international environment this kind of extension of power is taken as both obvious and good across the political spectrum and by practically all Americans in Roosevelt's time and now (contested is what should qualify as the American way of life and what are the appropriate means of conquest), the issue of the legitimacy of domestic hegemony in this *national identity* sense has been highly controversial, at least since the rise of mass participation in national politics.[27]

For Progressive intellectuals the issue of hegemony was especially pressing because so much of their political activity was explicitly directed to transforming intellectual and moral culture and to changing public opinion. The other side of this strategy was that much of Pro-

26. One of the first books to celebrate the Progressive victory and to disguise who was defeated is Benjamin Parke DeWitt's *The Progressive Movement* of 1915. Published by Macmillan as part of a "Citizen's Library of Economics, Politics and Sociology" series edited by Richard T. Ely, this book is now much maligned for giving credit to too narrow a band of leaders—indeed, for positing a coherent and unified movement at all. In fact, it is a beautifully crafted myth of inclusion. Part 1, "Origins and Development," has five chapters of almost equal length, each devoted to "The Progressive Movement in the (Democratic, Republican, Progressive, Socialist, Prohibition) Party." Part 2 recounts Progressive achievements in the nation (control of corporations, control of government, and measures of relief), Part 3, in the states (direct primaries, initiative, referenda, recall, and "measures to prevent and relieve social and economic distress"), and Part 4, in the cities (home rule, charter reform, efficiency, and purity). Seven of the thirty-two books published in the Macmillan citizenship series up to that point were written by four of the group highlighted in this study: Addams (two), Ely (two), Kelley, and Ross (two).

27. The issue here is when deference politics gave way to democratic interest group politics and cultural pluralism. See Formisano, 1974; Shefter, 1978; and Wood, 1987.

gressive political thought and reform was directed specifically against politics as a game, bounded only by written constitutions, elections, and formal procedures. For the Progressives, then, political reform consisted in directly calling for (and often seeking to impose) new and higher ways of life; both the Progressives and their enemies were quite outspoken on opposite sides of this issue. The last time this issue had arisen in a decisive way was, of course, with slavery. But both before and after the Civil War the standing national regime of parties and courts was largely legitimated by the claims of equal rights, limited constitutional government, and fair electoral procedures. Both the antebellum and the post-1876 regimes declared issues concerning ways of life off-limits in national politics. This is exactly what the Democratic party and the South claimed and the Republican party denied just prior to the Civil War and what even the national Republican party was usually forced to declare after 1876 in order to remain competitive.[28] In any event, with the exception of the Civil War period, there is a compelling logic in the liberal tradition of American political thought that would prompt one to conclude that the bare exposure of "hegemony" in national politics is proof of an infringement of rights and therefore a threat to democracy: hegemony is "aristocracy" and both are un-American.[29]

It is thus fair to say that discussion of what we today call "hegemony" was reintroduced both by Progressives on the offensive and by their opponents on the defensive.[30] The opponents claimed that a rights-based regime of limited national government and rule of law was

28. For example, even though a vast majority of *state* Republican party platforms called for prohibition in the 1880s and 1890s, the national platform did not even mention the issue until 1888, and then only following the main body of the document as "Offered by Mr. Boutelle, of Maine," which "sympathizes with all wise and well-directed efforts for the promotion of temperance and morality." In 1892, but by then in the main body of the document, it again sympathized with considered efforts "to lessen and prevent the evils of intemperance and promote morality." No mention of the issue appeared in 1896 or thereafter (Johnson and Porter, 1975).

29. The Democratic party, consisting of a coalition of more disparate cultures, religions, and regions than the Republican, was always a more consistent adherent to this egalitarian and "rights-based" language of liberalism. Theirs was a more consistent anti-hegemonic politics as defense against the increasingly powerful core economy and core culture. This difference will be discussed more fully in chapters 4 and 5 below.

30. This was standard party politics during the stalemate period, 1876–1896. Only as the Republican party became the permanent majority and Progressive ideas began to dominate political discourse both inside and outside electoral politics was the culturally defensive language of the Democratic party permanently subordinated under a new public doctrine. Although it is rather late in the day to try to get even, John Buenker calls this side of the Progressive project an "American Kultur-

in fact neutral as to ways of life and (with the exception of all women and all nonwhite races) neutral and agnostic regarding American citizenship: we are all equal members if we obey the law and display an appropriate democratic humility. "Equal rights for all and special privileges for none" applied not only to individuals, but to regions, religions, and subcultures as well. In this way, the defenders of the old regime exactly reproduced Tocqueville's observation that patriotism, or the sense of belonging to a single country, in early nineteenth-century America,

> is, so to speak, nothing more than an aggregate or summary of the patriotic zeal of the separate provinces. Every citizen of the United States transfers, so to speak, his attachment to his little republic into the common store. . . . In defending the Union he defends the increasing prosperity of his own state or county, the right of conducting its affairs, and the hope of causing measures of improvement to be adopted in it which may be favorable to his own interests; and these are motives that are wont to stir men more than the general interests of the country and the glory of the nation (Tocqueville, 1981, 83).

And in many respects, Tocqueville was right: pre–Civil War America was not one nation, even though Tocqueville thought that northern culture would inevitably prevail. To the Progressives, as to their abolitionist ancestors, fell the burden of trying to create one nation. To them, too, therefore, fell the task of overcoming Tocqueville's understanding of American citizenship and American identity. They provided the intellectual basis for concerted efforts locally and nationally, coercively and through "free institutions" (e.g., compulsory public schools), consciously to define, inculcate, and reward "national" ways of life over "local" ones. That they were more than willing to do so— indeed, their evolutionary social science rested on hegemonic assumptions and contained hegemonic strategies—is a most important horizon to consider, not the least because these Progressives are today so often exposed in current scholarship for doing exactly what they set out to do, namely, to exercise "social control."[31] The value of recent femi-

---

kampf" against "the urban immigrant-descended working class" who, after all, were really just as "progressive" (Buenker, 1978, 163 and 198).

    31. One of the most successful books in the social sciences was *Social Control* by Edward Ross. First published in 1901, it remained in print until 1932.

nist and neo-Marxist scholarship, then, cannot lie in its uncovering of vices that the exposed already knew as virtues. Rather, this contemporary scholarship of exposure is valuable because it has familiarized us today with a strategy of analysis used then by the Progressives. To them, too, the issues were whose horizon, whose hegemony, which ways of life. There can be no strict neutrality in these matters even when the way of life contended for is more cosmopolitan and universalistic than those of its opponents. Indeed, the Progressives claimed that the rights-based regime of nineteenth-century America specifically privileged narrow, conformist, and ignoble ways of life under the guise of neutrality and fairness. The perfect examples were the defense of slavery before the Civil War and the denial of women's rights after. Thus, the charge that the Progressives were "hegemons" seeking, not emancipation and justice, but social control and dominance[32] is very true but also very trivial both in the context of their own writings and for our understanding of them. And as creators of the role of university professor and journalist-intellectual as social guardians and social critics—replacing the New England clergy as the high priests of the religion of the American Way of Life—understanding the Progressives on these terms may teach us more than we care to learn about ourselves.

When John Adams was nearing the end of his life he was asked in a letter, "Who then was the author, inventor, discoverer of indepen-

---

Charles Cooley's *Human Nature and the Social Order* (1902) and *Social Organization: A Study of the Larger Mind* (1909) address these same themes. The latter book had a publishing life of twenty years. Ross (1918, 245) even translates the striving for high personal ideas into a form of social control: "The moralists with their 'self-realization,' 'beauty of virtue,' 'moral ideal,' assure us they are not *controlling* the individual, they are simply *enlightening* him. . . . They are merely trying to show the individual what is most worth striving for. That the *moral values* they commend to him tally so closely with *values for society* is a mere coincidence." Ross then adds that the sociologist must not be fooled by these disclaimers: "It is simpler and more elastic than certain outworn means of control. It is peculiarly compatible with that higher evolution of personality for which society exists."

32. American historical scholarship is a series of battles on this issue, especially regarding the Whigs, the abolitionists, and the Progressives. The arguments on each side—and even the patterns of evidence—are practically interchangeable. See an excellent discussion of this issue by Howe (1990). Because the subtext in all these discussions is the standing of the Puritan myth of America and the felt need or fear of collective duty, one can almost trace the present standing of this myth by seeing who seems to be winning the battle over history in any or all of these periods. On this measure, the Puritan myth of America has staged an amazingly rapid comeback since the final death of the New Deal in the late 1960s. A recent exception is Dawley, 1991, 191 and 254–94, resulting in a need to distinguish between "good" and "bad" Progressives.

dence?'' His answer is both deft avoidance and powerful expression of the New England narrative of America. He said that neither he, nor Jefferson, nor Otis, nor any of the other titular founders should take the laurels—all they did, singly and collectively, was to ''awaken and revive . . . the original fundamental principle of [seventeenth-century] colonization'' (Adams, 1851, 359). The task of discovering the ''inventors'' of what became the public doctrine of Progressivism will not go back quite that far. The search must go back far enough, however, to identify voices that are not simply parroting or popularizing the unamended ideas of others, whose arguments are deep criticisms of regnant national political ideas and institutions, and whose alternative ideas become constitutive of the new complex of public and private institutions and practices that were instrumental in bringing about a new regime.

This task meant that the search began much farther back in time than when party-political and political reform activities began. And insofar as Progressivism sought to destroy and supplant the prevailing system of parties, one must seek to discover the institutions and organizations that were to take its place. Innovation, then, is simultaneously intellectual and institutional; indeed, the new institutions embodied and represented new ideas and new ways of life, all of which were simultaneously seeking public recognition and public power.

From a variety of specialized studies of the intellectual and cultural life of this period, I generated a large list of potential candidates for the title ''inventor'' of Progressivism. From other studies of organizational and institutional innovation I discovered still more. I reduced the first list to those who wrote serious and largely original books and articles, beginning in the 1880s or early 1890s, that were deeply critical of prevailing American political and economic ideas and practices and that sought to redefine the way we view our moral, social, economic, and political life. My next task was to see how influential their writings were. Here I resorted to two measures of simple market success. The first is whether they had established their ideas and reputations sufficiently to write textbooks or other broadly definitive books in their special fields. The second test was to trace the number of years these books were continuously published. Through both bibliographical and biographical sources, I then explored the extent to which these same authors were organizationally and institutionally innovative. Did they write for a wider audience, organize professional associations, found specialized journals and academic specializations, and engage in other activities to spread and give effect to their ideas? This process was far less systematic in the doing than in the telling, but it did yield about twenty-five prolific and influential writers, most of them academics.

After dropping some of these for want of originality and others for lack of evidence that they and their writings were actively engaged in progressive reform activities and argument, I then turned to others who were not primarily academics, but who were organizationally innovative in ways that complemented reform ideas and activities. Here I added two innovative editor-journalist-publicists and four women who were both feminist intellectuals and actively engaged in progressive reform institutions and causes. The list is not intended to be "representative" in the sense of encompassing the entire range of reform movements, causes, or ideas. What it does represent is a core group of intellectuals whose writings and institutional innovations first defined the larger terms by which Progressivism was defined in all its inner variety and inner conflict. In that sense, the aggregate of *writings* of this group, but certainly not the *writers*, are more radical and more conservative, more religious and less religious, more utopian-romantic and more scientific-technical than most of the more programmatic and directly "ideological" writings and political activists that followed. That is the nature of formative ideas and institutions, and of theoretical activity generally. That is what distinguishes reflective and articulate ideas from serviceable ideology and, for that matter, hegemonic victory from passing fashion.

THE AUTHORS OF PROGRESSIVE PUBLIC DOCTRINE

HENRY CARTER ADAMS (1851–1921). Professor of political economy, University of Michigan (1886–1921). Grinnell (Iowa) College; Andover Theological School; two years at Heidelberg and Berlin universities; received the first Ph.D. degree awarded by Johns Hopkins. Born in Iowa, son of Ephraim Adams (New Hampshire descendant of early seventeenth-century English settlers, an early antislavery activist, cofounder of Iowa [Grinnell] College and member of the "Iowa Band," a group of New England evangelicals dedicated to erecting a Christian commonwealth in the Midwest). Cofounder of the American Economics Association in 1885, he was also the first to note America's unique administrative environment and attack the intellectual foundations of English political economy in "The Relation of the State to Industrial Action" (1887). *The Science of Finance: An Investigation of Public Expenditure and Public Revenues* (Holt, 1898–1924).

JANE ADDAMS (1860–1935). Founder and director of Hull House and writer. Rockford College; Europe, 1883–1885; and England, 1887. Born in Illinois, daughter of John Addams (Pennsylvania descendant of late seventeenth-century English settlers; prominent Republican state senator who had organized and led a military company during the Civil War). Active in the woman's political and labor movements. Founding member, American Sociological Society (1905). Seconded Theodore Roosevelt's nomination at the Progressive party convention (1912). Became a peace activist during World War I and received the Nobel Peace Prize in 1931. *Democracy and Social Ethics* (Macmillan, 1902–1926); *Twenty Years at Hull House* (Macmillan, 1910–1949).

WILLIAM DWIGHT PORTER BLISS (1856–1926). Editor, publicist, reform organizer, and writer. Amherst; Hartford Theological Seminary. Born in Turkey, son of Edwin Elisha and Isabella Holmes Bliss (both Congregational missionaries). Labor party candidate for lieutenant governor of Massachusetts (1887); founder of the Christian Socialist Society of the United States and the *Dawn* (1889); national lecturer for the Christian Social Union (1894); editor of the *American Fabian* (1895–96); president of the National Social Reform Union (1899). After serving two years as an investigator for the U.S. Bureau of Labor, he worked closely with Josiah Strong's American Institute of Social Service, 1909–1914. Compiled and abridged writings of British reformers John Stuart Mill and John Ruskin and edited a series of handbooks, yearbooks, and encyclopedias of American and European social reforms, reformers, and reform organizations. *Encyclopedia* and *New Encyclopedia of Social Reform* (Funk and Wagnalls, 1897–1910).

JOHN BATES CLARK (1847–1938). Professor of economics, Columbia University (1895–1923). Brown; Amherst; Heidelberg, Ph.D. Born in Rhode Island, son of John and Charlotte Clark (New England many generations; both children of clergymen). Cofounder of the American Economic Association (1885), and president (1894 and 1895). An early marginal-utility theorist, he translated that theory into a larger organic theory of social and moral progress in collaboration with his colleague at Columbia, the sociologist Franklin Giddings. Active in peace movements in the 1890s, Clark later directed research projects on historical and economic aspects of war for the Carnegie Endowment for International Peace (1910–23). *Philosophy of Wealth* (Ginn and Company, 1886–1904); *The Distribution of Wealth* (Macmillan, 1899–1913).

JOHN ROGERS COMMONS (1862–1945). Professor of political economy at the University of Wisconsin (1904–32). Oberlin; Johns Hopkins (no degree). Born in Ohio, son of John and Clarissa Commons (she was New England descendant of early settlers and a graduate of Oberlin; he was a descendant of North Carolina Quakers; both were ardent abolitionists). John Rogers was named after a sixteenth-century British Protestant martyr. Cofounder of the American Institute of Christian Sociology (1893) and, with Richard T. Ely and others, the American Association for Labor Legislation (1906). Assisted Ralph Easley, secretary of the National Civic Federation

(1902–4). Headed a research bureau for Milwaukee's socialist mayor (1911–13); appointed by President Wilson to the U.S. Commission on Industrial Relations (1913–15) to investigate causes of labor unrest. Conceived and drafted a series of innovative social reform measures for the state of Wisconsin: its civil service law (1905), public utility law (1907), and workmen's compensation act (1911), culminating in the formation of the Wisconsin Industrial Commission that same year. Served as president of the National Consumers' League (1923–35). *Races and Immigrants in America* (Macmillan, 1907–30); (with John B. Andrews) *Principles of Labor Legislation* (Harper and Brothers, 1916–36).

CHARLES H. COOLEY (1864–1929). Professor of economics and sociology at the University of Michigan (1894–1929). Michigan; Munich; Michigan, Ph.D. Born in Michigan, son of Thomas H. Cooley (New England descendant of mid-seventeenth-century English settlers; first dean of Michigan's law school; first chair of Interstate Commerce Commission). Founding member, American Sociological Society (1905), and president (1918). *Social Organization: A Study of the Larger Mind* (Scribner, 1909–29).

JOHN DEWEY (1859–1952). Professor of philosophy at the University of Chicago (1894–1904) and Columbia University (1905–52). University of Vermont; Johns Hopkins, Ph.D. Born in Vermont, son of Archibald Sprague and Lucina Artemisia Rich Dewey (both descendants of longtime Vermont farmers; in 1861, at age 50, Archibald sold his grocery store and enlisted in the Union Army, remaining in it until 1867). At Chicago Dewey was active with Hull House, the National Civic Federation, and Chicago's public schools. With his wife he founded the Laboratory School at the University. President, American Psychological Association (1899) and American Philosophical Association (1904). (With James Tufts) *Ethics* (Henry Holt, 1908–42); *Democracy and Education* (Macmillan, 1916–53).

RICHARD T. ELY (1854–1943). Professor of economics at Johns Hopkins University (1881–92) and the University of Wisconsin (1892–1925). Dartmouth; Columbia; Halle; Heidelberg, Ph.D. Born in New York State, son of Ezra and Harriet Ely (both New England descendants of early English settlers, including, on the father's side, a follower of Cromwell who fled to Connecticut in 1660). Cofounder with W. D. P. Bliss and secretary (1891–94) Christian Social Union; cofounder (1885), secretary (1885–92), and president (1900), American Economic Association; cofounder with John Commons and first president (1906), American Association for Labor Legislation. *Outlines of Economics* (Chautauqua Press, 1893–1908; Macmillan, 1908–39); (with George R. Wicker) *Elementary Principles of Economics* (Macmillan, 1904–34).

FRANKLIN HENRY GIDDINGS (1855–1931). Professor of sociology at Columbia University (1894–1928). Union College, A.B. and M.A. Born in Connecticut, son of Rev. Edward Jonathan and Rebecca Giddings (he was a New England descendant of mid-seventeenth-century English settlers). Editor, *Publications of the American Economic Association* (1891–93); editor, *Annals of the American Academy of Political and Social Science* (1890–92); founding member (1905) and president (1910–11), American Sociological Society. *Principles of Sociology* (Macmillan, 1896–1926); *Elements of Sociology* (Macmillan, 1898–1916).

CHARLOTTE PERKINS GILMAN (1860–1935). Feminist writer, lecturer, and editor. No formal education beyond grade school. Born in Connecticut, daughter of Frederick Beecher and Mary Westcott Perkins (he was the grandson of Lyman Beecher and New England descendant of early seventeenth-century English settlers). Charlotte was a relative of Henry Ward Beecher, Harriet Beecher Stowe, and Edward Everett Hale. Divorced in 1894, she married a cousin, George Houghton Gilman, in 1900. Founding member, American Sociological Society (1905). Although later active in the labor and feminist movements, she began her political career as a Bellamy Nationalist and wrote for W. D. P. Bliss's *American Fabian*. Before her path-breaking book on feminism, she wrote short stories and poetry. *Women and Economics* (Small, Maynard, 1898–1913).

ARTHUR TWINING HADLEY (1856–1930). Professor of political economy (1883–99) and president (1899–1921) at Yale. Yale, B.A. and graduate work; Berlin (no degree). Born in Connecticut, son of James and Anne Lording Hadley (he was a New England descendant of mid-seventeenth-century English settlers and professor of Greek at Yale). His 1885 study of American and European railroads was among the first to recognize the fallacy of Ricardian theories of prices in industries with heavy fixed costs. After he became president of Yale, he achieved the reputation as a sort of public moralist and lecturer throughout America and abroad. *Railroad Transportation* (G. P. Putnam's, 1885–1912); *Economics: An Account of the Relations between Private Property and Public Welfare* (G. P. Putnam's, 1896–1911).

EDMUND J. JAMES (1855–1925). Professor of public finance and administration, Wharton School, University of Pennsylvania (1883–96), and president, University of Illinois (1904–19). Northwestern; Harvard; Halle, Ph.D. Born in Illinois, son of Colin Dew and Amanda Keziah Casad James (he was the highest lay leader of the Methodist church in Illinois). One of the youngest among founders of the American Economic Association in 1885, he later cofounded, with Simon Patten, and was first president of the American Academy of Political and Social Science (1889–1901) and first editor of its *Annals* (1890–96). He was a leader in shaping professional education in business and finance and in establishing institutional and intellectual connections between businessmen, political leaders, and academics.

FLORENCE KELLEY (1859–1932). Social worker and general secretary, National Consumer's League (1899–1924). Cornell (no degree); Zurich; Heidelberg; Northwestern Law School (1895). Born in Philadelphia, daughter of William Darrah and Caroline Bartram Bonsall Kelley (she was a descendant of early Quaker settlers). Translator of Friedrich Engels's *Condition of the Working Class* (1887); associate editor, *Charities*; participant in Carroll Wright's survey of Chicago slums (1892). Active in woman's labor and political movements and child-labor issues; codrafter of 1912 Progressive party platform on social and industrial justice.

SIMON N. PATTEN (1852–1922). Professor of economics, Wharton School, University of Pennsylvania (1888–1917). Northwestern; Halle, Ph.D. Born in Illinois, son of William and Elizabeth Nelson Patten (he was a New York descendant of late eighteenth-century Scotch-Irish settlers). Cofounder (1885) and early president, American Economics Association; cofounder with Edmund James, American Academy of Political and Social Science (1889); founding member, American Sociological Society (1905). An early critic of British political economy, he introduced the importance of abundance and consumption choices into economic theory and applied those ideas to welfare economics and to theories of economic growth. *The New Basis of Civilization* (Macmillan, 1907–21).

EDWARD ALSWORTH ROSS (1866–1951). Professor of economics and sociology at Stanford University (1893–1900) and the University of Wisconsin (1906–37). Coe College; Germany; Johns Hopkins, Ph.D. Born in Illinois, son of William Carpenter and Rachel Ellsworth Ross (she was a Pennsylvania descendant of early nineteenth-century Scotch-Irish settlers). Founding member, American Sociological Society (1905), and president (1914 and 1915). The most prominent American social theorist of his day, he wrote the first textbook in social psychology and, through public lectures and popular writings, showed the relationship of social science to social reform. *Social Control* (Macmillan, 1901–32); *Foundations of Sociology* (Macmillan, 1905–26); *Social Psychology* (Macmillan, 1908–25).

VIDA DUTTON SCUDDER (1861–1954). Professor of literature, Wellesley College (1892–1928). Smith; Oxford (no degree); Smith, M.A. Born in India, daughter of David Coit and Harriet Louisa Dutton Scudder (Congregational missionaries related to E. P. Dutton, the publisher). Helped establish Denison House, Boston branch of the College Settlements Association (1890); founding member and lecturer for W. D. P. Bliss's Society of Christian Socialists; cofounder, Women's Trade Union League (1903). *Social Ideals in English Letters* (Houghton, Mifflin and Chautauqua, 1898–1923).

EDWIN ROBERT ANDERSON SELIGMAN (1861–1939). Professor of political economy, Columbia University (1888–1931). Columbia; Berlin; Heidelberg; Paris; Columbia, LL.B and Ph.D. Born in New York City, son of Joseph and Babette Seligman (prominent German-Jewish international private banking family with strong ties to the Republican party). Cofounder (1885) and president (1902–3), American Economic Association; founding member, American Sociological Society (1905). National Civic Federation executive council. Active in labor, immigrant, Negro, antiprostitution, and conservation organizations and movements, he coauthored the 1912 New York State Progressive party platform. One of the founders of the study of public finance in America, he also wrote extensively on economic competition and regulation and on theories of history and social change. He later became editor-in-chief of *Encyclopedia of the Social Sciences* (1930–35). *Essays on Taxation* (Macmillan, 1895–1925); *The Economic Interpretation of History* (Macmillan, 1902–24); *Principles of Economics* (Longmans, Green, 1905–25).

ALBERT SHAW (1857–1947). Editor and publisher, *Review of Reviews* (1892–1937). Grinnell (Iowa) College; Johns Hopkins, Ph.D. Born in Ohio, son of Griffin and Susan Shaw (he was a physician and Republican party leader; she was a New England descendant of early seventeenth-century English settlers). President, American Political Science Association; active in municipal reform movements of all kinds; close to Theodore Roosevelt and strong supporter of America as a world economic and military power. *Municipal Government in Continental Europe* (Century Co. and Macmillan, 1895–1906); *Municipal Government in Great Britain* (Century Co. and Macmillan, 1895–1907).

ALBION WOODBURY SMALL (1854–1926). Professor of sociology, University of Chicago (1892–1926). Colby; Newton Theological Institution; Berlin, and Leipzig; Johns Hopkins, Ph.D. Born in Maine, son of Rev. Albion Keith Parris and Thankful Lincoln Small (he was a New England descendant of mid-seventeenth-century English settlers; she was descended from Samuel Lincoln, Abraham Lincoln's earliest American ancestor). Founder and editor, *American Journal of Sociology* (1895–1926). Founding member (1905), and president (1912–14), American Sociological Society.

By 1915, this group of nineteen intellectuals had produced over one hundred fifty books, with articles, book reviews, columns, and pamphlets running in the thousands. The twenty-seven books written by this group are highlighted above both because of their publication frequency and life spans and because they dominated collegiate instruction and the ideas of more popular writers. Whereas most of this group's academic writing began in the mid and late 1880s, twenty-three of these books were first published between 1893 and 1910, ten alone in the period between 1895 and 1899 and another nine between 1904 and 1910. This tends to represent their more mature and authoritative work because the entire group of nineteen were born between 1847 and 1866. Eighteen of these twenty-seven books were published continuously for twenty years or more; eight were published for more than thirty years.[33]

Even though only thirteen of this group held academic positions, seventeen were founding members, journal editors, or presidents of academic professional organizations in economics, sociology, and political and social science formed in the period 1885–1906. Needless to add, their educational credentials and academic connections were impressive. All but one had college degrees; all but two also did graduate work, with eleven receiving Ph.D. degrees. Only one had a divinity degree, but he did not minister; three had law degrees, but they did not practice or teach law.[34] Fifteen spent at least a year abroad in travel and study, many spending two or more years. Twelve attended German universities, with four of them receiving German Ph.D.'s. Only one studied in England, but not for an academic degree. Using rather strict criteria (Dewey, for example, barely qualifies in this early period), we note that seventeen of this group helped form, actively participated in or wrote political material for specific Progressive reform causes, running the gamut from prohibition, woman suffrage, and antiprostitution campaigns, to urging initiative, referenda, recall, or proportionate representative legislation, municipal ownership of utilities, prohibition of child labor, trade union recognition and compulsory arbitration, to establishment of settlement houses and charity organization societies. And despite the prestigious academic affiliations of most of this group, seventeen wrote for the popular or semipopular press, with some becoming well known as a result. At some point in their careers, a good number of the academics ran afoul of university administrators and trustees for their "radical" political, social, or religious opinions (three lost academic appointments), but none of them suffered grievously or lost professional standing for their views.

This list of similarities among these people is only statistical and

33. Examples and discussion of political economy writings are found in chapter 5 below.

34. One should note here how different this group is from the membership and professional orientation of the American Social Science Association, formed in 1865 and disbanded in the face of academic professional associations in 1909. The ASSA was composed overwhelmingly of the reigning professions—law, medicine, divinity (Haskell, 1977, 77–90 and 104–10).

says nothing about their real intellectual and political connections to one another. It was only after this list was completed that I discovered how closely interconnected these people were and on so many different levels. In the language of C. Wright Mills, it was as if I had uncovered an incredibly tightly knit power elite—except for the fact that, at this time, they had very little power and were pitted against a prevailing elite. The most obvious connection is the academic one: nine of this group were founding members of the American Economic Association (AEA); four of these same nine, plus five others, were founding members of the American Sociological Society; two of the AEA founders in turn founded the American Academy of Political and Social Science and its journal, the *Annals*. Immediately following its founding in 1890, this journal became the meeting point for men and women from government, academia, labor, business, and finance to address the entire range of issues on the national political agenda for the next twenty-five years. In the period from 1890 to 1918, fully fifteen of this group had written a total of ninety-four articles or extended comments on articles in the *Annals*. Their connection through the *American Journal of Sociology* is equally close. Founded in 1895 and edited for almost thirty years by Albion Small of the University of Chicago, through 1917 this journal reviewed thirty-six books written by twelve persons from this group. Over this same period, ten wrote a total of one hundred twenty articles.[35] That only three held academic appointments in sociology suggests not only loose "disciplinary boundaries" but also that sociology served both as an integrator of the new social sciences and as the major source of theoretical grounding for Progressive reforms.

As an external test for the claim that this group of intellectuals was both coherent and central to the creation of Progressive public doctrine at its most articulate level, I ran two sets of "scholarly consensus vector" experiments. The first was to see how many of this group were discussed in three widely diverse books examining social reform in this period. The first is the 1908 *Encyclopedia of Social Reform*, a tome of more than thirteen hundred closely printed pages containing the history, organizations, writings, and ideas of social reform and packed with what seems to be every form of social statistics then known to Western man. The *Encyclopedia* also includes short biographies of prominent reformers, living and dead, mostly from England and America, but also from European countries. Fifteen of this group of nineteen are written up in the 1908 edition. A second source, Robert Crunden's

---

35. In the case of the *American Journal of Sociology* this must be qualified by the fact that Albion Small and Edward Ross account for eighty-five of this total, but each of the rest wrote at least two, and they average between four and five.

Ministers of Reform (1984), discusses Progressive intellectual, political, literary, and artistic culture. It includes discussion of fifteen from this group; with the *Encyclopedia*, the entire group is covered. Paul Boyer's 1978 study of urban reform and reformers in America from 1820 to 1920 includes nine of these intellectuals. In identifying the specific philosophical underpinnings of turn-of-the-century urban reform, Boyer discusses at some length writings by four academics, three of whom are included in the group above (Ross, Cooley, and Patten). The fourth writer he cites, Luther Lee Bernard, was a generation younger, studied under Albion Small at Chicago, and published his seminal work on social control in the *American Journal of Sociology* in 1911 (Boyer, 1978, 224–32).

But my criteria are more stringent than identifying Progressives as activists or even as influential ideologues for particular reform causes. If regime-changing political ideas are truly constitutive and in fact relocate the ways in which we see ourselves and our society, then this group must also be recognized by scholars who have charted the major changes in American philosophy, economics, and social and political theory over the course of American history. Do these studies feature members of this group? Dorothy Ross's recently published *Origins of American Social Science* and an earlier monograph include discussion of seventeen of these nineteen. Joseph Dorfman's classic study, *The Economic Mind of American Civilization*, vol. 3, includes discussion of fourteen from this group, with extended summaries of the writings from twelve. Sidney Fine's *Laissez Faire and the General-Welfare State* identifies all but one as laying the intellectual and moral foundations for the modern welfare state in America. Herbert Schneider's *History of American Philosophy* includes six from this group; Ralph Gabriel's *The Course of American Democratic Thought*, twelve.[36]

At this point an obvious question arises: why are Charles Beard and Herbert Croly absent from the list? The first and simple answer is that they came too late. Beard was born in 1874 and did not produce his first book until 1913, well after most of the serious intellectual innovation had already taken place and had dominated the universities. Croly was born in 1870 and did not produce his first book until 1909. But there are deeper reasons than chronology, and they involve no small degree of academic arrogance: both writers were derivative in both the content and the methods of analysis. When their first books appeared neither was seen as anything exceptional or new to this group of Progressive intellectuals. Moreover, both writ-

36. Addams, Dewey, Ely, Patten, Ross, and Small were the most frequently included, each appearing in seven of the eight. Those with six inclusions are Bliss, Commons, Giddings, Hadley, James, and Seligman.

ers were more directly "ideological" in a way that most of the earlier academics were not. This requires more explanation than will be given here, but it includes the fact that Croly and Beard wrote political histories of America that were already premised on the truths of Progressive public doctrine. Their histories, in other words, were retroactive political "proofs" of victories already envisioned for the immediate future and already clearly won at the level of intellect and culture. Ideology in this form of history is by definition parasitic on more fully articulated social theories. And this is true whether or not the decisive political victory was in fact won: activists and ideologues necessarily do a lot of whistling in the dark, presenting as inevitable futures they passionately wish to be realized. This same ground for exclusion is an implicit warning not to take as formative what might in fact be derivative. To analyze "Progressive political theory" by *starting* with Beard and Croly condemns the analyst to the reproduction of ideology because the texts used were written within a framework of ideas much more complex and deeply embedded in earlier work that the analyst might not know.[37] Symbolically put, without familiarity with the writings of the sociologist Albion Small and the economist Simon Patten, much of what Croly wrote regarding the sources of American nationality and democracy as well as his larger political economy arguments will be either misunderstood or ignored. And without knowing the writings of Seligman on economic determinism, the works of Beard will remain opaque.[38]

For the purposes of discovering the intellectual and cultural "horizons" of Progressivism, therefore, a list that excludes Croly and Beard is warranted; for the purpose of explicating and tracing the political implications of ideas within that horizon, the writings of Croly are absolutely essential and those of Beard always useful. Moreover, both writers would be central to any project seeking to understand the paradoxical passage from Progressivism to Wilsonian democracy and New Deal liberalism.

SOME PROGRESSIVE HORIZONS

It is now necessary to ask a final set of questions about these authors of Progressive public doctrine. How did this group and others like them find and recognize one another? What brought and held them together?

37. Stettner, 1993, 164–65, attributes to Croly the origin of the concept of "positive rights," when, in fact, it became a staple of academic and social gospel writings in the late 1880s. See chapter 6 below. And on 144–54, he treats Croly's writings on religion in the post–World War I period as a sort of Progressive disenchantment when, again, there were abundant academic and reform writings integrating "spirit" to reform in the previous three decades.

38. Barrow, 1992. This connection of Beard to Seligman strongly confirms Kloppenberg, 1986, 230–45, on the place of Eduard Bernstein.

From what common sources did they derive their identities, histories, and purposes of sufficient strength and energy to project them so powerfully into American academic, intellectual, and political life? In short, what horizons did they share? As creators and shapers of what became a new political identity for America and therefore the prevailing identity available for those who wished to become fully conscious of being an American, they superseded those who shaped and articulated the political values and personal identities of the earlier regime. Simply to say that they were "modern" or "advanced" because of their academic training will not suffice because they largely *created* the standards by which we now measure "modern" or "advanced" training and thinking. And insofar as *they* created much of *our* horizon, explanation by tautology—no matter how sophisticated or complex—the standard method by which histories of American academic disciplines are written[39]—will not give us knowledge of what they saw as *their* horizons and *their* origins. To say that they had widespread influence because they occupied powerful positions in academia and had strong connections to financial, business, and governmental elites is also largely circular[40] because,

39. There is either a pervasive "presentism" in these studies—the quest for origin as confirmation of present standards and practices—or a pro forma bow to "otherness" of origin at some (usually very early) point, and *then* the leap to discover their contributions to present-day fulfillment. The test for the presence of this kind of anachronism is usually the simple equation of professionalization and secularization. Bledstein, 1976; Coats, 1968; Fox, 1967; Haskell, 1977; Herbst, 1959; Hofstadter, 1955; and Veysey, 1965, are examples of this genre, disciplinary history as Ritual. A Populist or Marxian variant of "presentism" is to look for true or principled beginnings—often in religion or a passion for social justice—and then co-optation and sellout. In this way, one can at once criticize one's academic contemporaries, occupy higher or more advanced political ground, *and* claim adherence to traditional disciplinary origins. Lustig, 1982; Ricci, 1984; Ross, 1977; Schwendinger and Schwendinger, 1974; Seidelman, 1985; Silva and Slaughter, 1984, are examples of this genre, disciplinary history as Jeremiad. What both groups in this struggle over disciplinary history take for granted is that these academics and their writings *are* somehow constitutive of *our* horizons and *our* standards, but without serious explorations of those of *their* predecessors.

40. And if not circular, simply wrong: almost all of these writers shaped their definitive theoretical positions in the early 1880s through the mid-1890s, well before most of these "structures of power" were even in place. The only covering explanation here is that these men and women of incredible self-assurance and daring and energy quickly caved in at the threatened loss of some academic perquisites. This explanation better explains the much less self-assured generation of academic radicals in the 1950s than it does the Progressives. Populist critics of the new universities often tended to blame their regional isolation and therefore national weakness on powerful forces working against them in the emerging national universities while their faculties were among the few influential people outside populist regions of the country who understood the larger sources of populists' discontent and were often sympathetic to their cause, especially compared to the more traditional

again, members of this group helped create those academic platforms, those audiences, and the vocabulary in which they were addressed—and against both strongly entrenched opposition and other possible alternatives.

Their most obvious common bonds are party-political, regional, and religious. Even though all of them voiced antiparty ideas in one form or another, every one of them came from Republican party backgrounds, in many cases with exceptionally strong evidence of party loyalty.[41] This loyalty, however, was to the Republican party as a party against "parties," as the organized redeemer nation born in the abolitionist movement and matured in the Civil War and Reconstruction. With two exceptions, this group is not only Protestant, but overwhelmingly evangelical Protestant in family background. Here, their homogeneity is even greater than a most paranoid WASP-conspiracy theorist would have any right to expect. Fourteen of the nineteen came from Congregationalist families. To put this in perspective, as early as 1860 Congregationalists were already a distinct Protestant minority in America with 2,234 churches in comparison with Presbyterians (6,406), Baptists (12,150), and Methodists (19,883).[42] The remaining five of the group were Methodists (2), Presbyterian, Quaker, and Jewish. Two of the nineteen dropped all church affiliation, three switched to the Episcopal Church, and the rest remained in their family churches. Except for Seligman, who was German-Jewish, and Kelley, who was Scotch-Irish and Quaker, all were English in background. More surprising is that two-thirds traced their American beginnings to New England and more than half back to the period 1630–1660. Clergymen naturally loom large in these family backgrounds; indeed, the ministry was a career choice seriously consid-

---

faculty in the colleges in the North and East. This led to the strange affinity between, say, Henry George, Jr.'s, 1904 *Menace of Privilege*, a thoroughly reactionary tract against modernity, especially in social and political thinking, and post-1960s revisionist studies of the emergence of the modern university. The bridge between the two is, of course, the Texas populist C. Wright Mills, who wrote *Sociology and Pragmatism* as a doctoral dissertation in the early 1940s, well before he had read Marx. This legacy lives on: Barrow, 1990; Lustig, 1982; Ross, 1977; Silva and Slaughter, 1984; Weinstein, 1968. Appropriately, Mills then wrote *White Collar* in 1951, bewailing the decline of rugged individualism and independence caused by the rise of the modern corporation. See Zunz, 1990, 2–4, for an interesting analysis of this book and Richard Hofstadter's reaction to it.

41. The parents of some were party leaders, state legislators, or party appointees to office. Many had abolitionist backgrounds.

42. By 1900, this disproportion became many times greater: Congregational (5,604); Episcopal (6,264); Disciples (10,298); Presbyterian (15,452); Baptist (49,905); and Methodist (53,908). The Unitarians (455) and Quakers (1,031) declined even more rapidly than the Congregationalists (Gaustad, 1962, 43–44).

ered by at least six. As it was, twelve of this group wrote for the religious press, either in denominational or Protestant ecumenical publications or in scholarly reviews published by divinity school faculty (e.g., *Bibliotheca Sacra, The New Englander, Andover Review*).

Although New England looms large in their collective backgrounds, its importance rapidly diminishes in their foregrounds. Seven of this group came directly from New England, nine from the Midwest, and three from the New York area. But only two remained in New England, and no one moved there; nine ended in the Midwest and nine in the New York area. A factor related to this New England out-migration is that Harvard looms so small in this composite portrait. Given the backgrounds and later positions of this group and given the role that Harvard and Unitarianism had played in earlier nineteenth-century American intellectual culture, abolitionism, and immediate post–Civil War reform, this absence is significant.[43] Such was the strength of evangelical Christianity in the backgrounds of these Progressive intellectuals that only one of this group received a degree from Harvard, and no one taught there. Of equal significance to their horizons, no one was either raised a Unitarian or became one. This will become noteworthy when one explores the meaning of "secularization" when applied to Progressive social-scientific and political theories. When comparing, for example, this group of intellectuals with Ann Douglas's clergymen and female authors who dominated the popular and the liberal Protestant religious press in the two generations immediately preceding this one, the religious and regional differences are striking.[44] On a "progressive" reading of history-

43. Here, too, one should note the contrast to the earlier American Social Science Association (1865–1909) as discussed in Haskell, 1977, 132–36. Harvard, MIT, New England, and, presumably, Unitarianism dominated the membership and spirit of that organization. McPherson (1975, 3–10 and 396–408) studied the denominational affiliations of 284 "post-1870 abolitionists" active on behalf of the freedmen. This group preceded the Progressives in this study by one and two generations and includes a substantial number of nonevangelical Protestants, especially Unitarians and Quakers.

44. Although her group and these Progressives are not strictly comparable, each group tended to dominate moral discourse in the popular journalistic media of their day; each group was accorded the quasi-official status of "public moralists"; each group identified with and took some of their cues from their British journalistic and intellectual counterparts. Given the books they wrote, Douglas's clergymen played roles remarkably similar to those of Progressive academics thirty to fifty years later. Eighteen of Douglas's thirty women writers were raised Congregationalist and seven, Unitarian-Universalist. Fully fourteen of the Congregationalists, then a fully evangelical, if relatively liberal, church, switched to nonevangelical Unitarianism or became Episcopalians. Whereas this might constitute exceptionally strong proof for a thesis equating secularization and modernization in American intellectual life, it happened mostly before the Civil War and among those

as-modernization, a paradox immediately presents itself. The most innovative modernizers were from a religious subculture that appeared retrograde. Symbolically put, it was pious Congregational Yale that was the "national" university producing the future presidents of Cornell, Hopkins, and Chicago and serving as the model for education for the network of liberal arts colleges throughout the Midwest. Compared to Yale and its many "satellites," urban, urbane, and Unitarian Harvard was increasingly marginalized in the mid-nineteenth century, despite its stellar faculty and student body (Thernstrom, 1986, 115–20).

Although this will be discussed at length in another context later, it should also be noted that this group is singularly devoid of members of the legal fraternity. Judges, lawyers, law professors, and legal writers were not only absent from this network, they were studiously avoided and even treated with some measure of contempt. Here, Harvard's marginality can be further explained by the dominance of its law school. Just as Harvard was perfecting the case method of instruction and producing the shock troops of the emerging corporate law firms, America's innovating and leading intellectuals in economics, sociology, and political economy were writing epitaphs for formal-legal understandings of America and foretelling an age in which the artificial and arid world of law would be replaced by a real and luxuriant democratic faith.

Another way of isolating the horizon of these Progressives is to compare them to other contemporaries. This group of nineteen Progressives shared many characteristics with the leaders of the woman suffrage movement identified in Aileen Kraditor's study. The group of Progressive intellectuals includes some whose fathers or near relatives were quite prominent. Charles Horton Cooley's father, Thomas, was a noted legal writer, founding dean of Michigan's Law School and first chairman of the Interstate Commerce Commission. Edwin R. A. Seligman's father, Joseph, was a very successful international private banker in New York. Charlotte Perkins Gilman (also in Kraditor's group), whose de-

---

who wrote scores of feel-good hymns and sentimental-religious poetry and novels, not modern social science. Twenty-five of Douglas's sample came from New England; three from the New York area; two from the Midwest. Although this group moved a lot more than mine, almost all lived most of their lives in cities along the East Coast between New York and Boston. Her male theologian-clergyman sample of thirty contains fifteen reared as Unitarian-Universalist and thirteen, as Congregationalists. Four of the Congregationalists became Unitarian and one, Episcopalian via Unitarianism. Again, if this is taken as proof of the secularization of American intellectual life (which clergymen clearly dominated in that period) it is equally proof that this secularization became an increasingly isolated and provincial subculture in the post–Civil War period (Douglas, 1988, Appendix B and discussion, 80–117).

serted mother was very poor and who herself had only a grade school education, was the granddaughter of Lyman Beecher and thus related to Henry Ward Beecher and Harriet Beecher Stowe. Vida Dutton Scudder was also very poor, but was connected to the Dutton publishing family. Arthur Hadley's father was a noted professor of Greek at Yale. Kraditor's group of twenty-six is distinguished by a relatively greater connection to wealth (the Vanderbilt and McCormick fortunes are represented) and about the same social prominence (wives or daughters of a university president, a law school dean, a congressman, and some judges). Like the Progressives, Kraditor's group of twenty-six women, most of whom were born in the same period, were highly educated (sixteen with college degrees; nine with graduate work or degrees), well traveled (eight studied in Germany or England), and Anglo-Saxon (twenty-four).[45]

Given these similarities and differences, a final common feature of all these groups, including the abolitionists, is their incredible self-assurance and their ambition to lead and to prevail. This horizon is not self-explanatory for either the earlier or the later groups. With the partial exception of Douglas's clergymen (who themselves had just been disestablished), success and power were not achieved by rising within preexisting hierarchies of political status and power or entering preexisting networks of influence.[46] (Remember that none of them were practicing lawyers or judges or were political party bosses or held high electoral office.) The Progressive intellectuals who created ideas, institutions, audiences, networks, publicity techniques, and opinion-shaping organs were less a "meritocracy" than a new and politically emergent "clerisy"—national public moralists in thought, purpose, and deed. For more than a generation they went from victory to victory. In this circumstance, the better question to ask is who or what were the earlier models or examples they sought to imitate. What organizations, movements, leaders, and events from the past were exemplary? In negative terms,

45. Kraditor, 1965, Appendix, 265–82. No information is given on religious affiliation or changes in affiliation.

46. In contrast, Haskell, 1977, 77–90, 100–110, and 144–89, describes the earlier American Social Science Association as consisting of preexisting elites and professionals seeking to anchor their intellectual authority in the dynamic America of the postbellum years. Even though there was some overlapping membership between the ASSA and some of the founders of the academic professional associations, attempts of the ASSA to forge institutional links with the new graduate and professional schools failed. Moreover, centers of energy and power shifted over time within the sets of groups considered here: toward women, away from Unitarians and Quakers, away from Boston, toward Chicago, and so on. Fitzpatrick (1990) looks at the careers of four of the first female graduate students in the social sciences at the University of Chicago. Even more than the men, these women had to create their own institutions—in the case of Sophonisba Breckinridge, her own professional school—in order to occupy positions of power.

what sorts of institutions, ideas, leaders, and activities from the past did they hold in highest contempt? What counterparts of these did they see in the present and seek to destroy? These questions might seem more appropriate (and easier to answer) to put to Kraditor's women or to Haskell's American Social Science Association than to my more *arrivé* academics and intellectuals. It is necessary to interrogate Progressive writings with these questions, however, because even at their most abstract, Progressives anchored their ideas within a larger theory of evolutionary social and moral progress. These theories of progress contain images of fulfillment or triumph that they saw foreshadowed in earlier people and events and opposed by a rather large list of enemies. Putting the issue in this concrete a way—friends and enemies—is also useful because it attunes us to hear very specific political and moral resonances in their writings. Their political and social theories contain specific echoes from the past and, if we are prepared to listen, dissonant and even discomfiting chords for those—should one say, those of *us*—who followed.

There are many apparent paradoxes raised in studies of Progressivism. Perhaps the overarching one is this: why were these people—who, among all those active in national political affairs, were the most cosmopolitan, scientifically trained, philosophically sophisticated, informed, and deeply critical of prevailing institutions and practices—*also* the most moral, religious, spiritual, and even romantically mystical in their public doctrines? And why were their opponents—those nationally active public men (I use men advisedly) who were, by all measures, more traditionally religious and incomparably *narrower* in their education, experiences, and political imaginations—so secular-universalistic in their public doctrines, so modern and "liberal" in their discussion of rights and institutions? The Progressives, bearing the combined language of social science, social control, community, character, piety, and memory, created systems of knowledge and institutional structures on which much of modern "liberal" America now seems to rest. Their opponents, invoking the Bill of Rights and speaking the tough legal language of constitutional powers, defended ways of life and patterns of power we now associate with an America either quaint or dangerously reactionary. To speak today from the institutional platforms created by the Progressives is, perforce, to be a contemporary "liberal," a member in good standing of cosmopolitan culture. But to *say* today what they said then, and from the authoritative platforms they did so much to erect, would be a profound embarrassment to the audience—perhaps the result of some booking error, or maybe a deliberate parody to represent the "other," the enemy against whom contemporary liberalism now defines itself. Or perhaps this difference is much less great than it appears, the result of both misreading what they had to say and disguising from ourselves part of what we are saying.

2

THE NATION AS
HISTORY & DESTINY

We wish, fully and entirely, TO NATIONALIZE THE INSTITUTIONS OF
OUR LAND AND TO IDENTIFY OURSELVES WITH OUR COUNTRY; to
become a single great people, separate and distinct in national character,
political interest, social and civil affinities from any and all other nations,
kindred and people on the earth.
                        —*American Republican*, 7 November 1844

The idea of America as one nation with a common history and destiny was not an invention of the Progressives. It was, however, central
to their thinking, providing the ligaments that bound together their
theories of politics, society, and economy and connecting those theories to a serviceable public doctrine and program of action. On one
level, then, the Progressives were heirs to a New England narrative that
began with the Great Migration and the establishment of the city on
the hill as a world-historical event biblically foretold. On this reading,
America as "nation" was born of covenant, committing a unified
people to an errand, first to redeem the wilderness and then the world.
Insofar as this "myth of New England" came to constitute the "myth
of America" (Bercovitch, 1977; Bercovitch, 1978; Hutchison, 1987;
Miller, 1967), it provided the grounds for political nationalism evident
from the Revolution onward. Whether expressed in the biblical language of millennialism, the cultural language of the American Way of
Life, the economic language of plenitude, the ethnoracial language of
triumphant Anglo-Saxonism, or the liberal language of the extension of
freedom, it presupposed a politics of consensus, of one people.
  On another level, this idea of America as one people with a singular
mission and destiny, was attacked by the Progressive theory of nation.
America as singular too often implied an America exempt from history,
from the problems of the rest of the Western world. This reading of
American nationality as uniqueness counseled a complacent conservatism—when in danger always revert back to the "law" of the Constitu-

tion—and a dangerous kind of political irresponsibility and drift.[1] On this level, the Progressives attacked what they saw as false images of nationality, urging instead that Americans consider their country as only now entering the larger stream of world history, requiring new institutions, new ideas, and new practices both to insure older values and attain higher and better ones.[2] The overriding event in this contest of definition and direction was the Civil War. This event both confirmed the enduring strength of the covenant myth and appeared to destroy whatever merit inhered in the myth of America's exemption from history and the American as exempt from historic duties (Fredrickson, 1965, 135). In the formation of the Republican party the Progressives saw both the rebirth of the nation and the birth of a new nation finally prepared to enter the world stage on an equal basis with European nations.

PARTISANSHIP AND NATIONALITY

Whatever the Progressives' depth of disenchantment with the policies and practices of the Republican party after 1876, its rhetoric and imagery continued to be unmistakably national and not constitutional. In contrast, the Democratic party, before and after the Civil War, remained strictly constitutionalist and thus loyal to an individual-

1. Lincoln and Jackson offer interesting contrasts in this regard. Jackson's farewell address of 1837: "Our constitution is no longer a doubtful experiment; . . . we find that it has preserved unimpaired the liberties of the people, secured the rights of property, and that our country has improved and is flourishing beyond any former examples in the history of nations." Lincoln in 1838: "We find ourselves under the government of a system of institutions, conducing more essentially to the ends of civil and religious liberty, than any of which the history of former times tells us. We toiled not in the acquirement or establishment of them—they are a legacy bequeathed us, by a once hardy, brave, and patriotic, but now lamented and departed race of ancestors. . . . That our government should have been maintained in its original form from its establishment until now, is not much to be wondered at. It had many props to support it through that period, which now are decayed, and crumbled away" (from Levy, 1988, 190, 217, and 219). Croly, 1909, chap. 4, discusses the failure of the middle period to deal with the issue of slavery as the fault of Jacksonian democratic values. See also Major Wilson, 1967, 619–44, on concepts of time and the debate over slavery.

2. This is the central thesis of Ross, 1991. Given the rhetorical tradition of the jeremiad, which calls the nation back to its covenant *and* prepares the nation for new challenges and conditions, it is often difficult to place writings on a simple "left-right" ideological spectrum. This is a central theme in Bercovitch, 1978. In the apt words of Wellesley English professor and labor activist Vida Scudder, "We need all the courage the past can give us; we need all the consecration it can inspire." This was said in her support of "the victims of the modern slavery of trade" (1898, 211).

ist, localist, and "small republic" tradition. In the eyes of Progressive intellectuals, this combination disqualified the Democrats from the start as an agency for national renewal. And, given the strength of the Democratic party in the white South, that entire region was also disqualified from an active role in reform. The Democratic party reliance on the Constitution as a static legal agreement among states and its insistence on maximizing individual and local liberty necessarily precluded it from serious reflection on objects of national importance.[3] Contrasting the national platform language of the two parties in the post–Civil War period vividly illustrates this difference and serves as a concrete starting point for examining the Progressives' idea of American nationality.

In 1868 the Republicans officially called themselves the National Union Republican party. In 1876 they declared that "the United States of America is a nation, not a league"; in 1880, that "the people of the United States, in their organized capacity, constitute a Nation and not a mere confederacy of States." In 1908, invoking its language of more than thirty years earlier ("in the economy of Providence, this land was to be purged of human slavery"), the platform speaks of the Republican party as "this great historic organization, that destroyed slavery, preserved the Union . . . expanded the national domain . . . and gave to the nation her seat of honor in the councils of the world."[4] Its Whig and Liberty party origins remained intact.

The platforms of the Democratic party in this same period read like anachronistic documents protesting British colonial domination. In 1868, a long section paraphrases the Declaration of Independence as a bill of indictment against the presence of the national government in the South, "subject[ing] ten States, in time of profound peace, to military despotism and negro supremacy," and recalls the time that "the

3. Croly, 1914, 145, correctly calls this reading "the monarchy of the Constitution" because of its limited powers, its distance from popular majorities, and the concomitant dependence on mediating courts, lawyers, and party leaders. That Jefferson had exactly this ideal—that of a very limited, liberal "monarchy" at the national level in order to insure vibrant small republics and local democracy—is persuasively argued in Sheldon, 1991, chaps. 3–5.

4. Johnson and Porter, 1975. This language strongly recalls that of John Quincy Adams. In his understanding, "union" preceded the Declaration of Independence, making that document "a social compact, by which the whole people covenanted with each citizen of the United Colonies, and each citizen with the whole people. . . . Each was pledged to all, and all were pledged to each by a concert of souls, without limitation of time, in the presence of Almighty God, and proclaimed to all mankind" (1831, 17–18). The Constitution, as third and last stage of the Revolution (the war itself is the second), represents "the formation of the Anglo-American People and Nation of North America" (1836, 5). For a prominent Progressive view repeating this same logic, see James, 1896, 401–3.

people of the United States threw off . . . subjection to the British crown." From then onward the ideal image is of America as "a federal union of co-equal States." Its achievement demands that the nation "return to . . . constitutional limitations of power" (1872) to avoid "corrupt centralism" (1876). Throughout the 1880s and early 1890s the national platform language is unvarying, if less strident, on this theme, as befitted a party that had again become nationally competitive. In a paraphrase of Anti-Federalist writings almost a century earlier the 1880 platform warned of "a dangerous spirit of encroachment, which tends to consolidate the powers of all the departments into one, and thus to create [,] whatever be the form of government, a real despotism." In 1884 the same theme was sounded, but as "the preservation of personal rights, the equality of all citizens before the law; the reserved rights of the States; the supremacy of the Federal Government within the limits of the Constitution." Constitutional limitation was also the main theme four years later: "a plan of government regulated by a written Constitution, strictly specifying every granted power and expressly reserving to the States or people the entire ungranted residue of power." In the Democratic party platform of 1892 this idea was expressed as a call for "a return to these fundamental principles of free popular government, based on home rule and individual liberty" especially now that there was "a tendency to centralize all power at the Federal capital." By 1896 this language was compressed into the First Amendment ("freedom of speech, freedom of the press, freedom of conscience"), concluding with a call for "the preservation of personal rights, the equality of all citizens before the law, and the faithful observance of constitutional limitations." After 1896 and until 1916 the only expressed idea of nation was a section on states' rights and, in 1900, a philippic against militarism—"it means conquest abroad and intimidation and oppression at home . . . a large standing army and unnecessary burden of taxation."[5]

By the turn of the century both major parties moderated their respective languages of nationality. Indeed, in 1912 the Republican platform had no nationalist language at all, only a reference to the Constitution and federal courts as bonds of the country. In the Progressive platform

5. Johnson, 1975. The various Prohibition parties were even more explicit than the Republicans in their image of America as one nation. The first Prohibition platform refers to America as a Christian nation, and calls for national sabbath observance and national and state provision for public schools "for the universal and forced education of all the youth of the land," including "the free use of the Bible . . . as a textbook of purest morality" so "that our children may grow up in its light and that its spirit and principles may pervade our nation" (1876). Starting in 1888, they were also the first party to call for woman suffrage.

of that same year, however, the imagery of the earlier Republican party and the New England myth of America was revived. "The conscience of the people, in a time of grave national problems, has called into being a new party, born of the nation's sense of justice." This party founding is "the fulfillment of the duty laid upon us by our fathers" and the platform "our covenant with the people." Reviving the powerful image of the sovereignty of the whole people, the platform declares that "the people are the masters of their Constitution" (Johnson and Porter, 1975).

By 1916, with war raging in Europe and in the midst of preparedness campaigns, the Republicans rediscovered their nationalist roots. Given the circumstances and their prowar constituency, the platform language is quite moderate. Appealing to "all Americans, whether naturalized or native-born, to prove to the world that we are Americans in thought and deed, with one loyalty, one hope, one aspiration," it concluded by asking them to be true to "the great traditions of their common country, and above all things, to keep the faith." The Democratic party platform, under the heading "Americanism," was testimony to a conversion experience into the National Religion of the American Way. Recognizing "the assertion and triumphant demonstration of the indivisibility and coherent strength of the nation as the supreme issue of this day . . . it summons all men of whatever origin or creed who could count themselves Americans, to join in making clear to all the world the unity and consequent power of America." The virtues of the "small republic"—its homogeneity, its unstinting patriotism, its fraternal supremacy over all mere laws—were here translated to the whole nation. America was the gathered people, "the best of the blood, the industry and genius of the whole world . . . welded into a mighty and splendid Nation." As befitted its Tocquevillian articulation, this democratic celebration of unity was also a standing threat: "Whoever . . . creates discord and strife among our people . . . is faithless to the trust which the privileges of citizenship repose in him and is disloyal to his country."[6]

6. When Woodrow Wilson returned from the peace conference in 1919, his rhetoric appropriated in its entirety the Republican version from the Civil War period: "Our participation in the war established our position among the nations . . . the whole world saw at last . . . a Nation they had deemed material and now found to be compact of the spiritual forces that must free men of every nation of every unworthy bondage. . . . The stage is set, the destiny is disclosed. It has come about by no plan of our conceiving, but by the hand of God who led us into this way. We cannot turn back. We can only go forward . . . to follow the vision. It was of this that we dreamed at our birth" (quoted from Handy, 1984, 160).

THE BONDS OF NATIONALITY

The proof of hegemonic political victory in America is demonstrated not only when the defeated appropriate the ideas of the victors, but also when the result is written as democratic history, that is, as the necessary result of forces beyond the control or purposes of any identifiable group.[7] If Tocqueville is right, then the strongest evidence of the victory of Progressive ideas of nationality is neatly recorded in a book, *The Nation and the Schools* (1920), written by two highly regarded professional educators.

Every discovery of science, every invention in the arts, every advance in industry has worked throughout the country toward interdependence and unity, toward a multiplication of common needs, common ideals, and common aspirations, and toward an insistent demand for the kind of far-reaching collective action that will meet these needs and realize these ideals and aspirations quickly and effectively. It has been through the pressure of these forces,— impersonal, objective, and irresistible,—that the Federation has become a Union, and the Union a Nation.[8]

Those who struggled mightily for more than three decades to achieve this inevitability knew that they were up against formidable obstacles. Having experienced the results of the dissolution of the Civil War regime into a confused tangle of economic dynamism, social dislocation, and political impotence and having witnessed and recorded the results of German state building and British reform, they were deeply conscious of the institutional and intellectual barriers to the achievement of an authoritative nationality in America.

An analogous democratic fiction is to attribute intellectual discovery itself to necessity. A recent study of the formation of the professional social sciences speaks of the use of historicism, cultural organicism, and the concept of interdependence in American social theory at the turn of the century as a kind of "primitive recognition that the very constitution of the social universe had changed." The social experi-

7. "Historians who live in democratic ages not only deny that the few have any power of acting upon the destiny of a people, but deprive the people themselves of the power of modifying their own condition, and they subject them either to an inflexible Providence or to some blind necessity" (Tocqueville, 1981, 383).

8. Keith and Bagley, 1920, 2. Bagley was professor at Columbia Teachers College and coauthor with Charles Beard of a series of successful secondary school textbooks on American history written in the interwar period. This book, in fact, recounts a history of valiant political and cultural struggle to achieve public education in America from the Revolution to the time of its writing.

ence of reality itself, and not the values, traditions, and culture of the observers, it seems, produced the inevitable ideas that anchored the inevitable political and social reforms.[9]

In 1915, Albion Small wrote an essay, "The Bonds of Nationality," for the *American Journal of Sociology (AJS)*. This work can stand as a fair copy of the larger intellectual framework of Progressive discussion of American nationality, not only because of Small's standing, but because he integrated writings of so many of his fellow sociologists and political economists from the previous twenty-five years into this essay.[10] The article, he says, was written to "illustrate and elaborate two sociological concepts: first, that of 'social structure,' second, that of 'social achievement.' "[11] Small then moves to a third and integrating concept, "the social bonds," in order to ask how and why groups hold together over long periods of time. Asserting that these bonds must stand "for something more vital than the external accidents which are reflected in mere group forms (i.e., constitutions)," he concludes that external or institutional forms are expressive of and reflect the cohesive power of internal factors.[12] This static conception of social structure must be complemented by an analysis of social bonds as "group achievements," that is, the ways in which social structures alter their environments over time. Modifying Lester Ward's discussion of this dynamic, Small concludes:

These personal, or human or moral values . . . consist, first, in the control which men have gained and may gain over nature; sec-

9. Haskell, 1977, 15–16. In fairness to the author, this argument is soon retracted: "The systems of belief by which men live possess a tenacity so powerful that assumptions shape experience far more often than they are shaped by it. The lesson is not new, but never before [Thomas Kuhn's *Structure of Scientific Revolutions*] has it been taught so forcefully" (22). Given the remarkably homogeneous religious and cultural backgrounds of the early social scientists and their followers, understanding paradigms shifts in social theory in America is of a piece with understanding our cultural history more than our social-economic history. Only afterward do the material factors of wealth and power shape the reception and direction of that shift. And in pluralistic and democratic America, old paradigms never die, they only go underground for a time to emerge reformulated as if they were new.

10. In 1904, Giddings wrote a short article, "Sociological Questions," for *Forum*, a popular monthly, which is a precis of Small's themes and arguments. Giddings, 1904, 245–55.

11. Small, 1915, 629. These concepts are from Georg Simmel. Small refers here to thirteen of his previous articles in the *AJS* and to his *General Sociology* (1905), where he summarizes and discusses Simmel's work.

12. Small, 1915, 631. This is equally true for governments; Arthur Twining Hadley began his lectures on citizenship in 1903 with the statement that "form of government is an unimportant thing as compared with the spirit in which government is administered . . . this internal character or spirit of a government is far more important than any of its external characteristics" (Hadley, 1903, 1–2).

ondly, in the control which they have gained and may gain over themselves as individuals; thirdly, in the types of co-operation which they have achieved and may achieve, for more effective control of nature, and for more effective correlation of moral forces, to the end of progressive sublimation of human qualities, in progressively efficient combinations of activities for progressively higher ranges of achievement, in cycles to which our knowledge can assign no end (Small, 1915, 632).

Small quickly dismisses the first factor as significant independently of the other two social resources (mere "economic achievement" as control of material resources "would be halting at a point in the rear of the picket line of human progress") to turn to "control over the individual self, and control over human association" as the basis for discussing the bonds and progress of American nationality. Here, the individual as resource is treated almost as summarily as is power over nature. Noting that the individual is an autonomous resource only if he is loyal to others in systems of social cooperation, Small finds the issue becomes how individuals "by influences from within" maintain "fidelity to their posts in doing what their fellows have a right to expect of them." Thus, the issue is the difference between "adequate and defective individual working ideals of responsibility to the group." These ideals are socially constructed and maintained. Summarily stated, "a population of Herbert Spencers would probably perish of social sterility in a generation" (Small, 1915, 633, 635).

A corollary to this way of viewing the individual as social resource is that different individual qualities are demanded at different stages of human progress. Even granting that earlier in our history individual initiative and autonomy have been paramount in the economic sphere, Small says that this was never entirely true in our political life and even less so "in the realms of higher thought and religious belief." He recognizes that many claims of American individualism are bogus in any case (here he cites Tocqueville on our slavelike conformity to conventional ideas); even where they are true, especially "in our struggle for economic gain," they are no longer a social resource or bond of nationality. Indeed, the present circumstances of American life call for "transformation of these standards and corresponding remolding of individuals. . . . We are demanding that each shall fall into the ranks of the social battle."[13]

13. Small, 1915, 636–37. At about this same time, the historian Ephraim Douglas Adams of Stanford (and brother of Henry Carter) declared to a lecture audi-

It is only when he turns to group bonds that Small's analysis of nationality properly begins. The concept "group" or "association" quickly becomes "institutions" and bonds become "the social tradition."[14] Four "institutions" are then underlined as the embodiment of the most important social traditions for national cohesion. The first is a common language, by which he means a specifically "American language [as] the master key to American ideals" and therefore the means by which "spiritual communication of all with each" is achieved. Because "language carries the valuations of the group that uses it" we should not wonder that "conquering peoples have always tried to impose their language upon the conquered." Americans "believe almost fanatically in the efficiency of the American language in making Americans" both for its spontaneous effects and for its universal applicability.[15] This belief also explains the need for universal education and the system of public schools.

When Small turns to his second "institution," that of race solidarity, he first feels compelled to explain exactly what he means by race. Borrowing the term "consciousness of kind" from Giddings, Small's notion of race means only "that differences of ancestry cease to be mischievous in partitioning the population." Earlier, in fact, he used the term "melting pot" to mean the same thing. The creation of one people on these terms is not achieved spontaneously. Granting that "a population made up of successfully blended racial elements" will have great social strength, in the interim, he writes, "diversity of racial elements is in itself a national weakness" because of the expenditures of effort required to blend "heterogeneous stocks." Reminding the reader

---

ence at Yale that "industrial liberty, equality of opportunity, must yield in part, at least, to the organic sense of the nation—to fraternity" (Adams, 1913, 147).

14. Small, 1915, 639. Hadley used a Rousseauist image of general will in this same sense. Maintaining that the general will is a public sentiment constituting a people, he declares that this sentiment "includes all good men, minorities as well as majorities, who support the government not as a selfish means for the promotion of their own interest, but as a common heritage which they accept as loyal members of a body politic" (Hadley, 1903, 34); see also Hadley, 1901, 139–40.

15. Small, 1915, 643 and 641. This same idea carried one step further by Hadley, 1901, 141, is that sharing the same moral language is to substitute the power of public opinion for governmental coercion. "Just as in private morality there is an alternative between self-government by one's own conscience and the compulsion of external authority, so in public morality there is a similar alternative between self-government by public sentiment and the tyranny of a dominating power." And see Hadley, 1903, 74, where he says that the history of man is not the eighteenth-century version, that is, from "a system of authority to a system of liberty," but the more historically accurate one of "a passage from a system of obligations imposed by the community to a system of self-imposed obligations."

that "race solidarity in the strictly ethnic sense is largely imaginary," Small points out that even the term "Anglo-Saxon" is so capacious that only one or two generations are required to "assimilate citizens of the most heterogeneous origins" into "the amiable fiction that we are all of one blood." The psychic nature of unity should not detract us from the fact that felt diversity in matters of race "is functional disunity" and that so long as "minor groups distinguished by physical, mental or moral traits which are in contrast with those of the nation as a whole, *and which are thought of by the larger group as race traits*, the situation is relatively weak"[16] (Small's italics).

By far the longest section of Small's essay is devoted to the third source of national cohesion, that of "A Coherent Family Type." Depending upon the kinds of individuals produced by the family, a nation is strong or weak. The burdens Small places on the family are extensive but center on the need to inculcate the virtues of loyalty and service to others—in his words, "a quick sense of other people's values, and prompt response to requisitions upon obligation to respect those values." The best citizens, therefore, are those "men and women who are tempered and fitted to the loyalties implicit in the family association." There are many and varied threats to this key nation building institution, but the most dangerous enemy of the American middle class family "is the comparative freedom and desire to pursue individual interests." Whatever the source of this individualistic system of values, its power is such that, at present, "the American middle-class family is a dubious social asset" as producer and conservator "of the primary social loyalties."[17]

The last institutional bond of nationality is "a convincing religion." This may seem curious coming from one who abandoned the ministry and helped found academic sociology in America. But if one makes a firm and consistent distinction between "church" (dogma, ritual,

16. Small, 1915, 643, 644, 648. Small's reference here is to the South and the problem of Negroes. Until it is solved, the race question stands as a permanent barrier to unity among whites and also among blacks. W. E. B. DuBois, 1897, 6, expressed a national idea of race this way: "What, then, is a race? It is a vast family of human beings, generally of common blood and language, always of common history, traditions, and impulses, who are both voluntarily and involuntarily striving together for the accomplishment of certain more or less vividly conceived ideals of life."

17. Small, 1915, 650, 653, and 655–57. At this point in his discussion, Small digresses at length on the effect on the middle class of recent feminist attacks on the family and on child rearing and on the bad example set by the "pseudo-rich," that is, those whose incomes are such that they can mimic the marriage patterns of the idle rich without the stigma attached to the latter, and therefore serve as more effective transmitters of their vices to the middle class.

rules) and "religion" and then extends the idea of religion into something like "an integrated system of social explanation and personal meaning," Small's conclusion is both logical and central to his understanding of American nationality and national citizenship. To Small it goes without question that psychic unity and shared values are essential to nationality; the only question is the way in which these common beliefs are experienced and held. He insists that for a religion to be both convincing and powerful it must be voluntarily held "as the most plausible competitor among conceivable interpretations of the believer's [social] experience." This requirement precludes not only officially promulgated (church) creeds, but also the imposition of creeds based on the experience and interpretations of one people upon those whose "experience and interpretations have been of a different order." Although any conformity produced by these methods may "be effective for repression," they are poor substitutes "for the spur and lure of a faith which blends all one's mental and moral insights" (Small, 1915, 671, 673).

It is at this point that Small makes a significant turn, one that is essential for his larger argument and for Progressive social theory. Religions in America, he says, are not so much divided by denominations or faith traditions—for example, Baptists, Methodists, Catholics, Jews—as each of these, in various ratios to be sure, are divided by traditionalist and modernist understandings. And insofar as traditionalist views prevail, Americans will remain mired "in at least two worlds," that of their lived experiences and that of "their religious conventionalities" (Small, 1915, 673).

> The crucial problem at the present stage of religious development is not whether this, that, or the other doctrinal formula or system is correct; but the incalculably more radical problem is whether religion is a hand-out from an external authority or a deposit of the evolving output of men's objective experience and subjective interpretations and valuations (Small, 1915, 675).

The hope for a common religion, then, can only be sustained with the victory of modernism—what came to be called mainstream or liberal Protestantism—and this victory (here the reference to James and Dewey is obvious) depends upon overcoming the dualism between particular "church" traditions of religious belief and a faith-integrating common experience. But here he parts company with James and Dewey and turns to sociologists. Through their professional vocation, it is sociologists who have volunteered to represent among scholars the conviction that the world's knowledge . . . must be capable of demonstrating its objectivity in part by its composability into an organization of knowledge, each portion of which shall corroborate and vitalize every other portion. Nothing less than this is conceivably adequate intellectual support for a religion that should convince all men . . . [that it is] the only conceivable creedal basis for social unity at its highest power.[18]

On this series of steps Small has carried us to a central tenet of Progressive social theory as both national and personal identity and public doctrine. Whereas all religions are, ideally, "religions of humanity," only sociologists, by articulating the present condition of man's "social consciousness" in terms of its connections to "the remembered traditions of the race," can "invent"[19] a national religion as a national bond. Again, paraphrasing Dewey, this "modernism is not iconoclasm. It is conservation and renovation and reconstruction."[20] The political result of this national religion will be a democratic public.

On one level, Small is here calling for a project that had already been largely completed, intellectually if not institutionally and politically. The modernist impulse of the social gospel, beginning in the late 1870s, and historical criticism of the Bible, begun at Andover Seminary and Yale in the 1840s, had long since yielded a Christian social ethic and a Protestant ecumenical theology increasingly placed within a larger theory of social evolution (Kuklick, 1985, chaps. 11–13; Stevenson, 1986, chaps. 3 and 6–8). Indeed, twenty years earlier, the first two volumes of Small's own journal serialized what immediately became the most powerful single summary of this viewpoint, Shailer Ma-

18. Small, 1915, 676. This understanding of the purpose and function of social theory is radically at odds with the way disciplinary histories of sociology are now written. The same holds in discussions of John Dewey's achievements. See, for example, Haskell, 1977, 9–16. A good recent study of the relationship between sociology and religion is Curtis, 1991.

19. Small, 1915, 678. He deliberately uses the term "invent" in this context because earlier, in playing off of Voltaire's aphorism about the need to invent God if none existed, he had added: "That nation is weak in which the invention of religion is not a protected industry" (669). Although the meaning here is not entirely clear, he may be referring to the need for academic freedom and university autonomy.

20. Small, 1915, 680. This idea of preserving the past in the future as essential for progress was earlier stated by Giddings (1900, 53) this way: "Progress . . . is the continuous harmonization of a continually appearing unlikeness of feeling, thought and purpose . . . with a vast central mass of already established agreements."

thews's *The Social Teachings of Jesus.*[21] Thus, by 1915, Small is really codifying the results of a long-standing theological-ethical enterprise when he concludes that the symbolic centerpiece of this "new" national religion is the now historically recovered *"Weltanschauung* of Jesus"[22] excavated from barbarism, superstition, church, and dogma. Sociologists are not enemies or competitors to churchmen and should not ever "[assault] the minds of men in general with anything like ab-

21. *American Journal of Sociology,* vols. 1 and 2. Nine articles by Mathews, *The Social Teachings of Jesus.* To this must be added, in vols. 1–3, thirteen articles of what became E. A. Ross's *Social Control* (1901); see especially, chap. 16, pp. 196–218, on "Social Religion." In addition, books on social Christianity by Washington Gladden and Lyman Abbott were reviewed in those same volumes. See also Commons, 1894, 8–23, on Christianity and Sociology: "Sociology has rightly been said to be one half of religion; theology is the other half" (19–20). "[The minister] should begin with the organic nature of society, showing that it is based properly on Christian ethics; then the nature and functions of the State as a mighty force in furthering God's kingdom and establishing righteous relations among men; then the family and the home" (20–21). And Ely, 1889, chap. 1: "What has the Church done with the second commandment, which, in its elaboration, becomes social science or sociology?" (9). A meeting of Wisconsin Congregationalists in 1895 proclaimed "the right of sociology to demand that theology be ethicized" and declared that "the best book for social guidance is the New Testament; the best commentaries are the works of scientific sociology" (quoted in Thelen, 1972, 108–9).

22. Small, 1915, 680. Charles Horton Cooley, in his textbook on social psychology, put it this way: "The relative truth [religious creeds] once had . . . are now, for most of us, not creeds at all, since they are incredible; but creeds of some sort we must have . . . we need to believe, and we shall believe what we can. . . . The perennial truth of what Christ taught comes precisely from the fact that it was not a system, but an intuition and expression of higher sentiments. . . . All finality in religious formulas is discredited philosophically by the idea of evolution" (1909, 375–78). And see 191–203 on conflation of American democracy and this reading of Christianity. Simon Patten, 1899, 408–9, stated this same idea of democracy and progress as incarnation at the conclusion of his study of the history of English thought from an economic perspective. And see Patten, 1896, chap. 5, on the victory of abundance or the pleasure economy over scarcity or the pain economy running parallel with the victory of the "Christ ideal." See also Vida Scudder, 1898, 313–18, on the "remarriage" of democracy and Christianity in socialism. In the writings of a decidedly non-Christian Herbert Croly, this same ideal is expressed as a metaphorical parallel between America and New Israel. "The Law, as written in the books and as expounded by the holy doctors [lawyers, judges], had been [America's] schoolmaster, for whose instruction during their national religious adolescence they might well be grateful; but once Christianity was revealed, the schoolmaster lost his peculiar authority. Thereafter the high road to salvation was traced by an uncompromising faith, the constructive effect of which was incomparably greater than was conformity to any Law or the study of its learned commentaries. . . . A loyal progressive democracy is emancipated not merely from the authority of a legal formulation of social righteousness, but from bondage to a mechanical conception of social causation. The beauty of faith consists in the freedom with which it endows the faithful" (Croly, 1914, 169 and 174). For a discussion of this religious side of Croly's writings, especially in the 1920s, see Stettner, 1993, 148–59.

stract and doctrinalized modernism." Rather, as keepers of man's entire social and intellectual heritage, their task is *"never intentionally [to] undo a religious conviction, except through the process of enlarging the individual or group experience, and of assisting to reconstruct the conviction, so as to accommodate the new experience"* (Small's italics). Small ends his essay by quoting from one of his earlier university sermons. This vision of sociology he terms *"*a vision of *the American Religion"* (Small's italics), one that can be grafted onto the trunk of Catholicism, Judaism, and Protestantism so that "each might contribute to his rendering of religion all the spiritual force there is in his distinctive beliefs." This conclusion is, of course, an almost exact precis of Will Herberg's *Protestant, Catholic, Jew* written forty years later and hailed then as a "discovery" at once of American religious pluralism and, in what Herberg called "The Religion of Americans," a national religious unity.[23]

On another level, however, Small is already becoming somewhat anachronistic in his use of overt evangelical and explicitly biblical language. In John Dewey's writings, for example, "the method of democracy" becomes the "Religion of America," and the schools become the churches of the national democratic faith. In many other Progressive writings the sociological and economic "proofs" of the progress of this faith seem to overwhelm and even displace their religious causes.[24] In its stead, democracy itself becomes a faith in the American Way of Life, which includes, but now transcends, its earlier regional, denomina-

---

23. Small, 1915, 681 and 682. Small's colleague at Chicago, the theologian Shailer Mathews, put it most aptly when he called for making Christianity "a religion fit for [American] democracy" (Mathews, 1918, 121). Herberg, 1983, "The Religion of Americans and American Religion." This delay should not be surprising. In an article written in 1990, one of the most perceptive historians of American religion calls our attention to a "quid obscuram" that cuts across all organized religious communities in America, namely, traditionalism and modernism, and to the high church of modernism, which has been hegemonic in the twentieth century, the American university (Wuthnow, 1990). This "new" thesis receives contemporary political relevance in Hunter, 1991, where we are warned of an alliance of Protestant fundamentalists, Orthodox Jews, and Catholic conservatives against the Enlightenment tradition represented by secularists, reform Jews, and liberal Catholics and Protestants. A Catholic priest and ex-law school dean recently called for a new religious establishment consisting of all sensible Protestants, Catholics, and Jews against religious fundamentalism from whatever quarter (Mooney, 1990).

24. One should not make too much of this displacement. Evangelical Protestant pleas for the Christianization of the "West" were replete with social, economic, and demographic statistics and made the public schools as important as the churches in this task. See, for example, Beecher, 1977; Strong, 1963; and discussion in Handy, 1990, 281–301; and Ross, 1918, 175–79, on public schools and their religious functions.

tional, and even biblical formulations.[25] However formulated, Progressives insisted that democracy and democratic reform required a national will strong enough to generate bonds of sufficient strength to encourage sacrifice for social justice and the common good. Small's seemingly "conservative" formulation was an integral part of his economic "radicalism" as expressed in his contemporaneous writings on the social gradations of capital and on the transition from capitalism to democracy (Small, 1914; 1913; see also 1919).

WHEREVER CHILDREN
OF PURITANS ARE FOUND

A curious feature of Small's analysis of American nationality was a long digression on the legacy of the Hebrew ideal of family. Quite outside any framework of social evolution, Small states that the "Hebrew (i.e., Old Testament) conception of family loyalty . . . is far above the ideal practiced or professed by large sections of Americans" and that "the typical family life of modern Jews [is now] a salutary factor in American society." A similar philo-Semitism finds expression in Ly-

---

25. Dewey, 1916, chaps. 6–7 and 18; and Kuklick, 1985, chaps. 13–17, especially 242–46. See also Giddings, 1912, 585–89, on the same topic as Small's, in his presidential address to the American Sociological Association. The theme is national unity and fulfillment charted through mass consumption patterns, the triumph of scientific or universalistic views of nature, thereby purifying religion, and the assimilative effects of class struggle in the achievement of social justice through direct democracy. The origin of the term "Religion of America" or "The American Religion" used by Small and, later, Herberg, remains obscure, but E. D. Adams, 1913, 122, has a reference to a book or article by an English Catholic, William Barry, titled "The Religion of America." The famous expression, "nation with the soul of a church," is G. K. Chesterton's. The idea of American democracy as itself a faith is articulated throughout Dewey's writings. It also constitutes the somewhat mystical ending to Croly's 1914 *Progressive Democracy* and is articulated earlier in chapter 8 in contrasting faith to the "law" as external "works." Samuel Zane Batten, a social gospel theologian wrote, "There are many indications that the great movement for human freedom and social justice, begun in the Reformation, is about to take on new life and complete itself in what may be called the democracy of all life. . . . For democracy, we have come to realize, is less a form of government than a confession of faith; it is the confession of human brotherhood . . . it is the recognition of common aims and common hopes. . . . To confess this faith against the world, to follow this ideal . . . is the best evidence that man can give that he is working in line with the great purpose of God in the world" (1898, 253–54). Lyman Abbott repeats this same idea. America represents democracy in the world, but had not always been "conscious of the spirit which has possessed her." Now, however, we have come to realize that "Democracy is more than a scheme of government . . . a theory of economics . . . a plan of education . . . a form of religious institutions. Democracy is a great religious faith: a superstitious faith, if you will, but a great religious faith. It is faith in man" (1901, 196–97).

man Abbott's lectures on the rights of man and American democracy.[26] Framing all history as a struggle between Rome and Israel, he concludes that the modern age represents the final victory of Hebraism as democracy over Rome as aristocracy and imperialism. America as the New Israel of the Puritan founding is the exemplary Hebraic nation because it combines Christianity and Democracy, thereby making universal—in biblical language, "fulfilling"—the original Hebraic principles. Abbott puts this historical-evolutionary theory against the false one "that the consent of the governed confers authority" and, in so doing, makes American democracy the final achievement of history. As the fulfillment of this original Hebraic promise America is a kind of democratic theocracy "pervaded by the spirit, not merely of good will toward man, and of large hope for man, but also of faith in man."[27]

While expressions of this same Hebraic covenant ideal can be found in other contexts,[28] the primary source within American history is the Puritans. No matter what the context—economics, philosophy of history, sociology, psychology, or literary criticism—Progressive writings on American nationality are filiopietistic to the core. At first glance, this might appear somewhat paradoxical and even self-defeating. New England at this time was in cultural, economic, and demographic decline, its ancestral religion shrinking and many of its intellectuals either looking inward or living in imagination in England.[29] Like the

26. Small, 1915, 651. Abbott was editor of *Outlook*, a leading Progressive weekly, for more than three decades, and pastor of the leading Congregational church in America. This series of twelve lectures came with a bibliographical guide that constitutes a pantheon of Progressive intellectuals and their precursors: John Morley, T. H. Green, Lecky, John Stuart Mill, Sir Henry Maine, Frederic Harrison, and T. H. Huxley from Britain; Josiah Strong, Giddings, Hadley, and Ely from America; Hegel from Germany.

27. Abbott, 1901, 69 and 163–65. And see Ely, 1889, 11–12 and 92. This appropriation of the image of America as "New Israel" has a fairly continuous history in the nineteenth century. John Quincy Adams (1839, 119–20), in a discourse commissioned by the New York Historical Society on the fiftieth anniversary of the Constitution marked by the inauguration of George Washington, repeated much of the "unionist" and "covenant" theory of America referred to above.

28. The social gospel movement with its "kingdom" ideal is explicitly Hebraic and implicitly "theocratic" in a cultural sense. This equation is made in Ely 1889, chap. 2; Commons, 1894, chap. 4; and Batten, 1898, 235–53, and 1911, 207–27. And see Dombrowski, 1936, chaps. 4 (Ely), 5 (Protestant seminaries), and 13 (Herron); Crunden, 1984, 39–51 (Commons), and 56–68 (Dewey); and Handy, 1984, chaps. 4 (social gospel theology) and 6 (cooperative Christianity). And see Curtis, 1991, for a larger analysis of the social gospel and American culture.

29. Soloman, 1956, on response to Irish immigration and loss of political power. By 1906, Massachusetts, Connecticut, Rhode Island, and New Hampshire were all more than two-thirds Catholic. Another sign was the Boston-centered Anti-Imperialist League as a protest against the dynamism and expansion of America that left

South, New England was increasingly on the defensive against the dynamism of the core culture and economy represented by the twin poles of New York and Chicago. This ambivalence is nicely expressed in the conclusion to a book that was originally a Ph.D. thesis at Radcliffe at the turn of the century:

> When one notes how many of the cities and towns of New England are to-day controlled politically by those who have neither Puritan traditions, Puritan background of ancestry, nor Puritan ideals, one feels dismayed, for it would seem the old order had passed away save in memory and in history. But it is not an unintelligent and sentimental optimism alone which asserts that New England is still a living force, and Puritan traditions and ideals still working models. Such an assertion is proved to be undeniable fact when the sons and daughters of New England have been sought out in the West. The history of New England is not confined to six states; it is contained in a greater and broader New England wherever the children of the Puritans are found (Mathews, 1909, 272).

The study of what this author termed "Great Migrations" as a continuum of the great seventeenth-century migration to America traces the extraordinary influence of New Englanders in shaping the political institutions and culture of the dynamic states in the Midwest. This same idea was expressed in the 1920s by the president emeritus of the University of Colorado when he said that "Puritan standards have become the public standards of America, and you will find more of New England in Colorado Springs, Boulder, or Greeley (i.e., college towns), than in most towns of Massachusetts. This is not a partisan claim, but

---

New England behind. William James expressed this New England alienation in a way that repudiated both American expansion and American nationalism: "Damn great Empires! . . . I am against bigness and greatness in all their forms, and with the invisible molecular moral forces that work from individual to individual. . . . The bigger the unit you deal with, the hollower, the more brutal, the more mendacious is the life displayed. So I am against all big organizations as such, national ones first and foremost; against all big successes and big results" (Perry, 1935, 315). Boston's Anti-Immigration League expressed this same retreat. James's friend and fellow member of the Metaphysical Club, John Fiske, was its first President. Lasch, 1973, 70–79, discusses the anti-imperialism of both New England and the South in terms of their growing peripheral status. A third indicator was the demise of the Boston-centered American Social Science Association. Haskell's analysis (1977) of its rise and fall would be augmented by a combination of regional and religious analysis: the new academic professional associations were much more nationalist, expansionist, and "evangelical," thoroughly at home in the dynamic industrial core of America.

recognition of fact" (Grimes, 1967, xii). But the chief connecting link of Puritanism to Progressive conceptions of American nationality and Puritanism is Abraham Lincoln—"father Abraham"—and the Civil War.

Ida Tarbell, famous as a muckraking journalist, achieved even greater fame as a biographer of Lincoln. The culmination of her very successful magazine- and book-writing enterprise came with *In the Footsteps of the Lincolns*, which traces the progress of the family from New England to Illinois. As preface to this lavishly designed book is John S. Phillips's poem "Lincoln," written in 1908, part of which reads:

In him distilled and potent the choice essence of a race!
Far back the Puritans—stern and manful visionaries,
Repressed poets, flushed with dreams of glowing theologies!
Each new succession, out of border hardship,
Refined to human use the initial rigor of the breed,
Passing to the next the unconscious possession of a perfecting soul! . . .
Each axman and each plowman added
Another filament of ruggedness;
Unknowing minds dumbly cried for liberty;
Mute hearts strove against injustice. . . .
At last was ready the alembic, where Nature stored and set apart
Each generations finest residue,
Waiting for the hour of perfect mixture—
And then the Miracle!

In less grandiloquent terms, this use of Lincoln and the Civil War as bearer of the spirit of Jerusalem into the new dynamic core of America was restated in many forms in the writings of Progressive academics and intellectuals.[30] The new urban middle class evidently shared in this revival of the memory of Lincoln and the Civil War. The first of the new monthly magazines to achieve a large subscription base was the

30. Ida M. Tarbell, 1924, Preface. See Croly, 1909, 85–99 and 427; Hadley, 1901, chap. 1; E. D. Adams, 1913, chaps. 2 and 5, although, in fact, Adams's entire book, *Power of Ideals*, is simply a recounting of migration and nationality. The radical labor activist and English professor, Vida Scudder (1898, 204–6), charts our literary progress as fulfillment of American ideals, concluding: "To realize a spiritual democracy for the victims and outcasts of the Old World is a task before which we may indeed quail, unless we believe it to be God-given. But, turning back to the lives of our fathers, surely we see in the warfare against the slavery of the negro a prophecy of our larger conflict against evil less evident, but more deeply imbedded in the social body. The Civil War lies behind us as a great symbol, and its limited and clear-cut struggle may well inspire our generation as we face the more confused and widespread forces of industrial bondage that hold our laboring classes in a spiritual deprivation as complete in some ways as that of the slave" (210–11).

Century in 1888–89, with a series on the Civil War. Published later as a book, this series earned the Century Company more than a million dollars.[31] This success was followed by a book on Lincoln by Hay and Nicolay, first serialized in that same magazine, which earned the authors more than fifty thousand dollars. Other magazines and book publishers quickly joined this Civil War remembrance enterprise, a boom that lasted for twenty years. Significantly, the journals and book publishers that did this were also those that were the major vehicles for Progressive reform ideas and ideals (Mott, 1957a, 457–80, 510–16; 1957b, 589–607).

An earlier indication of the power of Puritanism and the rise of new conceptions of American nationalism was the popularity of books by John Fiske. Although he was too much of a Bostonian to be a Progressive,[32] his histories of the New England settlement, the American Revolution, and the constitutional founding were all placed within a social evolutionary and Hegelian-Christian view of history. The books on the colonial and the constitutional foundings were extraordinary publishing successes.[33] An earlier and more philosophical book set the theme for the three histories and established their interconnection; it was titled *American Political Ideas Viewed from the Standpoint of Universal History* and was published continuously from 1885 to 1917.

Within the horizon of Progressivism, biblical typology or evolutionary sociology (they were usually interchangeable) served as a theology of the fulfillment of America as a historic nation. Its future destiny is implicit from the start and can be traced back through the chain of obligations from those who preceded us and forward through the legacies given to our descendents. The sociologist Cooley wrote in an early textbook of "our need to recall vanished persons" as a primary cause of our ideas of goodness and justice (Cooley, 1902, 389). The psychologist James Mark Baldwin wrote in his textbook of the ways in which significant human actions are institutionalized and therefore constitute part of "the social heritage of our descendents" (Baldwin, 1906, 473). In a Hegelian-romantic rendering of this same idea, the germ of American nationality is the particularism of the first New England theocracies

31. The early success of this theme dictated the enormous scale of this project. Volumes 7 and 8 of the magazine, consisting of about 1,800 pages (including advertisements), include more than 250 separately written contributions, not including poetry. There were fourteen major articles on the deteriorating condition of the freedman in the South.

32. See note 29 above.

33. *Critical Period* remained in print from 1888 to 1916. The New England founding book, subtitled *"The Puritan Theocracy in its Relation to Civil and Religious Liberty,"* was published continuously between 1889 and 1930.

that, through the successive stages of ever higher dispensations marked by the great events of our national life, have grown into America as a great democratic nation. Social justice and human brotherhood are the modern fulfillment of this earlier spirit. Like the religious expressions preceding it, this spirit must never be entrapped within the formal confines of trained clergymen and institutional churches, but must pervade all aspects of life—the family, the school, the market, and the workplace.

THE ADVANCE GUARD
OF SOCIAL PROGRESS

American ideals of nationality shaped by Progressive academics and intellectuals might appear less contentious—and less politically relevant— when stated as history than when stated in terms of the contemporary political and economic struggles between regions, social groups, and institutions. For the Progressives, however, contemporary struggles were inseparable from this evolutionary history as prophecy. The connection becomes clear when one seeks in their writings the identity of the primary agents and agencies of nationality. The first and most obvious identity would be geographical: the vanguard regions of the country had become the mid-Atlantic and Midwestern regions of the country. One reading of this regional or geographical identity of the growth of American nationalism has already been suggested above: "wherever the children of the Puritans are found." Symbolized by Lyman Beecher's *A Plea for the West* and continuing through Josiah Strong's *Our Country* and *The New Era, or the Coming Kingdom*, the religious energies of New England were projected first into upstate New York and northern Ohio and then westward, following almost exactly the path of demographic and economic expansion. Almost every Progressive academic and intellectual highlighted in this study was a product of or participant in this movement and of the economic, cultural, and political institutions it left in its wake. Not a single one came from or identified with the South.

This sense that the dynamic core of America as a nation lay on an axis from New York to Chicago and from Chicago radiating south and west to the rest of the continent, can be expressed in a number of other images. The most obvious is the trunk line railway system, created in the first session of the first Republican-controlled Congress in 1861.[34]

34. Keller, 1977, 165–67. Between 1862 and 1872, the national government subsidized trunk line railroad construction with one hundred million acres of public

Less obvious are the ways in which national magazines, women's clubs, moral reform movements, and the planting of churches and colleges spread in this same way. This same core region was the site of the great electoral struggle for national political supremacy in the post-Civil War period: whoever won the Midwest conquered the political nation (Jensen, 1971). This same region was assumed by all to be the battleground on which church denominations fought for dominance and, later, when ecumenical and "parachurch" institutions worked more closely together, sought to Christianize the culture.[35] In the economic sphere, it was here that the great trusts and pools of investment capital were formed, mechanized agriculture thrived, the labor movement was first solidly organized, and the emerging patterns of industrial relations were established. And it was here that the great industrial cities of America were born and grew to immense size and power.

If America was to become a coherent nation; if America was to usher in the Kingdom of God; if America was to achieve social and economic justice; if America was to conquer the world for Christ or for democracy or for export markets for goods and capital, this geographical core would have to lead. But to do this, the core itself had first to be conquered, socialized, and organized. This required the creation of powerful national institutions in the core. These institutions had to then mobilize and discipline the intellectual, moral, and material resources for the task. Who would create these institutions and give them power and purpose? Who would point the way?

In the two decades following the Civil War the cultural answers to these questions seemed obvious: moral and intellectual leadership fell to the evangelical churches and churchmen. It was they who would provide the ideals, establish the organizational forms, and raise the money required to achieve the conquest of the West. But this obvious answer was also an increasingly wrong answer—and it was largely the theologians of the social gospel in alliance with Progressive social scientists who first showed how and why it was wrong.

Churches had separate institutional and denominational interests that compromised their larger social and political roles; most churchmen were wedded to particularistic theological and doctrinal systems that constricted the depth and reach of religion in the daily life of the larger society; many denominational colleges were parochial, defen-

---

lands and about one hundred million dollars in bonds and loans. See Hall, 1989, 191.

35. Chicago became the center of all these enterprises: theological schools, religious publishing, new universities, philanthropy, and social experiments.

sive, hopelessly unprofessional, and anti-intellectual. In the words of Washington Gladden, if "every department of human life—the families, the schools, amusements, art, business, politics, industry, national politics, international relations—[is to be] governed by the Christian law and controlled by Christian influences" (Handy, 1984, 140), churches as denominations and creeds and clergymen were hardly up to the task. Indeed, churches were as often barriers to the Kingdom as they were its harbingers, their "otherworldliness" a surrender to complacency and respectability in this one.[36] As Rauschenbusch, Ely, Ross, Commons, Dewey, and Cooley maintained from the start, churches and clergymen themselves needed to be "Christianized" (or democratized or socialized) on new terms.[37]

The import of this argument was not to reform the church and theology and clergymen so they could reattain the leading intellectual and cultural role in directing America.[38] Rather, if churches were to substitute a social ethic for theological creeds, they would be doing no less than what the Progressives expected *of all other* emerging national institutions and their leaders. If "social righteousness" was to permeate all life, then the role of clergyman in the church was hardly different

36. "Whenever an agreement has been reached between the Church and the world, the terms have been a division of territory as it were . . . the world has transferred the domain of dogma and the future life to the church, but has kept for itself the present life" (Ely, 1889, 53). Ely's book, *Social Aspects of Christianity* (1888) originally appeared as articles in the *Congregationalist* and was required reading in the major Protestant seminaries (Dombrowski, 1936, 50). Ely was one of the few academic Progressives who used the word "church" in the singular, but his meaning was never entirely clear in the American context. "While Christianity has awakened higher ideals of life among the masses and made them restless, the church has opposed the realization of those ideals in the life where they most are needed" (Commons, 1894, 10).

37. Rauschenbusch in Handy, 1984, 143–44; Commons, 1894, chaps. 1 and 2; Cooley, 1909, 5 and xxxii; Ely, 1889, chaps. 2 and 5; Ross, 1918, 208–17 and 370–72.

38. This is not entirely true. Before other reform institutions became firmly institutionalized, someone like John Commons in jeremiads to Protestant churchmen could say: "I long to see the day when the leadership in the social movements of our time will be taken from the lawyer and the newspaper and given to the Christian minister. We cannot expect to have a society based on righteousness so long as our social philosophy is given to us by editors and lawyers. They are put forward to favor special interests. But where is the advocate of the masses, of the great brotherhood of man? Where is the truly judicial mind, whose purpose it is to bring to pass the kingdom of God on earth? (1894, 23). This, in turn, must be qualified by what he said as preface to this hope: "The minister should devote one half of his pulpit work to sociology . . . sociology has rightly been said to be one half of religion; theology is the other half. . . . Theology considers man in his relations to God; sociology to his relations to his fellow-men" (19–20). But see Herron, 1894, 8, on the church as only one means among many to achieve "the kingdom of God, which is the just social order."

from that of the members of reform organizations, or the teacher in her school, or the businessman in his firm, or parents in their families, or social workers in settlement houses—or professors in their universities.

This identification of nationality with the institutions and values of the dynamic core of turn-of-the-century America sometimes encouraged a rhetoric of triumphalism in the writings of Progressive intellectuals. It was their reform organizations and institutions that appropriated the prefix "national" in their names as if by right.[39] The extraordinary growth of the evangelical churches and the success of their domestic, urban, and foreign mission activities in the late nineteenth century had already provided the language for this triumphalist rhetoric.[40] The wave of reform measures that swept the country in the period 1905–7 seemed especially to confirm that America was finally and permanently committed to a future Progressive intellectuals had marked out. By the end of the first decade of the twentieth century, their professional associations and journals were on a solid footing; their university departments and endowments were rapidly growing; their books and articles dominated intellectual and higher political discourse; their students and colleagues were actively sought by state and national political and reform bodies; and reform journals and journalists were disseminating their ideas to ever growing audiences.[41] Even

39. This was especially true of women's organizations. For a general sample of such organizations, Bliss, 1908, 806–10.

40. Methodist clergymen and theologians were especially outspoken in this regard, which is understandable given their phenomenal growth in the urban areas of the North and Midwest. James King of New York, in 1887: "Christianized Anglo-Saxon blood, with its love of liberty, its thrift, its intense and persistent energy and personal independence, is the regnant force in this country. . . . God is using the Anglo-Saxon to conquer the world for Christ" (Handy, 1984, 91). Daniel Dorchester, Methodist clergyman and editor of *Christianity in the United States* (an 1895 compendium which declared that, of the 165,000 churches in America, exactly 151,172 were evangelical): "Christ, reigning over a territory hitherto unrivaled in extent, great benevolences, awakened and sustained by a deeper religious devotion; rapidly multiplying home, city, and foreign mission stations, the outcome of intelligent consecration; magnificent departments of Christian labor, many of them heretofore unknown, and none of them ever before so numerous, so vast, or so restlessly active; the great heart of the Church pulsating with an unequaled velocity; the fires of evangelism burning with unwonted brightness . . . and a religious literature such as has characterized no other age, eminently practical, intensely fervid and richly evangelical . . . God has a living church within the churches, towering amid them all in its mightiness" (Handy, 1984, 101–2). As Handy wryly notes, "there is much implicit internationalism in social gospel thought" (1984, 146). These themes are discussed in chapter 7 below.

41. The clearest indications of popular success was the sudden growth and prosperity of the magazines featuring Progressive intellectuals and reform themes. In

Walter Rauschenbusch, the most programmatic of the social gospel theologians, declared in *Christianizing the Social Order* (1912) that, of the five great sectors of the social order, four had by then been largely Christianized, the family, church, school, and politics. Only business, "the seat and source of our present troubles," remained unredeemed (Handy, 1990, 296).

Among the Progressive economists and sociologists this triumphalism was less obvious, but it pervades their writings nonetheless. In their research monographs and textbooks they take great care in pointing out that the triumph of democracy and social justice would work only by a process of adopting the innovations produced by America's most advanced individuals and institutions. Charles Horton Cooley located progress in the opinions of specialized groups and, of these, only in those that "function through [their] most competent instruments," because the worth of all well-constituted groups "is nearly always superior . . . to the average capacity of its members." And in his discussion of social classes, he takes care to show that "the real upper class, that which is doing the most for the onward movement of human life, is not to be discerned by a visible sign. The more inward or spiritual a trait is, the less it is dependent upon what are ordinarily understood as class distinctions."[42] Jane Addams, no stranger to holders of great fortunes, held that the worth of contemporary large-scale individual philanthropy was not its material effects, but its freedom to innovate for

---

1906, Albert Shaw declared that his *Review of Reviews* had "the largest circulation in the world for any magazine not publishing fiction" (Mott, 1957a, 661). Mc-Clure's began its muckraking series of articles in 1903 and in 1908 announced that for ten straight years it had carried more advertising than any other monthly magazine in America. *Cosmopolitan*, another monthly vehicle for Progressive intellectuals, had more than a million circulation in the middle of that decade. The influence of women and the growth of women's magazines are other strong indicators of the growing popularity of Progressive ideas. With more than a million circulation, *Ladies Home Journal* had regular contributions from Jane Addams, Lyman Abbot, and Theodore Roosevelt. But it was Addams herself who clearly registered the popularity of Progressive values. Helped by her own publicity skills and by popular journalists such as Ida Tarbell, who dubbed her "The First Lady of the Land," she was voted "best woman in Chicago" in 1906. In 1908, *Ladies Home Journal* anointed her "First American Woman." In a poll of its members conducted by the New York Woman Suffrage Association to select the twenty-five "greatest women in history," Jane Addams came in third, but first among the living. In a 1913 readers' poll conducted by the *Independent* magazine to select the ten most useful contemporary Americans, Addams came in second to Thomas Edison, beating out Andrew Carnegie (Davis, 1973, 198–200).

42. Cooley, 1909, 124–25, 252, and 254–64. And see Cooley, 1902, chap. 9 on personal ascendancy and chap. 12 on freedom.

the rest of society.[43] The sudden explosion of wealth in the industrial urban centers was seen by most of these Progressives as as much an opportunity for as a threat to the attainment of social justice. Indeed, they witnessed and helped shape the rationale for the creation of the great charitable foundations and trusts that came into being at this time—and they, their students, and their universities were often major beneficiaries.[44]

In short, the signs of success that they saw were not only most evident in this new industrial core region of America, they were largely confined to that region and its mechanized agricultural extensions further to the west. The academic Progressives were not only at home in urban industrial America, they were among its first inhabitants and surely the first to seek a systematic understanding of its wealth and power.[45] And they equated this core with the authentic nation, saying

43. Addams, 1902, 161: "The danger of professionally attaining to the power of the righteous man, of yielding to the ambition 'for doing good' on a large scale, compared to which the ambition for politics, learning, or wealth, are vulgar and commonplace, ramifies through our modern life; and those most easily beset by this temptation are precisely the men best situated to experiment on the larger social lines, because they so easily dramatize their acts and lead public opinion." Her advice to them was to perform social experiments that exemplified a higher social ethic so that the larger public could decide whether or not to adopt them. "Such experiments," she says, "enable the nation to use the Referendum method in its public affairs" (164).

44. In obvious response to Veblen, Small (1915, 662) defends the philanthropy and social innovation of the responsibly rich families this way: "A brilliant contribution to historical and contemporary knowledge might be written under the title 'The Debt of Civilization to Its Leisure Class.' Some of the most important social services in progress in America today would be lacking if they were not performed by volunteers from our leisure class."

45. It seems curious to speak of Progressives as "small town" in reference to their origins and values, as if there were *others* in America who were not "small town," who were more "at home" in these new cities than they were. To say that their values were "traditional" is a variant of this, as if to say that there were others in America whose values were modern—say, peasant immigrants from Ireland and Southern Europe or Jews from Central Europe and Russia. This is the more curious because it was these same "small town" Progressives who provided the research, the intellectual framework, and the language by which urban America came to understand itself and who edited the journals and mass circulation magazines that explained industrial urban America to the rest of the country and made it acceptable. They were also the first to introduce European urban models to American audiences and to urge their study for use in America. Perhaps this characterization, which first came into use in the 1940s, was a way for academics of that era to use the cosmopolitan perspectives of Progressive social science to accuse earlier authors of being provincials in order to mark their own allegiance to New Deal liberalism and cultural pluralism. Charles Forcey, obviously drawing on Richard Hofstadter, says in his 1963 Introduction to Croly's *Promise*: "The reformers of Croly's day called themselves Progressives to indicate a bold grappling with the fu-

as their clergyman counterparts had in the mid-nineteenth century, that the future of the country rested on the power and justice of this core. Their persistent nationalism, therefore, was both a geographic regionalism of the core and a psychic regionalism of a covenant people that was being fulfilled in the institutions and practices of that core. In this double sense—children of the Puritans and founders of its reincarnated promise—the Progressives were at the cosmopolitan forefront of American life and spearheads of a region-as-nation conquest. Against this idea of nationality the parochial peripheries, through their party and legal spokesmen, had only the empty universalism of what Herbert Croly called a distant and abstract "monarchy of the Constitution"—a document that Progressives read as a barrier to democratic national purpose and a guarantor of local elites, small towns, and constricted lives.

---

ture, but historians have since agreed [!] that they looked backward more often than forward. Their ideals were largely inherited from a simpler American agrarian past. The great majority of Progressives feared strong governments and believed in laissez faire; they saw the individual and the protection of his rights as the beginning and the end of politics.''

3

THE NATION &
PUBLIC OPINION

Progressive intellectuals and reformers were acutely aware that the success of their projects depended upon their ability to gain popular acceptance. Distrustful of governing institutions dominated by political parties and disdainful of the stilted and artificial language of the courts, they pursued two related options: to appeal directly to a broad public and to dominate institutions that had or could achieve popular acceptance and autonomous political influence. This latter task was to some extent automatically accomplished insofar as the Progressives were powerful across the entire complex of Protestant religious institutions (including their colleges and universities), in most of the women's organizations, and in the graduate divisions of those universities that increasingly defined, produced, and certified the emerging class of professionals. And insofar as their values and purposes were transmitted through the new national monthlies and weeklies, the Progressives were extremely well positioned to dominate the shaping of the public agenda and to define the terms by which that agenda was discussed.

Across this open vista, however, lay two major barriers. First, in nineteenth-century America the meaning of public opinion rested on the presumptions that it represented majority opinion and that majority opinion, in turn, meant the preponderance of individual preferences. Second, the institutional test of whether these conditions were met was assumed to be either the market or the electoral system—both of which were driven by the irreducible element of individual preference. Thus, the first task of the Progressives was to redefine the meaning of public and public opinion and to give opinion the legitimate power to act *outside* of the two arenas that so overwhelmingly privileged local, isolated, and individual choices. In this process, the concept of public opinion could be transformed from an authoritative register of prevailing individual preferences into an engine of social control and transformation. In short, public opinion could become the authoritative will of a democratic nation.

PUBLIC OPINION AS PUBLIC GOOD

The one point at which all Progressives seemed to agree was that public opinion did *not* represent simple and ad hoc majority preferences. "Public opinion," Charles Cooley's sociology textbook states, "is no mere aggregate of separate individual judgements. . . . It may be as different from the sum of what the individual could have thought out in separation as a ship built by a hundred men is from a hundred boats each built by one man." One can combine "a very slight regard for most of what passes as public opinion with much confidence in the soundness of an aroused, mature, organic social judgement." A resort to "the average theory as applied to public consciousness is wholly out of place" and is, in fact, confession of failure: "If a group does not function through its most competent instruments, it is simply because of imperfect organization" (Cooley, 1909, 121–25 passim).

Franklin Giddings's sociology textbook distinguishes public opinion as "a rational like-mindedness" from mere public belief, which is emotional and grounded in habit and tradition (Giddings, 1898, 155). Public opinion comes into being when shared beliefs are subjected to informed criticism, leading to "an opinion . . . to which many communicating minds can yield their rational assent." The formation of public opinion, then, "can exist only where men are in continual communication, and where they are free to express their real minds, without fear or constraint." Thus, in a democratic society the "social mind" consists of "combinations of traditions with new thoughts," and together they constitute the "standards, codes, policies, ideals, tastes, faiths [and] creeds" of that society. For Giddings, public opinion is by definition an engine of reform constantly transforming prevailing beliefs and practices. And because "public opinion is almost wholly an intellectual product," the real reformers are intellectuals—those who subject traditional beliefs and practices to critical scrutiny—and their allies—those who help to communicate that critique to larger audiences (Giddings, 1898, 155–57 and 160).

In a 1901 lecture at Berkeley, Arthur Hadley defined authentic public opinion as public sentiment, the basis of democratic government by consent. "Even the fact that a majority may be willing to vote for a measure does not provide that it has this basis [of public sentiment]. The desire may be simply the outcome of widespread personal interest . . . opinions which a man is prepared to maintain at another's cost, but not at his own" (Hadley, 1901, 25, 27). Hadley equates authentic public opinion with Rousseau's general will: it literally constitutes individuals into one sovereign people, represented by a common public sentiment which includes all good men, minorities as well as majorities, who support the government not as a selfish means for the promotion of their own interest, but as a common heritage which they accept as loyal members of a body politic, in a spirit which makes them ready to bear its burdens as well as to enjoy its benefits.[1]

Public opinion thus becomes "a judgment formed in accordance with the dictates of . . . political conscience, and represent[s] a theory which a man is prepared to apply against himself as well as against others" (Hadley, 1901, 28). Hadley explicitly contrasts this understanding to the conventional one in which artificial electoral majorities or the results of business success are said to be democratically legitimated. This false understanding flows from Americans having been taught "to regard business and politics as games, with no obligations profounder than the rules, and no authority higher than the umpire" (Hadley, 1901, 31). Cooley best expressed their shared conclusion: "In politics communication makes possible public opinion, which, when organized, is democracy" (Cooley, 1909, 85).

In translating public opinion into terms such as public sentiment (Hadley), public conscience (Hadley and Cooley), rational assent (Giddings), reflective consciousness and purpose (Cooley), public will (Cooley), social judgments (Giddings), or organic social judgment (Cooley), these writers were implicitly turning the concept into an institution of conscious social purpose. Edward Ross's influential textbook, *Social Control*, published at the turn of the century, made this connection most explicit. Public opinion is the first topic he discusses under the larger heading "The Means of [Social] Control." Here, public opinion becomes a three-sided "public judgement" (the sanctions of opinion), "public sentiment" (the sanctions of intercourse), and "public will" (the sanctions of violence). After reviewing its advantages as a means of control (flexible, penetrating, preventive, prompt, cheap) and its disadvantages (unclear, reactive, static, lacking memory, rarely unanimous), Ross concludes that public opinion can be shaped into a progressive agency of the "Social Will" with education, respect for limits, and "the ascendancy of the wise."[2]

1. Hadley, 1903, 35; see also Hadley, 1901, 139–40.
2. Ross, 1918, 89, 95, 97–100, and 101–3. The logic of this body of doctrine regarding public opinion reaches a kind of fulfillment in Croly, 1914, chap. 15, where authentic public opinion is to receive its highest expression in the autonomous political executive, now freed from the constraints of party-dominated legislatures and lawyer-dominated courts.

OPINION AND LAW,
INFLUENCE AND POWER

According to these writers, public opinion would (or should) increasingly supplant law and other forms of external coercion in society even as organized cooperation replaced market competition in an increasingly interdependent economy. This conclusion was reached from a variety of different directions. For Ross, under a regime of public opinion ("long . . . schooled to act in a particular way") moral progress would be achieved because "the contents of the social mind are morally superior to the contents of the ordinary individual mind" (Ross, 1918, 365, 344). Functioning as a "social religion," public opinion will constantly confirm and enforce higher ethical standards.

Hadley's formulation was an Americanist gloss of Rousseau. The conventional but false history of freedom stipulates the "gradual passage of the human race from a system of authority to a system of liberty." A more accurate reading is that history "represents a passage from a system of obligations imposed by the community to a system of self-imposed obligations." Freedom lies not outside the law, but in its spontaneous fulfillment in a socialized conscience. "It is the ideal of a free community to give liberty wherever people are sufficiently advanced to use it in ways which shall benefit the public, instead of in ways which will promote their own pleasure at the public expense . . . and the most successful [i.e., progressive] communities . . . give freedom somewhat in advance of this ethical development."[3]

Ross termed the contrast between the rule by opinion and rule by law "ethical" versus "political" forms of control. Political forms of social control that operate through "prejudice and fear" are required in a society whose population is marked by "antipathetic and jarring" elements, where status and economic divisions are great and growing, and "in proportion as the parasitic relation is maintained between races, classes, or sexes." Ethical instruments, "being more mild, enlightening, and suasive" are appropriate to societies with homogeneous races and cultures, where "social contacts between all elements in the population are many and amicable" and where "the social constitution . . . conforms to common elementary notions of justice."[4] In the words of

3. Hadley, 1903, 74 and 82–83; see also Cooley, 1909, 403–4, on the relative merits and reach of "public will" versus "government."

4. Ross, 1918, 411–12; and see 106–25 on law. On the increasing power of opinion in a democratic society, Ross says: "We are come to a time when ordinary men are scarcely aware of the coercion of public opinion, so used are they to follow it"

John Dewey, common ends not arrived at by "common, free voluntary cooperation in process of achievement" are common in name only, requiring "bribes of pleasure, threats of harm, use of force" (Dewey and Tufts, 1908, 304).

The Progressive editor and publicist Lyman Abbott carried this argument one step further. Full liberty is achieved only in a pure democracy of literal self-government, "that in which the best in each man controls the inferior in each man. . . . The object of all government is to destroy the necessity of any government, by developing such a public conscience that no other force than that of conscience will be needed to protect the rights of man" (Abbott, 1901, 99–100). As in Giddings and Ross, the formation and power of public opinion constitutes an index of the progress of democracy; and insofar as public opinion requires intellectual leadership and guidance, the prestige and power of Progressive intellectuals and their institutions were indices of the existence and growth of public opinion.

The more that public opinion was conceived as a form of public conscience and therefore a shared commitment to a common good, the more it took on the characteristics of a new national ideal of American democracy. Although the religious expression of this connection is obvious in the "kingdom" writings of the social gospel and among the early social scientists such as Commons, Ely, Ross, and Small, it received a less overtly Protestant religious formulation in the social psychology writings of Giddings and Cooley. And well after most of these ideas were encoded in college textbooks, Herbert Croly and John Dewey drew out more clearly some of the political and intellectual implications. In Croly, the "law" represents a form of "bondage to a mechanical conception of social causation . . . which assumed an essentially automatic harmony between individual and social interests." Genuine democracy, in contrast, is a faith which "carries with it the liberation of democracy from this class of social pseudo-knowledge." This shared faith "is indispensable to social progress" because it encourages skepticism toward legal-individualist solutions to social problems and because its democratic expression is grounded in pragmatism and modern social psychology (Croly, 1914, 175–77, 183).

It has been reserved for recent social psychologists to give a concrete account of the way social minds are formed, and conse-

---

(105). About twenty years later, the reliance on the power of opinion over law becomes the concluding chapter in Croly's *Progressive Democracy*. There called "social education," its content and dissemination is in the liberal arts curriculum of the American university. Croly calls this opinion democratic "faith," but he does not go so far as to call the university its church (1914, 406–30).

quently to bring the idea of social minds into relation with the fundamental idea of society as a process. . . . Genuine individuality is also essentially an idea which does not become of great value to men and women except in a society which has already begun to abstract and cherish a social ideal [wherein society] is an end in itself [and] not merely a result of the harmony or the conflict of individual interests or wills. . . . The American nation is no longer to be instructed as to its duty by the Law and the lawyers. It is to receive its instruction as the result of a loyal attempt to realize in collective action and by virtue of the active exercise of popular political authority its ideal of social justice.[5]

John Dewey sought to explain why a reliance on commonly shared values informed and shaped by collective experiences not only furthered higher ethical and social ideals, but contributed to higher forms of individual freedom. The externally coerced harmony produced by law institutionalizes a false dualism of individual and society and prevents the application of shared intelligence to the solution of common problems. The agency of public opinion, in contrast, rests on the free acceptance of shared purpose.

Only a voluntary preference for and interest in a social good is capable, otherwise than by coincidence or accident, of producing acts which have a common good as their result. . . . [I]n truth a common end which is not made such by common, free voluntary cooperation in process of achievement is common in name only. . . . It has to be continually buttressed by appeal to external, not voluntary, consideration; bribes of pleasure, threats of harm, use of force. It has to be undone and done over.[6]

Earlier, Cooley had maintained that the ethical self "is not less a self for being ethical, but if anything more of a self, because it is a fuller, more highly organized expression of personality." The social is not opposed to the individual; rather, "the right is the social as opposed to

---

5. Croly, 1914, 197–99 and 210. Croly saw this process of replacement as a substitution of "pragmatism" (faith) for an abstract "intellectualism" (law).
6. Dewey and Tufts, 1908, 297 and 304. See Kloppenberg, 1986, 42–46 and 349–81, on Dewey in the larger context of American and European social theory; Kuklick, 1985, 230–49, on the religious origins and dimensions of Dewey's conception of democracy; and Westbrook, 1991, 144–48 and 154–56, on the philosophical basis of this argument.

the sensual.'"⁷ Dewey linked these same ideas in order to demonstrate the emancipatory nature of public opinion for individuals.

> Social influences enable an individual to realize the weight and import of the socially available and helpful manifestations of the tendencies of his own nature and to discriminate them from those which are socially harmful or useless. When the two conflict, the perception of the former is the recognition of duties as distinct from mere inclinations. . . . The conflict of duty and desire is thus an accompaniment of a growing self. . . . The phenomena of duty in all their forms are thus phenomena attendant upon the expansion of ends and the reconstruction of character. So far, accordingly, as the recognition of duty is capable of operating as a distinct reenforcing motive, it operates most effectively, not as an interest in duty, or law in the abstract, but as an interest in progress in the face of the obstacles found within character itself (Dewey and Tufts, 1908, 362–63).

FROM INFLUENCE TO LEADERSHIP

This stress on the internalization of common values and on the informal and spontaneous influence of opinion over the formal and conscious power of law might appear curious coming from those who were so concerned about the disorder and lawlessness they saw all around them. Although we will explore later some political and philosophical reasons for this emphasis, it is important to consider first some historical and institutional reasons. The political and religious culture from which these intellectuals came assumed that the "free institutions" of family, church, school, and township had traditionally held primary responsibility for creating the kinds of citizens required to sustain free government on a large and impersonal scale.⁸ Even after the early nine-

---

7. Cooley, 1902, 374 and 378; Patten, commenting on the need for family financial planning in the new industrial order, concluded: "This brings on a self-repression which is the essence of character building. The struggle for supremacy is now changed from a race and class struggle to an internal struggle for self-control" (1912, 339).

8. Discussion of these assumptions are found in Howe, 1990, 121–45; Stout, 1990, 62–76; and Bloch, 1990, 54–59. Lyman Beecher's *A Plea for the West* (1835), although its main enemy is the danger of Catholicism in America, is the locus classicus of this assumption as a political-cultural appeal. The republication of

teenth-century disestablishment of the churches in New England, clergymen, both in their official roles as ministers and as college and university professors and presidents and in their quasi-official roles as
public lecturers and moralists, served as the primary articulators and
guardians of shared societal values. Whereas these clerical roles were
no longer legally authoritative, throughout the antebellum period they
remained officially powerful and unofficially influential through their
domination of high literary culture and moral discourse. And even with
the spread of sectarianism within Protestantism and the arrival of large
numbers of Catholics, the residual power of this tradition continued after the Civil War, both through the older channels and in new ones
dominated by Protestant clergymen and their lay allies—imaginative
literature, the religious and secular periodical press, public school
boards, moral reform organizations, the women's movements, and the
new universities.[9]

In Ann Douglas's terms, this pre–Civil War shift in the ways in
which cultural authority was exercised represented both a retreat and a
''feminization.'' The shift from formal-legal ''power'' to informal ''influence'' especially typified the condition of northeastern and midwestern middle-class urban women whose families as institutions had
lost their economic and social roles and who were themselves reduced
to the privatized and isolated world of child rearing and consumption.
In alliance with the eastern liberal clergy—who had also lost formal authority—these women then sought to regain their lost ''official''
power, but indirectly, through influence. Through the Sunday School
movement, moral reform societies, and the writing of didactic short
stories, novels, hymns, and poetry, these women and liberal churchmen
dominated a powerful segment of moral discourse and spread a socialized and sentimentalized religion into popular culture.[10]

Beecher's book in 1977 was a striking symbol of how distanced liberal academics
had become from the horizons of their Progressive forefathers: it is part of the
''Anti-Movements in America Series'' published by a New York Times company,
which includes publications of the Ku Klux Klan, Joseph McCarthy, and a huge array of other anti-Catholic, anti-Asian, anti-Semitic, and anti-Communist writings.
The main readers of Beecher's book were those who powered the abolitionist movement.

9. Hall, 1982, 241–81; and see Tomsich, 1971, 1–93.

10. Douglas, 1988, chaps. 1–4. See especially her discussion of literary success
in novels, 103–15, and periodicals, 227–34, and their domination of hymn writing,
217–20. Hofstadter, 1962, 172–96, uses this same gender imagery to contrast the
Gilded Age reformer to the political boss, but then points to the new ''masculine''
image of Theodore Roosevelt, who also carried with him into the Progressive era
the tough-minded, no-nonsense academic expert.

Progressive feminist writers translated the equation of law : power = opinion : influence directly into gender as part of their claim that full equality for women is a necessary part of evolutionary moral progress. Charlotte Perkins Gilman states the case most forcefully.

> The coersive [*sic*] attitude is essentially male. In the ceaseless age-old struggle of sex combat he developed the desire to overcome, which is always stimulated by resistance; and in this later historic period of his supremacy, he further developed the habit of dominance and mastery. . . . The use of force is natural to the male; while as a human being he must needs legislate somewhat in the interests of the community, as a male being he sees no necessity for other enforcement than by penalty. . . . [T]he woman, the mother, is the first co-ordinator, legislator, administrator and executive. . . . Democratic government is no longer an exercise of arbitrary authority from those above, but is an organization for public service of the people themselves—or will be when it is really attained. In this change government ceases to be compulsion, and becomes agreement; law ceases to be authority and becomes co-ordination (Gilman, 1911, 180–85 passim).

Whereas Douglas tends to characterize this process as a retreat, invidiously contrasting it to the "real" (and thus masculine) worlds of party politics, economic development, and frontier revivals, a quite different reading of feminization is available in light of the abolitionist movement and the Civil War. Feminization as a realm of influence and feeling also carries forms of philosophical idealism, religious enthusiasm, and political romanticism that are hardly passive and often generate political movements that delegitimate and even destroy existing formal-legal political and economic institutions and practices. Indeed, major political transformations often require mobilization "out of doors" and the creation of new and counter social roles, cultures, and institutions. In these matters, nothing succeeds like success, so what might first appear as "feminine"—passive, indirect, outside the main channels of overt power—might suddenly become "masculine" in the form of new institutions of power. There was a close, even symbiotic, relationship between *Uncle Tom's Cabin* and *Battle Hymn of the Republic*—and both were penned by "sentimental" women.

FROM LEADERSHIP TO POWER

Feminists and clergymen were not the only ones to use these gendered images. Simon Patten's study of English moral philosophy in terms of a social evolutionary and materialist interpretation is organized by gendered typologies. As he traces and periodizes English social, economic, and political history, he writes of the rise of Puritanism as "womanly," given its stress on the home and family, against Cavalier communal pleasures. Later, he speaks of the supersession of Puritan values by the "manly" virtues of Wesley and Adam Smith. Finally, in addressing the moral and economic philosophy of John Stuart Mill, Patten speaks of Mill's temperament and sympathies as "womanly," and his Benthamism as "manly," resulting in an intellectual achievement which was unsurpassed in Mill's day in combining historical and psychological concreteness (woman) with the power of abstract reasoning (man) (Patten, 1899, 123-24, 138-39, 251-74, 286-96, and 318-43). These images were not meant to "rank," but rather to portray a dialectic of thought and history. What Patten terms the "stalwarts" will represent the final synthesis of the opposing principles. The victory of their way of life "will make character a test of citizenship, will exalt women and womanly standards, and intensify the 'home' ideal," resulting in a synthesis of each quality in every person when a just society is finally achieved.[11]

Progressive intellectuals and publicists shared many biographical, institutional, cultural, and religious connections to Progressive feminists and to the earlier New England genteel tradition. As with Douglas's women and clergymen and later the Mugwumps, there was an abundance of self-deprecatory contrasts of raw men of wealth and power to genteel people of ideas and moral sensitivity.[12] And there was often a parallel in the identification of their own claimed "powerlessness" with that of the direct victims of power—the laboring poor, the unemployed, the sharecropper, the tenement dweller.[13] But just as Ann Douglas's writers and intellectuals gained real power and success (and often fame and wealth) by this very strategy so, too, did many Progressives, especially in the new or expanding universities. Thus, a kind of intellectual pride and moral elitism could ride easily with declarations of "powerlessness," and together could be declared a morally superior and more democratic form of authority in America.[14] And as declared

11. Patten, 1899, 393 and see 394-98. Norton, 1986, interprets Puritan-Cavalier or North-South oppositions in exactly the reverse images. Whatever its plausibility, it makes both antebellum and postbellum women's movements in the North quite inexplicable.
12. Hofstadter, 1962, 188-96; Lasch, 1972, 44-55 and 80-99, uses these same gendered distinctions, but then condemns them all as finally unworthy.
13. This was especially true of those economists and sociologists who were closely tied to the social gospel movement, for example, Ely, Commons, and Small.
14. This same set of attitudes could also lead to conservative retreat, as in the

spokesmen of the great mass of the truly powerless and victimized in America, their own invisible influence would rightly increase in proportion to the achievement of social justice. As America increasingly democratized (or socialized, or moralized, or Christianized) its institutions and practices, the carriers of ethical influences would increasingly supplant the bearers of formal-legal authority and the holders of great wealth. The tie between feminism and Progressivism is here almost complete.[15]

This combination of humility and pride attached to the logic of "influence" was clearly embedded in discussions of social class and personal ascendancy found in the economics and sociology textbooks that came into wide use beginning in the 1890s. The most complete canvass of these themes is found in Cooley's discussion of social classes. After first distinguishing a rigid caste system from a more fluid class system, Cooley defends more open variants of systems of class differentiation typical of America because they provide outlets for social innovation and personal expression. Because "all organization is, properly, a means through which freedom is sought" so long as mobility is maintained within and between class organizations and so long as new forms of class organization can be created, these forms of differentiation and inequality will contribute to progress and justice (Cooley, 1909, 245).

Wealth gives disproportionate ascendancy to capitalists as a class but of a "pedestrian" kind, incapable of affecting "the profounder destinies of the race" and rarely accorded "enduring fame." Only because the man of wealth "goes attended by an invisible army of potential servitors, ready to do for him anything that the law allows, and often more," can money buy real power; and when allied through corruption to "shrewd and unscrupulous political ambition," this power can become formidable and "truly perilous." Money can gain power over public sentiment partly by its visible and tangible marks of success and partly by the indirect power of wealth on some professionals, especially lawyers and newspaper publishers. Capitalists as a class, however, are not only internally divided between those wanting to consolidate privilege

---

case of intellectuals in stagnant or declining areas of the country, for example, Boston. Thus, those who carried these traditions into the twentieth century were both more conservative and more radical than prevailing opinion. The most radical reading was given by Progressive feminists, some of whom combined claims of the superior moral natures of women with the powerlessness of those who live lives of atonement-victimization. Gilman, 1911, is the most comprehensive statement of this position.

15. Discussed in chapter 6 below.

and those needing to destroy extant forms to get rich themselves, they "are liable to moral deficiencies analogous to those of the conquerors and organizers of states[,] . . . a certain moral irresponsibility which is natural to those who have broken away from customary limitations and restraints" (Cooley, 1909, 268, 273, 259–60).

Real and lasting power is always "spiritual"—even the power that money can acquire. According to Cooley, "primary power goes for the most part unseen . . . much yielding only posthumous reputation and much . . . and perhaps the finest sort, having never any vulgar recognition whatever." Indeed, standing above his three-fold classification of classes based on occupation or profession, wealth, and culture and refinement is "the real upper class, that which is doing the most for the onward movement of human life [and] not to be discerned by a visible sign. The more inward or spiritual a trait is, the less it is dependent upon what are ordinarily understood as class distinctions" (Cooley, 1909, 265, 252).

The relationship between exalting the power of public opinion and asserting the influence of an unmarked and invisible spiritual elite was underlined in other writings as well. In Franklin Giddings's textbook the organizing category of his sociology is like-mindedness. "The social mind is that sympathy and concurrent intelligence of the like-minded which results in common purposes and concerted acts" (Giddings, 1898, 128). Given this perspective, he can ignore at the start the external and formal marks of power in his analysis of class and leadership and stress inner qualities almost entirely. There are, he said, three types of classes in society, categorized by vitality, personality, and social consciousness. Vitality is largely biological, marked by levels of fertility, longevity, and energy; personality, by levels of inventive power and willingness to change; and social consciousness, by the reach of sympathy and depth of caring for others, marked by leadership, self-sacrifice, and philanthropy (Giddings, 1898, 105–10). Noteworthy in this classification is the complete absence of class divisions based on formal-legal position and wealth. More noteworthy is that Giddings, like Cooley, then posits a small group standing above and cutting across the upper reaches of these three divisions, called "the preeminent social class." Imagine, he says, the qualities of those who are simultaneously in the upper reaches of all three groups:

Small as it is in numbers, it accomplishes the greater part of those undertakings which, in their totality, we call progress. It gives to society the new inventions, the improvements in law, industry, art, religion, and morals which make life richer in its achievements and larger in its possibilities.[16]

As Giddings expands his description of this "true elite," two characteristics loom largest. The first is the requirement of "an enormous amount of knowledge" to put its intelligence to productive use, especially knowledge of society and its constituent elements. The second is that the "power" of this group is informal influence, consisting of its ability to set exemplary standards for others in society to imitate, to generate new and original ideas that are then used by those immediately below them to organize and direct society, and, last, to generate higher forms of beauty and happiness.[17]

Feminist expressions of influence followed this same logic. Here the claim was that women qua women—at least those freed from the corruptions of power-seeking and male-dominated politics and economy—constituted a spiritual elite born of suffering and domestic servitude. Charlotte Gilman constructed an elaborate social-evolutionary anthropology to ground her conclusions, but its contemporary purchase was purely Progressive:

With the entrance of women upon full human life, a new principle comes into prominence; the principle of loving service. . . . The feminine attitude in life is wholly different. As a female she has merely to be herself and passively attract; neither to compete nor to pursue; as a mother her whole process is one of growth; first the development of the live child within her, and the wonderful nourishment from her own body; and then all the later cultivation to make the child grow; and all the watching, teaching, guarding, feeding. In none of this is

16. Giddings, 1898, 114. Toward the end of the book he concludes: "The stability of democracy thus depends, first, upon the acceptance of the many of guidance from those whose superiority is real because consisting in intellectual abilities and in moral character, not in artificial social distinctions or in pretentious claims; second, upon an unselfish activity on the part of the superior few. They must not only have the ability to plan and guide; but they must also put forth that ability, if need be at the sacrifice of their personal comfort and ambition" (321).

17. Giddings, 1898, 116–18. Lest one conclude that Giddings hid the power implications of this influence from himself and from his readers, note should be made of the conclusion of his next book, *Democracy and Empire*: "It would be a ludicrous ignorance of all scientific facts which should leave sympathy out of the inventory of manifestations of power. Not less are all the higher virtues—philanthropy, compassion, and forgiveness—manifestations of power. . . . It is only the men that have energy to spare who are normally altruistic. . . . The meek shall inherit the earth, not because they are meek, but because, taking one generation with another, it is only the mighty that are or can be meek, and because the mighty—if normally evolved—are also by differentiation meek" (1900, 351).

there either desire, combat, or self-expression (Gilman, 1911, 251–52).

Much of what Cooley and Giddings wrote regarding the relationship between the power of public opinion and the ascendancy of a new kind of elite was foreshadowed in a long series of articles by Ross, first published in 1896 and later collected into his book, *Social Control*. Though expressing traces of populist cynicism absent in these later books, Ross unravels the ways in which narrow groups can achieve control of society by controlling its opinions. Drawing heavily on ancient, medieval and modern European history, he gives the reader a rich catalogue of means by which some groups dominate others: ceremony, art, personality, religion, and illusion are examined in turn for their use and abuse as agencies of informal social control (Ross, 1918, chaps. 19–23). But inside this tale and determining its direction is a larger evolutionary theory of social and ethical progress. The genesis, selection, maintenance, and progress of "ethical elements" in social control are all attributed to various elites at different periods of history. And when Ross gets to the contemporary period, cynicism disappears. Many groups, he says, have a personal stake in preserving the ethical gains a society has achieved at any given point, but they also have an equal and even stronger stake in resisting new and higher ethical standards as well. Only an "ethical elite," defined as "those who have at heart the general welfare and know what kinds of conduct will promote this welfare," can underwrite both ethics and ethical progress: "The other groups in the party of order . . . want order, any kind of order, while the elite stand for an order that is right, one that squares with their instincts of sympathy and fair play." The contrast between this form of elite leadership and "class control" could hardly be more striking. The former rests on "special learning beyond the common ken" and lives within "a tradition embodying the ethical elements that have been contributed by the prophets and elite of the past." The latter is defined tersely as "the exercise of power by a parasitic class in its own interest."[18]

MATERIAL PROGRESS AND
HIGHER OPINION

Perhaps the most original explanation for the emergence of the power of opinion is found in the writings of Simon Patten, the Wharton School

18. Ross, 1918, 363, 369, and 376. Much of what Ross wrote was influenced by John Stuart Mill's *Logic of the Moral Sciences* and the writings of Mill's followers, especially those of Leslie Stephen and John Morley. See Eisenach, 1990a. Kloppenberg, 1986, traces these same ideas in the writings of T. H. Green, Henry Sidgwick, and Leonard Hobhouse.

economist well known even today for his innovative work in marginal utility theories of consumption (Dorfman, 1949, 182–88; Fox, 1967, 44–60). His wider influence lay in his theory relating economic changes to social forces and to social evolution. The foundation of this theory was the distinction he drew between a "pain" and "pleasure" economy, the former driven by scarcity and survival, the latter propelled forward by increasing abundance and more refined consumption choices. This materialist basis of his social theory would seem to have left little room for the role of intellectual elites, public moralists, and public opinion. But this was decidedly not the case. Following Lester Ward, Patten maintains that "the movement of a society to a more general environment lessens the dependence of its members upon the conditions of the objective [i.e., material] environment and increases their dependence upon the conditions of the subjective [i.e., mental] environment" (Patten, 1896, 55).

In the period of transition between a pain and a pleasure economy, the task of social theory is to "measure the influence of the forces of the pleasure economy toward which the race is tending, and see what effect the new conditions will have upon its ideals, impulses and institutions." This is best done by positing a hypothetical history of "normal progress" toward the social commonwealth of a pleasure economy and then measuring the institutional, intellectual, religious, and psychological barriers to its achievement. According to Patten, a Hobbesian world of law backed by fear of punishment and a Judeo-Christian God as ruler and punisher are the ideas appropriate to the older pain economy.[19] These beliefs and forms now stand as barriers to the achievement of the social commonwealth. This is especially evident in the realm of the economic motives. With abundance, competitive motives necessary to insure survival in the older economy of scarcity come increasingly into conflict with the social bonds created by the increasingly interdependent economic networks. But because even these new economic bonds rest on "the more or less conscious calculus of utilities," without the development of larger social bonds "there would be no check to the actions of individuals when their interests conflicted with the welfare of the race." A regime of law premised on "the conscious calculations of individuals" must be subordinated in the emerging regime to shared collective ideas as "social bonds" first expressed through art, then through morality, and, at their highest, through religion.[20]

19. Patten, 1896, 85, and extended discussion, 75–98; see also Patten, 1899, 144–57, on Hobbes, and 1–56, for an outline of this general theory.

20. Patten, 1896, 90 and 91–94. He concludes: "The citizens of [the future] social commonwealth would not understand what a state is if the word were used in

With Patten as with Cooley the religious beliefs appropriate for the coming age mirror the appropriate instruments of social control. Formal power and physical coercion are replaced by inner control enforced through shared ideas. The public moralist, the social scientist, and charity worker should all reflect the new image of Christ.

> He comes not as the ruler of men, but as their servant. He has so little power that a corporal's guard can crucify Him. [W]hen men are transferred to a pleasure world, their evils are internal. They are their own foes. They want relief not from persecution, but from temptation. The concepts of a powerful God and of a future retribution are of little help. . . . They want rather a model for imitation, one who remains pure even though subject to the passions and temptations of men. . . . [Christ] is a better ideal because he is powerless and helpless.[21]

In the coming era, "intelligence and self-control will be the great virtues" conveyed and spread through imitation and inspiration. Indeed, says Patten, this process is already evident in America. Everywhere one finds the development of higher "civic instincts," representing the standards or "type-producing forces" of those whose values are the vanguard ones for an economy of abundance. Those who meet these standards will flourish in the emerging order; those who do not, will perish. Whether the issue is work habits, consumption patterns (especially alcohol consumption), the use of leisure time, or the use of economic and political power, "when social co-operation becomes a requisite for survival [flourishing, progress], those persons against whom the civic instincts are aroused cannot remain a part of society. They must depend on their own exertions and these efforts are not sufficient to enable them to compete with those who are efficient parts of a society."[22] In this new environment, character and cooperation replaced cunning and combativeness as mechanisms of survival.

---

its present sense. Each institution would exert its own power in the way in which the family, the church and many other social and industrial organizations do at the present time"(98). This pluralist argument is developed further in a later publication, under the term "voluntary socialism" in Patten, 1912, 322–31.

21. Patten, 1896, 80. Note the affinity of this image to that of the liberal clergy and women in Douglas, 1988, 121–64; and, for its use in abolitionist literature, see Walters, 1977, 54–69 and 91–110; see also Cooley, 1909, 377; Addams, 1902, 275–77; and Vida Scudder, 1898, 305–18, for similar imagery.

22. Patten, 1896, 107–8, 137, and 136. There is even indirect support for a feminization thesis here: "The struggle for existence is now determined by other quali-

As part of this coming regime of affluence and influence, the work of helping the weak and other victims of the remnants of the pain economy took on a new urgency and required new methods. In an influential series of lectures for the New York Charity Organization Society, Patten proposed a new ethic of charity appropriate for an economy of abundance.[23] The leading motif was that charity should provide the means by which the standards of the larger society can spontaneously enter into the lives of the afflicted. "Character is acquired by example, not by blood; by the activities and amusements in the shop and street, not by restraints of church and home. . . . Social work has to do with the means of progress and not with its ends" (Patten, 1896, 215). With the change from a pain to a pleasure economy, charity work, too, must change.

> We encourage self-denial when we should encourage self-expression. We try to suppress vices when we should release virtues. We laud country life when we should strive for the improvement of cities. . . . We judge the poor by their family history when we should judge them by their latent powers. We impose penalties when we should offer rewards. We ask for the gratitude of the poor when we ought to point out their rights to them. . . . The aim of social work is democracy rather than culture; energy rather than virtue; health rather than income; efficiency rather than goodness; and social standards for all rather than genius and opportunity for the few.[24]

In Patten's theory of the evolutionary progress from external coercion to internal influence, public opinion becomes something like a theory

---

ties than appetite; and a new class of men gain the ascendancy, over whom the appetite has less control." Every increase of the food supply "allows men of weaker appetites to survive," and "[alcohol] abstainers will . . . gradually acquire a larger share of the land and capital of this country, and force the drinking-class into the less favored occupations. . . . The temperance people will increase in numbers and wealth until they are able to crowd out or suppress their opponents. The only question is whether drinkers shall be forced to reform, or gradually be crushed beneath the weight of their growing disadvantage" (Patten, 1889, 45 and 65).

23. *The New Basis of Civilization*, 1907. Edward T. Devine, one of Patten's students at Wharton and the most influential spokesmen of the "new" charity, borrowed heavily from Patten's ideas. See Boyer, 1978, 220–32; and Fox, 1967, 95–114.

24. Patten, 1907, 213. And, in the context of less advanced nations and races: "The characters of men improve, not by addition, but by differentiation. . . . Reform should . . . be directed toward helping the weak. The blocks to progress lie in the aggressions of the strong which prevent the weak from getting in the current of differentiation which evokes natural characters. A backward race does not have to be made over to fit it for civilization . . . the desired changes will come spontaneously if the initial evils are removed" (1903, 190). Jane Addams (1902, chap. 2) made many of these "new charity" arguments earlier.

of the incarnation—a term he in fact uses to describe the processes by which higher types of ethical standards and ways of life supplant lower ones (Patten, 1899, 408). And, as we have seen, these conflations of authentic public opinion into social conscience as the "Christ ideal" were both explicit and implicit in almost all of these writings. So, too, was an identity between the growth and power of public opinion, the growth of social intelligence, and the increasing prestige and power of exemplary groups and individuals. Moreover, insofar as public opinion as "social intelligence" took on the characteristics of a common faith and underwrote the growth of democracy, the values or content of this opinion became the measure of American identity and the political standard by which institutions and practices were measured. These shared perspectives should not blind us to some important disagreements. Progressive academic philosophers, sociologists, and economists differed over the meaning and operation of social knowledge and on the degree of activism and institutional power required of the vanguards of higher sentiments. They also disagreed over whether social knowledge, its creators and transmitters, were only indices and signs of moral progress—recorders of the progress of the spirit, as it were—or prophetic expression and witness to a higher religion and a more democratic social ethic. To take just the economists, Patten and John Bates Clark seemed to locate themselves more clearly in the former category, whereas Ely, Commons, and Ross seemed to belong in the latter.

Despite these differences, the poles separating them define the same axial principle and share the same social evolutionary assumptions. It is appropriate, then, to inquire of the entire group how they came to see *themselves* as qualified, both morally and intellectually, to define and articulate public opinion. What special qualities did they think they had that qualified them as members, or at least representatives, of an intellectual and moral elite? What warrants did they offer to back their claim that they were in a unique position to "see" what so many other Americans evidently failed to see concerning the causes of and solutions to America's political, economic, and moral troubles? What gave them motive and confidence to present themselves and their characteristic institutions to the larger public as exemplary of America's preferred future? On what basis could they claim to know the public good?

PUBLIC OPINION AND HIGHER LEARNING

I am . . . an aristocrat rather than a democrat; but when I use the word "aristocrat," I have in mind of course not a legal aristocracy, but a natural aristocracy; not an aristocracy born for the enjoyment of special privilege, but an aristocracy which lives for the fulfillment of special service.

These words, written by Professor Ely of the University of Wisconsin in 1894, were part of his defense of academic freedom in response to the charge in the *Nation* that he was teaching socialism (Herbst, 1965, 172). With a ringing defense of academic freedom from the Board of Trustees of the university, helped in no small part by Ely's personal standing in the state and among his professional colleagues, Ely's claim prevailed. The self-proclaimed aristocrat could continue his fight for social democracy. More than twenty years later Ely would serve on the committee on Academic Freedom and Tenure of the newly founded American Association of University Professors. Of the fifteen members of the committee, eight had studied in Germany.

At the 1904 Congress of Arts and Sciences in St. Louis, held in conjunction with the World's Fair, the world's academic aristocracy in the arts and humanities, the social sciences, and the natural sciences met to share the results of their knowledge. Organized by Albion Small of Chicago and Hugo Munsterberg, a German teaching social psychology at Harvard, the program consisted of the presentation of more than three hundred scholarly papers. The nationalities of the presenters included 202 from America, 41 from Germany, 21 from Great Britain, and 17 from France. More strikingly, 106 of those not from Germany (mostly Americans) were German trained, including half of the social scientists and historians and more than three-fourths of the chemists. Among the social scientists giving papers in addition to Small were John Bates Clark, Richard Ely, Franklin Henry Giddings, Arthur Twining Hadley, Simon Patten, Edward Alsworth Ross, and Edwin Robert Anderson Seligman.[25] All of these men except Giddings had studied in Germany, all were in their mid-forties through late fifties, all held professorships in well-established and highly respected universities in America and were recognized leaders of their respective disciplines and professional organizations. But their positions and the public recognition of their achievements were by no means foreordained. When these men and women began going to Germany to study in the 1870s, there were few or no academic positions in America corresponding to their specialized training. Indeed, many of those who went to Germany had

25. Herbst, 1965, 207–14. In a survey of all professional economists and sociologists in America done by Henry Farnum of Yale and published in 1908, of the 116 respondents, 59 had studied in Germany between 1873 and 1905 (Herbst, 1965, 130).

no intention of entering academic life on their return.[26] Nor was government service a real option at this time. Why, then, did they go to Germany to study, and why did they often return to pursue graduate work at Johns Hopkins or Michigan or Chicago when the vast majority of American colleges and universities had no places for them that would do justice to their learning?

Three general answers suggest themselves. The first is that their intellectual curiosity and demands could not be met or met nearly so well in America as they could be in Germany. They went to Germany for self-development, defined as disciplined and specialized theoretical study. As early as the 1860s, Americans who studied in German universities returned to launch powerful critiques of American colleges and universities and strongly urged adoption or adaptations of German models.[27] Thus, a second answer is that they studied in Germany to free themselves from what they saw as a confining intellectual atmosphere in America. Their critique of higher education broadened and blended into a critique of American intellectual and "spiritual" life generally, finally to become direct attacks on its leading political institutions and practices. And in so doing, a third answer emerges: study in Germany served as preparation for what Ely termed "the fulfillment of special service." This service was the cause of reforming—even redeeming—

26. The extent of their insecurity and the paucity of serious academic positions in America is well documented in Dorfman, 1949. This is especially evident in the case of Patten, who, after receiving his German Ph.D. in 1879, returned to live on his family farm in Illinois for four years, then served as a public school teacher for six before his appointment to Wharton in 1889 at the age of thirty-seven. James, the colleague at Wharton who rescued Patten, himself spent six years after receiving his German Ph.D. teaching in high schools in Illinois and free-lance writing (Dorfman, 1949, 160). For similar career shifts and job scarcities in Dorfman, see 162 (Ely), 276–77 (Commons), and 189–90 (Clark). Coats, 1968, 179–99, uses the life and career of Henry Carter Adams as a case study of the ambivalence of trained economists in this period, toward both their vocations and the American academic and intellectual environment they confronted. Among women such as Jane Addams and Florence Kelley, travel and study in Europe were undertaken with even more vocational uncertainty and did not include even the remote prospect of an academic career. This remained true for the first women graduate students in American universities until World War I; see Fitzpatrick, 1990.

27. Hofstadter and Smith, vol. 2, 1961, contains a good collection of these reform suggestions informed by German examples. The first (1890–91) volume of the *Annals of the American Association of Political and Social Science*, 78–102 and 272–88, carried a complete listing of all public and private lectures and seminars in both public law and political economy in every German university for the coming semesters, prefaced with an aggregate summary of numbers in each academic rank and total hours taught per week in each of the specialized subfields. That same journal regularly carried professional notes, notices of publications, and other professional news from the law and relevant philosophy faculties in Germany.

America. By the first decade of the twentieth century the connection between study in Germany and reform in America had become clear.

A comprehensive description of German university life written by an American academic was published in 1874. Based on the author's four years of study at three German universities in the mid-1860s and return visits in the early 1870s, it combines a narrative of his personal experience with a comparative analysis of German, American, and English higher education and German with American intellectual life generally.[28] After devoting long sections to description and personal experiences, the author takes up the issue of the meaning of a university in Germany. Immediately he makes clear to the reader that the German university, no matter what its size and number of courses, differs in kind and not in degree from *all* of its American counterparts, from the smallest college to the largest university. Because of their shared intellectual purpose, each German university has equal standing with all other German universities; each "aims at theoretical knowledge and meets the requirements of free teaching (*Lehrfreiheit*) and free learning (*Lernfreiheit*)." These conditions result in a very clear demarcation of what should and should not be studied and taught. Because universities are freed from "the practical and the technical," they can pursue a wondrous array of subjects in all their depth and subtlety and in whatever directions free minds will lead. All practicing professionals in Germany have gone through these universities where they are taught the real foundations of their practice and learn alongside those who study for the sake of knowledge only. "Hence the perfect *rapport* that exists in Germany between the lawyer and the jurist, the pastor and the theologian, the practicing doctor and the speculative pathologist." The purpose of the university is knowledge itself, and "all its energies are directed [to] the development of great thinkers, men who will extend the boundaries of knowledge."[29] In this sense, the university is a

28. Hart, 1874. James Morgan Hart (1839–1916) descended from mid-seventeenth-century New England ancestors, was from Princeton, completed his B.A. there, studied and received degrees in law and in philology in Germany, and taught modern languages and English literature at the University of Cincinnati, 1872–90, becoming professor of rhetoric and English philology at Cornell in 1890. The book was republished in 1878.

29. Hart, 1874, 250 and 258–59. The contrast to English universities is equally striking. The churchman Frederick Denison Maurice was recommended as a candidate for the Drummund Chair in political economy at Oxford in the 1830s. In a letter to a friend, Maurice agreed to stand in these words: "Finding there was no one else ready to come forward on this ground, that political economy is not the foundation of morals and politics, but must have them for its foundation or be worth nothing, I have consented to be proposed. . . . I shall of course endeavor to master the details of the subject" (quoted in Hilton, 1988, 47).

self-sufficient corporation, above and apart from the needs, contingencies, and demands of the larger society.[30] Recounting the ways in which graduate students, *Privat-docenten*, and professors freely circulate and rise within this enclosed university world, he concludes that the faculty "is thus a close corporation, a spiritual order" which is self-perpetuating (Hart, 1874, 257).

Given the weight and direction of this description, invidious comparison with American higher education—even at its best—inevitably follows.

> How many of our college professors have been professors, and nothing else? How many have qualified themselves directly for the respective chairs which they occupy, by a life of special study? How many of them formed the resolve while still students, to lead a college life forever, to devote themselves exclusively to instructing others in turn . . . ? How few of the hundreds and thousands of men, from New York to San Francisco, calling themselves professors, can say with a comfortable degree of pride: I selected my speciality in youth, I have pursued it without intermission, without deviation ever since, and I have produced such and such tangible evidences of my industry as a specialist (Hart, 1874, 255).

On the heels of this general comparison, Hart makes a specific one between a small German university and his own American alma mater. In student numbers and setting, Marburg and Princeton are almost identical, but there the comparison ends. Marburg has almost four times the number of professors and tutors, divided into four distinct faculties teaching students who have chosen them and who have proven their preparation for and dedication to specialized study. Its students "pass three and four years of their life in generous devotion to study pure and simple, without casting a single forward glance to future 'business.' "[31] Although he admits that some universities in America are now recruiting, training, and appointing

30. Hart, 1874, 252–53. Though he uses the term university in the singular, he makes clear that he means all collectively, both because of the constant circulation of students and faculty among them and because of the bonds of common purpose and standards within each discipline.

31. Hart, 1874, 258. And to make his point even more clearly, he says of Marburg: "its aim is not to turn out clever, pushing, ambitious graduates, but to engender culture" (257). The contrast in the position of the faculty is equally striking. Perhaps reflecting on some unpleasant experiences at Cincinnati, Hart idealizes his German counterpart in these words: "The [German] professor is not a teacher. . . . He is not responsible for the success of his hearers . . . only for the quality of his instruction. . . . The professor is his own master. His time is not wasted in cudgeling the wits of refractory or listless reciters. His temper is not ruffled by the freaks or the downright insults of mutinous youths" (264 and 267–68).

"energetic young men, enthusiastic in their vocation," America "is still indifferent, as a public. It is not aroused to the vital connection between the State and education in all its stages, highest as well as lowest" (Hart, 1874, 339–40).

But what has the "State" or politics to do with the quality of higher education in America? And why would reforming the American university be part of a larger political project? Hart makes an explicit connection between the individuality and freedom fostered in German universities and the disinterested devotion to self-development made possible by an ideal of professionalism as public service for the common good (Hart, 1874, 287–93). Are the shortcomings of American colleges and universities indicative of the absence of shared conceptions of public good and disinterested service on its behalf? Hart's proof that American colleges and universities have failed to embody high and disinterested *intellectual* standards is a *political* test—the failure of America to heed the call of Civil Service Reform, to elect better officeholders, to hold officials to high standards of conduct. But why this connection? Why the assumption that individual "emancipation" through disciplined study and self-development is of one piece with national social and political reform? His answer in the first instance is that America's low estimation of and even lower expectations put upon a college education simply reflect the larger fact that "the public does not perceive the importance of anything [that is] higher and more systematic." Indeed, American colleges often "exceed . . . the demands of their friends. They give more than is expected of them" (Hart, 1874, 339–40). A second answer is that the American dedication to the "practical" or the "useful," born of the pressures for individual success within a competitive business culture, corrupts both political and intellectual life.[32] This early critique, then, implicitly drew a connection

32. This critique of American colleges was by no means original with Hart. Henry Tappan, who became president of the University of Michigan in 1852, explicitly compared German and American universities in a book in 1851. In the context of discussing a report on Brown University, he praises parts of it for its attempts to move somewhat toward a German model. However, one part of the report speaks of adapting the institution to "young men who are devoting themselves to the productive professions," that is, business careers. This adaptation, Tappan warns, would subvert the very idea of a university at the start. "Shall we not have a large commercial institution, which, instead of gathering around itself classical associations, and impressing us with the worth and dignity of scholarship, shall only give us the hum of preparation for the business life in the industrial and productive direction? . . . Students seeking after science and philosophy for their own sake, and dreaming of high mental cultivation and profound learning, will be rarely seen, we fear, when candidates for the 'productive professions' form the overwhelming majority and create the *esprit de corps*" (quoted from Hofstadter and Smith, 1961,

between a liberal education as "emancipation" from low ends and American higher education as a political and cultural redeemer of America. This connection became a litany chanted by the next generation of German-trained American academics and reached a crescendo in the Progressive Era that followed.[33]

Thirty-five years after Hart's book was published and on the crest of a powerful wave of Progressive reforms, Herbert Croly repeated Hart's argument, but in the explicit contemporary context of reform. Economic and political life require "constructive regulation" in the form of "fruitful limitations on individual freedom" to provide a climate within which authentic individuality can flourish. In contrast, intellectual life in America requires much more individual freedom, not less. To reform economic and political life means to emancipate them from the more "stupefying and perverting" aspects of American intellectual tradition.[34] "The nation, like the individual, must go to school," but this school, consisting primarily of "experimental collective action aimed at the realization of collective purpose," requires teachers. Thus, a mutually sustaining relationship must be established between individual and collective intellectual emancipation. But where to start? How to break out of "a sterile and demoralizing Americanism—the Americanism of national irresponsibility and indiscriminate individualism" (Croly, 1909, 407, 426)?

Croly is aware that this process of emancipation and specialization was well on its way[35] and that the competent individual does not "feel

---

1:495–96]. As an ironic self-commentary, Hart ended his book with a series of "practical hints," not only regarding preparation in America before going to Germany, but in selecting courses of study there "with a knowledge of what the home-public will receive with favor" (Hart, 1874, 389).

33. And whose liberal echo was heard again as if for the first time in the late 1950s and early 1960s, symbolized by the success of Richard Hofstadter's *Anti-Intellectualism in American Life*, 1962, especially 233–52. Although this book did not seem all that different from critiques almost a century earlier, it received the Pulitzer Prize and went through eight printings or editions between its original publication in 1963 and 1974.

34. Croly, 1909, 421 and 424. At the start of this analysis he stated: "It is . . . essential to recognize that the individual American will never obtain a sufficiently complete chance of self-expression [freedom], until the American nation has earnestly undertaken and measurably achieved the realization of its collective purpose" (409). And see his earlier discussion of German nationality, 246–54.

35. Here it should be pointed out that Croly is simply wrong to assume that this "escape" from the confines of American exceptionalism by academics and intellectuals began in the 1870s and 1880s; this is the same mistake that Ross, 1991, makes concerning the origins of American social science. Two generations of American academics preceded the founders of American social science to Germany and for the same purposes (see discussion later in this chapter).

so much of an alien in his social surroundings as he did a generation or two ago." However, "his independence is still precarious" because it remains the political task to forge a clear connection between the discipline of self-development and the public good. The specialized and therefore emancipated individual

> needs to do what he has been doing, only more so, and with the conviction that thereby he is becoming not less but more of an American. His patriotism, instead of being something apart from his special work, should be absolutely identified therewith, because no matter how much the eminence of his personal achievement may temporarily divide him from his fellow-countrymen, he is, by attaining to such an eminence, helping in the most effectual possible way to build the only fitting habitation for a sincere democracy (Croly, 1909, 431).

FROM SECTARIAN CHURCHMEN
TO PUBLIC PHILOSOPHERS

In one sense, Progressive academics and intellectuals did not need to be told by Croly in 1909 what they not only knew but had vigorously practiced in their lives and writings over the previous thirty years. And by so pointedly contrasting a future national regime inspirited by common values to the fragmented one then artificially held together by law, they also already knew that expert legal knowledge, crowned by constitutional law, was a powerful standing intellectual alternative for defining public doctrine.[36] Moreover, along with Croly, these Progressives assumed that this intellectual tradition was both sterile and unfit to guide America to a more democratic future. That is why they were so energetic in founding graduate and professional schools and research degrees. Until those trained as lawyers first received the kind of emancipatory college education the Progressives were trained to give—this was not to become a regular practice until the late 1920s—the legal mind in America would remain about where it began in the mid-nineteenth century despite radically changed social, economic, and political conditions.

A second powerful standing alternative as a source of new and eman-

---

36. These same factors also help to explain why German-trained sociologists and political economists were so much more intellectually daring and theoretically creative than their counterparts in political science, a discipline in America historically bound to the Constitution and its articulation in constitutional law. See chapter 4 below.

cipatory public doctrine was the educated churchman and Protestant theology. Here the relationship was more complex and interesting. So long as a handful of Protestant denominations dominated American religious life, and their theological schools and colleges defined the higher reaches of moral philosophy, there always existed a powerful alternative vision of America—one which, in today's language, embraced more "civic republican" than "liberal-individualist" values.[37] And no better proof of the latent power of this de facto religious and moral establishment exists than the powerful critique of American life, symbolized by but not restricted to abolitionism, beginning in the 1830s and culminating in the Civil War. Insofar as Progressivism represented an attempt to recapture this spirit, its intellectual expression can be seen as a continuum of Protestant theology and moral philosophy. But insofar as Progressivism represented an attempt to transcend this earlier moment, its intellectual expression was in opposition to that theology and its moral philosophy. In either case and unlike their relationship to American legal and constitutional thought, Progressive intellectuals shared long-standing affinities to churchmen across almost every dimension that one might construct. This is why Richard Hofstadter could call academic reformers the "collateral heirs" of the New England clergy and compare the role of intellect during their ascendancy in colonial and early national America to that of the Progressives.[38]

One connection that has not been explored, however, is the way in which "churchmen" provided direct role models for Progressive academics. In the area of academic training, for example, American churchmen discovered German universities well before the Civil War. A surprisingly large number of Unitarian, Congregational, and Presbyterian churchmen who taught in religion departments and theological schools from the mid-nineteenth century on had German training. To take the most notable example: from Yale University, which the founding presidents of Johns Hopkins (Daniel Coit Gilman), Cornell (Andrew Dickson White), and Chicago (William Rainey Harper) attended as undergraduates, the list of faculty and presidents who studied in Germany at midcentury, which includes most of the history, theology, linguistics, and philosophy faculty, is quite astonishing (Stevenson, 1986, Table 1, p. 36, and Bibliography, pp. 200–205).

This training not only profoundly affected the direction of American theology and its relationship to moral philosophy, it also constituted a

---

37. The book which encodes this opposition, but as a *cri de coeur* for the American soul, is Diggins, 1984.

38. Hofstadter, 1962, 220; and see also 55–116, on churchmen, and 172–213, on the link between academic reformers and Progressives.

model of the relationship between trained intellect and public doctrine in America. Three of these German-trained churchmen-faculty (Dwight, Porter, and Woolsey) became presidents of Yale and continually addressed public issues in their books and in periodical literature. Woolsey helped to found the *New Englander*, a highly respected journal that bridged the intellectual worlds of churchman and philosopher and provided the major vehicle for addressing public issues at the highest level. Two others in this group, Fisher and Porter, also served in administrative and editorial capacities, with Fisher later helping to establish the *Yale Review*.

The academic model exemplified by Yale was not unique. Harvard Divinity School, under the leadership of Charles Everett during the last quarter of the nineteenth century, had a faculty of six professors, five of whom had studied in Germany beginning in the 1850s (Herbst, 1965, 93–94). The editors of the three leading American theological journals at midcentury had also received German university training: Charles Hodge, *Princeton Review* (editor, 1825–71) studied in Germany in the mid-1820s; Edwards Amasa Park, *Bibliotheca Sacra*, published by Andover Seminary and then Oberlin (editor, 1844–83), in the early 1840s; and Henry Boynton Smith, *American Presbyterian Review*, published by Union Seminary (editor, 1859–71) (Kuklick, 1985, 203–15). The *Andover Review*, although not part of this German-trained editorial oligarchy, was also a major vehicle for German philosophy and historical criticism. Those who later became Progressive academics had before them, in full view as it were, models of training, scholarship, publication, teaching, and public roles in the liberal Protestant churchmen who immediately preceded and overlapped them.

By 1900 these churchmen had been integrating German historical scholarship and German philosophy into American religion and moral philosophy for more than sixty years. Equally noteworthy is that just as Progressive social theorists were coming to the fore as articulators of public doctrine, churchmen suddenly began to disappear from the first ranks of American intellectual life. It was as if the pool of replacements to succeed them suddenly dried up, leaving successors who were no longer leaders in American thought at its highest levels. Very quickly and just as the German-trained social scientists were becoming "public" men, the successor churchmen were becoming "private," that is, increasingly confining their audience to their own denominations and no longer presuming to write for and to instruct the nation. Indicative of this retreat were the fortunes of their leading journals, which, from the 1840s onward, had published most of the sophisticated philosophical writing in America. First to fall was the *American Presbyterian Review* in 1871, absorbed by the *Princeton Review*, which in turn folded in 1888. Then, in three successive years starting in 1891, three more prominent journals ceased publication, *Unitarian Review*, the *New Englander* and the *Andover Review*.[39]

That churchmen as academics and intellectuals were the primary models available to the Progressives has a number of important implications. Although this is not the place to retrace their intellectual affinities,[40] it is important to note that it was German idealism and philosophy of history that were initially responsible for transforming American theology. And in so doing, the older millennial/national themes in American Protestantism became increasingly merged into theories of social evolution. Put differently, Hegel was the framework within which "Darwinism" was incorporated into religious thought, and German historicism was the means by which God's spirit was charted in both church and society. On this reading—and here the evidence in Progressive writings is simply overwhelming[41]—the social gospel was both the fulfillment and the death knell for academic theology as the highest expression of American thought. Its denominational

39. Despite this early demise, both John Bates Clark and Henry Carter Adams managed to publish in the *New Englander*, and John Dewey, Richard Ely, Arthur Hadley, Edmund James, and Vida Scudder published in the *Andover Review*. The demise of these theological journals in the East was partly offset by the formation of new ones in the Midwest—signaling both a regional and a denominational shift of influence. William Rainey Harper, president of the University of Chicago, founded and edited *Bible World* in 1893, and four years later, faculty at the Chicago Divinity School started the *American Journal of Theology*. These journals, however, never attained the influence and academic respect of those that had ceased publication. In 1900 the Disciples of Christ began what later became a very influential religious weekly, the *Christian Century* (Mott, 1957, 1: 301).

40. Kuklick, 1985, and Stevenson, 1986, are two excellent and detailed studies. Herbst, 1965, is an earlier study of the influence particularly of German historical thinking. Two older textbooks, Schneider, 1946, on the history of American philosophy and Gabriel, 1956, on the course of American democratic thought, remain the most richly documented and comprehensive studies of the ways in which articulate theological argument provided the primary means by which new modes of thought were received in America.

41. For expressions of the exhaustion of theology and of "creeds" for the furtherance of democratic values, see Cooley, Commons, Ely, Patten, Ross, Small, and also the social gospel writers themselves, especially Washington Gladden and Walter Rauschenbusch. For a late example of the latter, see Rauschenbusch's last book, *Theology for the Social Gospel*, from a lecture series in 1917, especially "The Social Gospel and Personal Salvation" (chap. 10) and "The Social Gospel and the Atonement" (chap. 19). Another factor is that the denominational framework for this theology represented an ever decreasing proportion of American Protestantism and American religion generally. Discussion of some of the implications of this merging of religious modernism and academia in America is found in George M. Marsden, "Preachers of Paradox: the Religious New Right in Historical Perspective," and Edwin Scott Gaustad, "Did the Fundamentalists Win?," both in Douglas and Tipton, 1982.

and church framework, the tendency toward internecine battle, and the inner logic of theological speculation itself combined to direct this demise. Social gospel clergymen contributed to this passage insofar as they read the church out of any unique institutional role in the achievement of the Kingdom and merged the gospel into sociology with hardly any doctrinal theology in between.[42]

The quick passage of John Dewey from the world of churchman to that of philosopher is both exemplary and causal. He most clearly pointed out how democracy and the methods of democracy themselves fulfilled the ends of a religious commonwealth.[43] Religion as creed and individual salvation were replaced, respectively, by democratic faith and democratic citizenship. But this passage was made possible only because those Americans who studied in Germany viewed the disinterested pursuit of knowledge as personally and socially transformative and the university as the redemptive engine of this transformation. Perhaps the best symbolic admission of this changing of the guard was in 1894, when the one surviving theological journal, Oberlin's *Bibliotheca Sacra*, added a subtitle: *A Religious and Sociological Quarterly.*

This same replacement of "churchmen" by "philosophers" also represents a more ambiguous kind of transferral. As legatees as much as conquerors, there was a decided blurring of roles. Just as the church pulpit was also a public lectern, so the university lectern became a public pulpit. The social gospel transition worked both ways, sacralizing sociology and philosophy and maintaining a powerful religious element in American public doctrine and national identity. In this sense, it is not at all clear who was a churchman and who a philosopher—whether Richard Ely or Jane Addams, for example, were less "religious" figures than clergymen George Herron or W. D. P. Bliss. All were quite consciously "public moralists" who worked through the variety of institutions and venues to fulfill their common redemptive vocations. Nor is at all clear whether liberal Protestant theology as the democratic "Religion of America" is a secularization or an indirect hegemonic conquest by Protestant theology now restated as public doctrine through academic social science and philosophy. That American Protestantism split down the middle precisely when the Progressive aca-

---

42. Herron, 1894, 8: "I would save the church from the false position of existing and working for its own glory and religious aggrandizement, from the fatal Jewish position of seeking to bring the world under the dominion of itself, and speak some word that would help to convert it to the Christian pursuit of sacrificing itself for the world." And "Jesus Christ offers sociology the only scientific ground of discovering all the facts and forces of life. That ground is his revelation of universal unity. . . . Sociology and theology will ultimately be one science" (23 and 32).

43. See Kuklick, 1985, 242–44; and Schneider, 1946, 365–80.

demics became the chief beneficiaries of theological "modernism"—occupying all the strategic institutional positions previously held by liberal churchmen[44]—may only indicate that religious modernism, in conquering new and valuable territory, was forced to yield some less valuable assets, namely, those denominations or religious factions that retreated from the task of reforming and perhaps even "reconstituting" America. Beginning around World War I, members of what later came to be called "fundamentalist" churches were increasingly consigned to the cultural equivalent of resident alien status. But it was modernized evangelical theology and the new social sciences and not secular liberalism that drew up the expulsion orders.

However this issue of transfer from churchman to philosopher is understood it is clear that Progressive intellectuals and earlier churchmen, as public moralists, shared a common audience, a common set of enemies, and a common view of their own political and intellectual importance. And both groups believed that their strategic advantage lay in their ability to see America from a comprehensive view, their capacity to raise issues and offer solutions that their intellectual competitors, whether jurists or party spokesmen, could not or would not address. But the Progressives, both as social theorists and as secular academics in a new kind of American university, were compelled to address their competitors more directly than had their churchmen predecessors. As more direct competitors for institutional political power (e.g., expert bureaucracy) and as intellectual underwriters and publicists for institutional reforms across every area of American political and economic life, they, unlike the churchmen, had to engage in direct combat with jurists and with partisan carriers of American political tradition. Although they did not always avoid "the narcissism of powerless moral superiority"[45] that sometimes characterized the pose of both churchmen and especially their female moral reform allies toward political and economic power, the Progressives often vigorously asserted their claims of moral and intellectual superiority over more traditional forms of political and legal thought in America. And to make those claims prevail—or at least directly competitive—they had to address this body of thought much more directly than had their clerical forefathers.

---

44. Even the great land-grant universities were initially headed by churchmen—Henry P. Tappan at Michigan and John Bascom at Wisconsin, for example—or by those who were active participants in modernist movements in theology, for example, Andrew Dickson White at Cornell.

45. From Diane Johnson's review essay, "Something for the Boys," *New York Review of Books*, 16 January 1992, 16.

4

NATION, PARTY GOVERNMENT, & CONSTITUTION

National political order in nineteenth-century America was dominated by two institutions, courts and parties. Corresponding to these
two institutions were two dominant frameworks of thought, constitutional law and democratic individualism. Both forms of thought received their distinct marks early in the nineteenth century, with constitutional law predating theories of democratic partisanship.
Symbolized by the figure of John Marshall as founder-statesman and
codified in the legal writings of Joseph Story, constitutional law possessed a "national" and even an "organic-historical" self-understanding.[1]

Democratic individualism, although deriving its theoretical origins
in the Jeffersonian opposition to the Federalists (and from earlier Anti-
Federalist writings generally), was institutionalized in the Jacksonian
invention of the mass-based and electorally oriented political party.
Tocqueville's *Democracy in America* held that democratic individualism was the natural product of a people born equally free and collectively sovereign, but only if freed from the prior constraints of the
"great parties" and elite leadership that marked the founding period.[2]

As dominant institutions and as dominant modes of political think-

1. This is understandable given its connection to common law, but constitutional law nonetheless grounded its reflections in the positive and authoritative
written text of the Constitution. There was an early and unsuccessful struggle, led
mainly by Story, to claim that adoption of the Constitution also entailed, for some
purposes, the "reception" of an unwritten and national common law. This battle
was decisively lost regarding a national common law of crimes and indirectly lost
regarding the civil law as well, except in some areas of commercial law. In civil law,
federal courts used state law, including the common law of the several states, in de-
ciding civil disputes in diversity cases. But common law understandings were routinely used in interpreting the Constitution, most notoriously in the use of the
"bad tendency" doctrine in determining the meaning of freedom of speech in the
First Amendment (Friedman, 1985, 289–90; Rabban, 1981, 1983).

2. Tocqueville, 1981, 88–93, 145–58, and 390–98; see also Formisano, 1974, and
Wood, 1987, on rise of party and decline of deference.

ing, this regime of courts and parties would appear inherently—even massively—at odds with itself. The institutional framework for constitutional law is formal in the extreme: a hierarchic system of state and federal appellate courts and court personnel, canonical casebooks and legal treatises, and, in various forms over time, systems of legal education, bar organizations, and standards of professional success. In contrast, the political party framework of democratic individualism is both informal and protean in organizational expression. Prior to Progressive regulatory reforms early in the twentieth century,[3] party leaders were informally chosen, were accountable to no body of officials, and exercised a constantly changing and bewildering number of powers. Attaching themselves to every level of government and all of its branches, forging ties to newspapers and magazines, ethnic and religious groups, and every conceivable form of economic interest, and adopting the vocabulary and styles of every expression of region and culture, party leaders made of the political party whatever significant numbers of voters and interests wanted it to become. During one election in 1854 in Hartford, Connecticut, twenty-three distinct party groupings ran candidates for office at the various levels of government (Billington, 1964, 390). Even in that most ritualized period of two-party competition following the Civil War, state and local party leaders were constantly innovating in organization and technique, if only to ward off the possibility of defection or third-party movements.[4] Party leaders, came (and went) in every conceivable guise, reflecting the inner variety of the electorate, the economic, social, and demographic changes over time, shifting patterns of coalitions and alliances, and the changing political values of the American voter.[5] With the exception of narrowly based "movement" parties, partisan political thought achieved coherence only at the national level and then less as programmatic guides than as encoded cultural appeals and as concessions to various interests in the coalition.

3. For example, in the five-year period 1903–8, thirty-one states passed legislation mandating direct primaries for political party nominations. McCormick, 1986, 343; and see Kelly, Harbison, and Belz, 1983, 438–43, for a range of antiparty measures at this time.

4. Jensen, 1971, is an excellent description of party techniques and strategies under conditions of hypercompetition and deep party loyalties. Kleppner, 1978, 49, speaks of parties as "political churches" in this stalemate period, 1876–96.

5. McGerr, 1986, 69–105, shows how party leaders began changing the tone and style of party appeals beginning as early as the late 1870s in response to the growing sophistication and antipartyism of the northern urban middle class. This kind of nonpartisan party appeal became increasingly common in the core regions of the country, with the Republican party emerging as the chief beneficiary and finally hegemonic victor in 1896.

These marked institutional and intellectual differences between parties and courts were most obviously played out in conflicts between state legislatures and state courts. And, insofar as the federal court system was heavily shielded from immediate partisan pressure and was staffed by those whose autonomous professional values were most strongly held, disputes between states and the national government were actually contests between state legislatures and national courts and therefore between the populist ideals of democratic individualism and the legal-institutional logic of constitutional tradition.[6] Finally, there were major ethnocultural differences. The federal appellate judiciary and most state appellate judges were not only WASP to the core, they vastly overrepresented mainstream religious denominations, especially Episcopalians, Unitarians and, later, Methodists. In contrast, party leadership and elected officials at all levels were much more ethnically, religiously, and economically diverse.

Given these marked differences, one would think that Progressive intellectuals would naturally gravitate toward and attempt to integrate their historical theories and reform ideas into the long-standing and rich tradition of constitutional law. The nationalism of the courts, the organic-historical features of the common law, the tradition of professional autonomy and public service of the bar and of legal education would all seem to have beckoned to reformers at this time.[7] But this was decidedly not the case. Constitutional law and the leading lights of American legal scholarship were treated by Progressive intellectuals with studied neglect as a kind of fossilized and symbiotic complement to the party system, which, in turn, they treated with studied contempt. While there are many historical-cultural reasons for the Progressive's neglect of the constitutional legal tradition—foremost is the antilegal sentiment deeply embedded in Calvinist theology—there is a

6. Friedman, 1985, 412–87 and 511–71; and Hurst, 1956. As Oliver Wendell Holmes cryptically expressed it: "We suppose this phrase [state police power] was invented to cover certain acts of the legislature which are seen to be unconstitutional, but which are believed to be necessary" (quoted in Keller, 1977, 410).

7. Earlier groups of reformers and intellectuals in the Gilded Age often included large number of lawyers, for example, the "Mugwumps" and the members of the American Social Science Association. John Commons, writing in the early 1890s, recognized this fact when he expressed the hope that he would "see the day when the leadership in the social movements of our time will be taken from the lawyer and the newspaper and given to the Christian minister. We cannot expect to have a society based on righteousness so long as our social philosophy is given to us by [party] editors and lawyers. They are put forward to favor special interests. But where is the advocate of the masses, of the great brotherhood of man? Where is the truly judicial mind, whose purpose is to bring to pass the kingdom of God on earth?" An earlier proviso is that the minister be trained in sociology (Commons, 1894, 23, and see 19–22).

deeper rationale to this result that only a few of the Progressives clearly recognized and then only quite late in the period.[8]

Despite the obvious differences between the forms of political thought institutionalized in courts and in parties, their separate fates were inexorably linked together in the nineteenth century. It is no accident that two of the most creative and original periods of American legal scholarship occurred at precisely those periods when parties and a lusty political democracy were most active and dominant. By the end of the Jeffersonian era the awesome energies of democratic individualism described so well by Tocqueville created an explosive demand for legal ideas and doctrines to channel and contain those energies. Both then and now, this period is viewed as a golden age of American legal scholarship, and one in which the lawyer attained a luster unmatched in the history of free governments.[9] Another extended period of legal creativity occurred during the Gilded Age, again when party was king and the energies of democratic individualism were unleashed. Here, too, a union of capitalism and the creative legal mind in America was forged, but this time the midwife was the corporate lawyer and the issue new forms of corporations, trusts, and financial instruments. The results for constitutional law were new legal doctrines making clear their way in a land still consisting of isolated localities of small-producer capitalists and realty interests. These older economic interests and economic regions both lusted for the benefits and sought to avoid

8. Croly, in *Promise of American Life* of 1909 has long sections excoriating government by law and lawyers, but only in *Progressive Democracy* of 1914, chaps. 6–8, does he portray the relationship between constitutional legal thinking and democratic individualism as mutually sustaining. "The particular expression of the conservative spirit to which progressivism finds itself opposed is essentially, and, as it seems, necessarily doctrinaire and dogmatic. It is based on an unqualified affirmation of the necessity of the traditional constitutional system to the political salvation of American democracy. . . . It has been and is being acclaimed . . . as a consummate system of law and government, framed under a final political philosophy, to satisfy the essential conditions of individual liberty and wholesome political association" (20–21).

9. For the self-congratulatory rhetoric from the upper bar during this period, Miller, 1962, especially lectures and orations by Joseph Story (1821 and 1829), Charles Jared Ingersoll (1823), James Kent (1824), Rufus Choate (1845), and David Dudley Field (1855). Given the Federalist-Whig values of the elite bar and given Tocqueville's characterization of the American lawyer as naturally "aristocratic," this mutual flourishing might appear paradoxical, but both jurists and Tocqueville knew that the more active the American democrat, the more dependent he became upon creative lawyers. Hurst, 1956, shows just how this mutually beneficial alliance between the lawyer and the American democratic capitalist was struck in the Middle Period. Louis Hartz (1954) anoints this alliance into a permanent bond, blessing the result as "the liberal tradition in America."

the competitive costs of the emerging national transport, industrial, marketing, and financial institutions.[10]

This association of the release of capitalist energy and legal creativity occurred precisely in those periods when, in the concurrence of contemporary observers and intellectual historians alike, the higher intellect in America was at an ebb and when intellectuals were least honored. The two golden ages of law in the nineteenth century, then, stood as a kind of paradoxical proof of American anti-intellectualism and provincialism. Although this story is complicated by other factors, most notably the democratization of professional entry and the lowering of educational standards in the Jacksonian period (Friedman, 1985, 303–22), American constitutional and legal thought could not escape this guilt by association with party and with the irresponsibility and excesses of democratic capitalism.

CONSTITUTIONAL LAW, POLITICAL SCIENCE, AND POLITICAL HISTORY

Despite the animosity between Progressive political and social theory and American legal thought, there were points of contact and attempts at intellectual mediation. Along with the political economists and sociologists so prominent in this study, there were distinguished American political scientists and political historians who also received German training and who studied and taught in the new American graduate schools. Political scientists and historians like John William Burgess (1844–1931) of Columbia, Herbert Baxter Adams (1850–1901) of Johns Hopkins, and J. Franklin Jameson (1859–1937) of Brown and Chicago, all linked history to politics through the study of the evolu-

10. This "battle of capitalisms" is the central thesis of Charles Beard's writings on both the founding and later periods in America. This same battle had its juristic counterpart in doctrinal and status battles within the legal community. On one side was the typical jack-of-all-trades lawyer—part-time land speculator, banker, politician, and judge—representing the older realty and small producer interests and, on the other, increasingly flanked by federal appellate judges, an emerging core of full-time law school professors, and some of the judiciary in the industrial states, the urban, college-trained, and highly specialized "corporate" lawyer (Friedman, 1985, 606–29 and 633–41). On this same battle as it was reflected in legal education and admission to the bar, see Stevens, 1983, 71–111; and Hall, 1989, 211–21. In 1876, Harvard Law School under Langdell introduced the case method and thus strictly national appellate court law in legal training. This started the Harvard model on its path to domination of legal training for the upper bar. Hegemonic victory for all of legal education was not achieved until the Great Depression and the demise of the nonuniversity law school (Stevens, 1983, 33–72 and 172–90).

tion of political and legal institutions.[11] And this list must include the most famous political scientist-historian-constitutional scholar of them all, Woodrow Wilson (1856–1924), a student of Herbert Baxter Adams and Richard T. Ely and a prolific writer and lecturer on these topics. In addition to these new academic connections to the study of American constitutional law, "realistic" constitutional histories informed by an evolutionary historical perspective were written in the 1880s and 1890s. In addition to Jameson and Wilson, George Curtis, Henry Jones Ford, William C. Morey, James Harvey Robinson, Simon Sterne, and Christopher Tiedman all wrote either constitutional histories or constitutional analysis from an organic-evolutionary perspective.[12]

Despite these seeming affinities, there are compelling reasons why Progressive scholarship was neither driven by nor even attracted to this body of work. The most obvious is that almost all the "realistic" histories of the Constitution stressed its "unwritten" aspects, to be sure, but often in order to attach party to Constitution, which at once legitimated the prevailing parties and party system and made of them a necessary instrument in the preservation of constitutional government. Insofar as the prevailing system of party government was seen as an obstacle to reform, the conservative thrust of this strategy is implicit.

This conservative tendency was augmented by the ways in which the historical antecedents to the U.S. Constitution were traced in this same literature. Whether tracked through British or American colonial institutional history or through dark Teutonic forests,[13] the destination reached was a constitutional product both antimajoritarian and of closely limited powers, again far away from the larger intent of the Progressives. Indeed, the necessary stress on legal and institutional "mechanics"—no matter what the protestations of the scholars themselves

11. Herbst, 1965, discusses each of these men and others. Burgess founded *Political Science Quarterly* and was first dean of the faculty of political science and public law at Columbia, having first taught at its law school. Jameson, a student of Herbert Baxter Adams and the recipient of the first Ph.D. in history awarded by Johns Hopkins, was one of the founders of the American Historical Association (AHA) and cofounder and managing editor of *American Historical Review*, 1895–1928. Adams, another founder of the AHA, began the *Johns Hopkins Studies in Historical and Political Science*, a major publishing vehicle of the German historical school in America.

12. Belz, 1969; Curtis, 1889; Ford, 1898; Jameson, 1889; Morey, 1891; Robinson, 1890; Sterne, 1882; Tiedman, 1890; and Wilson, 1908.

13. Of the writings considered here, Wilson's was the most studiously Anglophile, holding that the framers intended the Constitution "to be a copy of the government of England" (1908, 42). Most of the other historians laid more stress on the charters of the English trading companies in the American colonies, on colonial charters, and on early state constitutions. See Morey, 1891.

against "Newtonian" understandings—compromised any thoroughgoing historical and critical analysis. Thus, despite a Germanic gloss, these writers found it hard to ignore the obvious facts that most of our constitutions were "willed," usually written whole and changed whole, and that most of our political boundaries after 1789 were products of the draftsman's art, marching in grids across forests and prairies.[14]

Finally, constitutional history, no matter its grounding in new historical and evolutionary methods, necessarily focused on legally constituted political institutions, thereby raising artificial barriers between politics, culture, economy, and society just when Progressive scholars were attempting to lower them.[15] Indicative of this inner tension and the consequent isolation of constitutional scholarship from Progressive intellectual life is the fact that as early as 1885, the *Johns Hopkins Studies in Historical and Political Science* dropped its emphasis on political-institutional history. Its editor and leading political-constitutional historian, Herbert Baxter Adams, announced that he was switching to American economic history.[16]

Insofar as political science as a professional discipline was so strongly tied to the Constitution, it, too, could never quite free itself of these same disabilities. Except as political scientists became sociologists or political economists, their service to the shaping of Progressive public doctrine was either secondary and derivative or a conservative counterweight. In terms of the broader relationship between the universities and legal scholarship, the political scientists and constitutional historians might be credited with building some bridges over

14. Simon Patten's one foray into American constitutional issues from an evolutionary-historical perspective ended in hopeless frustration. In a short piece on state and local governments in America, 1890, he surveyed all the willed and arbitrary mismatches between "natural" economic, demographic, and cultural units and operative political boundaries (rivers should *connect*, not delimit, he almost shouts) and concludes that we must totally reconfigure our state and local boundaries (he even suggests "free cities" on the German model) or continue to suffer the decay and demoralization of local and state governments. He concludes that the greater the mismatch, the more the opportunity for party bosses to dictate policy because publics cannot find themselves, understand each other, and thereby become coherent, active, and powerful. *Annals* 1(1890): 26–42.

15. Kloppenberg, 1986, chaps. 2 and 3, discusses the philosophical foundations of this position in America, Britain, France, and Germany and, in chaps. 8–10, traces the political and programmatic consequences.

16. Herbst, 1965, 114. In a 1917 article in *The New Republic*, Charles Beard gave popular expression to this long-standing academic fact: "Political Science in the United States has always been under bondage to the lawyers. This is mainly due . . . to the nature of our system of government which places constitutionality above all other earthly consideration in the discussion of public measures" (quoted in McCorkle, 1984, 341).

which some law faculty and other jurists might cross, but the path on the other side seemed only to circle back to prevailing institutions and practices. In short, starting in the mid-1880s, Progressive horizons were decidedly not constitutional and legal. The stress on inner character, shared values, public opinion, social knowledge, and spiritual progress impelled the Progressives toward ever deeper critiques of American constitutional and party government and to ever more extensive reconstructions of democratic theory to accommodate new institutions and alternative practices in American political life.[17]

PARTY, PARTY GOVERNMENT, AND DEMOCRATIC THEORY

Much of the Progressive case against formal governing institutions in America was indirect. Given the tradition of antipartyism, attacking party was a way both to undermine prevailing formal-legal institutions—including the Constitution—and to reform them to serve Progressive ends. At first sight, this may appear paradoxical, for no institution in the nineteenth century was more powerful than the mass-based political party in overcoming the antimajoritarian features of state and federal constitutions and none more effective in mobilizing popular political participation. This "movement" or mobilizing feature of party was not forgotten by the Progressives, often making their critique of party a very selective one. As coalitions of state and local machines and their allied interests, however, most parties in America are not institutions of conscious national purpose. It was this coalitional and local-interest idea of party that was most excoriated.

Without always realizing it the Progressives were attempting to reverse Tocqueville's scenario of party in America as democracy gains more and more power. Tocqueville had predicted that democratic individualism spelled an end to "great political parties" that in the founding period had lifted adherents beyond their own narrow interests and ways of life under the "moral power" of great leaders. Democratic individualism both destroyed deference and created distrust of powerful government, leaving only small parties and therefore no party "which seems to contest the present form of government or the present course of society." Interests rather than principles and a multitude of minute and petty differences "upon questions of detail" animate parties premised on individualism and equality. The only difference between the

17. Kloppenberg, 1986, chap. 10, gives an excellent summary of this vision of a democratic society found in both American and in transatlantic progressive and social democratic thought in this period.

two parties, he concluded, is that one will seek to extend the authority of the people and the other will attempt to hold it in check. Neither will be animated by a larger conception of national greatness or the public good (Tocqueville, 1981, 89–91). As both parties become agencies of democratic individualism they reinforce the rights-based features of American constitutionalism and weaken coherent structures of national political authority.[18] As described by the new constitutional histories, parties enhance federalism, encourage the devolution of power, strengthen checks and balances, and require a politics of bargaining and compromise. What this system will not permit is critical inquiry and serious discussion of the common good. What neither "small" party can provide is a platform from which to measure and judge the quality of the standing regime. Together, the party system and the Constitution reinforce the status quo.[19]

The great exception to Tocqueville's logic and its implied prediction, was the formation and victory of the Republican party and the constitutional and political revolution of the Civil War. It was the memory of those events that served to keep alive the hope of another great national party. But it was this same memory that served to embitter those who witnessed the transformation of the Republicans into more and more of a "small" party after the war. This transformation was particularly evident in the Midwest, both because of the scale of economic and demographic change and because the parties were so evenly matched. It was this last factor that made the stakes so high. Whoever captured the Midwest and held it captured the national government. And because the axis from New York to Chicago was the increasingly dynamic core, arrogating to itself the wealth, talent, and population of the country, the core became more than a strategic prize on the way to victory; it was victory itself.

This combination of memory and hope gave Progressive antipartyism the aspect of a crusade and made of its rhetoric a jeremiad. This was not new. In 1835, the New England churchman Lyman Beecher had declared that "the West is destined to be the great central power of the nation, and under heaven, must affect powerfully the cause of free in-

18. Tocqueville also shows how the displacement of great parties with small ones contributes to the strengthening of state and local power and the weakening of the power of the federal government (1981, 265).

19. The theory that the opposition or "out" party normally provides a real alternative is refuted by the coalitional nature of this party and the logic of electoral competition in America. In a way, two-party competition is like oligopolistic economic competition in the American automobile industry in the 1950s: all the competitors assumed the same "automobile morality" and offered alternatives that differed only in chromium detail—until an exogenous automobile morality was offered in the form of the Volkswagen "beetle."

stitutions and the liberty of the world.'' With language indistinguishable from that of the 1890s, he described the West—now the Midwest—as ''a young empire of mind, and power, and wealth, and free institutions, rushing up to a giant manhood, with a rapidity and a power never before witnessed below the sun'' (Beecher, 1835, 11–12). For Beecher, Catholicism, not slavery or party, was the barrier to the conquest of the West for the American errand. After the Civil War, this same image of the Midwest became the image of America. In 1891, Josiah Strong repeated Beecher's call: ''Within the bosom of these few years is folded not only the future of the mighty West, but the nation's destiny: for . . . the West is to dominate the East.'' As this region is called to become the nation, so the call is to ''America for the world's sake . . . [because] ours is the elect nation for the age to come.'' The social gospel movement, Strong included, joined religious millennialism and political antipartyism to redeem the nation.[20]

Given this background, critique of party was suffused with moral and ethical passion. Samuel Batten, a prominent social gospel minister and college professor in Iowa, condemned the competitive party system because each party, in its single-minded desire for electoral victory, was constrained to take men as they are and appeal to their present selves and their immediate individual interests. The party system ''stands between the people and the government and makes a fully democratic government impossible.'' This ''subtle and silent . . . tyranny'' of party mirrors the despotism of the selfish appetites of the unredeemed American individualist. At its best, party government ''means stagnation . . . commonplace ideas and past issues''; at its worst, it ''spells compromise and not principles . . . it means mediocrity and inferiority where it does not mean cowardice and corruption. A good partisan cannot be a good citizen'' (Batten, 1909, 239–40).

Even Dewey's college textbook on ethics takes a poke at party government. Dewey first reminds the reader of the deep meaning of voting and other formal exercises of political rights: ''Political freedom and responsibility express an individual's power and obligation to make effective all his other capacities by fixing the social conditions of their exercise.'' He then turns to party organizations, recounting their past historical service for democracy and their present opposition to extending democracy. His disgust is not disguised.

---

20. Strong, 1893, 199 and 253–54. The barriers to victory for Strong were many and various, including Mormonism, the moral dangers of urban life, materialism, economic inequality, and Catholic alternatives to Protestant-dominated public schools. Even Tocqueville indirectly recognized the power of this hope: ''The civilization of the North appears to be the common standard to which the whole nation will one day be assimilated'' (1981, 265).

These agencies are the 'machines' of political parties, with their hierarchical gradation of bosses from national to ward rulers, bosses who are in close touch with great business interests at one extreme, and with those who pander to the vices of the community (gambling, drink and prostitution) at the other; parties with their committees, conventions, primaries, caucuses, party-funds, societies, meetings, and all other sorts of devices for holding together and exciting masses of men to more or less blind acquiescence.[21]

Among the Progressives, Croly's critique was certainly the most uncompromising and complete. Although almost all Progressives wanted to purge state and local government from the curse of party organization and corruption, most also thought that national parties for national elections were both necessary and good—in a sense, encouraging "great" parties by depriving them of temptations to pander to local and sectional interests while shielding states and localities from national party divisions. Croly, while admitting the force of this argument,[22] sought strong executive government at all levels to replace party across the board and to overcome jurisdictional limitations with a now unmediated democratic consensus.

American parties had been organized to work with the Constitution, and to supply the deficiencies of that document as an instrument of democratic policy. The organization of a strong official government would not only render the Constitution of less importance, it would also tend to dethrone the party machines. It would imply that the government itself was by way of being democratized, and that the democracy no longer need to depend upon partisan organizations to represent popular purposes. . . . The government itself, rather than the parties, is to be responsible for the realization of the popular will.[23]

Croly's argument held that political parties in America live in symbiotic relationship to a constitutionally fettered democracy in the same way that judicial review as "government by lawyers" does. Political

21. Dewey and Tufts, 1908, 474 and 478. Strictures of this type could be multiplied almost endlessly, both in the writings of Progressive academics and in the periodical press, starting early in the 1880s and reaching a crescendo in the first decade of the 1900s, when rhetoric turned to action and parties became increasingly regulated (Abbott, 1901, 238–42; Commons, 1894, 79–83).

22. See Croly, 1914, 330 and 334, for longer-range alternatives to national parties.

23. Croly, 1914, 124. "Just so far as a progressive political program is carried out, progressive social democracy will cease to need a national political party as an instrument" (336).

parties and constitutional courts exist because of defects in the institutions and practices of American democracy. Both have a stake in a discourse of rights, and not purpose, in a political universe where issues are discussed through the language of jurisdictions and formål powers, not merits. The result is stalemate, cynicism, and corruption. Paradoxically, then, parties both democratize the Constitution and keep alive its most democratically constricting features. But just as courts are giving way to legislative majorities, and legislative majorities, in turn, to direct democracy, so parties must now yield to democratic will, expressed as a coherent national program of social justice. Once "really democratic political institutions are created, the foundations of the two-party system are undermined."[24] Although Croly's hope that political parties would be replaced by strong government did not come to pass, the Progressives were surprisingly effective in subordinating party to government through regulation. Writing in 1920, the political scientist Charles Merriam described the cumulative effect of these reforms as "the gradual absorption of the party by government."[25]

Another way in which party was attacked was to encourage and legitimate other forms of mobilizing and educating the electorate. In a sense this replacement of party as the vehicle for effective citizenship was implicit in the very purpose of reform organizations, especially in alliance with standing institutions such as churches and universities. As these organizations and their journalistic allies became more directly active in politics, they not only forced a modification of party electoral strategy (McGerr, 1986, 69–106), they also weakened party government per se by creating governing bodies removed from direct party and electoral influence. And when one adds the decline of party loyalty, the transformation of the press, lower election turnouts, and the host of reform measures addressed against legislatures—the seat of party government—Croly's hopes to destroy party were not as overblown as might first appear.[26] The public, he said, must form "more permanently organized social and political groups" based both upon shared notions of public good (civic societies, voters' leagues, woman's

24. Croly, 1914, 311–12. As examples, Croly points to the enhanced power of state governors and strong mayor/home rule city governments to conclude that "executive leadership provides . . . an alternative official method of organizing a majority for purposes of government."

25. Merriam, 1920, 458; see also Kelly, Harbison, and Belz, 1983, 438–43; and McCormick, 1986.

26. Silbey, 1991, 224–41, locates the early 1890s as the end of the "partisan political nation" in American politics. See also McCormick, 1986, 197–227. The entire body of literature addressing the institutional changes caused by the realigning election of 1896 makes this assumption the foundation of its analysis.

suffrage unions) and upon shared national economic interests (farmers, wage earners) to supplant parties."[27]

A powerful ally in the attack on parties was the woman's movement in all of its many manifestations. Whether the object of attack was the liquor interests, employers of child labor, owners of substandard tenements, or adulterators of the food supply, at some point early in the battle, one or both political parties would emerge as a stumbling block for change.[28] Frances Kellor, one of Albion Small's first female graduate students at the University of Chicago and later a prominent Progressive party leader, summarized this position in no uncertain terms: "Politics in America had become a question of nominations and elections. Patronage was the key to success and power and hand maiden of the boss. Party lines were drawn, not by issues and policies laid down in platforms to be carried out, but by men who controlled conventions and competed for office" (Fitzpatrick, 1990, 151).

The dominant "feminist" wing of the suffrage movement was antiparty in its assumption that the women's vote would necessarily transform the ways in which parties could conduct their affairs and therefore the practices of government.[29] Gilman went further. Party government is politics considered as a game of combat with the winner enforcing rules by threat of punishment. Political parties are institutional expressions of "inextricable masculinity" in politics and are inherently opposed to women's political participation. Human government, or democracy, must replace "andocracy." This transformation will require women's full participation and will result in a political life

---

27. Croly, 1914, 313–17. This call for nonparty and even functional mobilization of the electorate combined with a powerful administrative bureaucracy is the reason Croly has often been called the architect of "corporate liberalism," that is, a national politics administered in and through its leading industrial, financial, and labor institutions.

28. As Susan B. Anthony put it in *The History of Woman Suffrage*: "Each of the two dominant parties is largely controlled by what are known as the liquor interests. Their influence begins with the National Government, which receives from them billions of revenue; it extends to the States, to which they pay millions; to the cities, whose income they increase by hundreds of thousands, to the farmers, who find in breweries and distilleries the best market for their grain. There is no hamlet so small as not to be touched by their ramifications. No 'trust' ever formed can compare with them in the power which they exercise. They and the various institutions connected with them control millions of votes. They are among the largest contributors to political campaigns. There are few legislators who do not owe their election in a greater or less degree to the influence wielded by these liquor interests, which are positively, unanimously, and unalterably opposed to woman suffrage" ([4:xix] quoted in Kraditor, 1981, 84, and see 60–61).

29. This aspect of the woman's movement is discussed in chapter 7 below.

wherein "a flourishing democratic government [could] be carried on *without any parties at all*" (Gilman, 1911, 187 and 221–22).

GREAT PARTY RESTORATION
AND THE EDUCATED MAN

In an early book on the role of the church in achieving social justice, John Commons stated that "almost every reform you can name is today blocked at the doors of municipal, State, and Federal legislatures." This blockage is laid at the feet of the "party machine . . . the organized clique of spoilsmen who feed upon the public storehouse" (Commons, 1894, 79 and 82). Whereas most of Commons's reform proposals are familiar ones—municipal ownership of utilities, unemployment and workers' compensation, temperance, "child-saving," and civil service reform—one proposal was directed at the political party itself, namely, proportional representation. This reform would not only break the grip of the two-party system by rewarding minority reform parties, it would transform legislatures by making them representative of the spectrum of opinions in the community.[30] No longer would the structure of party competition effectively screen out good citizens. And just as the women's movement claimed that their presence in electoral political life would in itself help to reform it, so did Commons and a host of others claim the same for "the educated man in politics" (Commons, 1894, chapter title, 51).

Commons creates a dynamic psychological profile of the contemporary college-educated young man in America and shows how he would logically progress from a college education to political and party reform. His starting postulate is that "the educated man is the Christian man," if not in formal creed, then certainly in ethics. As a result of his appearance in large numbers and his ethical values, America has witnessed the erection of massive structures of private benevolence, "the home and foreign missionary societies, the temperance unions, the churches and Sunday-schools, the associated charities and prison-reform associations." These efforts of individuals through voluntary associations soon teach the educated young man that "there are powerful underlying evil forces, which individual effort cannot reach and overcome." In this way the educated man discovers politics as "the cooperation of citizens for employing the sovereign power of government to crush the evil and promote the good

30. Commons, 1894, chap. 7. This and similar proposals were widely discussed in both scholarly journals and the periodical press in the 1890s and early 1900s. Initiative, referenda, recall, short ballots, and mandated party primaries proved to be more popular antiparty and legislative reform measures.

forces of society." In Commons's populist and social gospel version, this means that democratic political participation should be a kind of Christian witness: "[The educated man] should take the standpoint of the working classes, that is, of the class whose only means of livelihood is the daily labor of their hands."[31] With this standpoint he will combine inner conviction and the achievement of social justice.

Whereas Commons's particular version of the educated man in politics was more radical, his party-reform ideas more far reaching, and his merging of participation and atonement more evangelical than many other Progressive intellectuals, they, too, structured arguments about citizenship and participation around these themes. By the early twentieth century, this was the case even among established Republican party leaders. A published series of Yale Citizenship Lectures in the early 1900s provides a good sample of the influence of this kind of thinking on the political notables invited to instruct the Yale undergraduate. Like Commons, they all rejected an ideal of high-minded citizenship that stands aloof from the battle, and they urged democratic humility—a sort of threshold atonement—as the appropriate cost of entry. William Howard Taft, an early lecturer in the series, warned the rich among his audience that they had a handicap because they were under the temptation not to test their mettle in the larger world. He suggested to the poor graduate that he postpone marriage for eight or ten years in order to gain experience in the world through politics and to establish himself in a career. To both he said that experience in political life would prevent intellectual and moral self-indulgence—he used "parlor socialism" and laissez faire as polar examples—and suggested that the first step was getting to know one's fellow citizens:

> [The college graduate] must stand on an exact equality with men of less education and less advantages and must familiarize himself

31. Commons, 1894, 53 and 55. Although Commons may have exaggerated the college students' commitment to the working class, he was probably on the mark regarding their moral impulses, at least among college students in the Midwest. For example, in a straw vote among undergraduates at the University of Chicago for the presidential election in 1892 the winner by a large margin was the "fourth" party candidate, John Bidwell, with 164 votes, running on the Prohibition ticket, and not the Republican (151), Democrat (52), or Populist (3)(Jensen, 1971, 185). The Prohibition platform was economically populist (railroads and telegraph should be government controlled; restrictions should be placed on land ownership; commodity speculation should be prohibited), culturally nativistic (tougher immigration laws strictly enforced, compulsory English in public schools to "remain a homogeneous and harmonious people"), and politically antiparty ("Their protest against the admission of 'moral issues' into politics is a confession of their own moral degeneracy . . . their assiduous courting of the liquor power and subserviency to the money power") (Johnson and Porter, 1975, 92–93).

with the exact conditions that prevail in local municipal and broader politics. In many respects the college graduate has as much to learn from the workingman and the business man who have not enjoyed a college education as they have to learn from him (Taft, 1906, 29).

National parties held together by principle were the only effective means of reform. Any other kind of national party, that is, coalitions of separate local interests, no matter its rhetoric, will end up opposing effective national government and therefore will be negative, conservative, and nostalgic (Taft, 1906, 25).

The following year Elihu Root expressed these same ideas in a more muscular mode. Although democratic government rests on the stern virtues of self-control and national patriotism, these virtues must struggle for primacy in electoral combat where "manhood and self respect" do battle with "lust for power and savage instinct for oppression" and where "honesty and virtue" are pitted against "greed and cunning." Participation "is a matter of preemptory obligation which cannot be avoided by any intelligent man who has any understanding of the conditions under which he lives" (Root, 1907, 29–30). For this participation to be effective, however, "one must have a considerable degree of sympathy with [the] feelings and interests [of others]." To a degree "unequalled in any other association" political bodies include

men of widely varying conditions in life, with different opportunities for knowledge and capacity for reflection, with different prejudices and ways of thinking, differing widely in information, in previous reflection, in breadth and scope of thought, in motives, in characters, in tempers, in ambitions. . . . A rightly constituted man brought into association with a great number of others cannot fail to acquire some degree of proper humility (Root, 1907, 64, 66).

Root also ends with a call for "great" parties. His framework is the evolution of democracy from lower to higher stages: first factional struggle led by notable individuals, then coalitions of interests and principles with an incapacity to subordinate minor considerations, leading to endless bargaining, and finally, "two great political parties [that] oppose each other upon fundamental differences." Unfortunately, America is caught between the middle and highest stage because "an organization of active party workers for the distribution of offices" has been grafted on to "the great parties . . . organized for the advocacy of certain declared principles." Reform of party at state and local levels is already proceeding to address this barrier and reach a higher stage of democracy.

The last Republican party notable to speak in this series was Charles Evans Hughes. He begins like the others by warning the college graduate that he can easily forfeit effective citizenship: "A cynical disposition or an intellectual aloofness . . . while not marked enough to interfere with success in many vocations, or to disturb his conventional relations, largely disqualifies him from aiding his community." Effective political life requires that he "endeavor to understand the different racial [i.e., cultural] viewpoints of the various elements which enter into our population [and] be free from the prejudice of occupation or of residence. . . . He will look neither up nor down, but with even eye will seek to read the hearts of men" (Hughes, 1910, 11–12). Like the other speakers, Hughes defends great national parties, but with more sophistication and point, drawing on Maine's *Popular Government*, Lowell's *Government of England*, and *The Federalist Papers*. He concludes that great parties necessarily arose in America because of the constitutional fact of national presidential elections and the continuing presence of national issues and national purposes. But when great issues are resolved, what keeps national parties national? What keeps them from devolving into coalitions of "small" and locally oriented parties, thriving on "the stupidity, despotism, and corruption of party managers," and from driving good men into independence (Hughes, 1910, 75)?

Hughes does not so much answer this question (obviously reflecting the problems of the Republicans after the Civil War) as suggest that great parties can be restored only when educated and virtuous men lead them. Admitting that the present party system and practices have "created an irresponsible personal government not only unknown to the Constitution, but alike unknown to any admissible theory of government by party," he warns that reforms must be "consistent with . . . the maintenance of national party organizations." The restoration of great national parties can be achieved by "seeking to limit their activity to what properly belongs to [political parties], and thus to narrow the range of appeals to party loyalty where party concerns are not involved, and of opportunities to convert party loyalty inspired by national ideals to the personal advantage of [local] party leaders."[32] In

---

32. Hughes, 1910, 102 and 107–8. Hughes's specific proposals to achieve this severance read like a standard Progressive agenda: short ballots, nonpartisan city government and judicial elections, more appointed and fewer elective local offices, especially those touching law enforcement. His hope is that "in time, party nominations as such would be denied a place upon official ballots [for local office]" (114).

short, the reconstitution of great parties requires the nationalization of party and the prevention of local party scoundrels taking refuge in national party patriotism—and voters should not be placed in the position of purchasing their high-minded national party principles at the cost of subsidizing low-minded private and local interests.

The twin themes calling for the educated man in politics and restoring great parties of national principle linked Progressive academics and intellectuals uniquely with the Republican party and its immediate antecedents. The call for participation at all levels of partisan activity but in the name of national and higher ethical purposes—even if it meant helping to destroy one's own local machine—reflected the distinctive antiparty traditions of the Republicans who, in turn, inherited it from the Whigs and, earlier, northern Federalism. Not even after more than six decades of regularized two party competition could the Whigs and then the Republicans fully accept the democratic individualist theory that lay behind it. They had never fully believed in public good as an aggregate majority produced by registering individual preferences in a game with fair rules, whether in a political or an economic market.[33] If there is a common good it must be a consciously shared one and subjected to national discussion. Reliance on a "rights" discourse within the framework of neutral procedures defined by constitutions can as easily be a temptation to individualism and greed as a means of participating in the discussion and shaping of a common good. That almost all of these Progressive intellectuals acquired their early political educations through Republican families in the period between the early 1870s and the mid-1890s and in states with intensely close party divisions strongly reinforces this logic. An example of this Republican antiparty heritage and regional experience is a fixation on the earlier mugwump idea that a small group of virtuous and educated voters might serve as a strategic voting minority that can determine the fate of the nation—an assumption only credible in closely competitive two-party states that, in the national arena, could decide presidential victors and congressional majorities.

Following the election of 1896, the Republican party gained a firm grip on power in the Midwest and the industrial East. In this context

---

33. In this lecture series and in other writings, Arthur Hadley, by then president of Yale, made many negative references to politics considered as a "game" played by getting the most votes without getting caught violating the rules. This game aspect makes it "difficult for the good man to pursue high standards without sacrificing his chances for political efficiency." The same applied to business competition (Hadley, 1903, 163; see also Hadley, 1901, 11–14 and 30–31). Gilman, 1911, 107–25, explains the relationship between the "male" principle and combative games, 178–92, and explains how this distorts politics and business, 208–27.

the Progressives now saw themselves as a strategic group within the dominant party. As such, they could effectively make demands directly on local, state, and national governments through nonparty institutions and reform organizations. Moreover, under these changed conditions, playing electoral politics and manipulating party machinery became less important as the autonomous power possibilities of Progressive counterinstitutions grew more expansive. No longer seeing themselves only as a strategic minority dependent upon electoral results, they could now claim to stand at the head of a national reform movement consisting of an ever-growing complex of national institutions: universities, the periodic press, professional associations, and the host of local and national philanthropic and issue oriented groups.

Party and voter regulation and declining electoral turnouts further weakened the state and local parties, thereby increasing the strength of new and nonparty forms of political power. The Jacksonian universe of courts and parties appeared to be nearing its end and, with it, sectionalism and small-producer and agrarian capitalism. But what about the Constitution? Given the demise of party organization and the importance of elections, was it, too, destined for a kind of desuetude because it could not stand alone? Before this possibility can be addressed it is useful to examine the writings of Woodrow Wilson in this period. Although later placed in the pantheon of Progressives, Wilson, both as scholar and political leader, was usually seen by the Progressive intellectuals in this period as a conservative threat to their ideals. The best warrant for their view was Wilson's strong defense of the American Constitution allied with the prevailing party system as the guarantor of democracy, defined as the protection of individual rights. Wilson saw the mutual dependence of party and Constitution and sought to preserve both.

CONSTITUTIONAL LAW, INDIVIDUAL RIGHTS, AND WILSONIAN CONSERVATISM

In 1906, William Howard Taft, two years away from the presidency, reminded his Yale audience that despite his criticisms of party machines and patronage, great national political parties "are essential to the carrying on of any popular government" and that the more "efficient party [is one] in which the members are more nearly united on the great principles of governmental policy." Clearly making an appeal for the Republicans, he then concluded:

It is difficult to classify parties in this country as conservative and radical, because the facts do not always justify such a classification; but generally it will be found that the more efficient party in administration is the more progressive and more affirmative—more radical, therefore, in its policies. The opposing party is usually negative, declining to initiate new reforms (Taft, 1906, 24–25).

Under Taft's appeal to a consensual politics of "social harmony" that sublimated older ethnic, regional, and cultural appeals to the ends of shared national power and prosperity, it was clear that national public good was dominantly the values and interests of the urban industrial core.[34] Against this Republican core-as-nation victory, the Democratic party seemed to have no choice but to defend the independence of the economic and cultural periphery and to man the existing constitutional ramparts preventing further "colonization." Failure to do so would be to concede a permanent subordination of regions to nation as embodied in this core. And insofar as this core was defined and defended by those who increasingly dominated American intellectual life and its most sophisticated organs of public opinion, nothing less would suffice than a defense of the periphery in equally sophisticated and cosmopolitan terms.

In 1908, Woodrow Wilson, four years away from the presidency that he won against both Taft and Roosevelt, gave a series of lectures published as *Constitutional Government in the United States*. Anchoring the federal Constitution firmly in British tradition, beginning with Magna Carta, he locates the meaning of constitutional government in individual rights: "There is no such thing as corporate liberty. Liberty belongs to the individual, or it does not exist . . . [and] liberty is the object of constitutional government." Constitutional government protects liberty because "representatives of government have no authority except such as they derive from the law" (Wilson, 1908, 16, 18, and 20). After discussing the cultural and racial factors that make it possible for a "people" to sustain constitutional rule, he then asks whether and to what extent the United States is one people: "Constitutional government can exist only where there is actual community of interest and of purpose, and cannot, if it be also self-government, express the life of any body of people that does not constitute a veritable community. Are the United States a community? In some things, yes; in most things, no" (Wilson, 1908, 51).

American constitutional government is limited government; with

34. This consensual appeal originated with the McKinley campaign against Bryan in 1896 (Clubb, 1978, 61–79; Kleppner, 1978, 41–59).

federalism it is the sharing of limited government between states and the nation. So chary is Wilson of the idea of a single national community that when he does grant the growing power of national patriotism and purpose, he locates its origins only in the 1840s, symbolized in the famous speech by Whig Senator and Constitutional Unionist Daniel Webster.[35] And even granting the increasing power of national feeling, Wilson's commitment to constitutional government as protective of liberty constrains him to limit its political reach:

> There are natural limits beyond which such a [nationalizing process] cannot go, and our state governments are likely to become, not less, but more vital units in our system as the natural scope and limits of their powers are more clearly and permanently established. In a great political system like our own, spread abroad over the vast spaces of a various continent, the states are essential (Wilson, 1908, 49).

Concluding that increased perceptions of common interests will have more of a psychological effect than a political one, he predicts that while "the sphere of our national government will be . . . notably enlarged," this will not entail "any reconstruction of the system" (Wilson, 1908, 50).

Wilson's complacent prediction comes with an important caveat: constitutional government in America will effectively cease to exist *if the national government is given exclusive and broad powers to regulate commerce.* As the lectures proceed, this warning becomes more pronounced and its implications more ominous. In discussing recent commerce decisions by the federal courts, he says: "If the federal power does not end with the regulation of the actual movement of trade, it ends nowhere. . . . May [the national government] regulate the condi-

---

35. Wilson, 1908, 48–49. No clearer contrast to Wilson is provided here than Herbert Croly, who speaks of the "moral and intellectual cowardice" of leaders of all parties in the middle period, terming the leadership offered by the Constitutional Unionists "the least substantial" of them all. He then pointedly contrasts Webster's constitutional law nationalism to Lincoln's democratic nationalism. The starting points of Lincoln's analysis were that "a democratic nation could not make local and individual rights an excuse for national irresponsibility" and that "the Constitution was inadequate to cure the ills it generated" (Croly, 1909, 73, 75–77, and 86–87). Later he criticizes Wilson directly in these terms and with great force. Most pointedly he asks, "Does a real antagonism exist between the old order and the new order which some progressives are trying to substitute for it?" To answer no but to introduce a series of progressive reforms, as Wilson does, is intellectual cowardice and an act of bad faith toward his supporters who do not realize that the reforms subvert the democratic individualist ends proclaimed (Croly, 1914, 20). Thus the seeds of New Deal liberalism are planted.

tion of labor in field and factory? Clearly not, I should say[;] . . . that would destroy all lines of division between the field of state legislation and the field of federal legislation." This same theme is then repeated when discussing the states, warning that if national regulation or prohibition of child labor is constitutional, federal regulation "can be made to embrace every particular of the industrial organization and action of the country. . . . Should the Supreme Court assent to such obviously absurd extravagancies of interpretation," there would be no limits on the power of Congress except those "of opinion and of circumstance."[36]

Why did Wilson take such a reactionary stance? Why do his conclusions seem to fly in the face of more than two decades of economic teaching in America exposing the moral bankruptcy and intellectual absurdity of laissez faire as a national economic policy? How could Wilson be so at odds with his academic colleagues on such a fundamental issue? Although it may be a plausible answer to say that he was inoculated against the new social sciences by first receiving legal training at the University of Virginia, the better answer is supplied by Wilson's own arguments. If the commerce power is used by Congress to regulate labor and industrial conditions, regional autonomy and sectional self-direction will be lost. All of America would be subservient to its dynamic and industrial core. Extending the commerce power of the national government is to be resisted because a national politics of "social harmony" or common good is necessarily a politics of national economic planning. Whether planning is done by government, corporations, trade associations, finance, or trade unions is of course an important issue, but any conceivable combination would effectively destroy state police powers.

It would be fatal to our political vitality really to strip the States of their [police] powers and transfer them to the federal government. It cannot be too often repeated that it has been *the privilege of separate development* secured to the several regions of the country by the Constitution, and not the privilege of separate development only, but also that other more fundamental privilege that lies back of it, the privilege of independent local opinion and individual conviction, which has given speed, facility, vigor, and certainty to

---

36. Wilson, 1908, 171. On this logic, the New Deal court effectively destroyed American constitutional government by expanding the reach of the commerce clause.

the processes of our economic and political growth.[37] (emphasis added)

It is no wonder that Progressive intellectuals seldom viewed Wilson as an authentic reformer and that Herbert Croly in effect accused him of bad faith.[38] No serious reform could be urged within the prevailing system of party and constitution, both of which Wilson so vigorously defended.[39]

In his defense of constitutional law as the guardian of constitutional government, Wilson was at one with the upper bar from the Gilded Age to World War I. Like Wilson, they put both their American national identity and their trust in the Constitution and the courts. Although they tended to distrust partisan politics, they shared with Wilson the same institutional grounds of American nationality. By holding the Constitution above politics and beyond debate, they could legitimate the prevailing system of power and purposes as the fair result of neutral procedures. The Constitution is the game and we are all obligated to play by those rules. The president of the newly formed American Bar Association (ABA) declared in 1879 that the national Constitution was outside of politics and therefore belonged to the federal courts, in which repose "the sole determination and construction of the fundamental law of the land." He called on lawyers to "meet as on a common ground, in respect to all questions arising upon the national Constitution" and to oppose with all their strength "all efforts to transgress the true limits of the Constitution, or to make it at all the subject of political discussion." This refrain set the tone of the elite bar

37. Wilson, 1908, 191–92. He adds that the value of states' rights is not the protection of states, but of economic regions.

38. Croly does not mention Wilson at all in his book of 1909, which devotes a large space to discussions of contemporary reforms and reformers. But in that book he knows even better than Wilson what the stakes are: "The distinction between domestic and inter-state commerce which is implied by the Constitutional distribution of powers is a distinction of insignificant economic or industrial importance; and its necessary legal enforcement makes the carrying out of an efficient industrial policy almost impossible" (Croly, 1909, 351). In 1914, he takes Wilson's "New Freedom" vigorously to task as a "revival of Jeffersonian individualism," and therefore "a negative policy . . . opposing the extension of national responsibility . . . intrusting the future of democracy to the results of cooperation between an individualistic legal system and a fundamentally competitive economic system" (16–17). Bliss's *New Encyclopedia of Social Reform* of 1908 also fails to mention Wilson, let alone give him a biographical sketch. For a comparison of Wilson's economic views to the "new economics," Dorfman, 1949, 3: 336–42; and Fine, 1956, 276–79 and 239, on Ely's explanation of why his student failed to be influenced by him.

39. The implications of the rejection of a constitutionalist understanding of public good in Progressivism are discussed in chapter 6 below.

for the next three decades. Like Wilson, they could not envisage the political system functioning unless the traditional limits of the Constitution were placed outside of political discourse. Constitutional law, as one of their number said in 1912, "stands as an adamantine piece of reasoning and constitutes an invincible buttress of our nationality" (Foster, 1986, 55–56, 61).

No clearer indication of Wilson's distance from the moral and intellectual world of Progressivism was his strong defense of party. Given Democratic party fears of core domination through nationalization, Wilson's defense of constitutionalism as institution and constitutional law as political theory entailed a parallel defense of "small" party government and democratic individualism. He begins by stipulating an initial condition in our constitution making that we cannot alter: America chose not to create a strong executive responsible to a legislature upon whose advice and consent it acted. Constitutional separation of powers, therefore, mandates the political party as the only available source of governmental coherence and efficacy. Moreover, given the even greater dispersal of executive and legislative authority in the states "through the infinite multiplication of elective offices," party is also needed to weave these separated strands of power together. When these two factors are combined the necessary result is national political parties operating as coalitions of local and state party organizations. Two maxims flow from this result. The first is "whatever assigns to the people a power which they are naturally incapable of wielding takes it away from them," necessitating local party machines working across electoral levels and jurisdictions. The second maxim completes Wilson's defense of party:

> When the several chief organs of government are separated by organic law and offset against each other in jealous seclusion, no common legal authority set over them, *no necessary community of interest subsisting amongst them, no common origin or purpose dominating them*, they must of necessity, if united at all, be united by pressure from without; and they must be united if government is to proceed. They cannot remain checked and balanced against one another; they must act, and act together. They must, therefore of their own will or of mere necessity *obey an outside master*.[40]
> (emphasis added)

40. Wilson, 1908, 211 and 204, where he argues that American constitutionalism places government "in solution," which can be "solidified and drawn to a system only by the external authority of party, an organization outside the government and independent of it."

Whether by choice or necessity, constitutional government depends upon a system of party organizations outside the formal system of law and government. From this point on, Wilson's defense of party follows the inexorable logic of the nineteenth-century American regime. A hierarchy of party office "must supply the place of a hierarchy of legally constituted officials." National public opinion can only be produced through the separate national parties, and this, in turn, "depends upon their hold on the many localities of which it is made up . . . upon the petty choices which affect the daily life of counties and cities and States."[41] Efforts to change this condition will "always in the long run fail" because patronage and exchanges of favors, that is, party machines, "are absolutely necessary . . . for keeping the several segments of parties together." So bound together are local party machines, party government, and constitutional government that to attack the first is to subvert the last: "The disrepute in which professional politicians are held, is in spirit highly unconstitutional" (Wilson, 1908, 208–9 and 214).

With this defense, it remained only for Wilson to define the American body politic as held together by power and rules and propelled by "the restless strain of contest and jealousy." America is a disordered and jarring clash of interests that only the "network of parties" can compose. "The very compulsion of selfishness has made them serviceable; the very play of self-interest has made them effective." If we want to have constitutional government and individual rights then we must concede "that our national parties have been our veritable body politic."[42]

It is clear that Wilson's constitutional theory and his resistance to the nationalization of American political life were directly at odds with ideas that lay at the very center of Progressive self-identity forged earlier. Even if it is granted that many Progressives resisted handing over

41. Wilson, 1908, 207. A textbook with the revealing title *History of Political Theory and Party Organization in the United States,* published a year before Wilson's study of the Constitution, begins with these words: "Party organization in the government of a country exists in proportion to the recognition of freedom of thought and action among the people of that country. Where this freedom is denied, political activity has nothing upon which to rest" (Fess, 1907, 7).

42. Wilson, 1908, 220. Given this image of America, it is more than ironic that academic scholarship on the left now attributes to Wilson and the Democratic party the more "radical" and "state-building" side of reform in the Progressive era (Buenker, 1978; Dawley, 1991; Sanders, 1990; and Sarasohn, 1989). Given these types of arguments from Wilson, surely the most cosmopolitan and progressive spokesmen of the Democratic party of his day, any defense of the Democrats as progressive in this period necessarily requires that "Progressivism" have no intellectual or programmatic coherence at the national level. This is precisely the starting point of these studies. See discussion in chapter 1 above.

powers to the national government, their fears were exactly the opposite of Wilson's. They feared that an unreconstructed national government would regulate the nation as if it were *not* a nation, but a collection of localities, states, and regions held together by an intricate system of corrupt bargains, threats, and bribes. The very values of "separate development" that Wilson sought to protect were, to the Progressives, barriers to national integration and so many excuses to evade the responsibilities of American citizenship. So, too, did they treat a political discourse premised on the constitutionalist language of checks and balances, of federalism, of jurisdictional rights, state's rights, property rights, and even individual rights, a rhetoric of evasion and bad faith.[43] If the competitive and unreconstructed political party system is not our veritable body politic, still less are governmental institutions under its control. But if the "small" party-state can never represent the nation as a democracy, what sort of state structure can?

WHERE IS THE STATE?

It has been said that a maxim of the party reformers from the Gilded Age onward was "strike at parties / strengthen government" (McCormick, 1986, 258). Herbert Croly seems to confirm and strengthen this maxim in the Progressive Age: "The overthrow of the two-party system [is] indispensable to the success of progressive democracy, because, under American conditions, the vitality of the two-party system has been purchased . . . at the expense of administrative independence and efficiency" (Croly, 1914, 349). The maxim as revised by Croly might now read: "strike at parties / weaken party-government and legislatures / strengthen bureaucrats and executives and independent regulatory agencies." This equation has fueled a huge body of literature on the

43. Their critique of this language, especially in the Democratic party, parallels that of the women's movement. The editors of *History of Woman Suffrage* contrast a list of Republican platform planks on rights of women (but not the right to vote) in the 1880s and 1890s to platforms of the Democratic party, concluding: "No Democratic national platform has recognized so much as the existence of women, in all its grandiloquent declarations of the 'rights of the masses,' the 'equality of the people,' the 'sovereignty of the individual,' and the 'powers inherent in a democracy'" (quoted from Grimes, 1980, 81; from *History*, 4: 437). Wilson's argument here, but without party, replicates Jefferson's constitutional theory almost exactly. Local liberty or the virtue required of small republics is the guarantor of individual rights. Given slavery and southern gentry politics, Federalist charges of hypocrisy naturally followed.

"statist" proclivities of Progressive thought[44] that, in light of its heady sense of nationalism and German influences, would seem particularly apt for the Progressive intellectuals highlighted in this study. And given the way in which they sought to transform the idea of public opinion and popular consent into organic social judgments with constitutive powers, it would seem that a Rousseauist or Hegelian State as embodied Nation would necessarily follow. When to all of this is added the sacralization of the "bonds of nationality"—a Religion of America— the sacralization of the National State could not be far behind. This conclusion receives added support from the language used by Progressive sociologists and political economists with close ties to the social gospel movement.[45] George Herron saw the birth of the authentic democratic state as a collective religious conversion from corrupt law to pure faith: "Except the state be born again, except it be delivered from pagan doctrines of law and government . . . [and] from merely individual theories of freedom, it cannot see the divine social kingdom" (White and Hopkins, 1976, 194). His fellow Iowan, Samuel Batten, in *The Christian State*, declared that "'in the last analysis the State is the organized faith of a people, and where there is no faith, . . . the State crumbles into dust; . . . the State is the sphere in which the religion of a people finds its full and final expression.'"[46]

Perhaps the most widely cited example of Progressive state theory is Mary Follett's *The New State*, published in 1918. Starting with now familiar ideas from the new disciplines of sociology and social psychology, Follett minces no words:

> The old idea of natural rights postulated the particularist individual; we know now that no such person exists. . . . As an understanding of the group process abolishes 'individual rights,' so it gives us a true definition of liberty. . . . We see that to obey the

44. Dawley, 1991; Lustig, 1982; Sklar, 1988; Skowronek, 1982; and Weinstein, 1968. The argument is not that a corporate state was achieved (there was not a powerful enough state to accomplish this), but that both the pattern and the logic of some reforms pointed to the permanent institutionalization of the national government and national economic organizations.

45. See Herbst, 1965, 149, on Patten and Clark; Ross, 1918, 175–79, on the state's replacing the church as educator of citizens; Commons, 1894, 53–54, on the coercive power of government as a moral force; Ely, 1889, 72–80 and 92–93, on the Christian doctrine of the state and on government as "coercive philanthropy"; and Patten, 1916a, 8–9, on the need of the state to protect American culture and values.

46. Batten, 1909, 326. Batten's book is interesting in that it draws so eclectically on German, American Progressive, and British writings. Among the British used most prominently in the book are John Morley, John Stuart Mill, and Bryce; among American Progressives, Small, Abbott, and Ross; and among the Germans, Bluntschli.

group which we have helped to make and of which we are an integral part is to be free because we are then obeying ourself. Ideally the state is such a group, actually it is not, but it depends upon us to make it more and more so. The state must be no external authority which restrains and regulates me, *but it must be myself acting as the state in every smallest detail of life* (1918, 137–38, emphasis added).

This same logic was at the heart of one of John Dewey's earliest essays, "The Ethics of Democracy" of 1888:

If, then, society and the individual are really organic to each other, then the individual is society concentrated. . . . If society be organic, the notion of two classes [governors and governed], one of which is inferior to the other, falls to the ground. The basal conception, here, is of unity, and all distinctions must occur within and on account of this unity. The organism must have its spiritual organs; having a common will, it must express it. . . . In democracy . . . the governors and the governed are not two classes, but two aspects of the same fact—the fact of the possession by society of a unified and articulate will. It means that government is the organ of society, and is as comprehensive as society.[47]

THE NATION, THE STATE, AND PARASTATES

What is most problematic about these and other Progressive paeans to the "state" is the uncertainty of its location.[48] Given their distrust

47. Dewey, 1969, 237–39; see also Kloppenberg, 1986, 349–73, for a discussion of these same themes in the context of American and European thought.
48. Giddings's sociology textbook defines the state as consisting of "public corporations," but these include all bodies at all levels of government, with the lower subordinate to the higher. Even this broad definition gets broader: "The functions of the state are coextensive with human interests," no matter attempts "to prove that the functions of the state ought to be limited to a comparatively narrow sphere, leaving all other things to individual initiative and voluntary organization." He concludes that "the primary purpose of the state is to perfect social integration," thereby giving it power in economic and cultural life, the latter including religion and education (Giddings, 1898, 202–3). Small's sociology textbook is thoroughly Hegelian in its stress on antagonisms in the process of state formation and in the struggle of states to realize themselves as states. "Any given stage of na-

of formal laws and constitutions, why would distant and impersonal rational-bureaucratic structures suddenly appear to Progressives as attractive solutions? Given their vision of substituting the higher ethical means of informal persuasion for the lower means of external coercion, why should they suddenly turn to rules written by faceless agents of a *Rechtsstaat*? Where is the "state" to be found? For Follet, Dewey, and most of the Progressives, the state is first "located" in the good citizen who, *in whatever role and location*, spontaneously acts according to consciously held—and shared—ideas of the public good. This is precisely Herron's notion of a "reborn" state and Batten's notion of the organized faith of a people. A good citizen is "state-oriented" in the sense of seeking to achieve a larger public good in his actions in every sphere of life.

Some citizens are more state-oriented than others: they are the better citizens. Some regions of the country and some institutions are led by good citizens and some are not. Where is the state? Wherever good citizens gather, organize, and act. Rather than raise again the question of the "failure" of Progressive academics—especially political economists—to become state-centered social democrats (or at least English Fabians) and then look for sources of corporate-capitalist corruption in universities,[49] it may be more fruitful to explore what Progressives mean by "state" and speculate more fully on its probable locations.

From their writings on American nationality and on the meaning of public opinion, the first location, prior to any external expression, must be an internalized idea of membership and shared values. There can be no "state" without a "people" and no people without good citizens sharing common ends and integrating those ends into their individual purposes, including their rights claims.[50] This is the individual-

---

tional development is a struggle of that which has come to be regarded as the common interest, and thus the spiritual substance of the State, against all and several of the contesting interests which dispute for place within the civic order. . . . Civilization, so far as it is bounded by national limits, consists in the enlargement of the content of the common spiritual substance, until it approaches inclusion of all interests, so far as they depend upon concerted conduct; leaving scope for independence only in those activities in which free individual movement best realizes the common interests" (1905, 248). Following (249–51) is an utter dismissal of American constitutionalist theory of the state based on the primacy of rights.

49. A sampling: Barrow, 1990; Mills, 1964; Ross, 1977; Schwendinger and Schwendinger, 1974; and Silva and Slaughter, 1984.

50. One of the clearer statements of this idea was in Florence Kelley's review of recent "ethical gains" made through legislation. Under the heading "right to leisure" through half Saturdays, eight-hour days, and mandated holidays, she treats the justification of this right as a requisite for citizenship: "Self-help and self-edu-

ized meaning of the term "social ethic" and its collective result in "social justice" as described in the sociology and psychology textbooks. In contemporary terms, they argued that the individual capable of bearing and exercising rights is "socially constituted"—and this is true whether those rights are exercised in socially benign or socially destructive ways.

John Dewey puts this same internalized idea in philosophical and ethical terms. Individualist claims of right against the prevailing practices and norms of the society are admissible to the extent that they are a means by which more inclusive ideas of common good come to be "socially embodied . . . [and therefore become] a means of social reconstruction." He contrasts good and bad citizens in these terms. Bad citizens "regard their actions as sanctions [i.e., normative] if they have *not* broken the laws. . . . The intelligence that should go to employing the spirit of laws to enlighten behavior is spent in ingenious inventions for observing their letter. The 'respectable' citizen of this type is one of the unsocialized forces that social reformers find among their most serious obstacles" (Dewey and Tufts, 1908, 432 and 467). Good democratic citizens and true democratic states are mutually dependent creations, consisting of "the development of a comprehensive and common good." After reviewing American constitutional and party barriers to the creation of a democratic citizenry and state, Dewey then reverses the causal flow. The state is "the emancipation of personal capacities, . . . *securing to each individual an effective right* to count in the order and movement of society as a whole." From the standpoint of ethics, the moral test of a practice or a law is whether it "sets free individual capacities in such a way as to make them available for the development of the general happiness or the common good" (Dewey and Tufts, 1908, 474, emphasis added).

Both Follett and Dewey made of the democratic state an achievement to be won in the future. Neither the American national government nor many state and local governments had seriously begun to achieve the

---

cation among the wage-earners are as dependent upon daily leisure as upon daily work. . . . Instead of educating the worker, the breadwinning task of today too often stupefies and deforms the mind; and leisure is required to undo the damage wrought in the working hours, if the worker is to remain fit for citizenship in the Republic" (1905, 108–9). In the early 1880s, Richard Ely drew up a proposed constitution for a "society for the study of the national economy" modeled after the famous German *Verein fur Sozialpolitik*. Part of the section addressing the increasing differentiation of the laboring and capitalist classes reads: "Public interest demands that the sanitary and industrial conditions of the laborer shall be such as will enable him to develop in himself and perpetuate in his family the qualities necessary to make him a desirable citizen of a great republic" (Ely, 1938, 297).

status of "democratic states." But if that is the case, where is the good
citizen to find a place to exercise citizenship? The standing answer is
first to exercise citizenship in order to be able to exercise citizenship by
reforming constitutions, governments, and parties. But if much of this
exercise fails or becomes self-defeating, what then? There are two Progressive responses. The first has already been touched upon: the good
citizen "officially" participates in those governmental institutions
that contain or are mostly likely to come to contain substantive public
goods. In short, some public institutions are or might become authentic state structures by virtue of their purposes and policies, whereas
others cannot or will not. This accounts for some of the fascination
with autonomous political executives (e.g., strong-mayor or city-man-
ager forms of urban government) and expert commissions and bureaucracies. National citizenship exercised in and through these executive
institutions may well consist only of supplying expert knowledge and
policy advice, whether to a mayor, a state commission, or a federal bureau. National citizenship, in short, can be exercised at any level of
government because reform as "social reconstruction" is the result.
Thus, for example, municipal ownership of a trolley company is a "national reform"; using federal tax money and national legislation to pay
off an electoral debt to a particular interest is not even a national act,
let alone a national reform.[51]

But if national citizenship can be exercised in and through these vari-
ously located governmental bodies, why not through nongovernmental
bodies? Why is teaching English to immigrants in a Cleveland, Ohio,
YMCA not an act of citizenship, whereas voting in Cheyenne, Wyo-
ming, for the party that promises a tariff on wool is? In a profound
sense, it was women's participation in politics well before they had the
vote that gave credence to this "influence" theory of political action
and to this higher ideal of citizenship as public service. And this was
the case whether or not women engaged directly in a politics of influence. The mother in the family, the teacher in the public school or the
Sunday school, and the charity worker were all participating in the task
of acting out ideals of public good and therefore "acting as the state in
every smallest detail of life." The earlier roots of this ideal of citizenship were the early-nineteenth-century idea of "free institutions."
These included town, church, and school, as well as the earlier Puritan
notion of the family as "a little commonwealth." Translated into a
state ideal with multiple locations, the new formulation would make

51. Ely's draft of a constitution for the forerunner of the American Economic
Association read, in part: "Sovereignty resides in the people and is one in its nature, whether exercised by a local or general government" (Ely, 1938, 296).

of these institutions something like "parastates," in the sense of being supportive of the government both by producing good citizens and by themselves carrying out the substantive ends that would be desired by an ideal state. In the words of the title of an article by Jane Addams in the early 1890s: "Hull House, Chicago: An Effort toward Social Democracy."[52]

In Progressive thought, these older free institutions are forced to share place with new parastates in the form of labor unions, moral and political reform movements, settlement houses, and universities. In that sense, the older "parachurches" of the ecumenical religious establishment are a sort of way station, mixing with and merging into the newer parastates. Together, these parastates, like all historical states, have a tendency to seek conquest, but in this case, not always through laws and coercion. To borrow a phrase from Theodore Roosevelt, "ethnic" conquests are always more durable than mere "political" ones. One might electorally "conquer" various official governments and turn them into instruments of the common good by conquering the hearts and minds of the majorities of their voting citizens. If this tactic fails, one might conquer these same governments by dominating the agenda and information of powerful bureaucracies or executives who, through political reforms, have become somewhat independent of electoral and legislative majorities. One might prepare for these conquests by dominating enlightened opinion through journalism and teacher training and social research. *In short, these institutions as "parastates" will do exactly what political parties as "outside master" (Wilson) had routinely done in nineteenth-century regimes.*

Progressive parastates, despite their greater reliance on indirect influence, are even more various, more protean, and more resourceful than political parties. The most basic of these units, the family, illustrates the method and reach of this new conception of politics. Insofar as the family is the first training school for citizenship, to monopolize respectable ideas of motherhood, health, child rearing, and preschool education also represents a parastate conquest if those ideas carry with them a "social ethic." This is exactly how Florence Kelley, Jane Addams, Charlotte Gilman, and the "new charity" intellectuals saw their political task. Gilman, one of America's most influential feminist intellectuals, saw no conflict between espousing the emancipation of wives from housekeeping roles and writing *A Clarion Call to Re-*

---

52. Addams, 1892. Patten, 1912, 322–31, used the term "voluntary socialism" in contrast to "state socialism," saying that a reliance on the former would avoid the need for the latter.

deem the Race; the Burden of Mothers.[53] Just as Dewey had argued, freedom for women—in Gilman's case the release of their energies from housekeeping routine—is justified only if those energies are placed in the service of the larger society. Jane Addams's advice to mothers is hardly different.[54] What holds for the family as parastate holds even more for larger and more extensive organizations: schools, churches, trade associations, women's clubs, and even nationally organized economic interest groups.

Progressivism in both thought and deed represented the partial victory of the "parastate" over "party-government" but at the cost of locating citizenship and the exercise of power increasingly outside of constitutionally mandated boundaries. Put differently, party reinforced constitutional formalism whereas parastates circumvented and subverted it. But to the charge of extraconstitutionality, the Progressive might reply: Isn't party government also outside the Constitution, and isn't it the exercise not of informal influence, but of invisible power? The power exercised by parastates, whether within or outside constitutional boundaries, is "public" in the most important senses of that word: visible, based on widely known and shared moral, educational, and scientific standards, and exercised by people who willingly communicate and defend their ideas in the larger society through means accessible to all. Party power is not only deliberately disguised and exercised in rooms filled with smoke and shadow, its leadership augments its power by making secret and corrupt bargains with other hidden sources of power in the society. The alliance of powerful and corrupt parties with equally powerful and corrupt economic interests has entangled constitutionally authorized officials in ever-tighter networks of corruption, holding the voter hostage to his lowest self. "Behind the ostensible government sits enthroned an invisible government owing no allegiance and acknowledging no responsibility to the people. To de-

53. Gilman, 1898 and 1903, on emancipation of the housewife; Gilman, 1890, Shaker Press. Florence Kelley states the civic connection more directly: "It is clearly the duty of the parent to support his children; that is his obligation to the Republic" (1905, 69).

54. Gilman, 1898, 160–68, 268–69, and 319–40; and see Kelley's charge to "prosperous women" with "unsought leisure" (1905, 112–16), and Addams's discussion of the duty of the mother to her college-educated daughter. Addams begins by showing the connection between personal ethics ("righteousness") and social justice, telling the reader that her book is a study "of various types and groups who are being impelled by the newer conception of Democracy to an acceptance of social obligations involving in each instance a new line of conduct." One of her six chapters is directed to mother-daughter relationships and another to household management and the ethics of employing maids (1902, 1–3 and 11; see also 70–90 and 105–36).

stroy this invisible government, to dissolve the unholy alliance between corrupt business and corrupt politics is the first task of the statesmanship of the day" (Progressive party platform, 1912).[55]

Party government's symbiotic relationship extended beyond constitutional government. The democratic individualism of party, restrained only by the fragmented and externalized constraints of Constitution and courts, was repeated in the economic sphere. There, too, democratic individualism, under the blessings of constitutional legitimacy and property rights, had produced huge "machines" as well, equally unaccountable to the people, equally invisible in their inner workings, equally corrupting, and equally powerful. They, like party organizations, needed regulation. They, too, needed to be both socialized and democratized.

55. Johnson and Porter, 1975, 175. Croly, 1914, 92–95, gives a trenchant analysis of the cause of this alliance, born of the failure of Republican national industrial policy to change regime values and political institutions while encouraging economic institutions and practices that in fact can benefit all.

5

NATION & ECONOMY

Economic theory concerning the relationship between government and economic life in America was transformed by a small and identifiable group of Progressive economists. Although their connection to actual changes in economic policies in the decades following their original work is less direct, by 1900 their domination of professional training and scholarship in economics was virtually uncontested. Following their studies in Germany and the assumption of academic positions in newly established American graduate programs in political economy, economics, and sociology, a stream of articles and books came to constitute the boundaries and landmarks of the new economics. In 1885 Simon N. Patten, four years before he was able to obtain his first academic appointment, published a defense of national economic planning in a treatise on political economy. The year following, he outlined the first systematic explanation of the effects of consumption choices on economic growth and welfare. The first coherent theoretical defense of public ownership of utilities was an article written in 1886 by Edmund J. James, who brought Patten to the Wharton School. That same year, Richard T. Ely, still at Johns Hopkins, wrote the first scientific study of wage labor and labor organization in America. Also in that same year, John Bates Clark at Columbia provided the theoretical foundations for understanding relationships between monopoly pricing and wealth distribution. A year later, Henry Carter Adams at Michigan wrote what became the definitive monograph on the relationship of the state to the new industrial economy. Thus, in the space of just three years in the mid-1880s these five young economists had carved out whole new territories for scientific exploration, shaping not only the disciplines of political economy and economics, but the emerging fields of social psychology and sociology as well.[1]

1. Fine, 1956, 221–50, for summaries of the early writings and careers of each of this group; and see Dorfman, 1949, 296–98 (Adams), 190–204 (Clark), 161–64 (Ely), 160–61 (James), and 182–88 (Patten).

The shared perspective in these early writings was already anticipated in the founding of the American Economic Association (AEA) in 1885, essentially by these same five economists and E. R. A. Seligman of Columbia. The first plank of its proposed platform, written by Ely, reads: "We regard the state as an educational and ethical agency whose positive aid is an indispensable condition of human progress. While we recognize the necessity of individual initiative in industrial life, we hold that the doctrine of laissez faire is unsafe in politics and unsound in morals; and that it suggests an inadequate explanation of the relations between the state and the citizens."[2]

As this group defined the scope and methods of the new political economy, so did they and their professional colleagues write the definitive textbooks and monographic studies in the field: Clark's *Philosophy of Wealth* was in print continuously from 1886 to 1904; Henry Carter Adams's *Science of Finance* on public expenditure and revenues, from 1898 to 1924. Ely's economics textbooks were the clear favorites, both for college students and for a broader audience of concerned citizens. His *Outlines of Economics* was first published by the Chautauqua movement in 1893; after nine printings or editions, a switch to Macmillan publishers, and a name change to *Introduction*, the textbook saw another twenty-eight printings or editions through 1939, for a total of forty-six years of continuous publication. When one adds to this list the publishing success of books by Patten, Seligman, Hadley, and Commons—and to this list, books by those trained in economics who wrote texts in sociology, Giddings, Ross, and Cooley—the conquest of "the economic mind" of America would seem beyond doubt.[3] Their editorships of professional journals and monograph series were added elements in their production and control of professional economic knowledge.

In addition to the expanding collegiate and university markets, an

---

2. Ely, 1938, 136. This statement was thought too extreme, so in the interests of attracting more traditional economists and others, it was revised to read: "We regard the state as an agency whose positive assistance is one of the indispensable conditions of human progress" (140).

3. Patten's *New Basis of Civilization*, 1907–21; Seligman's *Essays on Taxation*, 1895–1925, and *Principles of Economics*, 1905–25; Commons's *Principles of Labor Legislation*, 1916–36; Hadley's *Economics, An Account of the Relations between Private Property and Public Welfare*, 1896–1911, and *Railroad Transportation*, 1885–1912. As a group, the sociologists were even more successful. Giddings's *Principles of Sociology* had a run of thirty-two years, *Elements of Sociology*, eighteen years; Ross's *Social Control* was in print for thirty-one years, *Foundations of Sociology* for twenty-one; and Cooley's complex and demanding *Social Organization, A Study of the Larger Mind*, was published for twenty years. Ely's *Introduction* sold 30,000 in the first decade, with total sales over half a million. Fine, 1956, 238–39; and see Dombrowski, 1936, 50–53, on Ely's larger audience.

audience and vehicle for new ideas in political economy also existed in the social gospel movement. The founding meeting of the American Economic Association in 1885 totaled fewer than fifty people. Twenty-three of the charter members were Protestant clergymen (Ely, 1938, 138; Fine, 1956, 201). During this same period, many of these academics and clergymen multiplied their influence by joining with other reformers in new publishing, educational, and organizational ventures. Some of the AEA academics and clergymen became members of one of the many local branches of Josiah Strong's Evangelical Alliance founded that same year, which was dedicated to spreading the gospel of Social Christianity through the medium of the new economics and sociology. In that same decade other organizations were formed on similar lines, such as the Convention of Christian Workers and the Christian Association for the Advancement of the Interests of Labor (CAIL).[4]

The 1890s saw even greater organizational and publishing innovation. Ely became founder and first president of the American Institute of Christian Sociology. Under his editorships, Crowell Publishers brought out sixteen books on politics and economics between 1888 and 1902 and, through Macmillan's Citizenship Series, thirty-seven books on reform themes between 1900 and 1915.[5] W. D. P. Bliss, whose *Encyclopedia of Social Reform* (1897 and 1908) did so much to establish the reputations of the new economists in the larger reform community, founded the American Fabian League in 1895. Two years later, with fellow Christian Socialists, he attempted to create an umbrella organization of all reform forces, the Union Reform League, later renamed the National Social Reform Union, in order to put combined pressure on the political parties to adopt more serious reform measures.[6] The popu-

4. Fine, 1956, 171–72; Dombrowski, 1936, 96–120. In light of all of this associational, literary, and publishing evidence by the founders and leaders of the American Economic Association, it is quite inexplicable that Haskell, 1977, 187, can conclude that "the AEA's commitment to reform was extremely superficial," reduced "to the irascible personality of one man, Richard T. Ely." Without doubt Ely was irascible, and most of his colleagues did not wear their reform hearts on their sleeves as he did. Nonetheless, the line between political economy and sociology—the new discipline that Haskell admits was the leading edge of professionalized reform values—was extremely blurred, and social evolutionary theory pervaded both fields. The fact that the leading founders of the American Sociological Society were German- or Wharton-trained political economists further attests to this connection. The influence of Patten was critical in this regard.

5. Ely, 1938, 309–17. The Macmillan series included books by Addams (two), Commons, Kelley, and Ross (two).

6. Fine, 1956, 171–72 and 349–51. On the special importance of Ely in connecting the new economists to the social gospel, Dombrowski, 1936, 50–53. Bliss's umbrella group was seeking to influence the Democratic party; given the closeness

lar and influential social gospel theologians Walter Rauschenbusch and George Herron also founded reform organizations and publication programs in the 1890s.[7]

Two other overlapping audiences, consisting of the larger intellectual community and the new urban middle class, were also reached by the professional economists and sociologists. Through both the "highbrow" periodicals (e.g., the *New Englander, Yale Review,* and *Andover Review*) and the serious weeklies and monthlies (e.g., *Arena, Atlantic Monthly, Century, Cosmopolitan, Forum, Harpers Monthly, Independent, Outlook, Review of Reviews*) these academics and allied reform intellectuals reached ever-wider circles of readers. The fast-growing weeklies for women also became outlets for their reform messages.[8] Popular journalism in turn created a demand for books consisting of collections of previously published articles. That these collections mixed together pieces from professional journals, highbrow reviews, and the popular press is indicative of their broad audience and of the relationship these academics saw among scholarship, citizenship, and public service.[9]

---

of its original name to the Union League Clubs of the Republican party during the Civil War, a name change was necessary. Prominent at its great convention in Buffalo in the summer of 1900 were George Herron, Richard Ely, John Commons, Jane Addams, Florence Kelley, Henry Demarest Lloyd, and Eugene Debs (Crunden, 1892, 47).

7. Fine, 1956, 172 and 193–96; Crunden, 1984, 45–51; Dombrowski, 1936, 171–93. At Grinnell, Herron's Department of Applied Christianity and its publication, the *Kingdom*, had John Bascom, an economist from Williams and later president of the University of Wisconsin, John Commons, and Josiah Strong as associate editors. Contributors included Richard Ely, Jane Addams, Graham Taylor of Chicago, Commons, and Henry D. Lloyd (Dombrowski, 1936, 110–13).

8. For example, Adams and Clark wrote for *New Englander*; James, Hadley, and Ely for *Andover Review*, and Patten, Hadley, and Ely for *Yale Review*. Adams, Ely, Giddings, Hadley, Seligman, and Small all wrote articles for *Forum*. Ely regularly contributed to *Harpers*, and also wrote for *Atlantic Monthly, Independent,* and *Century*; Giddings and Clark wrote for the *Independent*. Albert Shaw, a Hopkins Ph.D. in political economy and an expert on European city governments, founded and edited the *Review of Reviews*; Ely, James, Commons, and Hadley contributed to it. Periodicals such as *Forum* and *Review of Reviews, Cosmopolitan, Century,* and *Outlook* all had circulations larger than 100,000 at the turn of the century, many with considerably larger circulations in the next decade. Ely was the most active; in a banner year for such efforts, 1901, he wrote five articles for *Cosmopolitan* on topics such as public control of private corporations, tax reforms, and the steel trust. At this time, *Cosmopolitan*, a woman- and family-oriented monthly, had a circulation of over half a million with more than 100 pages of ads per issue (Mott, 1957b, 480–505).

9. Ely's *Studies in the Evolution of Industrial Society* (1903) contains materials previously published in an AEA monograph, *International Journal of Ethics, Yale Review, North American Review,* and *Boston Evening Transcript*. Giddings's *Democracy and Empire* (1900) has materials reprinted from commencement addresses, *Political Science Quarterly, International Journal of Ethics, Science,* the *Chautauquan,* the *Independent,* and *Ethics*.

Through these venues and in public lectures, the Progressive academics urged a fairly common program of administrative and economic reforms. All of them heaped scorn on the idea that the fundamental principle of economic life and of the relationship of government to economics should be competitive markets and laissez faire. While they differed at the margins, almost all agreed on the need for legally recognized trade unions and arbitration of labor disputes; unemployment and worker compensation and state employment bureaus; municipal ownership of utilities; national ownership or regulation of transport and communications; national incorporation laws and corporate regulation; the use of tariffs as a tool of national economic planning; the national compilation of industrial, agricultural, and financial statistics; state and federal regulation of hours and wages; public inspection of factories, mines, and tenements; federal and state progressive inheritance taxes; state and federal controls on use of natural resources; public land use policy; and compulsory public education and free technical training.

This agenda of progressive economic reforms could be expanded or contracted depending upon the individual, and inferences might then be drawn regarding where on a spectrum of "radicalism" or "socialism" he or she might fall. The same could be done regarding their individual stands on banking and currency issues, public ownership versus regulation of monopolies, and trusts. And from these data, one might construct a sort of "populist versus progressivist" index to calibrate the relative affinities of these academics toward more equitable redistributions of wealth and power or toward managerial strategies and public policies directed to production and efficiency. One might even cull from their writings friendly or hostile mentions of the word "socialism" to place one or another of these Progressive academics.[10]

This sort of exercise, however, would not lead to a clearer under-

10. This type of analysis has been the staple of the many disciplinary and intellectual histories of this period. From these studies, in turn, one might construct a "socialist (or populist) nostalgia-socialist (or populist) betrayal" index of their authors. Ross, 1977 and 1991, 98–140, offers the most thorough analysis from this perspective. Equating, for example, the acceptance of marginal utility theory with the rejection of socialism, one finds it difficult, nevertheless, to discern what is meant by the "socialism" being rejected. Gilded Age variants were very different visions of society than were Marxist or centralized and bureaucratic forms of European state socialism. Kloppenberg, 1986, 199–246, explains why American Progressive economics was so removed from Marxist and revolutionary socialism by showing the different philosophical, ethical, and religious sources of their writings, referring especially to those of Ely and Rauschenbusch. Moreover, this revisionist view carries over to Europe as well, in the economic writings of the "new liberals" and Fabians in Britain and the social democrats in France and Germany.

standing of their economic ideas or to Progressive public doctrine generally. To measure the economic writings of this group by looking at their agenda lists and policy stands ignores two difficulties. The first is that the "left-right" measure used now does not necessarily reflect contemporary choices or projected outcomes, nor can it measure the intensity of this group for or their sense of the feasibility of any given set of reforms. The second difficulty is that their individual stands on the salient issues of the moment are an untrustworthy guide to their larger theoretical and historical arguments. This placement exercise does, however, have one unintended benefit: to ask why this interpretive strategy is misplaced and distorting is to open us to a clearer contextual understanding of what they did write and how they related their theoretical insights to the formation of public doctrines regarding the nation and economic life. In this way we can both see their own horizons and understand the ways in which Progressive reform ideas are related to the liberal ones that followed.

LAISSEZ FAIRE, DEMOCRATIC INDIVIDUALISM, AND GOVERNMENT

The first difficulty in seeking to understand the economic writings of these Progressive academics through agenda items measuring their distance from "laissez faire" is that they often saw these issues in quite a different light from many of their supporters and their opponents—and certainly from post–New Deal academic historians. These were, after all, cosmopolitan scholars with a deep commitment to get outside the prevailing framework of discussing economic issues in America; they were conversant with the work of British and European economists and political historians, their explanatory frameworks, and their economic theories.[11] Moreover, as some of the earliest American compilers and users of comparative-national economic data, both historical and contemporary, their ideas regarding policy choices were often driven by their concern for macroeconomic and overall social effects over long time periods—concerns that few reformers and even fewer party-political leaders fully appreciated. Related to these cosmopolitan economic views was their concern with the relationship between economic activity, moral character, and citizenship. This last

11. A good antidote to agenda-ideology perspectives is to read their introductory textbooks and scan their suggested bibliographies. See especially Ely, 1893 and revised editions through 1915; Hadley, 1896; and Seligman, 1905. For their larger projects and perspectives learned from German historical economists, Herbst, 1965, 121–52.

concern did tie them directly to the social gospel and Christian Socialist movements in America and to the new liberal, Fabian, and social
democratic intellectuals in Europe.[12] These affinities rested more on
shared moral-psychological and historical-evolutionary assumptions
than on specific forms of economic methods and understandings.

Moral and evolutionary factors suffused the economic analysis of
these Progressive academics. Their attack on the doctrine of laissez
faire in economic theory was rarely an attack on capitalism itself or the
prelude to a call for public ownership of property. Indeed, a standard
strategy was to criticize laissez-faire theory as the ideology of small-
producer capitalism, ending with a critique of democratic individualism and moral shallowness in American public life and policy. But even
when these two attacks are related in a broader "anticapitalist" sense,
the sincerity and commitment of the attacker cannot then be measured by some separate but related position, namely, the use of "the
state" to address the problem.[13] To understand their writings as the
Progressives understood them is to consider the possibility that in
some cases a resort to government and coercion *is a confession of the
failure of "socialist" ideals and not their fulfillment.*[14] These new
economists, their teachers, and their political colleagues abroad neither began nor, for the most part, ended with state socialism. Neither
did they ground their economic theories or their political prescriptions
in class conflict.

A second order of difficulties in understanding the writings of Progressive academics from a laissez faire–government intervention per-

---

12. Dorfman, 1949, and Fine, 1956, are both historically accurate and culturally
astute in emphasizing these relationships regarding the Progressives' shared moral
case against laissez faire. Both are much less convincing, however, when they attempt to array these American movements along a left-right spectrum derived from
European thought. Again, Kloppenberg, 1986, 199–297, shows the separate origins
and logic of American economists and their counterparts in Europe.

13. The classic statement of these distinctions, especially between laissez faire
as dogma and free competition as an effective principle is Adams, 1954, 67–83 and
90–125, on forms of state interference to counter the pernicious effects of free competition. It is difficult to exaggerate the importance of this early essay in shaping
the fundamental postulates and reform ideas of the new economics.

14. Patten, 1924, 290–93, explicitly contrasts voluntary and state socialism in
America, saying the former is indistinguishable from progressive democracy:
"When a progressive democrat maps out a program, it is the same as the program
of an evolutionary socialist." And see 322–31, on the ways in which "voluntary socialism" becomes interest group pluralism. Social problems like divorce and
drunkenness were addressed by many Progressives with a similar ambivalence regarding the use of legal coercion versus social coercion through education. This
ambivalence should not be foreign to contemporary American intellectuals who address problems of AIDS, drugs, and single-parent families.

spective concerns their own shared assessments of the political and economic context in which they saw themselves. Two of these assessments or "background" assumptions are particularly relevant here. The first is that, except when exhorting audiences of well-off Protestant clergy and laymen in the rhetorical mode of the jeremiad, they gave little evidence in their writings of fears of class warfare, not to speak of revolution, in America.[15] Indeed, precisely the opposite was more often the case. Most of these academic political economists and sociologists knew European labor history and were clearly aware of differences between Europe and the United States in the contemporary period. Not only was there little fear of working-class revolution in America from this source, there was an expressed fear of its opposite, namely, that American belief in social mobility and the values of individualism would drain the wage earners of effective leadership and strong organization. The lack of worker solidarity was of more concern to them than its excess.[16]

Behind this complacency concerning class conflict lay their knowledge of an American revolution in industry and transportation yielding ever-increasing productivity and the reduction of average living costs, which translated into higher wages. Here again, one finds repeated attempts by these economists to call to the attention of the larger reform community the welfare and economic class effects of falling prices, increasing consumer choices, and a growing "social surplus" available for education and leisure. The important policy choices concerning productivity growth and its moral effects might be only tangential to

15. Ross, 1977 and 1991, 98–140, places heavy emphasis on the defeat of William Jennings Bryan in 1896 as causing a shift from fear of revolution to complacency. There is little evidence in the writings of these sociologists and political economists to support this contention. There is strong evidence, however, that it was not until the 1890s that a clear distinction began to be drawn between centralized state socialism and populist nostalgia. The Progressive academics viewed the former as an impossibility, given American federalism and the party system, and the latter as a contradictory and futile dream—a sort of gigantic democratic patronage state living off the manna of the industrial economy it was attempting to dismantle.

16. Cooley, 1909, 241–46, 274–76, and 284–89; and Patten, 1924, 291; see also Jane Addams, 1902, 142–48, on the Pullman strike. Croly, 1914, 391, while very clear on what he means by good and bad unions, argues that, good or bad, they require long struggle in order to wrest recognition from employers and share a measure of their property right: "It requires for the purpose of this warfare a much more general and intense feeling of class consciousness and responsibility than it has at present, and a much more tenacious and enlightened class policy." This, from an exponent of "liberal corporatism" and a politics of consensus and common good, does not suggest a fear of socialist revolution.

any current reform agenda.[17] These Progressives, almost alone in America, first charted, projected, and understood the massive changes in the structure of the American economy.[18] As they shared this social knowledge with their students and the larger reform audience, they also sought to show the relationship between these changes and the declared ends of social justice all reformers were seeking to achieve. Sometimes there was a substantive fit between the current reform agenda and this social knowledge; at other times, there was more of a symbolic connection; and, in some instances, there was a misfit.[19]

A second background assumption is also related to the issue of the role of government in economic life. To assume that because these economists attacked laissez-faire economic doctrine with such vehemence they must have favored in principle government intervention in wide areas of economic life is simply unwarranted. Indeed, they argued that an economics of laissez faire *combined with a partisan politics of democratic individualism*, usually led to excessive governmental expenditure and the reckless expansion and corrupt use of government. More generally, their attack on laissez faire was often directed against the explanatory powers of classical economics and not its policy imperatives regarding governmental intervention. And, knowing European economic history, they also knew that liquid and transparent markets might well require massive governmental intervention and the use of authority both to establish and to maintain them. Even more to the point, while their attacks on laissez faire were often attacks on small-producer capitalism they were also in defense of large, privately capitalized and managed economic units and monopolistic trade unions. This form of attack on laissez faire gives us a rather different view of what

17. Ely, 1903, 461–89, is a good example of this educative attempt. And see Patten, 1902a and 1907; and Cooley, 1909, 218–97. This educative task necessarily included the acceptance of large scale and centralized economic units and the abandonment of the language of natural rights arguments for economic justice.

18. Chandler, 1990, 52–89; and Zunz, 1990, 37–102, both describe the organizational features of the new corporations and patterns of consolidation and merger but fail to discuss the rich descriptive and theoretical literature produced by the professional economists writing at the time.

19. An example of a substantive fit between social knowledge and reform would be national and state inheritance taxes, which flowed naturally from the economist's analysis of wealth distribution, theories of economic justice, and efficient frameworks of incentives. An example of a symbolic connection would be the prohibition of alcohol; as expressive of a collective responsibility to provide the conditions for decent family life, this reform would be only one (and perhaps not at all the best) measure contributing to this end; others might include tenement inspections, public parks, half-Saturday work, and so on. Examples of a misfit would be laws prohibiting state-chartered corporations from owning property out of that state or from owning stock in other corporations.

these economists saw was wrong with our economic system and its political supports.

The battle was in large measure an ethical one directed against the corrosive effects of competitive individualism under modern industrial conditions. Wage labor in huge industrial combines, they maintained, is a much better teacher of civic virtue, competence, and cooperation than the isolated and undercapitalized farm. Many of these economists were raised on farms or in small market towns in the Midwest, so they had few illusions about the joys of rural life or the moral education of Main Street. The ranks of urban clerks and layers of managers in a large retail department store called on a much higher range of qualities, skills, and individuality than an equivalent number of proprietors of hundreds of little shops.[20] (Thorstein Veblen's iconoclasm rested on a large body of respectable academic opinion.) Thus, quite aside from the issue of economic growth and efficiency, laissez faire as a defense of small-producer capitalism was attacked as a morally corrupting barrier to an emerging social ethic. In the language of the social gospel, laissez faire stood as a barrier to the coming of the kingdom of righteousness. Under contemporary conditions, those economic structures were to be encouraged that helped to break down the psychologically false division between individual and society. Those structures, both "public" and "private," flourished in urban, industrial, and financial centers.

JEFFERSONIAN SOCIALISM

Because of these background assumptions the founders of Progressive economic doctrine saw what later generations of historians and social scientists had great difficulty seeing, namely, that many popular calls for "socialism" in America at this time were calls on government to restore or subsidize democratic capitalism whether in the form of Main Street or the small farm. These populists and socialists also disliked political parties, but for reasons exactly the opposite of those of the Progressive economists: for making deals with and therefore permitting large corporations to flourish. American populism and the more parochial variants of Christian Socialism were permeated by this combination of Jeffersonianism and Christian brotherhood. A statement of principles by one of the more radical Christian Socialist orga-

20. Zunz, 1990, 125–48, discusses the ways in which middle management and clerical work was organized to ratify and reward the values of those who filled the positions, thus strengthening native American middle-class values and extending the reach and power of those values.

nizations in America nicely captures this spirit of restoration in both
the biblical and the individualist sense:

> The law for the social life is revealed in the Old Testament. . . .
> The God was the Universal Father; every man of the theocracy a
> brother. Property in land was not absolute; the land was conceived
> as belonging to God. No individual could own it in fee simple. He
> could only use it. *In its use he was inalienably protected. It came
> to him through the family as an inalienable inheritance.* If,
> through poverty or misfortune, he temporarily parted with it, it re-
> turned to him in the year of jubilee. . . . No permanent mortgage
> indebtedness was, therefore, possible on either land or capital; that
> is, *the law was truly socialistic in providing in the name of orga-
> nized society for both land and capital for every family.* . . . [We]
> therefore, favor the reclaiming of the land for the use of all the
> people, by taxing land values on a graduated scale, and increas-
> ingly, every few years, till finally the whole value of the natural re-
> sources of the earth be taken for the people, and not for the favored
> few.[21] (emphasis added)

The new economists shared antipartyism, a concern for social justice, and an evolutionary theory of history with many of these groups,
but their analyses and their prescriptions increasingly diverged. Even a
moderate new economist would see himself as much more "radical"
than the most outspoken and self-proclaimed socialist of this type,
whether it be George Herron, Henry George or, arguably, Eugene Debs.
And except for some academics tied to W. D. P. Bliss and Christian Socialism, the new economists did not treat William Jennings Bryan as a
reformer at all but only as a symbol through whom discontent could be
expressed. They saw the "radicalism" of these groups as dangerous

21. Bliss, 1908, 204. The group was called the Christian Socialist League, organized in 1906 in Louisville, Kentucky. Bliss calls this statement "a correct representation of the principles and actual methods usually advocated by avowed and
radical Christian Socialists." An early example of Jeffersonian socialism was the
United Labor Platform of 1888, discussed in Johnson and Porter, 1975, 84–85. Another way to see this relationship between socialism and individualism is to trace
the rhetorical overlap between the more fervent social gospel ministers and the
leaders of various labor and socialist movements: both had few traces of state socialism but many of small-producer and agrarian capitalism. George Herron and
Samuel Batten often repaired to this rhetoric even as they cited the new political
economists as authoritative. See Herron, 1894, chap. 1, and Batten, 1909, 235–36
and 247; and on labor, Gutman, 1976, 79–117. A third connection is simply to
chart where socialist newspapers were published and where socialist mayors and
state legislators were elected in the period 1900–18 (Weinstein, 1976, 94–102 and
116–18).

largely in its capacity for fostering illusion and for the train of disruptions and dislocations that would necessarily follow in governmental attempts to bring back individualism under the guise of equal-rights socialism. Both Patten and Ely, for example, vigorously criticized Henry George, not for his "socialism" in urging confiscatory taxation of capital gains from land values, but for his unreconstructed individualism in assuming that all other forms of differential economic gain by individuals in competition would be merited and fair, once the evil of "monopoly rent" was destroyed.[22]

There is strong evidence of this same tension between the new economists and sectors of the social gospel movement, most notably in the writings of Ely, Commons, and Ross. The economists tried to turn the clergymen's axis of debate away from indignation over particular "wrongs" or "sins" (as if each issue could then be settled by legislating "rights" or "righteousness") and toward consideration of the relationship between larger evolutionary changes, social dislocation, economic growth, social and economic knowledge, and civic responsibility. The range and organization of topics in Ely's influential *Evolution of Industrial Society* is a model lesson in this regard.[23]

In contrast to the Jeffersonian socialists on the periphery, the economic theories of Progressive feminists were thoroughly at one from the start with those of the new political economists.[24] Gilman's concept of "socialism" was much closer to Patten's than to George's, for it rested on the extension of large-scale industrial interdependence and the demise of small-producer economic units, with their rights-oriented discourse of justification. Feminists like Gilman equated economic democracy with more organized and complex forms of cooperation and both with the emancipation of women.

We are entering upon a period of social consciousness. Whereas so far almost all of us have seen life only as individuals, and have re-

---

22. Patten, 1916, 211: "If the income from a corner lot is a surplus and can therefore be described as unearned, the income of a man of better heredity, education or opportunity must also be regarded as a surplus income and therefore unearned." The policy implications of Patten's position are, to say the least, more unsettling to a liberal individualist order than those of George's, and still are. No stronger statement of this argument can be found than in Croly, 1909, 148–54, "The Logic of Reform," followed immediately by an analysis of Bryan within that logic.

23. Ely, 1903. See also note 17, above.

24. Feminist writers such as Charlotte Perkins Gilman, Florence Kelley, and Vida Scudder, as well as their allies in academia, labor, and the settlement house movement were closely tied to the political economists through their journals, especially *Annals* and the *American Journal of Sociology.*

garded the growing strength and riches of the social body as merely
so much more to fatten on; now we are beginning to take an intelligent interest in our social nature. . . . In this change of systems a
government which consisted only of prohibition and commands
. . . is rapidly giving way to a system which intelligently manages
our common interests, which is a growing and improving method
of universal service. Here the socialist is perfectly right in his vision of the economic welfare to be assured by the socialization of
industry, though that is but part of the new development; and the
individualist who opposes socialism, crying loudly for the advantage of "free competition" is but voicing the spirit of the preda-
ceous male. . . . An economic democracy must rest on a free womanhood; and a free womanhood inevitably leads to an economic
democracy.[25]

ADMINISTRATIVE INCAPACITY, PATRONAGE, AND ENTITLEMENTS

Another set of misreadings often made is to equate the new economists' attacks on laissez faire theory and practice with favoring the creation of a centralized and general welfare state. Although it would be
difficult *not* to find in their writings discussions of state and national
systems of health and unemployment insurance and public employment schemes, old age pensions, worker's compensation, and even
child allowances, one also discovers a systematic skepticism regarding
their feasibility and even desirability in America *by the national government as presently constituted*. Their resulting hesitancy was neither from lack of political nerve nor from unconscious entrapment in
the American liberal tradition or conscious commitment to value-free
social science but was a natural product of their own professional
knowledge and a realistic appraisal of known conditions.[26]

A recent study of this period concludes, "At this point in American
history [from the 1890s to 1915], modern social-spending programs

25. Gilman, 1911, 191–92 and 260; see also 57–58.
26. The order of explanation that follows from this standpoint is in explicit contrast to the ones supplied by Ross, 1977 and 1991, 99–140; and Haskell, 1977, 144–
210. Both explain intellectual methods, styles, and shifts against a larger "ideological" background: Ross, on the spectrum of liberalism versus socialism, and
Haskell, on the spectrum of inherited political commitments versus professionalism.

were neither governmentally feasible nor politically acceptable."[27] Put differently, when the party system and courts were performing as they were expected to perform, and within the prevailing rules of constitutional law, national administrative incapacity and governmental incompetence was a necessary result. Starting with the railroads, those who addressed the governmental and administrative tasks required by the new industrial economy were fully aware of this condition.[28] This equation held true whether the issue was distributive, as in social spending programs, or regulative, as in business and labor legislation. And even if legislation was rationally framed and deemed constitutional, such were the huge and growing gaps between the industrial and other regions of the country that no common standards would be politically acceptable, given the decentralized party system.[29] An even more dangerous probability was that economic regulation issues would sim-

27. Orloff, 1988, 53; see also Orloff and Skocpol, 1984; and Skocpol, 1984, part 2. Skowronek, 1982, 39-162, documents the systematic failures of the national government in the late nineteenth century to carry out tasks routinely done by European national governments. The Progressives' ambivalence about the capacity of the national government both in setting norms and in fairly administering social spending and regulation programs can be understood more clearly if one would ask of today's liberal academics whether the functions of the educational "trusts" should be nationally regulated or even assumed by the national government. Here one thinks of the College Entrance Examination Board (SAT, LSAT, GMAT, GRE), the law schools (AALS), and schools of public policy. Suggestions to follow British and European practice in supplying a permanent higher civil service through nationalized training are not even mooted, let alone seriously proposed; rather, we trust to the exercise of public responsibility by the self-perpetuating trusts that require monopolistic or oligopolistic market positions in order to carry out their tasks.

28. Skowronek, 1982, 133-38. Within months of the passage of the Interstate Commerce Act, Seligman (1887) simply and correctly showed exactly how and why, by outlawing pooling, it would probably fail.

29. For example, the census of 1900 showed that of the nearly half a million women engaged in agricultural labor, 96.8 percent were from the South and almost 80 percent of the national total were Negroes (Nearing, 1912, 123-24). In 1900, 36 percent of white farmers and 75 percent of black farmers were tenants or sharecroppers, again, almost exclusively in the South (Sanders, 1990, 186). A *Century* magazine report on the 1880 census illustrates the relationship between the erosion of the relative wealth of the South and the growth in the number of farm units. Alabama, for example, went from 55,000 to 136,000 farms between 1860 and 1880; Georgia from 62,000 to 139,000; and North Carolina from 75,000 to 158,000 (Walker, 1882, 920-26). Per capita income levels also varied significantly by region and increased after the Civil War. In 1900, the ratio of the South Atlantic states to the national average was 45 and the East South Central states, 49. New England (134) and the Middle Atlantic states (139) were by far the richest (U.S. Bureau of the Census, 1975, 242). It is estimated that average per capita cash income for the bottom three-fourths of the southern population in the 1880-1900 period was in the range of $55 to $64 a year (Sanders, 1990, 186).

ply become battles for marginal economic advantage among the regions of America, corrupting at the start any possibility of coherent planning and policy.[30] A final factor was that some of the more advanced industrial states had long and effective records of business regulation and a more competent bureaucracy to support and administer the programs than did the national government.[31] In all these ways, national market laissez faire as *policy* protected Progressive gains in the eastern states that were the first to become urban and industrial. These same policies encouraged the more rapid growth of modern economic institutions and practices throughout the country.[32]

There was one final background factor that acted as a decisive barrier to nationally run social spending programs such as old age pensions, health and unemployment insurance, or workmen's compensation. Ignored until recent policy histories brought it to light is the fact that for over thirty years prior to World War I *the United States national government ran the world's largest and most expensive disability and pension system in the world.* Funded by a treasury surplus from high tariffs and expanded by congressional acts of retroactive inclusions, eligibility expansions, and private bills, by the turn of the century it covered approximately half of all native-born elderly males outside the South, a coverage comparable to or higher than that in European countries at that time. The program was, of course, the Pension Fund for Union Army soldiers and their dependents. In 1913 Great Britain, with a population of about 46 million, spent only one-third as much on pensions and disabilities as the American federal government, serving a population of about 78 million. In 1907 Germany, with 60 million people, spent DM 91 million (US$21.6 million) on its national pension plan, or less than one-fifth the ratio of the United States.[33]

30. This is Ely's argument against nationalization of railroads in America (1903, 248–52); see also Hadley, 1903, 141–44, and 1901, 14.

31. The best example is Massachusetts. See Blodgett, 1966; and McCraw, 1984, chap. 1, on Charles Francis Adams.

32. Recent studies in public policy history at the state level have recovered for us what was expert knowledge then, namely, that many American states were legislating regulatory and welfare reforms parallel to those of Great Britain when they reached comparable levels of urbanization and industrialization. Orloff and Skocpol, 1984; and Orloff, 1988, for both data and bibliography.

33. British figures from Skocpol, 1992, 102, and see 131–35 for other comparisons. German data from Bliss, 1908, 850 and 887. In the banner year of 1900, great numbers of new recipients were made eligible and given retroactive lump sum payments totalling $38.7 million. The number of "invalids" and the amount spent more than tripled between 1880 and 1890. In an indignant article on the political cynicism and moral shabbiness of the expansion and retroactive payments in 1890, titled "Pensions and Socialism," a *Century* magazine writer pointed out that our

It is difficult to exaggerate the growth, scale, and profligacy of this social spending program. By expenditures, the Pension Office was the
largest civilian bureau in the world. In 1890 it consumed 34 percent of
the entire federal budget (with Civil War debts and other veterans' expenditures, 45 percent). By 1900, there were still more than one million recipients; by 1910, thanks to increases in payouts, expenditures
were higher than in the early 1890s. They did not drop until after World
War I. Originally a program to aid the war wounded and the most immediate dependents of the dead and wounded, it quickly became the
keystone in a vast edifice of Republican party patronage. The Pension
Office of more than 6,000 patronage employees coordinated and deployed the hosts who lived off the scheme: 60,000 pension attorneys
and claims agents and 4,000 examining surgeons battened off its locally documented and loosely monitored standards for eligibility. As
the Civil War receded into the past, and as its veterans died off, the pension recipients' organization known as the Grand Army of the Republic
(GAR) nonetheless grew larger. From about 60,000 members in 1880
($30 million and 200,000 pension recipients), the GAR peaked at
428,000 members in 1900 ($140 million and 900,000 pensioners).[34]

In the dynamics of the pension scheme was a perfect symbiosis of
democratic individualism, the party system, and a weak national state,
producing an almost ideal conflation of Jeffersonian rights and socialist
idealism. Congressmen of both parties (more than one-third of northern and border-state congressmen were Union veterans) lived off the
Pension Fund through constituency favors and electoral victory. Rules
of eligibility were mandated by legislative acts, and these rules became
ever looser and further removed from the Pension Act's original intent.
Additionally, through private bills, ever more voter-recipients could be
enrolled outside even these increasingly generous standards. In one session of Congress in the mid-1880s, 40 percent of all legislation in the
House and 55 percent in the Senate were private bills to award pensions; by 1910, Congress was passing almost a thousand such bills per

---

total pension and military expenditures in 1890 equaled 80 percent of what the
"militarist" states of France and Germany combined spent on armaments that
same year. "We bemoan their sad fate and the oppressive burdens under which the
men, women and children of old Europe groan. But this is the pass to which we
have come: 86,000,000 of French and Germans pay $265,000,000 for armaments
and pensions—63,000,000 Americans already pay $226,000,000" (Sloane, 1891,
185–86).

34. Skocpol, 1992, 102–51, on the political history and dynamics of the Pension
Fund and organized interests having a stake in it.

session.[35] When this first experience in a nationally administered welfare system is placed alongside patronage in the largest federally owned utility—the Post Office—it would be difficult to expect too much enthusiasm on the part of professional economists and reformers generally for federal ownership or for federally run social spending programs.[36] This dramatic growth in government took place mostly during the 1880s and 1890s, the heyday of laissez faire and democratic individualist public doctrine.[37]

One must be clear on the implications of this experience for Progressive economists and for the larger understanding of "welfare state" values in America. These economists not only did not equate expansion of government with victory over laissez faire, they saw government and laissez faire as mutually dependent.[38] In the case of pensions and Post Office patronage, the "state" was not exercising authority over "pri-

35. Keller, 1977, 311; Orloff, 1988, 47; Skocpol, 1992, 122, shows the relationship between the Pension Fund and patronage through the numbers of Congressional requests to the Fund to bend rules or expedite service. In 1891 these requests averaged 500 per working day. A writer in *Century*, following the most rapid expansion of the plan a year earlier, shows clearly that the Fund started to become a patronage and electoral scheme only in 1879. Before that, both the rolls and the expenditures were shrinking. The writer is so incensed at the chicanery and lack of honor implicit in making benefit claims that he condemns the pension plan as the product of both hyperindividualism and dangerous communist beliefs (Sloane, 1891, 179–88).

36. Rapidly increasing federal revenues (400 percent between 1878 and 1908 versus a population increase of 84 percent) only whetted party appetite to create patronage jobs in the Post Office. Growing from 56,000 employees in 1881 to 136,000 twenty years later, the postal service dominated federal employment (57 percent in 1901) the way the pension system dominated federal expenditures—and both were driven by the patronage and organizational needs of the party system and quite within the formal limits of prevailing theories of the Constitution and federalism (Keller, 1977, 310).

37. Another example of dramatic growth is the Agriculture Department between 1884 and 1887, as summarized by Keller, 1977, 314.

38. Adams's 1887 monograph is a classic statement of the reverse theses that determined the basic assumptions of the new economists on this issue. Laissez faire in economics weakens and corrupts government, turning it into a battleground of private interests. In this sense, it encourages "the multiplication of laws" and expansion of government, but in order to achieve private interests (Adams, 1954, 89–90 and 116–25). Washington Gladden, writing in 1892 on urban poverty in Britain and America from the perspectives of Booth's report on London, concludes: "Large powers are given for such purposes to the municipalities of Great Britain, and they are trusted to use them for the public welfare. Here, it must be confessed, we encounter our most serious difficulty in dealing with the problem of poverty. Our existing governments are not, as a rule, bodies of men to whom such powers could be safely entrusted. . . . It is simple fatuity to go on sowing the seeds of pauperism by the municipal machinery, thinking meanwhile to extirpate it by such voluntary forces as we can bring to bear" (255).

vate'' economic life, but almost the reverse: locally based partisan interests had captured the government and turned a large part of public revenues into private patronage schemes. In the process even the tariff lost most contact with coherent public policy; providing 57 percent of federal revenues by 1890, it had become transformed into a fiscal imperative of the pension system. When the Democratic party came back into national power in the 1880s, there was no real choice except to adopt this system but try in the meantime to stop its growth by lowering tariffs. Democratic party opposition to the tariff is today presented as a "progressive" reform in the name of economic justice and the regional redistribution of income. In truth, this principled stand was a side benefit of undercutting the patronage base of the Republicans (Keller, 1977, 307; Skocpol, 1992, 113–18 and 124–30).

In nineteenth-century America, laissez faire as principle at both the national and state levels never inhibited the spending of public money for distributive purposes if the party-political system required it. At the state level throughout the nineteenth century, laissez faire easily coexisted with persistent government intervention in the economy as land, money, credit, and sovereignty itself was expended to promote settlement, develop industry, and subsidize transportation (Hartz, 1948; Hurst, 1956; Kohl, 1989, 186–227; Pisani, 1987; and Scheiber, 1972 and 1973). The most bizarre example of this is found in Cincinnati, Ohio. In the 1880s the state legislature authorized the city to construct a railroad, 300 miles long, running through Tennessee and Kentucky to link Cincinnati to Chattanooga. When completed, Cincinnati Southern cost $18 million or the equivalent of about 4 percent of the yearly national budget (Low, 1892, 731). Most of the expansion of the federal government in the Gilded Age, one of the larger peacetime expansions in our history, was of this same order and can be read not as an expansion but as a contraction or diffusion of sovereignty. To those who looked back to the Civil War regime of Lincoln, later expansion of governmental activity represented a clear loss of public authority, suggesting the paradoxical slogan, "expand government, weaken the state." Only well into the twentieth century and as a result of the marked decline of the party system and the rise of national "parastate" institutions could thoughtful reformers begin to equate federal expansion with the growth of a new social ethic and a response to the new political economy.[39]

39. Skocpol, 1992, 321–24, suggests an interesting variant to this thesis. Because women and children were perceived as outside the party-electoral system, social programs on their behalf in the late nineteenth and early twentieth centuries were much more successful and more predictive of future welfare state programs than those dealing with adult men.

A rather different set of issues presented itself regarding direct federal regulation of the economy. Social spending and promotional programs benefited individual and group interests under conditions where government asked little or nothing from the recipients and the party sponsors asked only the vote in return. No "rights" seemed to be threatened. Regulation of the corporate economy, in contrast, not only required huge resources of public authority and concentrations of political will, it coerced substantial obligations from the recipients in exchange for the privileges and protections granted. These requirements were made even more daunting because the units to be regulated and privileged consisted of huge interlocking combinations of capital, often in the form of "trusts" whose very right to exist was being powerfully contested. Given the weakness of public authority and the power of decentralized parties, the potential for replacing the "honest corruption" of individual voters and localities—democratic individualism plus party and governmental patronage—with a corrupt alliance of bosses from parties, industry, finance, and labor seemed more than the American individualist could bear. One solution was to avoid the problem by destroying trusts and reinstating the honest corruption of American innocence. This was not what the Progressive new economists had in mind.

"PRIVATE BUSINESS IS A PUBLIC TRUST"

The Sherman Antitrust Act was passed in 1890. The vote in the Senate was 52–1 and in the House, 242–0 (85 not voting)—prima facie evidence that no clear economic or industrial policy was contained in the bill and that substantive decisions regarding the meaning of the act were to be decided by default in the federal courts. The federal courts, in turn, were caught in a sort of Bermuda Triangle whose points were vague statutory language, traditional common law doctrine, and constitutional law stipulating extensive state police powers and federal power over interstate commerce.[40] To adhere to the act itself was no guide at all because it criminalized and punished many of the very private economic behaviors that, in the prevailing political system, made possible the public benefits the legislators and their constituents wanted to maintain. But to seize the reins of constitutional interpreta-

40. Sklar, 1988, 105–46; Kelly, Harbison, and Belz, 1983, 386–90 and 428–35; Chandler, 1990, 71–82; Keller, 1981, 64–72; and W. Letwin, 1965, 71–77, on the analysis of antitrust policy by the economists Adams, Clark, Ely, Hadley, James, Patten, and Seligman.

tion by expanding the national commerce power to include production and finance capital to get at predatory market-share monopoly would be to annul state police powers in one stroke and, according to Woodrow Wilson and most of the American legal community, to destroy constitutional government itself. To rely on common law precedent and proceed case by case would turn the Supreme Court into a de facto national industrial planning board, a role neither constitutionally envisioned, politically possible, nor professionally appropriate.

In fact, in some critical areas of economic decision making the federal courts were forced into this role by default.[41] If they had not taken strong initiatives in antitrust policy, the emerging national industrial economy would have been picked apart by the insatiable demands of state legislatures, which had every incentive and few restraints to use police powers to blackmail ''foreign'' sources of wealth in order to do business in their states.[42] Moreover, insofar as new industries required very large amounts of fixed capital, they were under the twin pressures of needing to attract this capital and to maintain production to pay the bond interest. In this context of competitive political and economic markets a sort of Gresham's law of corporate and governmental behavior was inevitable: for a small investment, a company might conquer or maintain markets through political means that it might fail to achieve by price and efficiency alone.[43]

The earlier experience of railroads, America's first example of the need for large pools of fixed capital (mostly foreign) and a predictable

41. Kelly, Harbison, and Belz, 1983, 386–90; and Chandler, 1990, 71–79. Trusts and holding companies are unique to America, invented in the 1880s as a response to state legislation protecting small-producer capitalism by prohibiting corporations from holding stock in other companies or owning out-of-state property. Without the holding company laws in a few friendly states, the investment of foreign capital and the creation of national industries and marketing structures would have been severely curtailed. Excellent comparative descriptions of the legal basis of American and European industrial organization are found in *The Encyclopaedia of the Social Sciences*, 3: 234–43 and 15: 111–21. Horwitz, 1992, 65–107 and 145–67, provides an excellent history of the change in legal conceptions of the corporation and property in this period. Croly recognized the role of the courts by democratic default even in the pre–Civil War period (1914, 140 and 149), because constitutional law underwrote the framework of democratic individualism and small-producer capitalism without making independent demands of national citizenship; this becomes the centerpiece of his critique of the modern period (127–83; and see 1909, 351–60, on the courts vis-à-vis state police powers).

42. Although many other Progressives recognized this feature of what might be termed the lost virtue of small republics in a national industrial economy, Croly's analysis is by far the most trenchant (1909, 351–54).

43. Or, as in the case of some distribution and marketing innovators, a small investment could achieve cost efficiencies that lower prices to the consumer, in some cases dramatically (Chandler, 1990, 58–62).

environment within which to operate, was not encouraging. Even with the gold standard to guarantee steady flows of foreign investment and the establishment of the Interstate Commerce Commission (ICC) in 1887[44] to override state beggar-thy-neighbor competition for low rates, such were the statutory ambiguity and the multiple demands placed on the Commission by regional competition for low rates that railroad bankruptcy was the norm. And, until the ICC was given substantial new authority in 1906 and 1910, it fell to masters appointed by federal bankruptcy judges to restructure by fiat entire regional and national systems of rail transportation.[45]

Given this political and economic context, as their first priority the new political economists tried to change the terms of discussion of trusts and monopolies away from that defined by regional economic competition, the party-political system, and the language of constitutional rights. Indeed, to stay within the boundaries of *that* discourse was to forego coherent discussion at the start. Moreover, these same economists had a very successful German model of industrial policy before them that they clearly understood from their own experience abroad, their graduate training, and their current reading and scholar-

---

44. The Interstate Commerce Act was forced on Congress by the Supreme Court in the *Wabash Railroad* case of 1886, which struck down Illinois state law prohibiting rate discrimination as intruding on the federal commerce power. Pooling, rate-setting, and market-sharing arrangements among the railroads were the only ways to avoid mutually assured bankruptcy. It was the railroads that finally prevailed on Congress in 1903 to prohibit rebating and other deviations from published rates (Kelly, Harbison, and Belz, 1983, 383–84 and 436). As it was, the Supreme Court gutted the powers of the ICC in response to legislative (i.e., shipper interest) intent, thereby insuring ruinously low rates and massive railroad bankruptcies during business downturns. Much of this result was predicted by Seligman (1887), who wrote two long articles on the economics of railroad regulation the year the Act was passed, pointing especially to the necessity of pooling agreements, referring to European experience and the logic of increasing returns. That same year, and in the same journal, Seligman's colleague at Columbia, John Bates Clark, published "The Limits of Competition," that strongly defended pooling as a way both to benefit from competition and to avoid its destructive aspects in all industries which benefit from increasing returns on fixed investments. On railroad bankruptcy and regulative policy, Galambos and Pratt, 1988, chap. 3; Keller, 1981, 66–67; and Skowronek, 1982, 150–62.

45. Berk, 1990, 130–50. Berk suggests that a viable regional railroad system alternative existed (150–61), an alternative that no Progressive political economist seriously considered or defended. This nostalgic possibility would, however, be in perfect accord with Wilson's "privilege of separate development." Here again is the radical gap between the conflicting imperatives of the party-political system and the economy. Bensel, 1984, takes up this condition in the 1880s and traces the politics of economic sectionalism for the next century.

ship.[46] They were quite aware that the real stakes in economic policy and industrialization were not primarily regional-domestic but national-international and that the real issue was not present distributions but continuous expansion and lower per-unit costs.

As Hadley and others reminded their own classically trained and British-oriented colleagues, the father of *political* economy was Adam Smith, whose primary concern was the wealth of the nation.[47] Rejected as doomed from the start was any Wilsonian or Democratic party notion of "separate development" by semiautonomous economic regions of the country. The industrial and financial system, the railroads, and retail marketing, although located on the New York–Chicago axis, reached everywhere. The fortunes of every other economic region of the country necessarily and absolutely rested on the success of that system.[48] For either the South or the West to prosper and maintain economic autonomy would require the systematic subsidy by massive transfer of industrial profits from the core to these regions. Some would call this economic justice; the new political economists would call it foolhardy plunder. Trusts and monopolies were the engines of innovation and economic growth generating the social surplus to invest in the society to insure future growth. At the managerial and clerical level, the aspirations, values, and fortunes of the middle classes rode on their success. Aside from the new universities, these financial, business, and industrial corporations were the only institutions in America willing and able systematically to reward training, loyalty, and self-discipline. For most of the new immigrants, wage labor in these industries and their dependencies was the only possible pathway to economic security and a decent life. The right behavior and success of the "trusts" were essential to achieve any national conception of public good.[49]

46. It is difficult to appreciate the reliance on non-American materials and scholarship during this entire period. A good indicator is *Annals*, which not only regularly reviewed books by foreign scholars but even kept its readers current on individual German economists' career movements and research and publishing projects. See note 27, chapter 3 above.

47. Hadley, 1901, 52. Originally an article, "Socialism and Social Reform," *Forum* (1894).

48. Zunz, 1990, chaps. 1–3 and 6–7, on the role of the new corporate white-collar middle classes in spreading the influence of corporate business culture to small towns and farms, especially in the growing Midwest. One could even say, with the somewhat mystical Simon Patten, that the fulfillment of the Kingdom as the victory of the "pleasure" economy rested on the social surplus of the industrial core and the dominance of the values that it produces and that it requires for its production. See chapter 2 above for discussion of his evolutionary theory.

49. This was recognized even before the Populist party was formed. In 1890 Ely argued in a popular monthly magazine that, *unlike all other economic interests,*

Some of the obvious ways to address the problem of trusts and monopolies were also the most politically difficult to achieve. Since all corporations rested on chartered privileges granting limited legal liability to stockholders, one solution would have been to require national charters for all corporations of a certain size doing interstate business.[50] This privilege of national incorporation would have entailed reporting requirements and charter provisions regarding standards of competitive behavior. Another possibility would have been to treat all major trusts as public utilities, like railroads, with an independent commission or bureau overseeing their activities. Both of these obvious responses were entirely too centralizing and "statist" for the prevailing political system. Moreover, given the doubts about the integrity and quality of public administration and its lack of autonomy from legislative interference, even the economists recommending such solutions were skeptical regarding any gains in economic growth or social justice. A third approach would have been to regulate large corporations and trusts indirectly through strong national regulation of the financial system, labor relations, tariff policy, and natural resources. If combined with central banking, this system would have radically expanded the power of the national government to regulate by manipulating the larger economic environment to achieve public ends. And the capacity for this coordinated manipulation would have given the national government all the tools it needed to determine national industrial development policy. Again, however, these solutions required too much centralized authority and too radical a shift of power from Congress to administrators and the presidency. All of these visions were literally in-

---

the problem of wage labor and meeting its interests is inseparable from the public good (1890, 939). Croly's entire analysis of economic policy rests on this analysis, stated in terms of core profits and peripheral rents: he condemns the utter bankruptcy of Democratic party solutions based on equal rights as a cover to plunder core profits for peripheral land values and thereby undermine the possibility of industrial peace and increasing productivity (1914, 107–21; and see 1909, 352–57, on use of state police powers for purposes of blackmail and plunder). Croly got most of his profit and rent arguments from Patten. On the role of state legislation to prevent direct sales from manufacturers and legal challenges to these restrictions by the new corporations, McCurdy, 1978.

50. Croly, 1909, 357–60, clearly recognizes that this act would give large firms even clearer advantage over local ones than they already possessed. Many leading business and financial leaders favored national incorporation, as did Theodore Roosevelt, to avoid incoherent state regulation and to make possible business rationality without such complex legal maneuvering. Chandler, 1990, 71–81, shows how much organizational, legal, and financial innovation was required to achieve this in comparison to Great Britain and Germany, but it was achieved, with dramatic results in productivity and lowered costs.

conceivable within the Democratic party and only distant visions in some sectors of the Republican. In the event, under Roosevelt's and Taft's presidencies, some initiatives were taken in these directions and, in some respects, the courts went along.[51]

INDUSTRIAL PARASTATES
AS VOLUNTARY SOCIALISM

Despite these hopes, doubts, and efforts, the burden of governmental trust regulation lay primarily with the courts, ruling after the fact on a case by case basis. Coherent and rational reform usually suggested the national state; the localized and sectionalized party-electoral system fostered continuous illusion and therefore national governmental incapacity (Croly, 1914, 65–69, 92, and 100–101). Thus, another Progressive approach to the trust question was to urge "parastate" solutions. Given that control of large corporations was increasingly divorced from ownership, could not the managers and the investment bankers and their corporate-legal staffs be "socialized" by publicity, education, and fear of adverse regulation? So many other areas of American life had been socialized (democratized, Christianized) into parastates, why not the trusts and their investment bankers? There were extant and successful models. The national reform press was on the verge of achieving the quasi-official status of definer of American identity and public doctrine. The formation and purposes of the new universities and professional associations presumed this possibility, as had the host of national religious and reform associations earlier. But this projected solution suggested two rather different paths. The stress in most of the social gospel literature was on "just" distributions of present profits, not on long-range economic growth. Social gospel was more often addressed to wealth disparities than to increased productivity, lower prices, and new wealth creation. Proponents often seemed to ask that corporations and banks act as nonprofit charities, risking the jobs and fortunes of thousands on an economics of atonement.[52] The other path,

51. Kelly, Harbison, and Belz, 1983, 426–35; and Sklar, 1988, 184–203, regarding the Bureau of Corporations established in 1903; and Rosenberg, 1982, 52, on the Payne-Aldrich Tariff Act of 1909 transferring some tariff-making authority to the president.

52. See, for example, Abbott, 1901, 117: "For the true wealth of the community depends far more on the equity of the wealth distribution than upon the aggregate amount of wealth produced." In this respect at least, the current environmental movement is a sort of reborn social gospel movement, with the same tensions between the economic atonement values of much of the active members and the economic efficiency constraints recognized by much of its expert leadership.

shared by the new economists and many of the social gospel writers, stressed trusteeship: "Private business is a public trust."[53]

Hadley, whose primary expertise was the economics of railroad regulation, defended trusteeship by contrasting it with an economic theory of individual rights. If one begins from the perspective of the primacy of competitive self-interest, there is simply no solution to the problems of the new industrialism. The public will rightly refuse to punish labor violence and illegal conspiracies because it can perceive immediately the disparities of power between labor and capital, each with legitimate but incompatible "rights." And, under that same assumption, but applied to trusts and monopolies, "we shall be simply attempting to punish someone else for doing effectively on a large scale what we, on our own part, having been trying to do much less effectively on a small one." State socialism is a solution, but it involves a kind of paradox when viewed against the background of American political democracy and administrative incapacity and decentralization: "If we grant that a socialistic state is managed by citizens who subordinate their own interests to the common interest, and hold their power as a public trust, most of the evils under which we now suffer would be avoided. But so they would under the present conditions of capitalistic enterprise if we had this habitual exercise of public spirit and recognition of public obligation."[54]

Since, under present conditions, this is not true of our political life, it is probably better to have the state intervene periodically and by regulation to enforce standards of trusteeship on business enterprises. To have public ownership, whereby a ring or party would then control both politics and industry, would leave the public with "no outside means of checking [this concentrated power] except through the agency of revolution."[55]

As institutional analysts of industrial society, the new economists had another and more compelling argument in their defense of trusteeship—the logic of the financial market. Until not long before, manufacturing corporations had access only to localized capital consisting of

53. Small, 1895, article title in the first volume of his *American Journal of Sociology*. In that same volume , he published "The State and Semi-Public Corporations" (1895a).

54. Hadley, 1903, 143–44. Patten, 1912, 307 and 331, uses the term "voluntary socialism" for this habitual exercise, referring to banking, railroads, trusts, and labor unions as examples of cooperation within groups leading to cooperation between them: "The real choice of the American people lies between voluntary control and coercive state control." Under the former, "the state merely registers what mutual assent has already attained."

55. Hadley, 1903, 143; see also 1901, 11–14.

rich individual investors who knew the managers and trusted them. With industrial trusts taking on more and more the characteristics of railroads in their need to amass large amounts of investment from throughout the country and abroad, managers had increasingly to adhere to higher standards of stewardship simply to meet the new standards of stock and bond marketability then prevailing for railroads.[56] Combined with the wage pressures of strong labor unions and the price pressures of domestic competition and wise tariff policy, only those manufacturing industries that behaved responsibly could survive. And although he grants that some monopolies may well fall under public ownership, Hadley is indifferent to this result and predicts that the public will be similarly indifferent. As consumers in an increasingly consumer driven economy, the public will hardly make a principled choice between prices charged by monopolistic private businesses that borrow long-term money at four percent and those charged by public businesses that could borrow at three.[57]

Even those economists who urged more extensive public ownership and control than Hadley were often reluctant to rest their case on cost or economic justice alone. Ely, for example, praised German public ownership of telegraph and telephone services because the required formal training and competitive examinations taught employees habits of self-discipline and responsibility. And, in exchange for life-long careers, they had to continue this discipline and training to earn promotion. He and others urged municipal ownership of local utilities as much to encourage habits of solidarity and responsible citizenship as to redistribute wealth, income, or power.[58] Whether at the national or the local

56. Hadley, 1901, 44. As the acknowledged American expert on the economics of railroad investment and regulation, Hadley knew what he was saying. He assumed, however, that manufacturing corporations would never require the regulatory apparatus of natural monopolies, only that manufacturing enterprises would voluntarily adopt many of the fiduciary standards of regulated railroads. Zunz (1990, 125–48) discusses the increasingly high standards of personal behavior demanded of white-collar employees of the new corporations and (91–121) the attempts of the Metropolitan Life Insurance Company to become a social service agency and leader for progressive reform. Chandler, 1990, 58 and 79–82, confirms Hadley's contemporaneous analysis.

57. Hadley, 1901, 46–49. He is assuming taxpayer vigilance in the latter case, i.e., lower prices would not be achieved by subsidy. The notion of a mandated "floor" beneath competition was outlined by both Clark and Adams in the 1880s. Clark, however, was a stronger believer in some natural laws of economics and therefore wanted both to limit government regulation more than his colleagues and took a much more hostile stance toward trusts. His colleagues continually pointed out that these two positions were somewhat at odds.

58. Ely, 1903, 242–48 and 225–37. Municipal ownership would teach the citizenry that they would have to select a much better class of public officials if those

level, the political system was more of a barrier to the new economists' reform ideals than their own economic imaginations or the practices of the corporations themselves. This same sense of political limits was widely shared by Progressive political officeholders and leaders.[59] And for both political activists and political economists, this same combination of political limits and the potential welfare benefits of increasing productivity, economic surplus, and the growth of a consumer economy was evident in their discussion of economic justice for labor in America.

THE DISCIPLINE OF LABOR
IN THE NEW INDUSTRIAL ECONOMY

Once focus shifted in the direction of "trusteeship" for the large business organization, the obligations shifted accordingly and spread beyond ownership and management of business corporations to include the entire work force. In one of the earlier discussions of the industrial economy from this perspective the term "trust" was used as a metaphor to facilitate the inclusion of labor in the network of obligations. "We are living in a half-developed system, and in the law of its

---

new enterprises were to function efficiently. To take away the implication that the average citizen had to be tricked or bribed into virtue by these means, Ely added that the entire municipal franchise system created conditions where good citizens found it difficult to reform city government. See also Ely, 1890, 950–51; and Commons, 1894, chap. 6. As Kloppenberg, 1986, 199–297, shows, these same noneconomic values permeated the economic arguments of the new liberals and Fabians in Britain and the social democrats in France and Germany.

59. Hughes, 1910, 37–55 and 102–7. As with the economists, Hughes stresses the ways in which demands for regulation and public ownership entail much greater civic discipline and hierarchy, for example, a professional civil service, more power to executives, and the reduction of the number of elective offices. William Howard Taft praised the annexation of the Philippines for exactly this same reason. Since the whole world was watching and the patriotic pride of the average American was put at risk, Congress was forced to permit the executive to appoint qualified and competent administrators abroad (Taft, 1906, 80–87). This logic is carried to an extreme when one confronts authentic socialists of the European variety in America. Laurence Gronlund, in a circular to professional economists urging a secret society of young men dedicated to the extension of governmental functions, told his readers that "socialism, under the auspices of the intelligence of the country, is providentially destined to be our future social system (not the socialism which is in the interest only of the weak and the inefficient, but that which will create glad and willing obedience to all—ORDER—and thus is even more in the interest of the competent)" (quoted from Dorfman, 1949, 154). This relationship is most evident in the writings of the British Fabians like the Webbs; see S. Letwin, 1965, 365–78.

growth may discern . . . an outline of the form that it will ultimately take." The modern industrial system increasingly rewards intellect more than muscle, and character more than both: "The largest stipends that it offers are for fidelity to trusts. . . . In cheapened production, which is never appreciated, and is often blindly resisted, lies, according to this social law, the chief hope for modern workers. . . . The outline of the coming industrial state has the shape neither of despotism nor democracy; it is the outline of a true republic."[60]

But how were trusteeship values in management and labor to be determined and enforced in an industrial regime of "free contract" between employer and employee? Again it was Henry Carter Adams who first provided the theoretical formulation that framed Progressive economic thinking about industrial wage labor.[61] In his 1896 AEA presidential address, "Economics and Jurisprudence," Adams summarized this position in three propositions. The first is that individualism "fails to express the moral necessities of the present industrial order," thereby causing an unbridgeable gap between the required morality and prevailing legal doctrine. The second is that "the principle of [contractual] responsibility, which is the cornerstone of English jurisprudence, is incapable of industrial application under existing industrial conditions." His final proposition is that to realize industrial liberty for the worker will require that the worker himself possess "industrial property" (Adams, 1954, 140).

The facts of modern industrial life that nullify the individualist presumptions of the older economics are easily stated. The modern corporation can expand to the limits of its markets for goods and services. By receiving increasing returns on fixed increments of capital, they "destroy the conditions under which competition is alone able to perform its beneficent service," which is to compete to lower prices.[62] More-

---

60. Clark, 1888, 50–51. In the words of Giddings, in the emerging economy the relative weight of "moral forces" are increasing at the expense of "competitive forces" in determining the distributions of profits because it is largely "the moral quality of the people" that increasingly determines productivity and therefore the absolute amount of wealth (Giddings, 1888, 68).

61. Adams's AEA presidential address of 1896, "Economics and Jurisprudence," in Adams, 1954. Hadley remarked following the address that Adams "put with so much force many things that we have all been thinking" (163). Giddings remarked that this formulation was a "conservative" or minimalist "view of the policy that industrial communities will have to adopt in order to bring about industrial peace" (164–65).

62. Adams, 1954, 146. This is the essence of the modern corporation and is the core of his earlier critique of classical economics and of his justification for state interference (Adams, 1954, 109–14). The influence of this 1887 monograph is difficult to overstate. His analysis of the "three classes of industry," their legal status,

over, modern corporations "now conceive of themselves as business associations of perpetual life" and "plead the interests of a perpetual existence" to defend their rights. How is it that "a [temporary] body of men organized for the purpose of private gain" can make claims of perpetuity—claims that in earlier periods of history were made only by the state? Finally, corporations as artificial legal entities do not practice the restraining personal virtues that the older economic order required as "essential for continued business success." In the old order, morality, economic rationality, and jurisprudence were in harmony because all centered on the individual and his ethical and legal capacities and responsibilities. In the new industrial economy, individuals are held responsible for social effects they cannot control; they must come under a new regime of social ethics enforceable by a new legal order (Adams, 1954, 146–47).

The next step in Adams's argument is the centerpiece of his larger economic theory. The prevailing jurisprudence is based on individual rights expressed in voluntary contracts. When the state coercively enforces these contracts by assessing penalties for their breach, society acting through the state *is not mandating some separate duty originating in its own will* but only "exacting . . . the penalty [expressly or tacitly] recognized in the contract . . . and voluntarily assumed by both parties in the agreement." In these voluntary contracts, then, there is a responsibility or duty behind each individual's exercise of liberty, and "the nature of that responsibility must, of course, conform to the nature of the liberty it is designed to control" (Adams, 1954, 151).

Herein lies the great gap between contemporary economic life and law. In the new industrial order, the responsibilities voluntarily agreed to in labor contracts cannot be enforced for the simple reason that "the great body of workmen . . . have no property, privilege, or advantage that they can place in jeopardy as a pledge for the fulfillment of a labor contract," making "enforcement by the orderly procedure of (common law) jurisprudence" impossible.

> In the situation thus portrayed, do we find the explanation, first, of the reckless manner in which workmen frequently urge their claims [i.e., alleging breach of contract]; and second, of the ten-

---

and their patterns of competitive activity runs through the entire literature. Albion Small's 1914 article, "The Social Gradations of Capital," justly noted for its implicit radicalism, is largely a restatement of Adams's three classes into "tool-capital," "management-capital," and "finance-capital," the latter undercutting all legitimate claims of exclusive private property rights and its proceeds (see especially 732–34 and 739–43).

dency on the part of employers to appeal to force [to enforce their claims]. The workmen are reckless because in the evolution of modern industry they have been bereft of all proprietary interest in the plant that gives them employment; the employers appeal to force because there is nothing else to which they can appeal for the restraint of propertyless men (Adams, 1954, 152).

The appeal to force on both sides "is an admission that the law of property has reached the limit of its evolution" and constitutes a de facto abandonment of the English [i.e., common law] system of jurisprudence. The appeal to force is a tacit rejection of "a society *whose moral code is expressed in the language of rights*" and the tacit acceptance of "a society whose *moral code is expressed in the language of duty.*" In sum, the solution cannot lie in either management coercion that enslaves the workers or in worker violence that destroys the investment. Any viable solution must lie in creating new forms of "workmen's property" sufficient to restore moral responsibility commensurate to the liberties claimed in the labor contract. These new property rights necessarily void the absolute rights to property claimed by corporate owners and exercised through their managers.[63] These new rights could be possessed and exercised only collectively, through legally established and publicly accountable labor organizations.

The conclusion to this argument is simple. The moral basis of this new property right flows directly from economic theory, which postulates that wealth is created socially and that *"the source of the increment of product is the new [social] relations that men enter into."*[64] These new property rights will be established first through collective bargaining, requiring of employers union recognition and of unions the

---

63. Adams, 1954, 152–53, emphasis added. Adams then goes on to dismiss as wholly irrelevant questions mooted in court battles between labor and capital such as "How many men in how many ways may make how many kinds of conspiracy?" Although questions of this type establish rights of belligerents in war, "they are uninteresting to the student of economics because they add nothing to the evolution of industrial jurisprudence at the point where evolution is necessary in order to bring industry and law into harmony" (153–54). Croly, 1909, 351, similarly dismisses legal and constitutional argument regarding intra- and inter-state commerce as "a distinction of insignificant economic or industrial importance."

64. Adams, 1954, 159, emphasis added. This is an argument with a complex background in theories of just shares from labor, capital, and rent. Adams extends in a socialized way the argument that innovation or "entrepreneurial profits" are also earned, therefore, all men have a proprietary interest or "right" in wealth created by accumulated knowledge, hereditary transmission of aptitudes and skill, or any other collective and historical source contributing to the wealth of a nation. This argument corresponds to Patten's critique of Henry George who only asserted the social creation of the profits of land rent.

enforcement of contracted duties on their members. Second, it will be necessary to create arbitration boards whose decisions over time will create the equivalent of common law rights to property over which the workers become group proprietors. These possessions and privileges would constitute motives to "become a responsible party in the world of industrial association." Last, a subsidiary law of industrial agency that defines the duties of corporations, trusts, and unions to the public at large must be imposed directly by the state. Only with the "state interest" clearly enforced can the subsidiary structures of unions, collective bargaining, and arbitration be held to account (Adams, 1954, 159 and 161–62).

Note that Adams's entire discussion of the "rights" of labor lay within a framework of collective duties and the conditions of their enforcement. This model was fully developed by the 1890s and ruled for all subsequent discussions of the labor problem by these professional economists, their students, and their larger reading public.[65] The duties incumbent on owners, management, and labor had to be performed because the combination of wage labor and concentrated capital was the material foundation for the public good. Framed in this way, the Progressive economists' labor policy agenda can be understood quite apart from the abstracted ideological question of socialism and capitalism or the question of competing "rights."

Three years after Adams's 1887 monograph "Relation of the State to Industrial Action," Richard Ely, with the assistance of New York reform mayor Seth Low, wrote "A Programme for Labor Reform" for *Century* magazine. Such is the importance of labor relations to America's future and such are the present day conditions of wage-earners and their families, said Ely, that *"whenever we truly advance the interests of wage-earners we necessarily advance the interests of all society."* This is not Ely as Marxist, but Ely as Progressive who firmly denies that the labor problem is "merely a class problem." What he is asserting is the institutional dependence of all other economic sectors in America on the success and growth of the new industrial economy, which, in turn, depends on the quality, discipline, and character of the

---

65. Examples of this are John Commons, who served from 1902 to 1904 as general secretary for the National Civic Federation, whose purpose was to establish networks of mutual rights and obligations among labor, industry, and finance (Lustig, 1982; and Weinstein, 1968). The most powerful articulator of this position was Herbert Croly, 1909, 385–96, and 1914, 378–405. See also Walter Weyl, 1914, 292–93. Weyl, who joined Croly on the *New Republic* in 1914, was one of Patten's doctoral students.

industrial labor force.[66] "This cannot be said for any other social class," each of which, he points out, seeks to better its own fortunes "by the promotion of special interests in legislative halls and elsewhere, while society as a whole may languish."[67]

Ely's larger point is that the most productive economies in the world are regulated in order to enhance productive forms of competition, innovation, and skills while preventing their opposites.[68] The entire catalog of evils to be addressed was premised on these arguments. Child labor, women in factories, substandard urban dwellings, Sunday and night work, occupational disease and accidents, excessive and unplanned immigration, overspecialization, and early marriages, family breakdowns, and the resulting social pathologies are the evils to be addressed. These evils are substantive and pragmatic and can neither be described nor addressed in the language of rights.[69] The same holds for Ely's catalog of remedies to address these evils.

The remainder of Ely's reform program for labor is largely addressed to what I have called "parastate" institutions. Ely addresses in order, the church, the family, and the schools, paying particular attention to German and Swiss examples of compulsory school and youth training programs. Only then does he turn to the role of government, but even

66. Ely, 1890, 939, emphasis added. This is exactly what Croly came to argue in 1914, 119 and 121: "The aim of the whole program of modern social legislation is at bottom the creation of a new system of special privilege intended for the benefit of the wage-earning rather than a property owning class . . . [but] they must be worth their salt. Insofar as they are not worth their salt, they must be helped, trained and sometimes coerced to become so." This is not the language of rights. Toward the end of his book, he treats trade unions as parastate institutions that must play a central role of national governance, concluding: "The creation of an industrial organization which will serve to make individual workers enlightened, competent and loyal citizens of an industrial commonwealth, is most assuredly a task just as essential as the creation of a loyal and enlightened body of voters" (379).

67. Ely, 1890, 939. This argument could be and was understood by an audience attuned to the social gospel and Christian Socialism on quite another level, that of Christian atonement and sacrifice for the common good. Ely goes on to show how, in England, legislation forbidding child labor, restricting the hours and conditions for women and youth, securing safe working conditions and decent living conditions, and similar reform immediately redounded to the public good through increased productivity, convincing such liberal individualists as Gladstone to recant their earlier opposition and even causing Cobden to waver.

68. Ely, 1890, 949. Here he refers to Adams's 1887 monograph for proof.

69. Patten, 1912, 316–17; and 1889a, 36–70, also stresses the role of social and family values determining consumption choices and self-discipline as evolutionary adaptations contributing to economic growth and better distributions of income and wealth.

here the stress is on dwellings, factory laws, savings banks, and honest administration of law.[70] While calling for "labor organizations" and labor arbitration that presumes their institutionalization, Ely's dislike of special interests and rights claims by economic classes and sectors is such that he is as much concerned about repressing the evil features of unions as he is about encouraging their good features.[71] He reserves his strongest condemnation, however, not for labor violence, but for the violence and illegality of corporations that employ "spies and informers" and court anarchy with their "armed bands of hirelings" (Ely, 1890, 496).

Ely shared with his professional colleagues a fixed conviction that the labor problem was the decisive proof of a "diseased social body." Any solution to that problem must address the disease itself.[72] At the

70. Ely, 1890, 947–50. Ely is incensed less by the lack of legislation than by the lack of enforcement and obedience to the most basic laws governing civil and responsible behavior. Croly (1914, 63–65, 69, 92, 100, 158, and 300) is so exasperated at this inherent trait in our party-political system that he coyly suggests that the entire political system would be overthrown and the party system dissolved if honest law enforcement were ever seriously undertaken.

71. Croly's argument twenty years later is almost the same as Ely's. Both corporations and unions are forms of privilege granted by the state in exchange for the performance of specified duties; there is no "right" to monopolize labor markets any more than there is a "right" to monopolize markets in goods and services or *a right to own land and collect monopoly rent*. All rights are conditional on the achievement of common good and therefore constitute privileges in exchange for special obligations (Croly, 1909, 126–31 and 385–98). This argument gets refined by Croly (1914, 109–26), after he read Patten's "Reconstruction of Economic Theory."

72. Ely, 1890, 946. Ely concludes with a long section on "monopolies and corporations" in which he suggests a host of reforms, particularly municipal ownership of utilities, protection of public property, and strict incorporation laws, with criminal penalties. But here, too, it is the party-political system and its lack of administrative capacity, not capitalist ideology, that he identifies as the chief barrier to reform. "The weakness of States and cities is well known. . . . Not a city in the Union is strong enough to force street-car lines to lay properly grooved rails. . . . Not a State in the Union is strong enough to protect the traveler by foot or by horse against dangers from steam railway [crossings]. . . . Not a State in the Union is strong enough to make corporations bear their due share of public burdens." Ely's call for municipal ownership, then, is to teach citizens and political leaders "how to manage their own affairs." Once this civic capacity is learned, it will then be "easier for State and nation to perform . . . their legitimate functions. It might perhaps then be possible even to leave railways in the hands of corporations, instead of placing them directly under the management of the Federal Government." If this is "socialism" it is certainly of an ironic kind: public ownership is required to create the state and national capacity sufficient to insure responsible regulation, thereby preserving private ownership. German political economy meets the American political and constitutional system and not American "capitalist ideology." Washington Gladden, in the same *Century* series on current problems, has a similar complaint regarding poverty relief policy. Showing that current policy in American cities is more generous regarding "outdoor" relief than London, he nevertheless bemoans the barriers that the political system erects to the achievement of systematic and effective efforts to address the deeper causes of poverty (Gladden, 1892, 255).

deepest level of their analysis of the labor problem, then, was the insight that a politics of democratic individualism produces a political and party system incapable of addressing the problems either of labor or of industrial and finance capitalism. Brute force and reaction are the mirror image of populism, socialism, and anarchism. Like the issue of slavery earlier, the issue of wage labor, although in appearance a "sectional" issue (in this instance, the urban Northeast and Midwest), was *the* national problem. And, like the issue of slavery earlier, the prevailing party-political system was incapable of addressing the issue in national terms, requiring the destruction of one national regime and the institution of a new one.[73] Had the Civil War regime been maintained, of course, solution would have been at hand.

MONOPOLY RENT AND
DEMOCRATIC VIRTUE

When Charles Beard distinguished between "capitalist" and "agricultural" ("realty") interests in his analysis of the struggle over the U.S. Constitution and later party divisions in America, he was referring to two forms of capitalism. In the earlier language of the new economists the conflict was between earned "profits" and unearned "rents."[74] Stated in this way, and not in terms of capitalist power versus democratic innocence, they confronted dominant American political assumptions with some ironic and sobering conclusions regarding the relationship between democratic virtue and privilege. Beard's redescription of American political history is an application of those conclusions.

Excess earnings that flow from monopoly market positions in industry and transport are a form of rent, but these benefits are usually short

73. This is exactly Croly's analysis (1914, 101). The Democratic party is committed in principle to the earlier system while the Republican party is trapped by residues of it in seeking "to impose a constructive democratic policy on the nation without eradicating a large residue of negative democratic methods and ideas in its own composition. *It built up a national economic system beyond the fortifications of the Constitution; but it wanted that system to enjoy both the privilege of unlimited expansion and the shelter of impregnable and definite walls"* (emphasis added).

74. Beard, 1913 and 1915. His *Economic Interpretation* was reviewed in *American Journal of Sociology* 19 (1913): 405–8. Noting that the journal's readers would find that "neither the theory nor the viewpoint will be new," the reviewer nevertheless praised the book because it "scrupulously avoided any moral issues [and] refrained from commendation or condemnation." Beard's outlook was very close to Croly's across a whole spectrum of economic and constitutional issues. See Barrow, 1988 and 1992; and McCorkle, 1984.

term, governmentally regulated (if natural monopolies) or avoidable through substitution in economies of abundance.[75] The prospect of getting and keeping this rent is a constant spur to effort and innovation. A related form of "rent" is entrepreneurial, the excess earnings derived from new forms of business organization, the introduction of more efficient production processes, or from *any possession of special skills which command a wage or salary premium on the market.* These forms of rent are also productive but usually short-lived because of innovation, competition, and substitutability.[76] The one form of rent or excess earnings that cannot be avoided is that which rests on the finitude and immovability of space, the rent represented by the value of land in excess of what it would earn by producing goods in a larger competitive market. This is the setting for a three-sided battle between the Progressive economists on one side, peripheral-populist "radicals" on another, and core laissez-faire "conservatives" on a third.

From at least the late eighteenth century onward the agricultural economy in America has always had three separate components. The first form one might call a subsistence-welfare or equal opportunity agricultural economy. If one had few skills, little talent, no capital, and no connections, both a living and independence from any superior could be hazarded through the availability of cheap or free land. The earliest colonial grants of housing plots and farmland, the sale of state lands in small parcels cheaply or on credit, the post hoc land titles granted to those who had simply taken it, and, finally, the homestead acts and land runs were the "equal opportunity" and welfare policies of democratic America as a small-producer and agrarian democracy. It was presumed that the labor of one's body and the use of one's own tools in a localized economy of simple exchange produced goods sufficient for a minimally decent life if one acted responsibly and diligently. In this economy, like that of any independent professional, there is no concept of "profit," only of work and return (Patten, 1912, 312). So long as one stays put, the market value of one's land is irrelevant, the market value of any salable surplus only marginally important, and the gross amount of the product absolutely crucial for survival and flourishing.

75. As the new economists put it, this is monopoly (oligopoly) in competition with monopoly (oligopoly) in any economy where consumers are rich enough to make choices.

76. Whereas almost all of the new economists dealt with these themes, Adams, 1954; Clark, 1886 and 1887; Clark and Giddings, 1888; and Patten, 1889 and 1902a defined the framework of this discussion. Patten (1902, 33–128) outlined this basic theory and applied it in all his later works. In a work of 1912 he refers to this rent as "super-profits" and "super-wages" in new industries that have a temporary advantage.

Although there was, in fact, often little relationship between work and return (the land was poor, the weather unpredictable), the rise of a second agricultural economy often supplemented and "saved" the egalitarian and virtue assumptions of the first.[77] This second economy was commercial agriculture, where most value is derived from income from the regular sale of agricultural and even simple craft products in a market. This economy presumes regional, national, and perhaps even international markets as well as infrastructures of transportation for access to these markets and of credit to fund the investment and production costs of specialization. Profit represents the difference between production costs and competitive market prices. The cost of the land and the availability and cost of credit are crucial in this second economy. Where this economy is not strictly local or regional, pressures for efficiency and self-discipline can be quite unrelenting and the struggle for regional comparative advance quite fierce. So, too, as the southern planters and slaveholders were the first to learn, is the struggle over credit.[78] Significant premiums or "rents" are available to those whose land is near cheap transportation and large markets. Thus, part of the politics of this second agricultural economy is to induce government to privilege particular localities by making provisions for cheap credit, by constructing roads, canals, or railroads or, on a national scale, by expanding domestic and international markets for their products so that their profits will rise faster than those of their competitors. Commercial agriculture of this type provides an increasingly friendly environment for commercial and industrial investment.[79]

77. McCoy, 1980; and as reflected in legal thought, Ellis, 1974.

78. Beard uses this analysis with devastating effect in explaining the resistance of the South to an effective national government following the break with Britain. He argues, and contemporary charges support him, that much southern support for independence was motivated by the hope to escape indebtedness to British creditors. At the signing of the Jay Treaty in 1794, which committed the national government to assist in the collection of this debt, private debtors in the five southern states owed just short of 90 percent of the total American debt to Britain, with Virginia accounting for half of that. Southern state courts and legislatures continued to frustrate collection under the Treaty. Earlier, efforts had been made by Virginia delegates at the Constitutional Convention to bar federal courts from enforcing treaty provisions respecting private debt. These debts were never paid by those who owed them. When Jefferson was elected president he bailed out southern realty interests by negotiating a convention that shifted payment to the federal government, thereby subsidizing the world of individual and states rights and agrarian virtue. This precedent and its attendant bad faith became a tradition in defending the civic virtue in what Croly termed "territorial" and Beard "realty" democracy. The most recent chapter was the national bailout following the savings and loan crisis in the 1980s (Beard, 1915, 296–98 and chap. 10).

79. This system embraces the first two of Small's "three grades of capital," ear-

This second form was the dominant agricultural economy of the Jacksonian and immediate post–Civil War periods (Kohl, 1989; McCoy, 1980). Simple forms of industry and commerce create regional networks of exchange and the growth of large regional market cities. But it was precisely the growth of these other sectors that raised to prominence the third component of the agricultural economy, the speculative land economy. This agricultural economy had always existed and thrived on the big rewards derived from the market value of land alone and not from the sale of goods or the provision of subsistence. Winning in this economy was both a kind of lottery and a bonus on virtue. Both commercial agriculture and its subsistence-welfare parent linked success with good health, good weather, and hard work. And in the second economy, there was a sort of moral interdependence operating: the more hardworking and responsible your neighbors, the richer you became. In the third or realty economy, however, success depended on none of these factors directly, but solely on rises in land values and access to credit to cash in. "Capital" in this third economy is not risked on future actions promising a profitable return, in the way commercial ventures are planned, but is instead leveraged as a wager to produce further speculative returns. This process is identical to that of adding speculative incentive to buy a house when down payments are low, interest is cheap, and real estate prices are rising.[80]

This third economy depends on factors quite extraneous to the ability to produce value on a particular parcel of land. It rests instead almost entirely on location, land scarcity, and the activities of third parties. For example, a trunk line railroad capitalized by London banks and federal land grants locates a depot in X space. The town expands and the prices of all adjacent farms, whether well or ill managed, triple. Commercial and residential property values in the expanding town in-

lier termed by Adams "industries of the first and second class" by virtue of relationship of investment and returns. Patten, 1912, 301, is excellent here: "America has no rent class. Land is an investment and its income is not distinct from that of capital. Few know what part of their income is rent and what profit or interest."

80. The only virtue components to justify the capital gains from housing are that one saved for the down payment and kept a job to pay the mortgage. But these virtues are properly their own reward; identical buyers in different housing markets, when they sell, receive radically disproportionate rewards that bear no relationship whatsoever to their invested virtues. The same is true for some farmlands, except the stakes are higher. Rising values are leveraged to buy more land, illustrating Abraham Lincoln's wry comment that the farmers he knew had the modest ambition to acquire only the lands adjacent to their own. After the New Deal invention of low-interest thirty-year mortgages and GI loans, the modest homeowner equivalent only wanted a new house every five years, worth 30 percent more than and financed by the capital gains from the old one.

crease even more. Everyone wins a piece of a lottery, yet each winner thinks his or her individual virtue has at last been properly rewarded. Under these conditions property ownership per se represents, not a "use right" with its market rewards, but an increasingly valuable privilege. *And because all land ownership is a form of monopoly, all gains from buying and selling, or all leasing income beyond its actual productive value, is unearned rent.* Like the grant of an exclusive and perpetual unregulated franchise to provide a necessary service (for example, the Charles River Bridge), this monopoly rent is permanent, increasingly valuable, nonsubstitutable and, in comparison with industrial monopolies and regulated utilities, produces no commensurate collective benefits in return. Because all three of these agricultural economies operate simultaneously, both illusion and moral confusion are easily fostered, for these three land-based economies combine democratic monopoly, democratic capitalism, and democratic virtue. Monopoly privilege spread this widely becomes indistinguishable psychologically and morally from equal rights and equal opportunity. Personal greed, personal virtue, and public good as collective prosperity are equally difficult to disentangle. Unearned speculative gain becomes confused with the just deserts of hard work and speculative loss with either theft or larceny.

But what happens when these three economies become separated both in space and by region? What happens when it is not local effort and diligence and cleverness that sustain land values and generate local speculative gains—the only source of significant fortunes in these non-industrial regional economies? What happens when the exogenous sources of growth—population, income, productivity, investment capital—are caused by actions in one part of the country (the industrial core) and the potential recipients of the unearned increments (the commercial and realty economies) are everywhere?

So long as almost the entire economy was small-producer capitalist, the exogenous causes of increased monopoly rent were spatially and psychologically indistinguishable from the commercial economy. *The real productive efforts of each underwrote the speculative gains of all.* This is exactly the world Tocqueville described when he spoke of the virtuous materialism and enlightened self-interest of the average American.[81] It is exactly this same world that the Progressive econo-

---

81. Tocqueville, 1981, vol. 2, bks. 2 and 3. Both Croly and Beard restate this alliance of interest and virtue with an edge of bitterness. "The pioneer, in spite of his aggressive uninformed individualism, was essentially a good citizen. . . . His individual purposes had not betrayed him into an anti-social attitude toward his fellow-countrymen. . . . Competition was keen; but it was competition less for subsistence than for the largest killing" (Croly, 1914, 96). And see his use of

mists called dead and gone forever—in the words of one of their more apt pupils, "a type of economic society such as had never before appeared in the history of the world and can never exist again" (Beard, 1928a, 132). Our lucky accident of the endless space that created this world is translated into a Jeffersonian curse on the modern era, a curse in the form of political mendacity and constitutional illusion. This is what Beard and Croly learned from the new political economists.

In simple and positive form, the lessons of the new industrial economy are these. To enrich the local realty or "rent" economies beyond their own increased productivity and efficiency requires gaining access to industrial profits. These profits are earned by adding real value to the economy, providing wages, new investment, dividends, and interest. Job growth also constitutes the major market for agricultural products and therefore underwrites the prosperity of all of the towns and cities in the productive agricultural parts of America. To redistribute politically from these profits in order to increase (or even to maintain) the wealth of the nonindustrial sector is simply shifting national income from earned profits to unearned rents, with small gains for the general welfare and larger losses of future economic growth. And land rent, unlike all other forms of unearned rent such as special skills or talents, has very little redeeming economic value. Most nonland rent and all profits are earned and productive; all capital gains from land not tied to increased investment and productivity are unearned speculative gain. And although it is true that this redistribution would also increase land values in the industrial core region, the recipients, landowners participating in commercial agriculture and living in the core, know that they will be equally or perhaps more enriched if the redistribution does not take place. These recipients know their dependent relationship; those on the economic periphery do not. This was the basis of the Republican party in the North after the Civil War. It was this same combination of finance, industry, industrial labor, and mechanized agriculture that achieved hegemonic victory after 1896.[82]

The implications of this economic analysis are both profound and profoundly disturbing in the context of the American political system. Simon Patten put the case most systematically, and Croly, who studied Patten's work, put it most forcefully. First Patten:

Charles Beard to refute J. Allen Smith's populist and sentimental *Spirit of American Government* (ibid., 47–62).

82. Zunz, 1990, 149–74, shows the penetration of the railroads and agricultural machinery corporations into the daily lives of Midwestern farmers. The contrast of this penetration and its absence in the South is striking.

The real struggle is not between two classes [i.e., management and labor] but between two forms of industry. Industry either exploits some general advantage, in which case its surplus is profits, or it exploits local advantage the resulting income of which is mainly rent. Centralized industries divide those interested in it into two classes, the controllers who direct, supervise or manage, and the machine workers upon whose activity the industry depends. The one class is interested in centralized profits; the other in personal super-wages. Between these two forms of income there are no fixed limits. Either can grow at the expense of the other. Every new struggle leads to a new compromise in which some advantage comes to the workers. . . . [The other form of industry consists] in the exploitation of local advantage . . . which unites the rent of situation with the super-wage of efficiency. . . . Such a capitalist does not think of his joint income as arising from distinct funds: he blends it by a recomposition of values into one fund and thinks of it as due to his activity. . . . This class grows with the rise of rent and loses with the increase of centralized profits. . . . The present struggle is not between the rich and the poor but between centralized and localized wealth.[83]

Whether called "centralized industry," "the new industrial economy," or "the leading institutions of 'voluntary socialism,'" public good in America rests on the profits and investments generated from this sector. The interests of wage labor are inseparable from this economy; insofar as their welfare and interests are not heeded, the national interest suffers. Parastate institutions such as the National Civic Federation expressed this same assumption (a sort of holding company of voluntary socialisms).[84] The need to organize wage labor in the core economy and even ruthlessly to discriminate against the unorganized worker is on the same order of urgency as is the need to shield this entire economy from the raids and depredations of the periphery. Just as the strikebreaking scab in the core must be banished so that he cannot

83. Patten, 1912, 303 and 336. These views were formulated much earlier by Patten in his historical critiques of Ricardo, Malthus, and Mill. See Patten, 1889a, 19–32, and 1902, 88–93. His 1912 formulations are used here because this is what Croly read and cited in his *Progressive Democracy*.

84. John R. Commons, the pioneer labor economist at Wisconsin and intellectual founder of the "Wisconsin Idea" of allying the university to the state for political reform, was executive secretary of this organization from 1902 to 1904. Headquartered in Chicago, it brought together labor unions, investment banking, and large monopolistic or oligopolistic industries and utilities. For a "Jeffersonian socialist" critique, Weinstein, 1968; and in much broader terms, Bensel, 1984.

destroy "workman's property" and responsibility,[85] so too must small businessmen and farmers on the periphery be prevented from looting this economy so that they can raise their local land values under cover of democratic virtue.[86]

What Croly calls "territorial democracy" is the politics of local advantage as monopoly rent in the economic periphery. This model of conflict outlined by the Progressive political economists becomes, in the hands of Beard and Croly, the analytical tool by which to explain American political history and outline contemporary political choices. The resulting "Progressive" history could, therefore, cut both ways: a defense of the modernizing, Hamiltonian tradition (Croly, Beard) or a defense of traditional and localized ways of life that the prevailing system of "rights" always tends to protect. Croly's summary is a precis of Beard's *Economic Origins of Jeffersonian Democracy*:

> Thus, the policy of the territorial democracy in attempting to destroy the privileges enjoyed by organized capital cannot fairly be described as one which seeks to abolish all privilege. Rather is it an attempt to do away with one particular kind of favoritism in order that another particular kind of favoritism, which operates in the interest of a larger class, may be released from inconvenient encumbrances. . . . Local advantages are quite as much a matter of

85. Croly, 1909, 386–87: "To incorporate [the labor union] into the American legal system, is equivalent to the desertion by the state of the non-union laborer. . . . A democratic government has little or less reason to interfere on behalf of the non-union laborer than it has to interfere in favor of the small producer. As a type the non-union laborer is a species of industrial derelict." The parallel to national recognition and incorporation of large industries and trusts is almost exact: "It is not an explicit discrimination against their small competitors, but amounts to such discrimination. If the small competitor is to be allowed a chance of regaining his former economic importance, he must receive the active assistance of the government. Its policy must become, not one of recognition, but one of recognition of conditions which would impair the efficiency of the large industrial organization" (358). This is what Patten meant in his cryptic statement: "The choice is between a political socialism that would absorb all profits and such direct action on the part of [wage] laborers as will insure them a share in the social surplus" (Patten, 1912, 305; see also 307–8, for his critique of wage policy discussion in the ICC).

86. When Wilson became president and the income tax law was passed, these conflicts were quickly resolved in favor of realty interests and the periphery. At the original 1913 rates, Chicago alone paid more income tax than all eleven of the ex-confederate states combined, while four states, New York, Pennsylvania, Massachusetts, and Illinois, paid 60 percent of all corporate and income taxes (Sanders, 1990, 191).

privilege, in their effect upon their proprietors and society, as is an exclusive franchise or a protective duty.[87]

Having surveyed the economic arguments from the Civil War to the time he was writing in 1914, Croly concludes that the Democratic party had become simply too self-contradictory and ill equipped, as a party, to sustain any serious reform.[88] And the regular Republicans, having successfully sponsored the new industrial economy, returned to defending laissez faire and private property rights under the myth that their policy bestowed equal benefits and "rights" for all. Both Democrats and Republicans were wrong in assuming "that no necessary privilege attaches to property as property, that a system of equal rights wrought in the interest of property owners can be kept an essentially unprivileged system by withdrawing the active encouragement which the government has been granting to specific productive agencies" (Croly, 1914, 109). Only if policy choices are not viewed legally, as bestowing particular rights (privi-lege = private law), are not seen "as a right of possession," but are viewed functionally "as an opportunity of achievement," can the prevailing system of privilege "be gradually socialized in the manner of [its] exercise" (Croly, 1914, 113–15).

Croly, like the new economists before him, clearly recognized that the post–Civil War Republican party consciously discriminated in favor of the industrial core and comparatively disadvantaged the South and West through a policy of high tariffs. This the economists viewed, however, as a kind of de facto national economic planning under cover of laissez faire and substantive due process of law, arguing that both the South and the West received more absolute benefits from this system than they might have from any regionally based alternative. And the nation as a whole benefited even more. To be sure, with a strong state and national administrative capacity, the distributive results and the economic growth would have been much improved (as in Germany) but this fairness and growth would still have remained within the core. Indeed, the new economists viewed the world of subsistence and tenant farms and the persistence of subsistence wage labor as a world that gradually had to be destroyed by relentless economic pressure. That world, marked by agriculture in most areas of the South and parts of the

---

87. Croly, 1914, 111–12. It took another ten years for these ideas to penetrate the American legal mind, but when they did, the results were shattering: Morris Cohen's "Property and Sovereignty" of 1928 is a brilliant example.

88. That Wilson could accomplish some authentically progressive reforms was due to his totally dictatorial position in a heterogeneous party of localities: each locality depended upon Wilson and his progressive appeal to win. That Wilson was a benign dictator does not detract from this conclusion (Croly, 1914, 335–46).

West, was one without hope and without a future.[89] *Those who live off that world and who seek to maintain it for their own benefit under the guise of rights or claims of social justice, i.e., local economic and political leaders in the periphery, do not deserve a serious hearing and must be defeated for the national good.* This was done in 1896 but could easily be undone in the future.

The other threat to the national economic interest was resistance to the improvement of the conditions and rewards of wage labor. So highly did Croly regard the improvement of industrial wage labor and the necessity of its complete organization and integration into the society, that he was quite willing to see the agricultural regions of the country become a kind of economic training ground for those currently unfit for the rigors and benefits of urban industrial society.

> If all, or almost all, the industrial labor of the country came to be organized in the manner proposed, the only important kind of non-union laborer left in the country would be agricultural; and such a result could be regarded with equanimity by an economic statesman. . . . If the supply of labor were regulated, and its efficiency increased as it would be under the proposed system, agricultural laborers would not have the opportunity of finding industrial work, except of the most inferior class, until their competence had been proved. . . . Moreover, farm labor is, on the whole, much more wholesome for economically dependent and mechanically untrained men than labor in towns or cities. . . . If they can be kept upon the farm until or unless they are prepared for a higher class of work, it will be the greatest possible boon to American farming.[90]

The political economy of Progressivism encoded an epitaph for democratic individualism in its most characteristic home. The small subsistence farm, that locus classicus of equal opportunity and manly independence, capitalized by little but muscle and hope, finally became a supplier of cheap nourishment and a reform school for the industrial

---

89. Patten, 1912, 302, calls those who live in that world "toilers" competing in the older, Ricardian economic world of "wage funds," rather than workers. He goes on to argue that social evolution will gradually spell their doom because their ways of life, if left unchanged and passed from generation to generation, will put them at increasingly severe disadvantages. Social policy should not prolong the agony of their eventual demise by subsidizing those ways of life.

90. Croly, 1909, 396. He, like the Progressive academics, many of whom were raised in the centers of successful capital-intensive agriculture (Patten, James, Commons, and Ross), saw the future of agriculture in specialization and in national and international markets. Zunz, 1990, 149–74, shows how right they were.

economy. And where it did not adapt to these conditions, it was consigned to the worst fate of all, a slow but unmourned death. This was the intellectual banishment much of the agricultural South and Southwest suffered, not only in the writings of the professional economists, but in the popular Progressive press generally. The curse of the post-Civil War South was its gradual reenslavement of the freedmen and poor whites in the grinding poverty of agricultural tenancy and subsistence farming. Every decade after the war ended, the number of farms in the southern states *increased*,[91] and every decade per capita income fell relative to the national average. In contrast, agriculture in both the "old" and the "new" Midwest was thriving in partnership with the new corporations. Farms were declining in numbers and rapidly and systematically increasing their productivity.[92] From the 1870s onward, both materially and morally, they were becoming an integral part of the new industrial economy.

THE NEW WOMAN AND THE NEW ECONOMICS

No survey of the horizon of Progressive political economists can be complete without addressing their treatment of women and economics in their writings. Although this issue will be considered separately in a

91. The superintendent of the 1880 census, Francis A. Walker, reported in a *Century* magazine article in 1882 that in eight southern states (Alabama, Arkansas, Florida, Georgia, Louisiana, Mississippi, North Carolina, and South Carolina) there were 369,000 farms in 1860, 490,000 in 1870, and 888,000 in 1880. Personal income fell from about 70–75 percent of the national average in the pre–Civil War period to less than 50 percent by 1900, and even this disguises the depth of poverty of the small and tenant farmers, given the great income disparities within the states of the old Confederacy. Other comparative data from the 1880s in James, 1992, 168. On income disparities in the South, Kousser, 1974, 246–50 and 267–68. This fall was not caused by the post–Civil War tariffs any more than it was reversed by the lowering of those tariffs when Wilson came into office (U.S. Bureau of the Census, 1975, 242). Contrast this portrait with Zunz, 1990, 149–74, on the integration of agriculture and the new corporations in the Midwest.

92. Zunz, 1990, 149–74. The Great Plains states increased their share of total agricultural production from 6 percent in 1869 to 30 percent in 1909. By 1920, 73 percent of the farm units in Iowa had automobiles. Many hundreds of salaried agents of the McCormick Company and International Harvester were to be found among all the market towns in these states, but not many were found in the South. United States Department of Agriculture county agents were stationed *only* in the South until after legislation in 1911, but they were concerned primarily with soil erosion and social welfare issues, not with scientific farming. In the first decades of the twentieth century Harvester alone had more agents in the field than did the USDA, but almost all were located in the Midwest. These agents were both part of the local community and carriers of a disciplined corporate ethic.

later discussion of feminism and woman's rights, it is important to introduce it here as a dramatic counterpoint to the tale of peripheral decline and subordination. A new and triumphal voice began to be heard in the land, that of the new woman of the urban industrial core and her allies throughout the small towns in the North and Midwest. In the eyes of the political economists the victory of the new industrialism and social justice required the efforts of both wage laborers and women. In turn, the new industrialism created the conditions for both female and labor emancipation. Some early feminists simply conflated the condition and future of women and the condition and future of wage labor: "Two great movements convulse the world today, the woman's movement and the labor movement. Each regards the other as of less moment than itself. Both are parts of the same world-process."[93] Many women's rights and feminist leaders were active in labor movements, including, but not restricted to, organizing women's labor organizations. The organizational and institutional affiliations of feminism, social reform, and labor were thoroughly intertwined.[94] Jane Addams both symbolized and helped create these interconnections.[95]

If any group in American society saw itself as enthusiastically committed to modernization and economic development along Progressive lines, it was the new feminist intellectuals.[96] Indeed, they and the new political economists were the first to recognize and integrate the woman question and issues of family life into economic analysis[97]—women had been as invisible in classical economic theory as they were in classical liberal political theory.[98] Most of the leading women Pro-

93. Gilman, 1911, 190–91; see also 260. Skocpol, 1992, 311–423, charts exactly this relationship, terming it "a maternalist welfare state," but showing how its vision was deflected by deep-seated political factors into protective legislation for women and children only and pensions for mothers.

94. There is a large and growing literature on this topic; a good summary is found in Davis, 1973, 92–109, on the role of Hull House; and Cott, 1987, chaps. 1 and 2. Scudder, 1898, and Gilman, 1898, each provided theoretical grounding for this equation; democracy is the fulfillment of both women and wage laborers.

95. From the very start, Hull House was a center of organizational initiatives on behalf of women workers; see Addams, 1892.

96. Gilman, 1904, was particularly enthusiastic about technological progress and the wonders of modern industry; like Patten, she saw this progress as a fulfillment of the kingdom of God in the victory of the "Christ ideal" on earth.

97. Those who wrote most extensively on women, the family, and economics were Simon Patten, Albion Small, and Charles Horton Cooley. Scott Nearing, Patten's student and fellow faculty member at Wharton, wrote extensively on women's issues, at least once with his wife, Nellie Nearing, who had a master's degree from the University of Pennsylvania.

98. The literature on this is immense and growing. A good recent summary is in Shanley and Pateman, 1991.

gressives who wrote on economic topics did so in the journals and through the organizational networks founded and run by these economists.[99] And when these women wrote in the popular magazines, they shared the same venues and usually the same values as these economists.

A good proof text for a summary of the relationship of women and Progressive views of the economy is *Woman and Social Progress*, coauthored by Nellie and Scott Nearing in 1912. Incorporating ideas from Lester Ward, Charlotte Perkins Gilman, Edith Abbott, Cicely Hamilton, Havelock Ellis, and G. Stanley Hall, it smoothly merges calls for freedom from older marriage and family patterns with new careers for women and the opportunity for educated women to be a vanguard in the fight for moral progress.

Physically robust from the splendid course in physical training, and the invigorating games of college life; trained to think accurately and clearly; learned in method of study and presentation; effective through the power of cooperation; and thoroughly alive to the desirability of making time and life count, these college girls furnish the most optimistic argument for the future of women. The college girl with her atmosphere of efficiency and capability, has penetrated every group of women who have the time and intelligence to think. Whether college educated or not, the women of America are taking their cue from the college graduate. *They see in her the prototype of what they might have been, and they take from her successes new inspiration for their efforts. The college girl is the type of the future for women.* But what shall she do? She can do anything she pleases.[100] (emphasis added)

99. Florence Kelley and Jane Addams each published books in the Macmillan Citizenship Series, edited by Richard Ely. Albion Small's *American Journal of Sociology* regularly opened its pages to both Addams and Kelley as well as to Charlotte Perkins Gilman, the leading feminist theorist of her day. From 1899 to 1924 Florence Kelley ran the National Consumer's League (NCL), of which John Commons was president in the early period. An excellent summary of the activities of Kelley and the NCL is in Skocpol, 1992, 383–96. Hull House was a center where academics, women's labor leaders, and reformers from the various women's and feminist movements often met and forged cooperative ventures.

100. Nearing and Nearing, 1917, 236. This triumphalism has a strong regional bias. Only in the North Central states, for example, did women play important roles in college education, accounting for 60 percent of all women faculty in the country in 1903–4. Only in this same region and in the West were women strongly represented in colleges. In the North Atlantic states, the ratio of men to women attending college was more than 7 to 1; in the North Central states, less than 2 to 1; and in the West, 3 to 2 (Bliss, 1908, 427). In 1900, more than half the undergraduates at the University of Chicago were women.

This triumphal conclusion is foreshadowed by a long analysis, borrowed largely from Gilman, on the ways in which technology and the industrial economy have gradually emptied the home of economic production, leaving in its wake fewer children to raise and more money and leisure to consume. The fact that middle class women can now work outside the home (or remain single or not establish households at all) means that the political economy of the marriage relationship has been permanently altered. For these women, as well as for stenographers and retail clerks and even factory girls, marriage need no longer be seen as a "trade," in the double sense of gaining a livelihood and selling one's body for economic security.[101] The industrial economy also empowers women within the marriage relationship in the same double sense. The home, now "a deserted workshop" (Nearing and Nearing, 1912, 41), emancipates women from the household economy as it opens new career opportunities in the national economy. These new opportunities can be either paid careers alongside or in equal competition with men[102] or, for women who may or may not wish to work

101. Nearing and Nearing, 1917, 78–87. This was the whole point of Gilman, 1898, stated in terms of anthropology and social evolution, and of Gilman, 1903, in terms of urban and industrial America. Gilman, 1898, 110: "She gets her living by getting a husband. He gets his wife by getting a living. It is to her individual economic advantage to secure a mate. It is to his individual sex-advantage to secure economic gain." In Nearing and Nearing, 1917, 161–70, the balance of power has now shifted, especially for the college woman: it is she who now can determine the future of the race because, having options outside of marriage, she can choose the fittest mate. Here again, the industrial economy has altered the sexual one, with a clear gain for morality and self-discipline: "The men who believe in sowing their wild oats cannot yet reconcile themselves to the new standard required of them . . . and consequently the better educated women may marry less often than their non-college sisters. But this is merely a transitional stage. As the demand grows— and it is growing—men will be compelled to meet the requirements of the college-woman standard" (114). This same ideal is expressed earlier in Gilman, 1898, 332–40 and, referring to Gilman, Ely, 1903, 172–73.

102. Nearing and Nearing, 1917, stress the ubiquity of women across jobs, careers, and skills in America at this time. Part of this display was deliberate government policy by Progressive officials to encourage more participation by women in the larger economy, for example, the 1907 Census Bureau publication, "Statistics of Women at Work, 1900." Zunz, 1990, 116–21 and 125–48, shows the relationship between the new corporation, its work environments and values, and social mobility for lower-middle- and middle-class single women. Unlike the Nearings' portrayal, Zunz's shows that white-collar clerical employees were rigidly separated in the new corporations (often separate entrances, lunchrooms, and the like) but suggests that the rigorous separation and moral supervision of young women by businesses such as Metropolitan Life were to insure a steady stream of young women employees because parents were reluctant to see them employed by strangers at a distance from home. Additionally, the overwhelming percentage of both male and female white-collar employees in these corporations had native-born parents and eagerly sought middle-class respectability.

for income, full-time careers in social service. This last type of career is the more interesting to explore here, because it holds out for women the prospect of social reform as a vocation, what Gilman termed "social motherhood." This higher vocation was symbolized by Jane Addams and was the major cause of her becoming a popular icon in this period.

Although the notion of careers in social service has often been portrayed more as a limit than as an opportunity for women, at that time and for these feminists it was seen as a direct path to independence, status, and power. Organized philanthropy, professionalized by the new graduate schools in social work and criminology; women's industrial unions and other labor organizations; suffrage organizations; and the entire complex of new social and civic organizations constituted a rich and challenging field of choice for the woman college graduate. Whether these vocations were in addition to marriage or not, they were products of the new industrial economy that, in turn, made possible the emancipation of women from the earlier domestic economy of the household.

This focus on the college woman and her career choices does not do justice to the larger argument of either the new economists or the feminists. Suffice it to say here, however, that both groups thought that the needs of society and the promise of the collective goods that a social surplus is able to supply were too pressing to tolerate the waste of the talents that all women could come to possess. The contempt that the Nearings, Gilman, Addams, Kelley, and others express for unproductive women of leisure was mirrored by their praise of the factory girl, the secretary, and the sales clerk over the hired domestic.[103] Not everyone was fortunate enough to do well by doing good, but everyone had a duty

---

103. Addams, 1902, 116: "The domestic employee is retained in the household largely because her 'mistress' fatuously believes that she is thus maintaining the sanctity of family life." Kelley, 1905, 112, refers to "the unsought leisure of prosperous women" as "a free gift of the new industrial order," which must be paid in the coin of social service and social responsibility in employment, expenditure, and socially responsible consumption. Gilman, 1898, 120–21: "As priestess in the temple of consumption, as the limitless demander of things to use up, her economic influence is reactionary and injurious . . . this false market, this sink into which human labor vanishes with no return." Nearing and Nearing, 1917, 54–55, make the choice that of "voluntary sex parasitism" or vocation: "If women use their leisure to develop what gifts they may possess, to do the work which opportunity offers, then will the blandishments of the parasite sink to their real value, and righteousness prove its own reward through the blessedness of constructive effort." This contempt is mirrored in a hatred of prostitution and anger at the need for virtuous women to compete for men in a corrupt market of appearance and eroticism. Gilman, 1911, 60–61, 140, and 176, speaks of this condition as constituting "humiliation," "degradation," and "ignominy" of such depth that "angels weep." For further discussion of this theme in the context of the new ideal of marriage, see chapter 6 below.

to contribute to the common good up to her capacity. And those with the most talents and energy had a special duty to point the way, both by their own examples and by helping to create the political and economic environments that aligned personal and public purpose. In this sense, Progressive feminists were direct heirs of abolitionism, which combined emancipation of both women and slaves from economic and sexual bondage.[104]

104. Walters, 1977, 70–110. The radical labor activist and professor of English literature at Wellesley, Vida Scudder, made this connection explicit. "To realize a spiritual democracy for the victims and outcasts of the Old World is a task before which we may indeed quail. . . . But, turning back to the lives of our fathers, surely we see in the warfare against slavery of the negro a prophecy of our larger conflict against evil [of the modern slavery of trade] less evident, but more deeply imbedded in the social body." Scudder ends with a depiction of this new emancipation as socialism, the realization, after centuries of estrangement, of a perfect remarriage between Democracy and Christianity (1898, 210–11 and 318). The sexual imagery following from this is discussed in chapter 6 below. These feminists and their ideas did not at all sink into oblivion. Gilman's name and ideas lived on into the 1950s through Mary and Charles Beard's popular American history text (Beard and Beard, 1927, 2: 431 and 721).

6

NATIONAL DEMOCRACY
& PERSONAL FREEDOM

Across the range of Progressive writings and throughout this entire period one finds a persistent attack on rights and individualism as worthy foundations for American national democracy. In their economic writings Progressive intellectuals constructed a powerful case against theories of property rights premised on natural rights. All rights to property, they argued, should be seen as granted by the community contingent on the performance of duties set by the community. The rejection of natural rights as a foundation for moral or political reasoning was not even considered to require a defense; what was contentious was their claim that rights per se should be considered as neither primary or autonomous. This denial of the primacy of rights took many forms and was deployed in many different settings, but behind these forms and settings is a psychological, social, and political theory in explicit opposition to the "rights talk" that legitimated the regime of courts and parties in the nineteenth-century polity. The direct form of the Progressive critique was familiar enough: any social evolutionary view of man and society must reject as a starting point both the autonomous individual and the idea that there is a fundamental dualism between society and the individual. The indirect critique of rights consisted in linking rights-based thinking to the institutions and practices in the United States most condemned by informed moral opinion.

The most obvious form of this latter critique was to link rights claims to individualism and individualism to selfishness and greed. Here, the most powerful counter discourse was that of Christian citizenship expressed as the social gospel. Simon Patten, for example, lists as one of the ten principles of social Christianity "the doctrine of social responsibility, in contrast with individual rights." The northern Baptist theologian and ecumenical leader, Samuel Zane Batten, declares in *The Christian State*, "just so far as democracy means the enthronement of self-interest and the apotheosis of individual desire . . . so far it becomes an iniquitous and dangerous thing." George Herron declared more than a decade earlier that "the law of self interest is the eternal falsehood which mothers all social and private woes; for sin is pure individualism." Until political life is emancipated "from merely individual theories of freedom, it cannot see the divine social kingdom."[1]

Rights as individualism was also attacked as the source of social disintegration. John Dewey, in one of his earliest essays, "The Ethics of Democracy," maintains that a theory of democracy premised on isolated individuals and aggregate majorities is

> in effect, simply an account of anarchy. To define democracy simply as the rule of the many, as sovereignty chopped up into mince meat, is to define it as abrogation of society, as society dissolved, annihilated. When so defined, it may be easily shown to be instable to the last degree, and so difficult that a common will must be manufactured—if not by means of a contract, then by means of a combined action of the firm of Party and Corruption.[2]

Charles Horton Cooley, Dewey's colleague at Michigan in this early period, showed the ways in which individual rights rested on formal-legal assumptions about social and political institutions. This combination is false both to life and to the requisites for moral and political order. Writing what must stand as one of the most biting criticisms of a "constitutionalist" understanding of American political life contained in a standard college textbook, Cooley declares:

> Formalism goes very naturally with sensuality, avarice, selfish ambition, and other traits of disorganization, because the merely formal institution does not enlist and discipline the soul of the individual, but takes hold of him by the outside. . . . The lower "individualism" of our time, the ruthless self-assertion which is so conspicuous, for example, in business, is not something apart from our institutions but expresses the fact that they are largely formal and unhuman, not containing and enlarging the soul of the individual. . . . In so far as it is true of our time that the larger interests of society are not impressed upon the individual, so that his

---

1. White and Hopkins, 1976, 133, quoting Patten; Batten, 1909, 215; Herron, 1894, 110; White and Hopkins, 1976, 174, quoting Herron.

2. Dewey, 1969, 131. This 1888 essay was a review of Sir Henry Maine's *Popular Government*, a favorite in earlier Mugwump culture and featured in Godkins's *Nation*. Batten, 1909, 247, calls the doctrine of "individualism and atomism . . . a doctrine of anarchy and confusion and can never bring social peace and progress."

private impulses cooperate with the public good, it is a time of moral disintegration.[3]

Although these critiques of democratic individualism abounded,[4] they shared the feature of equating rights discourse with what today is called "negative" liberty, the freedom *from* the authority of other persons and institutions. The alternative starting point for the Progressives was a conception of democratic citizenship informed by values of "positive" rather than "negative" liberty. Batten, while granting that the initial struggle for liberty "is almost wholly a story of negatives," insists that "true liberty is a positive thing, and to consider its negative aspects alone is to miss its high and divine significance. . . . True liberty means the voluntary sacrifice of self for the common life." Democracy must become "positive and constructive, . . . must now declare what are the things that are truly honorable and authoritative; it must now define and illustrate the true titles of nobility and worth" (Batten, 1909, 217, 219, 244).

This dichotomy was a litany in Progressive writings, voiced in the languages of economics, ethics, sociology, and religion. The economist Richard Ely defines "true liberty" as "the expression of the positive powers of the individual," which is possible only within a framework of "social solidarity." And because we can "thrive only in a common wealth . . . we fulfill our own mission and develop ourselves in body and mind" through obligations to others, through subscribing to a "social ethic." It is this ethic which unites "self and others, the individual and society . . . in one purpose."[5] Dewey's college textbook *Ethics* makes this same distinction.

3. Cooley, 1909, 349 and 351; see also his 1902, 422–31. Thomas M. Cooley was his father; one of the foremost constitutional scholars of his day, he was founding dean of Michigan's law school, first chairman of the ICC, and author of *A Treatise on the Constitutional Limitations Which Rest upon the Legislative Power of the States of the American Union*. Herbert Croly calls down an anathema on those who would reform by appeal to a rights-based vocabulary: "They do not realize . . . how thoroughly Jeffersonian individualism must be abandoned . . . and they do not realize how dangerous and fallacious a chart their cherished principle of equal rights may well become" (Croly, 1909, 153). And see his critique of the Bill of Rights as the basis of political theory (1914, 217–19); and Beard, 1928a, 106–11, for his complacent discussion of their lack of applicability. In a 1915 article in the *New Republic*, Croly summarized these same ideas in still another way: "Any graduate student fresh from the political science department of a contemporary university can triumphantly perform the work of demonstration. Abstract rights of any kind have ceased to command very much reverence" (quoted in Stettner, 1993, 111).

4. See, for example, Abbott, 1901, 68–100; Hadley, 1903, 73–99 and 126–49; Ross, 1918, 214–17 and 269; and discussion in Herbst, 1965, 118–20.

5. Ely quoted in Kloppenberg, 1986, 280 and 289. Croly calls for "the ideal of individual justice . . . being supplanted by the ideal of social justice" to express this same contrast (1914, 146).

Although negative expressions of liberty were necessary "in the struggle in which the moral personality has gradually won its way," it is only a sense of duty to society that "enable[s] an individual to realize the weight and import of the socially available and helpful manifestations of the tendencies of his own nature and to discriminate them from those which are socially harmful or useless. . . . [These] phenomena of duty in all their forms are thus phenomena attendant upon the expansion of [individual] ends and the reconstruction of character."[6] Like the social psychologists James Mark Baldwin and Charles Cooley writing earlier,[7] Dewey adroitly turned negative rights claims into an argument for positive liberty. The recognition and moral legitimacy of claims against society and government, he says, reside only in their predicted capacity to "be socially embodied" in new and higher duties. Disembodied claims for liberty, in contrast, are superficial and often destructive of social bonds because the agent seeks only to avoid liability defined by external rules. True liberty—what Dewey calls "effective freedom"—requires "positive control of resources . . . trained powers of initiative and reflection requisite for free preference and for circumspect and far-seeing desires" (Dewey and Tufts, 1908, 432, 438). In the concluding chapter in his sociology textbook, Cooley rejects the common notion of freedom as "the absence of constraint" as "not especially pertinent to our time and country."

If the word is to have any definite meaning in sociology, it must therefore be separated from the idea of a fundamental opposition between society and the individual, and made to signify something that is both individual and social. . . . The definition of freedom naturally arising from the chapters that have gone before is perhaps this: that it is *opportunity for right development*, for development in accordance with the progressive ideal of life that we have in conscience (Cooley, 1902, 422, 425, 423).

Significantly, Cooley then equates this notion of personal freedom to an equally developmental and progressive notion of collective freedom: any notion of personal freedom "that is not part of the general onward movement of society is not free in the largest sense." And if this is the case, "the social order is antithetical to freedom only in so far as it is a bad one. Freedom can exist only in and through social order . . . because nothing else can supply the multifarious opportunities by means of which all sorts of persons can work out a congenial development

6. Dewey and Tufts, 1908, 153 and 362–63. And see his 1888 essay in Dewey, 1969, 235–38. See Hadley, 1903, 126–28, contrasting early-nineteenth-century America to the present.

7. Baldwin, 1906, 551–52 and 562–67; Cooley, 1902, 422–31.

through the choice of influences.'' It only remained to show, then, that the matrix of free institutions—''government, churches, industries, and the like''—have as their primary purpose the growth of human freedom ''and in so far as they fail to perform this function, they are wrong and need reconstruction.''[8]

Whether this critique of negative liberty was put in economic, historical, psychological, or philosophical terms, the claims made for positive liberty were all anchored in strong conceptions of social or associational membership and political citizenship. One form of this expression was to say, with Batten, that ''personal freedom can come only through social regulation'' exercised by a matrix of political and social institutions. Another way this idea was expressed was to say with Dewey that, as the social order becomes more comprehensive and organizationally diversified, the opportunities for freedom are multiplied—but only if one also multiplies obligations to and through those organizations. Because institutions shape and empower individuals for action, Cooley concludes that ''all innovation is based on [institutional] conformity, all heterodoxy on orthodoxy, all individuality on solidarity.'' In the words of Hadley, freedom is ''an institution rather than a principle; a help to the realization of public morality, rather than a postulate of morality itself.''[9]

FREEDOM, EQUALITY, AND THE SOCIALLY CONSTITUTED SELF

Positive liberty is socially constructed and maintained by institutions. In the political sphere this relationship is often readily granted: political freedom substitutes self-government for external restraint, but the purpose achieved is still governance. This argument lies at the basis of the conclusion that political freedom is a hard-won historical achievement. In Lyman Abbott's words: ''Self-government is not an assumption on which we are to start in framing a government; it is the goal which we are to reach by means of government'' (Abbott, 1901, 100).

External political freedom and internal moral self-discipline are inseparably connected both as modes of self-government and as individual expressions of socially constituted and institutionally sustained

8. Cooley, 1902, 426–28. This sociological formulation mirrors Dewey's ideal of a pragmatic liberalism as a method combining social and individual development in a democracy. This formula has been forcefully restated in Anderson, 1990.

9. Batten, 1909, 245; Dewey and Tufts, 1908, 436; Cooley, 1909, 314; and Hadley, 1903, 44.

values. In a democracy the good citizen must strive to embody regard for the entire community, what Dewey called a *"generalized* individualism . . . which takes into account the real good and effective—not merely formal—freedom of *every* social member" (Dewey and Tufts, 1908, 472, emphasis added). This requisite of political democracy cannot be supplied by politics alone but requires the coordinated institutional power of the entire society. Indeed, proof that one is capable of self-government on these terms would necessarily require that one work actively to insure that all members of the society do in fact have the resources to participate as equal members. A "generalized individualism" is inseparable from "the democratic movement of emancipation of personal capacities, of securing to each individual an effective right to count in the order and movement of society as a whole" (Dewey and Tufts, 1908, 481). The very term "ethics of democracy" entails this notion of self and freedom; without this entailment, democracy would only be a mechanical register of individual preferences. Its citizens, lacking "powers of intelligent self-control . . . will be in bondage to appetite, enslaved to routine, imprisoned within the monotonous round of an imagery flowing from illiberal interests, broken only by wild forays into the illicit" (Dewey and Tufts, 1908, 438).

Charlotte Perkins Gilman begins her feminist analysis of work by identifying the "ego concept" as the basic error in social analysis. Whereas all people have separate desires and personal consciousness, we have them as (natural) animals and not as (social) persons: a distinctly "human consciousness is collective." People, like all animals, have either female or male sexual characteristics and impulses, but our common humanity and therefore our identities as persons—as women and men—are constructed in and through society. As social influences and interests increase, so each person enlarges his facilities and capacities, becoming more distinctly human. Sexual equality, then, emancipates everyone from a biological individualism powered by ego and sexual drives into a higher sphere of consciousness and human relationships.[10] Duty to our humanity is both the precondition and the

10. Gilman, 1904, 59; see also 79–124. In *Reconstruction in Philosophy* (1920), Dewey makes this same argument: "When the individual is taken as something given already, anything that can be done to him or for him can only be by way of external impressions and belongings: sensations of pleasure and pain, comforts, securities. . . . Only in the physical sense of physical bodies that to the senses are separate is individuality an original datum. Individuality in a social and moral sense is something to be wrought out. It means initiative, inventiveness, varied resourcefulness, assumption of responsibility in choice of belief and conduct. These are not gifts, but accomplishments" (1982, 191).

cause of progress; the victory of human consciousness is the victory of social consciousness.

In the modified Hegelian language of Cooley, without anchoring the self in social institutions that contain and transmit authoritative ideals of life, "we are ruled by native impulse and that private reason which may be so weak when detached from a rational whole; . . . it is as if each one should sit down to invent a language for himself." And like the "beautiful soul" excoriated by Hegel, Cooley contrasts the "whining questions" constantly afflicting those who seek to evade their clear social duties as husband or wife or worker or parent to the "pride in . . . self-devotion" of those who "know what their duty is and have no other thought than to do it." Without the ethical resources of free institutions by which and through which to discover and express one's identity, the individual will have no choice but to be in perpetual opposition to the larger society, "and in turning against others he destroys himself. The embittered and distracted individual must be a bad citizen."[11]

RIGHTS AS RESOURCES
AND RESPONSIBILITIES

The ethical resources necessary for the exercise of positive liberty in a democracy must be complemented by many other resources essential for a self-determined life. In the textbooks on philosophy, sociology, and economics and in reform writings intended for the larger public, discussions of rights as positive liberty became calls for the social provision of resources deemed essential for their exercise. In this way, an individual-rights language reappeared but now firmly tied to its positive origins within the framework of social duty. This relationship is most clearly seen in the earlier discussion of industrial wage labor. Society has a duty to restrict working hours and Saturday labor, and workers should demand these restrictions as a right; but these claims can only be honored in the context of the requisites for equal participation in a democratic society. Regular and organized leisure is a necessary resource for self-help, self-improvement, and "sustained intelligence in the voting constituency" (Kelley, 1905, 109). Society has a duty to encourage and support trade unions and workers have a right to form and join them because "the creation of an industrial organization . . . will

11. Cooley, 1909, 353–54. This mirror's Gilman's contempt for those who condemn the rich for being social parasites, but "who would do the same thing if [they] had the chance" because they share the same individualist economic and social theories (1904, 346).

serve to make individual workers enlightened, competent and loyal citizens of an industrial commonwealth'' (Croly, 1914, 379). Society has a duty to provide and make universal compulsory public schooling, and every child has a right to an education because ''this is a precedent to self-government.'' Just as monarchies provide for the education of the king's children, so democracies must provide for the education of their future rulers: ''the children of the people are educated by the state because they are to rule the state. In America we all belong to the royal family; therefore the state educates us all.''[12]

Educational rights, industrial rights, women's rights, and political rights were all justified ''positively'' as resources necessary for effective participation in a democratic society. Indeed, discussions of the social requisites for individuality and the economic, social, and political requisites for maintaining free government were of one piece. In a book on wealth creation, Simon Patten discusses the distribution of income as modified by economic rights and the ways in which their guarantee underwrites future economic growth in an industrial economy. He most naturally starts with ''market rights'' to insure openness and transparency of exchanges, security of property, and freedom to cooperate in economic undertakings; but then he adds three other categories of rights as resources. Included under ''social rights,'' Patten lists rights to a home, to homogeneity of population, and to decisions by public opinion; under ''rights to leisure,'' recreation, cleanliness, and scenery; and under ''exceptional rights,'' those of the poor and unemployed to relief and those of women to independent provision of income.[13]

Dewey makes a similar argument for the provision of material and intellectual resources in his discussion of the ways in which freedom and responsibility can be understood in their ''positive central meaning.'' For Dewey, social progress and democracy consist in the continuous process of translating formal-legal rights exercised by the few into universally available positive ones.

> It is the possession by the more favored individuals in society of an effectual freedom to do and to enjoy things with respect to which the masses have only a formal and legal freedom, that arouses a sense of inequity, and that stirs the social judgement and will to . . . reforms [to] transform the empty freedom of the less favored individuals into constructive realities (Dewey and Tufts, 1908, 439).

12. Abbott, 1901, 153–55. Abbott explicitly rejects both charitable and in loco parentis justifications for compulsory schooling, and he insists that moral education must be a central part of the curriculum (164–65).
13. Patten, 1902a, chap. 3. See also Abbott's discussion of ''industrial rights,'' 1901, chap. 4.

These rights include physical rights to decent living conditions and personal security and rights to economic welfare, especially the right to work. But note the conflation of right and duty: "Until there is secured to and imposed upon all members of society the right and the duty of work in socially serviceable occupations, with due return on social goods, rights to life and free movement will hardly advance much beyond their present largely nominal state." This same right or duty obtains for "rights to mental activity" or freedom of thought. So long as the spiritual treasures of mankind are the property of the few and while most men do not have sufficient leisure, even rights of speech and conscience remain only formal and ineffective (Dewey and Tufts, 1908, 445–48).

A not-so-hidden corollary of treating rights as effective resources for their positive exercise is that their equal provision carries with it a much heightened demand for self-discipline. Equal rights read in this way is another way of saying that to the extent that they are insured, the average American runs out of excuses for irresponsible and socially destructive behavior. The possession of these rights, like the possession of property or of extraordinary talents, is a trust, even when the possessors include most members of the society.[14] And every extension of positive rights carries with it an expectation of higher average standards of behavior. In today's language, Progressives treated emancipation as empowerment but added that empowerment entails expectations of more social responsibility and greater self-discipline. Given their institutional analysis of the socially constituted self, this relationship is implicit. Given their theories of the relationship between individual and social reform, this relationship is necessary. And given their commitment to democracy as the enhanced capacity for self-government, this relationship is a good to be desired and struggled for. Nowhere are these parallel arguments made more clearly than in discussions of women and freedom.

"WHEN THE MOTHER OF THE RACE IS FREE"

Framing Progressive discussions of freedom from the standpoint of the woman question reveals both their differences from the nineteenth-century discourse of rights and the relationship Progressives sought to establish between personal freedom and national democracy. From the beginnings of mass political parties associated with Jacksonian democ-

14. This understanding of rights was also implicit in much of the earlier abolitionist literature and underlines the inseparability of emancipation and social control. See Walters, 1978, chaps. 5 and 6, and discussion of hegemony in chapter 1 above.

racy there was a perverse dependence of democratic individualism on the denial of rights to Negroes and women.[15] Their legal subordination constituted the unbridgeable dividing line above which all white males were equal. Thus, both the pride of citizenship and a distinct American political identity were constructed in opposition to both nonwhites and women. Paradoxically, then, to urge emancipation for either women or slaves (or equal rights for Negro males in the North) was seen as a threat to equal rights and democratic individualism.[16] All white men were equal because each stood in the same superior relationship to all women and to all Negroes. If that foundation of equality were removed, "aristocracy" as hierarchy could soon reappear in political life. In the case of freed slaves, voting qualifications would necessarily be reintroduced, qualifications that some blacks would meet and some whites would not. In the case of women, suffrage would not only further empower many women who already possessed resources far superior to those of most men—witness the success of prohibition in states and localities— it would undermine the political role of the father in the family. Without the resource of that form of patriarchal authority and identity, the average American white male would have little else to fall back on. With that resource he could have pride in his citizenship and his freedom without the need to make any substantive demands on himself.[17] Equality and negative freedom were his from birth. Democracy on these terms made the costs of citizenship, like the costs of public lands following Indian removal, very cheap.

If it can be said that all horizons privilege, then the horizon of nineteenth-century equal rights was the privilege all white men had over all

15. Peterson, 1966. Most anti-Jacksonian political movements were products of evangelical culture and espoused values closely associated with later feminism. See also Watson, 1992, on this "ambiguous legacy" of Jacksonian democracy.

16. Howe, 1979, 23–68 and 181–209, on differences between Jacksonians and Whigs; Peterson, 1966, 137, 143, and 214–33, on the relationship between the achievement of universal white male suffrage and new restrictions of male Negro suffrage in New York; Morgan, 1972, on slavery and democracy. Both Jeffersonian and Jacksonian thought was liberal-individualist at the national level, but would allow strong and intrusive government, and thus "civic republican" virtues, within homogeneous regions, states, and communities. This same duality informed Jacksonian ideas of the proper constitution of the Democratic party as discussed in Jaenicke, 1986.

17. This is exactly what Tocqueville saw as the weakness of American individualism and what Croly sought to overcome with a national democracy. Kann (1990, 57–62 and 72–77) argues that this burden fell largely on women who, without formal political power, were held responsible for inculcating civic virtue. Underneath a formal liberalism was a hidden and largely gendered civic republicanism. This argument, in the context of the welfare state, is amplified in Skocpol, 1992, 311–72.

women and all people of color.[18] Hints of what an alternative national horizon might be are found almost everywhere in writings urging the extension of women's rights. Anna Howard Shaw, president (1902–15) of the National American Woman Suffrage Association (NAWSA), argued that American women needed the suffrage more than French women or English women because the latter two were ruled by their own kind whereas "in this country American women are governed by every kind of man under the light of the sun. There is no race, there is no color, there is no nationality of men who are not the sovereign rulers of American women."[19] A parallel argument, made in terms of character, was voiced in the authoritative *History of Woman Suffrage*, edited by Susan B. Anthony and Ida Husted Harper.[20]

These arguments were buttressed by more explicitly feminist ones as well. Voting rights for women would materially and symbolically augment a distinct and needed voice in American politics. Even without the vote, women reformers, with their many allies and with extensive organizational and communication networks, were already a powerful force in the land, starting with the prohibition movements of the late 1870s and growing by the year. Indeed, extensions of women's rights requiring only (male) state legislative changes or (male) judicial decision and not constitutional change requiring popular majority assent, were an unalloyed success story, at least outside the South.[21] Moreover, legislated reforms of a broader nature dealing with mothers' pensions, child

18. Given federalism, for many Americans there were really two separate horizons, regional or local, and national. The latter, under the Constitution as a "neutral framework," also legitimated as equal these separate and more provincial identities. In this way, a southern yeoman or slaveholder could see himself as the independent and equal citizen of his county and state in the same way that the New England citizen could see himself in his town meeting: and, for that reason, both could see themselves as free and equal Americans as if no horizon existed at all.

19. Quoted from Kraditor, 1965, 126. The NAWSA was by far the largest and most powerful of the woman suffrage organizations at this time. Under the leadership of Shaw, the organization grew from about 17,000 members in 1905 to more than 100,000 in 1915. Ibid., chap. 1, for an overview of women's rights organizations and state suffrage laws. It was no accident that the white South and the ethnic-Catholic North found a common home in the Democratic party.

20. Quoted in Kraditor, 1965, 94: "A real democracy has not as yet existed, but . . . the dangerous experiment has been made of enfranchising the vast proportion of crime, intemperance, immorality and dishonesty, and barring absolutely from the suffrage the great proportion of temperance, morality, religion and conscientiousness; that in other words, the worse elements have been put into the ballot-box and the best elements kept out" (from vol. 4, 1902).

21. In the preface to vol. 4, *History of Woman Suffrage*, Susan B. Anthony declares complete victory, except for the vote, for the 1848 program, that is, "to acquire an education, to earn a living, to claim her wages, to own property, to make contract, to bring suit, to testify in court, to obtain a divorce for just cause, to possess her children, to claim a fair share of the accumulations during marriage" (quoted in Kraditor, 1965, 79).

labor, delinquency, and prostitution—all viewed as the special concern of women and urged by women's organizations—were successful even without woman suffrage. A final "constitutional" victory, however, would symbolically legitimate that voice and, perhaps, bestow increased power and prestige on the organizational expressions of feminist values in the society.

Furthermore, their victory would be a victory of northern ideals of the family, evangelical Protestant ideas of morality in politics, and Federalist-Whig-Republican ideas of antipartyism and national citizenship. By the early twentieth century, these values were already clearly ascendent. Woman qua woman, an ever-growing audience was told, embodied many of the values of increasing importance in the modern age: the entire logic of social evolution favored the traits that women already possessed. For Gilman, political rights for women would correct the distortions in political practices and institutions caused by male monopoly of them:

Men have made a human institution into an ultra-masculine performance; and, quite rightly, feel that women could not take part in politics *as men do.* That it is not necessary to fulfill this human custom in so masculine a way does not occur to them. Few men can overlook the limitations of their sex and see the truth; that this business of taking care of our common affairs is not only equally open to women and men, but that women are distinctly needed in it (Gilman, 1911, 223).

As early as the 1880s Frances E. Willard declared that "woman's evolution has carried her beyond [men]" but with the spur of equality, men will be able to "climb to the same level some day."[22] The equation of women with advanced morality and self-control was symbolized by the canonization of Jane Addams. In a contest in 1906 to discover "Who is the best woman in Chicago," Addams not only won, but she and fellow settlement-house workers monopolized the first four positions.[23]

But the clearest relationship between freedom for women and reform-

22. From Davis, 1973, 91. This difference, she adds, gives him "a sense of larger liberty and her an instinct of revulsion," perhaps explaining why "the loves of women for each other grow more numerous each day," especially now that "any capable and careful women [sic] can honorably own her own support" (90–91).

23. Davis, 1973, 199. The contest rules stipulated that contestants be restricted to unmarried women because "unless a married woman ignores the wishes of her husband it is difficult for her to achieve the same degree of goodness that the unmarried woman does."

ing the nation—between rights and substantive power—was in discussions of the marriage relationship. Like John Stuart Mill, who commented upon it in his 1869 essay on the subjection of women, American feminist intellectuals and their male allies knew that the prevailing political economy of marriage would forever frustrate the achievement of the society they envisioned. Without major changes in the marriage relationship, distinctly feminine virtues in American public life could be directly expressed only by unmarried women (or those few married women in decidedly unconventional marriages), leaving their married counterparts with the secondary task of socializing males to higher ideals through their roles as wives, mothers, and Sunday school teachers. And given the increasing socialization of life and therefore the demand for a higher social ethic, women in traditional marriages would be increasingly less positioned to understand and to inculcate that ethic.[24] In Gilman's language, men are in fact "more human" than women because of their privileged opportunities to participate in the larger society, even though women qua women have precisely those values that the larger society needs to make it more human.[25] Like Mill, these feminists viewed the economic and psychic dependencies in the marriage relationship as one of the last remaining barriers to the achievement of a true democracy. Within the context of the implicit exchange of sex for support and all of the competition for wives and husbands, the family that occurred was portrayed exactly the way Mill portrayed it, "a school of despotism" that undermines and distorts the better lessons taught in the larger society and culture. If families could become transformed into schools of national democratic citizenship, progress in all areas of American life would be insured.[26]

Gilman was the most influential exponent of this explicitly feminist

24. This is the larger message of Addams, 1902, chaps. 1–4; and Gilman, 1903.

25. Gilman, 1911, 184 and 235. Her larger argument, of course, is that male or "androcentric" culture has appropriated and therefore distorted the socially created and distinctly "human" sphere of life (22–25 and 132–35).

26. Mill, 1970, 174. Gilman, 1911, 40, echoes this depiction: "The child should receive in the family, full preparation for his relation to the world at large. His whole life must be spent in the world, serving it well or ill; and youth is the time to learn how. But the androcentric [male dominated] home cannot teach him. We live to-day in a democracy—the man-made family is a despotism." Mill (1970, 160 and 166) was not reticent about the content of this despotism. The family is the last enclave where animal passion can be expressed without discipline: "He can claim from her and enforce the lowest degradation of a human being, that of being made the instrument of an animal function contrary to her inclinations . . . this power seeks out and evokes the latent germs of selfishness in the remotest corners of his nature . . . offers to him a license for the indulgence of those points of his original character which in all other relations he would have found it necessary to repress and conceal, and the repression of which would in time have become a second nature."

position, but muted variants of her argument were voiced by Progressives generally.[27] The reason for her influence was less her claims for women's legal rights than the fact that her feminist vision was seamlessly interwoven into a social evolutionary perspective that ratified the new industrial economy, embraced the cosmopolitan perspectives of the new sociology, and recommended the same order of socialized discipline to bring about social fulfillment. Her case for the restructuring of the marriage relationship on the basis of equality did not rest on any claims of natural or human rights or on any a priori assumption of sameness deserving of legal recognition in marriage.

Her entire argument is shaped within a social-evolutionary perspective resting on a materialist theory of moral advance. Historically, the economic dependency of women on men and the male need to struggle against other males for economic sustenance was a natural necessity—and remains a necessity in most parts of the world. Like Patten's depiction of the structural and value requisites of a "pain" economy, Gilman's story of the transition to conditions necessary for a new marriage relationship is the achievement of the abundance, surplus, and leisure that comes from the physical, intellectual, and organizational mastery of nature.[28] This mastery is not of external nature alone: democracy and moral progress require a parallel self-mastery. But whereas the conditions of the larger society now warrant the hope of achieving an order within which equal and authentic freedom can be experienced by every member, the traditional family relationship necessarily prevents its fulfillment. Men will never be able to exercise full self-mastery over their instincts so long as they continue to enjoy such a "cheap and easy lordship" over their economically dependent wives. Wives, in turn, will lack the psychic and moral resources to fulfill their goal "to make more feminine, and so more human, the male of the human race." So long as their self-interest and security depends upon being "over-sexed" to compete in the marriage market and to maintain the marriage relationship, that long will women remain a barrier to human progress.[29]

A further connection between Progressive discussions of freedom

27. Patten, a close student of Mill's writings, had already gendered Mill's entire economic theory, especially pointing to the influence of Harriet Taylor in introducing the role of "social ideals" (Patten, 1899, 336–39; see also 318–35). Because of the close publishing dates, there is no evidence that either Gilman or Patten was aware of the other's work, even though they run strikingly parallel. One explanation is that both Gilman and Patten had been heavily influenced by Lester Ward.

28. Gilman, 1898 and 1911, on the distinctly feminist argument; 1904, on the economic or material preconditions for sexual equality.

29. Gilman, 1898, 337 and 132; see also 31–39. This same argument is restated in 1911, 26–43, in terms of a three-sided distinction of male, female, and human, with the third category a restatement of Progressive political economy and sociology.

and feminist discussions of rights was a shared religious vision. As befitted the relative of Harriet Beecher Stowe and Lyman Beecher, Gilman's argument about "androcentric" or male-dominated distortions of human development and social advance is also a story of female atonement and humanity's salvation.[30] Although this is most clearly expressed in her discussions of the triumph of the "Christ ideal" fulfilled in a truly socialized consciousness,[31] her gendered story of evolution makes the age-old sacrifice of the woman in the household the precondition for eventual triumph. This atonement story begins with a disclaimer that "a purely feminine culture would have advanced the world more successfully" or that to men can be attributed "a wholly evil influence." Rather, like biblical history generally, and certainly through its Hegelian gloss, sacrifice and suffering are necessary to vouchsafe ultimate victory.

> The mother instinct, through nature, is one of unmixed devotion, of love and service, care and defense, with no self-interest. The animal father, in such cases as he is of service to the young, assists the mother in her work in similar fashion. But the human father in the family with the male head soon made that family an instrument of desire, and combat, and self-expression. . . . We have to-day reached a degree of human development where both men and women are capable of seeing over and across the distinctions of sex, and mutually working for the advancement of the world. Our progress is, however, seriously impeded by what we may call the masculine tradition.[32]

The triumph of humanity is the victory of race over sex, race meaning "human race" at its highest levels. Although women grievously suffered within the "sexuo-economic" despotism of the family, this suffering prepared the way for progress and eventual equality in a common humanity. "If the female [from the start] had remained in full per-

---

30. The relationship among feminism, moral reform, and a Christ-centered atonement theology is long standing. Douglas, 1988, 124–28, on major books marking this theology, especially Horace Bushnell's *The Vicarious Sacrifice;* Kuklick, 1985, 161–230, on this theology from Bushnell to John Dewey; and see Patten's formulation, 1899, 359–60.

31. Gilman, 1904, 119–21, concluding that this emancipates us from "the narrow limits of personal life, that poor animal existence" and gives us a victory over death because the distinctly human "I" is "Human Life," which is immortal.

32. Gilman, 1911, 131–32; see also 193–207; 1904, 267–372; and 1898, chap. 7. Douglas, 1988, 128, discusses the way in which Sara Hale in the 1850s also portrayed the drama of the Atonement in sexual terms, with woman's vicarious sacrifices for man's sins finally assuring her "salvation [of] . . . the race."

sonal freedom and activity, she would have remained superior to [the male] and both would have remained stationary." Now, however, "the period of women's economic dependence is drawing to a close," making possible the substitution of "inter-human" rather than merely "inter-sexual" love. Under these conditions, the "primitive form of sex-union chafes and drags," preventing as it always had marriages between "the best individuals . . . a union between man and woman such as the world has long dreamed of in vain" (Gilman, 137–44, passim). In teleological terms, "the relentless responsibilities of her duty as a mother" can now be fully realized; woman as the "race type" is now in the position to choose her mate, thereby fulfilling her destined role in heeding "the clarion call to redeem the race" (Gilman, 1911, 34, 49–50, 247; 1890).

Although Gilman's anthropological theories were not always accepted, her atonement story was integral to the Progressive mind. America redeemed is the race redeemed: "Women [in America] are growing honester, braver, stronger, more healthful and skilful and able and free, more human in all ways." Since women are able to select which kinds of men and which kinds of characteristics will be reproduced, the marriage relationship will no longer stand as a barrier to race improvement. "A new grade of womanhood we can clearly foresee; proud, strong, serene, independent; great mothers of great women and great men. These will hold high standards and draw men up to them; by no compulsion save nature's law of attraction" (Gilman, 1911, 250).

This beatific vision combined the new ideal of marriage with democracy in a union of ethics, religion, and politics. Gilman concluded her early book with the prediction that "When the mother of the race is free, we shall have a better world, by the easy right of birth and by the calm, slow, friendly forces of social evolution." In a poem dedicated to Jane Addams, biological and social motherhood is fused in this same imagery:

> Mother of races fusing into one,
> and keeping open house with presence sweet
> In that loud city where the nations meet
> Around thy ample hearth when day is done,
> When I behold the wild tribes thou hast won
> And see thee wooing from the witching street
> By thy own saintly face the erring feet,
> I know Love still has power beneath the sun (Davis, 1973, 205).

Vida Scudder ends her study of English and American literature by showing how its development points to the "marriage" of Christianity and democracy in an America of one united and equal people. As preface to this union, Scudder clearly sets the problem:

> Belief in democracy is the last demand of idealism. We are not likely to forget this: we whose national Credo must be spoken in the presence of the seething throngs of the outcasts of Europe. To look our national situation squarely in the face and say that the cure for democracy is more democracy requires a reverential trust toward humanity at large such as only the mystic who avoids men has in the past been able to hold with any degree of steadiness (Scudder, 1898, 246).

Writings such as the "Fabian Essays" in Britain and the flood of reform writings in America now bear "important witness to that invasion of the world of action by the idealists which we have signaled as one of the significant symptoms of these latter days." In Scudder's version, the marriage of democracy and Christianity in "these latter days" is socialism as the triumph of equality and justice.

> It is difficult, it is impossible, to define or describe a tendency of which we are all disciples; but so much it is safe to say,—that with the intellectual impulse toward the reconstruction of social theory, and the practical impulse toward the activity of social service, is blending more and more a spiritual impulse deeper than either of these, imperatively desiring and seeking the realization of the Kingdom of God on earth (Scudder, 1898, 287, 314).

Each of these tendencies are "imperfect alone [but] united they become a power." They are now "rushing together" and, once united, will constitute "a sacramental union" that "draws to a close . . . the long separation between democracy and Christianity" and makes possible "freedom for more perfect collective expression than has ever yet been seen on earth" (Scudder, 1898, 314, 318).

While voiced in terms of equal suffrage and legal equality in the marriage relationship, feminist claims for a recognition were also made in the name of a substantive vision of political and economic life that the exercise of these rights would bring into being. Democratic individualists in nineteenth-century America were fully aware of this. The connection between women's rights and Progressive goods posed a deep threat to their identities and impelled them to deny women and Negroes the vote to keep that vision from becoming a reality. In opposing women's rights they were not only opposing "the firm though loving government of heroic women,"—to use a phrase from an 1882 handbook for charity workers (Boyer, 1978, 153)—they were defending the very basis of the nineteenth-century polity, which declared that the national government under the Constitution was to be strictly neutral as to ways of life, just as it was to religious belief. And insofar as nongovernmental "parastates" and the media sought to step in where formal government was thought constitutionally barred, these institutions, too, were charged with rights invasions.

But much more was involved here: the proponents of women's rights were not different in kind from Progressive intellectuals generally. They spoke the same language across the range of their discourse, and they certainly shared the same enemies.[33] In this sense the "extremist" demands for woman's rights were also the moderate claims for Progressive goods. Like their abolitionist ancestors, women were often conflated with Negroes, clergymen-intellectuals, and even Christ in a common image of powerlessness, suffering, and redemption. Both feminists and Progressives were fully aware that when Gilman, for example, spoke of the female principle against the male in order to insure the triumph of a distinctly human or social ethic, her effective reference was the myth of New England and all those of both sexes who were authentic members of the redeemer nation. She and they knew that abolitionism was also a "female" principle against the slavemaster-husband-despot, North and South, and that as many men as women were abolitionists. In short, "women" in Gilman's writings meant "progressive" and progressive in the larger literature meant a program of reform to defeat what Gilman called "androcentric" politics and culture—the party system, competitive economics, politics as a game, a wholesale reliance on law and punishments, a religion of threat and damnation.[34]

33. Albion Small, although he did not always agree with Gilman, opened the pages of his journal to her and her allies and wrote on the relationship between women's educational opportunities, the family, and social progress. At the turn of the century more than half the undergraduates at the University of Chicago were women and one-third of all Ph.D.'s awarded to women in the social sciences before 1900 were awarded by Chicago (Fitzpatrick, 1990, 84 and 75). The *Annals* was equally open to women's issues. Patten wrote at least three articles in the periodical press on themes supportive of Gilman's general theory (*Independent*, September 1906, 674–81, and December 1904, 1244–49; and *Twentieth Century Magazine*, July 1912, 254–62) as well as in the *Annals* itself (56 [1914]: 111–21).

34. The fact that this critique was often expressed in gendered terms does not limit it to feminist demands; the alliance of romanticism and socialism was often expressed the same way. Charles and Mary Beard (1927, 2: 431 and 721) easily blended Charlotte Perkins Gilman into their larger narrative of American reform and progress. Their textbook became a standard, published continuously from 1927 to 1954. Charles Beard also wrote a pamphlet, "The Common Man and the Franchise," in 1912 for the Men's League for Woman Suffrage, a cause in which his wife Mary was very active.

PROGRESSIVE FREEDOM AND
CONTEMPORARY LIBERAL THEORY

Recent critiques of liberal political philosophy within the anglophone tradition offer instructive points of comparison to Progressive writings critical of rights. Except for some feminist writers and some students of John Dewey, discussion today is conducted in happy ignorance of Progressive writings and therefore reproduces unawares many of the same logics and arguments. While this veil of ignorance has some advantages for constrained discourse, it has the disadvantages that the contemporary variant often lacks concrete historical and institutional locations and therefore is without a crucial political dimension and an institutional memory.

The Ontological Argument

Three patterns of contemporary criticism are of particular value for comparison with Progressive writings. The first is what Charles Taylor and others call the ontological argument, the presuppositions about the "selves" who make rights claims and who are the bearers of rights. What degree of social solidarity and prior agreement are individuals presumed to have before they can begin to discuss rights and justice? While many defenders of liberal individualism (Nozick, Larmore, Ackerman) respond today that issues of identity and community are irrelevant to liberal justice, both feminists and "communitarians" have insisted that some such presuppositions are made willy-nilly and that a denial of this constitutes a de facto advantage for certain ways of life over others under the guise of neutrality.[35] Moreover, any liberal theory of distributive justice, such as Rawls's, "which involves treating the endowment of each as part of the jointly held resources for the benefit of society as a whole," must presuppose some meaning or "horizon" to the term "society as a whole."[36] Furthermore, given the range and intrusiveness of the activities of the modern liberal state, how is normative sense to be made of those activities under the assumptions of a "neutral framework" open to all citizens equally? In short, how can a rights-based dis-

---

35. On the communitarian critique, Galston, 1991; Sandel, 1984; Taylor, 1989; on the feminist critique, Okin, 1989; Shanley, 1991; for the use of these arguments against a discourse based on rights, Glendon (1991), whose book is subtitled "the impoverishment of political discourse."
36. Taylor, 1989, 162; see also Galston, 1989, 711–26; and Rawls, 1985, 223–31.

course premised on disembodied selves serve to make sense of our own lived experiences in a democratic society?[37]

A liberal "view from nowhere," so this critique goes, leads either to willful blindness as de facto obligation or to an alienated perfectionism and the withdrawal from political life as a corrupt world of raw power. Thus, an ontological critique of liberalism, especially when combined with a theory of language and human agency (Taylor, 1985), charges that no viable political order, democratic or otherwise, can be built on a foundation of equal but disembodied citizens. The polity that underwrites personal and civil rights first requires a people to constitute the polity. Attempts to explain and to justify any standing regime outside of this connection either hides a social ontology (often male or rich) under the cover of neutrality or unconsciously draws upon the normative reserves of a particular tradition to sustain its claimed universality. In short, a regime that takes rights seriously needs "a sense of mutual commitment . . . sustained . . . by encumbered selves who share a strong sense of community."[38] Once this "need" is recognized, the twinned issues of nation and identity immediately present themselves. What ways of life are to count as valid tickets for equal membership? What common "horizons" or values constitute the boundaries of the community within which membership is claimed or sought? Feminist critiques of rights have stressed the identity and equal-respect implications of this argument, whereas communitarians have stressed the issues of civic education and patriotism. Neither, however, can avoid both sets of issues because identity issues are also issues of membership and loyalty, and vice versa.[39]

At the most abstract level, critiques and defenses of liberal individualism now and in the Progressive era differ very little. What is strikingly different are the institutional and social assumptions lying just below the surface of these two discussions. In late-nineteenth-century defenses of liberal individualism, the institutional guarantor of "neutral

37. Glendon, 1991, 14: "The most distinctive features of our American rights dialect are the very ones that are most conspicuously in tension with what we require in order to give a reasonably full and coherent account of what kind of society we are and what kind of polity we are trying to create."

38. Taylor, 1989, 162. Dewey, 1982, 190–91, anticipates Taylor's larger ontological critique this way: "The real difficulty is that the individual is regarded as something given, something already there. Consequently, he can only be something to be catered to, something whose pleasures are to be magnified and possessions multiplied" (emphasis deleted).

39. See, for example, Galston, 1989; and Okin, 1989. Glendon, 1991, 146–70, comparing American and European court decisions on homosexual rights, faults American rights talk for forcing either-or decisions on whose ways of life are to be accorded respect, thereby preventing discussion, compromise, and inclusion.

frameworks" and disembodied but equal citizens is the United States Constitution, a document radically restricting the reach of the national government in domestic affairs. But even the most hard-bitten nineteenth-century defender of a rights discourse at the *national* level simply presumed a "goods"-based politics at the *local* or *regional* level. What Croly derisively termed "the monarchy of the Constitution" was a limited and liberal formal-legal empire astride countless virtue-based "republics" (states, localities, churches, schools, families). In short, the reach and depth of nineteenth-century liberal individualism was highly constrained. The point of insisting that the federal Constitution be interpreted as a neutral framework of limited government was precisely to legitimate nonneutral—and therefore "illiberal" or particularistic—persons, localities, and regions. This equation, federal : rights = states : goods, mirrored an economic one that severely constrained the power of the national government to interfere with free markets and contracts but gave states all but free rein to intervene in these areas and elsewhere through police powers. Woodrow Wilson's "privilege of separate [economic] development" had a cultural dimension as well: the Constitution and the party system combined to permit regions and localities to impose their own "community" cultural and moral values, including racial segregation.[40]

Progressives insisted that social progress required the conscious adoption of "nonneutrality" *at the national level*; democracy now required national, not regional-local "embodied selves"; national, not local, patriotism and citizenship; and national, not party-local, institutions of civic mobilization and political education. The male-dominated family (especially in the white South and among the newer immigrants in the North) and the local political party were both barriers, not because their values were illiberal but because they were wrong, preventing the growth of an inclusive and national public good and therefore a democratic America. Both families and local party machines were "despotic" because they enslaved their participants in ways of life that both limited them and led to self-destructive national politics.

Today's defenders of neutral frameworks and a national rights-based

40. This norm was so strong that Walter Lippmann, writing at the time of the Scopes trial in 1925, assumed that the federal courts had no authority to review the state legislative decisions regarding what would be taught in the schools (Steel, 1980, 216–17). This tradition of federalism causes some paradoxical results in contemporary discussions of civic education in America. Compare Gutman, 1989, 30–31, defending the right of government coercively to intervene in Amish education, to Galston, 1991, 252–55, defending the right of the Amish to be left alone. The former defends liberal neutrality as the basis for civic education, but urges state intervention; the latter defends the right of the state to teach substantive values, including patriotic and religious ones, but urges toleration and restraint.

regime can find little historical support in nineteenth- and early-twentieth-century American example except in a reading of the federal Constitution that limited its reach far short of protecting individuals from state and local enforcement of shared community norms. Those who defended ''rights'' in the late nineteenth century were also defending these parochial and local virtues; those who urged a national democratic community and national virtue were those who did battle with parochial and local virtue. Against this history, to insist on a *national* regime of neutral rights is to warrant ever-increasing incursions of federal power into private and local affairs, universalizing local conflicts and compelling all to act as if they were cosmopolitans.[41] In this sense today's liberals are every bit as ''imperialistic'' as yesterday's Progressives but in bad faith: liberals' compulsion is presented as a value-free defense of neutrality against illiberal local attempts to compel nationally contested definitions of substantive goods. Nationalizing rights in this way undermines local democracy and even some forms of cultural pluralism without giving national democratic and national patriotic reasons commensurate with the local loss.

On this reading, the local virtues celebrated in the ''civic republican'' tradition become provincial and undemocratic vices from a national perspective—*whether that national perspective is framed in terms of Progressive "goods" then or liberal "rights" now.* Contemporary defenders of communitarian values often instinctively mirror their rights-based opponents. Stressing the value of the local, the regional, the plural (participatory democracy, the democratic family), they refuse to insist on the kinds of governmental and moral authority that might be required to instantiate those same values as national norms.[42] Progressive academics and intellectuals, along with their feminist counterparts, were nationalists to the core, but their's was a substantive nationalism, a view of America as a coherent democracy with shared purposes and a shared project in the world.

The Civic Republican-Communitarian Argument

A second critique of liberal individualism today is directly related to the ontological one. This is a critique premised on the contrast of ''civic

41. Walzer (1983) is the one participant in the contemporary discussion who takes into account this logic of nineteenth-century America in twentieth-century institutional terms.

42. The only nineteenth-century model for clear national norms is the Civil War, whereas all twentieth-century models are foreign wars or cold wars; none but the most romantic and conservative of communitarians would base a national liberal polity on the need for enemies.

humanism" or "republicanism" to liberal individualism. Through which "paradigm" should America be read and freedom be understood? What intellectual traditions and what philosophical arguments explain and justify public expressions of freedom as opposed to private defenses of right? Historical arguments over the meaning of the revolutions in seventeenth-century Britain and eighteenth- and nineteenth-century America are also arguments over contemporary meanings and relationships of political freedom and private rights. "Liberal" readings tend to stress the bourgeois and economic components of this history and to underplay the importance of both religious and democratic elements.[43] "Republican" or civic humanist readings stress political mobilization and the public and participatory sides of revolution. They go on to insist that the primary idea of freedom is "public freedom," in contrast to despotism. Only as "communal liberty" is secured and maintained can private rights confer security, dignity, and meaning. Read this way, both in origin and in priority private rights are subordinate to public purpose just as private ends and purposes are subordinate to the rights and obligations of citizenship.[44] Put in terms of ontology, even this is a false way to state the relationship: the "self" as claimant of rights is already a civic self, forged in the fires of conflict and participation. Citizenship is not a separate identity in competition with a private self, but an integral part of one's personality. Without the identities and bonds created through collective action and commitment, the resources and motives necessary to protect the rights of others as well as one's own would be lacking. This same civic humanist reading has been used by those who stress the role of Puritan religious millennialism, specific theological traditions, and nongovernmental sources of civic education (churches, schools, families) in British and American ideas of freedom.[45]

43. Or, critics stress the victory of the liberal paradigm to show the betrayal of authentic democratic visions that did make their appearance (Marxist version: Locke beats the Levellers, the Constitution betrays the Revolution) or to show the barrenness of modernity absent its classical-Christian roots (Straussian version: secular founders, godless Constitution, Hobbesian turtles all the way down). Locke is almost required to be misread in both versions, that is, without acknowledging his writings on theology, church, and family.

44. The pervasive reach and power of juries in colonial through nineteenth-century America is testimony to the power of civic republicanism. Selected at random and claiming powers to judge both fact and law (often in courts presided over by elected and/or untrained judges), juries institutionalized the dependence of rights on the political community.

45. Glendon (1991, xiii) perfectly replicates the republican side of this historical debate in her critique of contemporary rights talk by referring to the "seedbeds of civic virtue . . . families, religious communities, and other primary social groups." And see Glendon, 1991, 171–83. Noll, 1990, selections 1–8, contains an excellent

The historical arguments are more explicitly political than are the battles over textual interpretation in the history of political thought. The civic humanist side of both arguments, however, places a much greater stress on intellectual elites and cultural institutions, whereas the liberal side stresses the role of property and the ways of life appropriate to a market society.[46] Viewed through the earlier lens of Progressivism, these differing understandings are no accident. The Progressive critique of the nineteenth-century American regime was clearly a national-democratic "civic humanism," not only in its stress on public virtue and higher citizenship, but in its reliance on tradition, both religious and politico-cultural. Civic humanism, both ancient and modern, enshrines patriotism, and patriotism requires narrative discourse and collective memory. Just as Machiavelli required of every republic founding events and exemplary deeds to "make a memory," so civic humanism asks every citizen to defend the republic and save it from degradation and despotism by making new memories emulating the old and thereby "refounding" the original memory. Both the myth of New England and its refoundings in the Revolution, Constitution, and Civil War—and the biblical-historical framework of evangelical Protestantism, with its jeremiad rituals of civic religion—are integral to Progressive understandings of American nationality and the public doctrines Progressives shaped. They would have found it quite preposterous even to entertain the idea that America was built on "Hobbesian" or "possessive individualism" foundations.

These same national understandings gave Progressive intellectuals a huge popular audience and a historical pedigree for their modernist civil religion and their doctrines of social justice. Their conscious location within this system of national memory was both a political strategy and a form of expressive political action crucial to their own identities, their intellectual projects, and even their claims to scientific objectivity. Their most "modernist" readings of Christianity and their most "materialist" readings of the advance of moral progress betray this histori-

---

summary of the terms of this historical debate as it relates to the role of religion; Kramnick, 1990, and Appleby, 1992, participate in and review the terms and implications of this debate. Because the issue of federalism is so often ignored, the debate often has an unreal quality. One recent article that has refreshingly altered the terms of discussion at the national level of American political history is Wood, 1987.

46. Marxists are often befuddled here. Because civic republicanism has been used against certain forms of liberal capitalism, it is also taken to be more "democratic." Using that assumption to interpret American political history, especially without addressing the national-local problem, creates numerous contradictions, for examples, Norton, 1986.

cist impulse and link their public doctrines to a strong national republican reading of America as a historic people with both a history and a destiny requiring political expression in the larger world. This same impulse links them directly to their claimed ancestry and puts them in deep opposition to Jeffersonian localism and secular-constitutionalist readings of the nation. If the logic of civic humanism seems to require thick notions of time—whether classical-cyclical or Christian-apocalyptic—the logic of liberal individualism suggests the timelessness implicit in a view from nowhere: the image of America ever restored to native innocence as it pushes westward or the freedom of the rational actor who owes nothing to his ancestors and little to his posterity. As John Quincy Adams, the original anti-Jacksonian, put it, the democracy of his day was radically deficient and radically evil because it "has no forefathers, it looks to no posterity, it is swallowed up on the present, and thinks of nothing but itself."[47]

The Democratic Individuality Argument

For all of their emphasis on the socially constructed self and the need for subordinating individual interests to a common good, Progressive academics and intellectuals also had a robust theory of individuality. By stressing social complexity, cultural tradition, and the social provision of resources, they argued that a democratic society would provide much greater scope for the flourishing of individual differences and talents than did the current rights-based regime of nineteenth-century America. This is the third theme that resonates in contemporary discussions of the meaning of freedom.

Contemporary critics of liberal individualism replicate this argument in a variety of ways. One form is to link individuality—as opposed to individualism—with deeper forms of pluralism. Progressives stressed "difference" as one of character, marked by specialization and service. Both feminists and multiculturalists today stress cultural and sexual differences and insist that these differences be publicly ratified. They maintain that a society of substantial gender, racial, and ethnic equality will make possible a "humanist" liberalism where differences will no longer be suppressed under the veil of neutral institutions but will be

---

47. Quoted in M. Wilson, 1967, 107. For a general discussion of the paradigms of "time" and "space" in pre–Civil War America, M. Wilson, 1974; and Greenstone, 1986. Tocqueville (1981, 396) depicts the effects of democratic individualism in almost the same words as Adams: "The woof of time is every instant broken and the track of generations effaced. Those who went before are soon forgotten; of those who will come after, no one has any idea: and the interest of man is confined to those in close propinquity to himself."

encouraged by the legal and cultural protection of minority ways of life (Okin, 1989; Shanley, 1991). With or without taking their cues from earlier Progressive feminists like Gilman, they reproduce her vision of a society where higher forms of individuality are only possible if women (and, today, minority cultures) are emancipated.[48] In any case, there is a shared vision of democratic—some would say "romantic"—individualism in a society reconstructed by new family and new social relationships, once women and minorities attain equal standing and respect.[49] Today's discussion is framed in terms of "the politics of identity and difference," (Connolly, 1991) rather than in the Progressives' language of the conditions for full self-development, but images from Whitman and Emerson float just beneath the surface of both discussions.

Comparing recent attempts to recover traditions of democratic individuality with Progressive writings also provides an instructive benchmark. John Dewey and Charles Horton Cooley outlined the ways in which a more comprehensive and authoritative national community would provide conditions for a higher individuality. Their attack on "dualism" in psychological and social theory was also a defense of the proposition that only a shared social ethic can sustain a society both democratic and complex and thus support the resources required for individuality to flourish. For Dewey and Cooley, differentiation and specialization were preconditions for higher forms of individuality, but this differentiation would necessarily yield hierarchy and class distinction unless both talents and identity were constructed within a larger social purpose. Dewey's call for individual "moral initiative" and Cooley's call for those with special talents and energies to immerse themselves "in the deeper currents of the general life" attested to their common belief that there is "no essential conflict between democracy and specialization in any sphere." Dualistic conceptions of man and society and a

---

48. Contemporary feminist writers are increasingly discovering the limits of a rights discourse in justifying institutions and practices that both protect and encourage their substantive values. Put differently, one response to the charge that recent feminist arguments do not take rights seriously enough is to admit it, but point to ways in which more communal and pluralist ways of construing democracy will result in more equal measures of respect for various ways of life. Some contemporary feminists are even rediscovering the family as an institutional resource for both feminist values and individuality, again reproducing some of the Progressive argument about its centrality. See, for example, Lange, 1991, using Rousseau to suggest new forms of democratic feminism. Perhaps Camille Paglia will soon be depicted as voicing dangerous pagan doctrines of sensuality and individualism inseparable from a pure rights discourse.

49. If these contemporary claims are expressed only in a individual rights and equal justice language, they self-destruct as claims for group privilege—a fact gradually being recognized in the literature, which is increasingly compelled to speak in the language of a larger public good.

legal order premised on that dualism stand in the way both of democracy and of individuality. "Democracy is an ethical idea, the idea of a personality, with truly infinite capacities, incorporate with every man. Democracy and the one, the ultimate, ethical ideal of humanity are to my mind synonyms."[50]

Herbert Croly raised these same themes in his discussion of "constructive individualism." In the nineteenth-century rights-based regime of democratic individualism, distinction and personal development were always devalued and subverted by the commercial-competitive standards of small-producer capitalism; "intellectual individuality and independence were sacrificed for the benefit of social homogeneity and the quickest possible development of American economic opportunities." The talented and specialized individual was continuously forced into the position "of selling his personality instead of fulfilling it." In a commercial society everyman must be part salesman. For individuality and personal distinction to flourish in a national setting, the social critic must carry on "an incessant and relentless warfare on the prevailing American intellectual insincerity" and be "unscrupulous" in cultivating "a genuinely individualistic practice and ideal."[51] Only in a positive and constructive national political democracy will individuality be seen as a virtue and not an aristocratic threat because the whole range of human talents and energies will be placed in constructive relationship to the common good. There must be established for Americans "a vital relation . . . between the assertion of intellectual independence or moral individuality and the adoption of a nationalized economic and political system." Genuine intellectual emancipation and individuality in the past rested on highly differential access to humane culture—often only to be found by going abroad. And precisely because it was isolated from democratic culture, this traditional culture, both in Europe and America, was often narrow, defensive, and sterile. Social education in a genuine democracy, therefore, "must be, above all, a liberal education" to accomplish "for the mass of the people a work of intellectual and moral emancipation" that, in the past, it accomplished

---

50. Cooley, 1909, 139; Dewey, 1888, 248. Dewey ends his essay by quoting from the Emersonian poet James Russell Lowell. Cooley maintains a running argument with Tocqueville over the issue of whether democracy can permit personal distinction and higher forms of individuality. And see Cooley, 1909, chap. 15; and Dewey, 1982, 190–201.

51. Croly, 1909, 422, 444, 449, and 451. And see Stettner, 1993, 27–32 and 50–56, on the influence on Croly of a powerful novel, *Unleavened Bread*, which explored the conflict of professional standards and the demands of the marketplace for a gifted young architect.

for a few and often with antidemocratic results.[52] As in Dewey, Croly here suggests that a democratic society can liberate the individual only as it liberates political and social ideas because political and moral knowledge is a constituent element of human agency and freedom.

Recent discussions of democratic individualism and recent scholarship on "romantic-individualist" elements in the history of British and American liberal political thought (Eisenach, 1981, 192–215; 1987; and 1990a; Kateb, 1989; Rosenblum, 1987 and 1989) have highlighted many of these earlier Progressive ideas. The one factor that was integral both to these earlier writings and to the Progressives, but that tends to be lost or subordinated in contemporary readings, is the tight link between these ideas of individuality and a shared sense of purpose. Whether one draws on Emerson or Whitman, reinterprets John Stuart Mill, or reexamines Gilman's transgendered idea of freedom, the single element shared by them all is a vision of a new kind of "connectedness," a shared sense of human destiny—even a religious conception of democracy. Croly draws explicitly on Mill at the conclusion of *Progressive Democracy* to declare this important teaching of "the progressive democratic faith":

> Every victorious selfish impulse, every perverse and cowardly thought, every petty action, every irresponsibility and infirmity of the will helps to impoverish the lives of other people as well as our own lives. We cannot liberate ourselves without seeking to liberate them. . . . [This democratic faith] finds its consummation in a love which is partly expressed in sympathetic feeling, but which is at bottom a spiritual expression of the mystical unity of human nature (Croly, 1914, 427).

Emerson might have said this as well;[53] Gilman and John Stuart Mill already had, and a whole host of British "new liberals," drawing on both Mill and T. H. Green, were saying it too.[54]

52. Croly, 1909, 422; and 1914, 417. In this way, Croly echoes the calls made to Yale undergraduates by reform Republicans, discussed above, chapter 3.

53. In his study of Emerson, Irving Howe remarks, "He starts from where people actually are—slipping away from but still held by religious faith—and helps them move to where, roughly, they want to go: an enlightened commonality of vision justifying pride in the republic, a vision akin to, yet distinct from, religious faith. The remains of religious sentiment—ideality, yearning, spiritual earnestness—thereby become the grounding for a high public culture" (quoted in Wills, 1987, 387).

54. Freeden, 1978, 25–75 and 170–84; Kloppenberg, 1986, 64–94 and 132–95.

FREEDOM, INSTITUTIONAL
BOUNDARIES, AND
CONSTITUTIONAL LIMITATIONS

An important question remains concerning Progressive ideas of freedom, one that shadows contemporary critics of liberalism as well. Were their attacks on "rights" strategic, self-standing, and integral to their larger public doctrine, or were they only using a critique of rights tactically, in order to get at their real foes, the interests, institutions, and practices of the standing regime? One can repeat this question from the other side: to what extent could the nineteenth-century regime of courts and parties legitimately be defended by the language of rights and liberal neutrality? This problem is not merely the abstract one of the relationship between ideas and institutions; it forces us to confront more directly the regime contexts of political theory in America and the intellectual difficulties one encounters when examining them. A test case is the defense of slavery (and the patriarchal family), a practice tacitly ratified with the Constitution and integral to the way federalism was instituted and practiced. To say that most Americans merely misread the meaning of rights in this case (and later in the case of women, wage laborers, and freedmen in the South), however, does not evade the larger difficulty. Where does the misreading stop? Can it ever stop? *Every* past regime in America defended by a constitutional or a rights vocabulary soon becomes exposed as hiding, but enforcing, specific clusters of substantive goods and ways of life. Does the same hold true for every future one?[55]

If national constitutional law is treated as if its overriding purpose is to instantiate the liberal ideal of a neutral framework maximizing rights, it would be politically self-defeating to attack the specific enemies of national political democracy without also trying to overturn the theory of constitutional rights that protects and privileges those enemies. Prevailing rights always shield a particular social order and its substantive goods and ways of life. Constitutional law, almost by definition, can hardly avoid legitimating reigning values and practices: that is what we mean when we call them reigning. In this tautological sense, a defense of prevailing rights is usually "conservative"—at least in expressing the interests and powers of extant national leadership.

---

55. Huntington, 1980, is both a recognition of and a capitulation to this relationship. He declares the "American creed" incompatible with durable and legitimate governing institutions. This is evident, he reasons, during every "creedal passion period." Significantly, his analysis does not include abolitionism and the Civil War as a "creedal passion period" and makes of Progressivism a periphery populism and not a movement to create and strengthen national institutions.

Over time, then, constitutional rights legitimate the standing regime in universal terms, but each regime it legitimates is a particular horizon of institutions, interests, and values. The Progressives, like many feminist and communitarian critics of liberalism today, deny from the start this constitutionalist mode of legitimating our politics. They are all claiming to be making principled and not tactical arguments. But the corollary to this stance is that they themselves must then forgo seeking to legitimate their own regime in this same constitutionalist language. When or if they win, the victory must be claimed on the basis of a new public doctrine that is a substitute for constitutionalism and not merely a change in constitutional interpretation.[56]

On this reading, the victory of Progressivism on its own terms signaled the overthrow of constitutional government. There is some truth to this. Some attempts made to justify Progressivism (and twentieth-century American political life) constitutionally are doomed from the start. Some institutions and practices inseparable from twentieth-century American political life are simply incompatible with traditionally understood rights-based argument.[57] Progressive public doctrine really did foreshadow "the end of liberalism" in America even before twentieth-century liberalism such as the New Deal was conceived. Thanks to the Progressive critique and Progressive reforms, much constitutional law soon became a dead letter—as did the party system that both depended upon and enforced constitutional powers and constitutional boundaries in the nineteenth century. Here is Charles Beard's reading of the American Constitution, probably written in 1914, in the leading textbook on American government from its initial publication in 1910 through the 1930s:

> No longer do statesmen spend weary days over finely spun theories about strict and liberal interpretations of the Constitution, about the sovereignty and reserved rights of states. No longer are men's affections so centered in their own commonwealths that they are willing to take up the sword . . . to defend state independence. It is true that there are still debates on such themes as federal encroachments on local liberties, and that admonitory volumes on "federal" usurpation come from the press. It is true also that conservative judges, dismayed at the radical policies reflected in new statutes, federal and state, sometimes set them aside in the name

---

56. This is the whole point of Croly arguing that the real revolution required in America is an intellectual one, overthrowing "the monarchy of the Constitution."

57. That is, extending the loss of constitutional protection over economic rights, which occurred in the 1920s and 1930s, to the entire system of governance.

of strict interpretation. But one has only to compare the social and economic legislation of the last decade with that of the closing years of the nineteenth century, for instance, to understand how deep is the change in the minds of those who have occasion to examine and interpret the Constitution bequeathed to them by the Fathers. Imagine Jefferson . . . reading Roosevelt's autobiography affirming the doctrine that the President of the United States can do anything for the welfare of the people which is not forbidden by the Constitution! Imagine Chief Justice Taney . . . called upon to uphold a state law fixing the hours of all factory labor. . . . Imagine James Monroe . . . called upon to sign bills appropriating federal money for roads, education, public health . . . and other social purposes! . . . Why multiply examples?[58]

What constitutional law had legitimated and political democracy through the party system enforced was a world of institutions and practices that has largely ceased to exist. On this institutional reading, then, the conclusion that the Progressive critique of rights prevailed does not seem absurd. We have had a revolution in constitutional law such that even its most liberal component, the Bill of Rights, no longer appears to limit Congress and certainly does not limit the president. Since the 1950s constitutional law has become an engine of nationalization, imposing what are, in effect, modified Progressive and cosmopolitan standards on states and localities.[59] And certainly, the institutions of the twentieth-century American state, the political economy, and the larger culture are much too hierarchic and bureaucratic to be either understood or contained in the language of individual rights.

These historical and institutional arguments, however persuasive, still avoid the central issue. Despite Progressive attempts to find a new

58. Beard, 1928a, 100–101. Note that all his nineteenth-century examples are from the "democratic" party. He was equally complacent about justifications for protections for free speech: "It is a hard, cold proposition: by what process are we most likely to secure orderly and intelligent government?" (36). His review of government control over speech, from the 1798 Sedition Act to the sentencing of a girl of twenty-one to fifteen years imprisonment "for taking part in issuing a circular severely attacking President Wilson's policy of intervention in Russia" is done without any questioning of the government's right to do so (107–9). In his *Economic Interpretation* Beard has no kind words at all for the position of the Anti-Federalists and doesn't even mention their greatest contribution, the Bill of Rights (McCorkle, 1984, 333–34).

59. A frank recognition of this result is Macedo, 1990, 60: "In order to vindicate its overriding status, a liberal political morality will have to speak directly to illiberal personal ideals, arguing that these are false or less important than competing liberal values, or that they can be mended and made compatible with liberalism." And see Gutman, 1989, on democratic education.

language, are not our public doctrines and our political discourse today about rights or, at least, rights as "liberal virtues?" On this intellectual and philosophical level the assertion that the Progressives have prevailed seems absurd on its face. Surely their attack on rights could only have been tactical; they could not really have believed all the bad things they said about them? And even if they did, who in America today speaks their organic, nationalist, and mystical-religious language?[60] But here, too, there are some not-so-hidden ironies and therefore some more subtle possibilities. The contemporary institutional bastions of a language of rights and of cosmopolitan liberal culture generally are precisely those that Progressive public doctrine helped to create and served to legitimate: governmental bureaucracies; universities; professional and trade associations; corporations; trade unions; consumer groups; public interest groups of all kinds; a nonparty national media; and a kind of trans-Protestant and inclusive national civil religion, now expressed as liberal internationalism—the American commitment to freedom in the world.[61] To defend a regime of rights once these state and parastate institutions are firmly on top (and locally based values and political parties are not) is, perforce, to defend a new regime of "goods" or "virtues" in the constitutional law language of neutral rights.

Such liberal virtue does not go unpunished in America. If rights are primary, then a democracy will insist on equal rights. In the absence of a common and consciously held identity within that horizon, that is, a national democratic community, these "liberal-establishment" institutions and practices are vulnerable to attack. Every appearance of ways of life and purposes not equally included in the matrix of prevailing institutions both "public" and "private" is soon a claim for equal recognition and inclusion. And insofar as these specialized and hierarchic establishments are largely the product of a public doctrine that treated individual rights as secondary, they are hardly designed to withstand strict scrutiny from within a discourse they initially rejected. The only way to deflect the charge of hypocrisy, of not living up to one's own proclaimed values of neutrality and equal rights, is to proclaim some higher value than equal individual (and now group) rights—for example, economic necessity, national defense, common

60. And if the temptation to do so ever occurs, Holmes, 1989, is there to show what dangerous company we keep. Stettner, 1993, 92–99 and 164–65, valiantly tries to save Croly for later liberalism by trying to show that his *Progressive Democracy* of 1914 was much more respectful of democracy and rights than his earlier *Promise*. In fact, it was World War I and its aftermath that belatedly taught Progressives the value of a strong defense of rights—but that was when Progressives were demoralized and on the defensive.

61. This is the irony of Holmes, 1989: almost every illiberal intellectual sin he condemns was committed by the founding social science and theological faculty of his university.

sense. Contemporary liberals have been loath to do this. The Progressives were not; in many ways and on many different levels they articulated an ideal of a national democratic community where equality was achieved more by sharing projects in common and by participating on the basis of equal respect than by being equally protected in one's rights against others. Contemporary liberal public doctrine is deeply distrustful of political democracy defined as shared values. Progressive public doctrine, in contrast, was premised on this definition.

The clearest expression of their "national" reading of shared values is the social-evolutionary method itself. Freedom, whether collective or individual, is agonistic and located within historical boundaries and choices that cannot be wished away. This perspective is not only a way of countering formalism and dualism, it suggests as well a way of combining personal and national self-understanding that is both realistic and emancipatory. The older idea of individual rights, as Progressives never tired of reminding us, presumed an automatic harmony of interests, both in economic life and regarding ways of life. National history read on these complacent terms was inseparable from a kind of nondemanding virtuous materialism; because of our boundless space, America was exempt from history—nature's nation was a free lunch. The Progressives, standing in the footsteps of their clerical ancestors, would have none of this illusion, this good-old-boy mendacity. America must be understood as a historical nation with what Walt Whitman called "terrible duties" left us by our ancestors.

Indicative of the power of this historical understanding are the ways in which Croly and Beard went to great lengths to discredit neo-Jeffersonian and populist critiques of the Constitution that began to appear in academic literature at the turn of the century. This alternative critique of late-nineteenth-century America—here termed "Jeffersonian socialism"—wanted to resuscitate the more lusty rights language from the Revolution in order to charge that the Constitution was designed from the start to favor rich and powerful capitalists against such simple democrats as farmers and small businessmen (and slaveholders). American populist cum socialist intellectuals had discovered Anti-Federalism. Although we often associate Beard with this position, we are simply and even radically wrong to do so. It was, in fact, Beard who launched one of the first and still the most convincing historical offensives against its first and most powerful scholarly expression.[62]

62. McCorkle, 1984. For Beard's critical review of J. Allen Smith's *Spirit of American Government*, Beard, 1908, 136–37; and discussion in Barrow, 1988, 253–66. An alternative strategy in this literature was to argue that judicial review was neither intended nor adopted in the Constitution. Again, Beard, 1912, utterly demolishes this argument, singling out Madison's and Jefferson's Virginia and Kentucky Resolutions for special scorn.

Without question, he admits, the Constitution established a powerful national government that marginally advantaged one kind of property and one kind of capitalism over another—just as the states had done the reverse under the Articles of Confederation. But the fact that neither President Jefferson nor President Jackson chose to amend the document despite overwhelming political majorities and the fact that political parties could easily nullify almost any parchment barrier to national party coalitions of local democratic wills, demonstrate the absurdity of blaming the document for America's present discontents. Indeed, the victory of agrarian and small-producer capitalism and its appropriate public doctrine of democratic individualism constitutes the major barrier to present day reform. The Anti-Federalists quite rightly saw that the best defense of their economic (reality) interests lay in opposing the adoption of the Constitution (Beard, 1915). Having failed, they turned the battle to elections and constitutional interpretations. Here, the rise of mass political parties and the sanctification of the Bill of Rights meant that, in crucial ways, the Anti-Federalist spirit won the nineteenth century, and we are all now paying for it.

Beard, Croly, and most of their Progressive teachers associated Federalist and early constitutional theory with the institutionalization of nationality, awaiting a real fulfillment in the democratization of that ideal. They, like Fiske earlier,[63] truly admired the Federalists and had little patience for either the Anti-Federalists or Jefferson. The curse of the nineteenth century was precisely in lending credence to the Jeffersonian (and especially southern) illusion that the mere expansion of rights by weakening national institutions would automatically underwrite equality, economic welfare, and distributive justice. The radical ahistoricism of this nineteenth-century self-image of "nature's nation" is of a piece with a view of the Constitution as either freedom's holy writ or some original defilement of the democratic garden. Both of these misreadings, said the Progressives, have now borne fruit: justifications for unjust corporate power and economic privilege are now made in the name of the Bill of Rights and substantive due process of law. Populist critics of the Constitution as an undemocratic document are paradoxically criticizing the use of its most democratic feature and "do not realize how dangerous and fallacious a chart their cherished principle of equal rights may well become" (Croly, 1909, 53). If they were

63. Fiske's *Critical Period of American History, 1783–1789* was an immediate success, remaining in print from 1888 to 1916. A year after *Critical Period*, he published *The Beginning of New England; or the Puritan Theocracy in Its Relation to Civil and Religious Liberty*, which was published continuously through 1930.

sincere democrats, they would recognize this contradiction and support disciplined and powerful national institutions allied to a reconstituted and democratic public good. But this, alas, requires the abandonment of democratic hypocrisy and democratic individualism and the end of the "pattern American."

Jeffersonian and Anti-Federalist "nationalism" was so thin because it was so liberal; neutral, because it was too weak to take a stand. Without strong "aristocratic" enemies at home or abroad, its national ideal of personal freedom increasingly became empty and undemanding, an abstract "spirit of freedom" without national institutions or national purpose to give it definition, discipline, and substance. The Progressives insisted that freedom must have both a national and a world-historical location: without those horizons, personal freedom could as easily warrant greed, violence, and cowardly betrayal as it could reflective self-discipline, equal justice, and the willingness to defend those values. If the Progressives' writings often sounded like repetitions of John Winthrop's seventeenth-century political sermons on liberty and authority, they were, but on a radically altered contextual and institutional level. If they sounded like the Federalist clergy, praising a politics of consensus and covenant and excoriating the partisanship and irreligion of the Jeffersonians under the banner of equal rights and local virtues, they were; but again, on another level. And if they often sounded like Lincoln and the abolitionists, with their ancestral piety and their millennialist hopes in a fallen world of virtuous materialism and pervasive irresponsibility, they stand equally convicted. In short, their ontological arguments voiced in the psychological and philosophical language of the social self form a larger argument that America ought to be understood as a historic nation.

WHOSE FREEDOM? WHOSE HISTORY? WHOSE IDENTITY?

To link personal freedom to national democracy—a substantive and inclusive public good—not only placed issues of rights within a framework of national institutions, it redefined the idea of citizenship on those terms as well. This topic was familiar in arguments about the admission and assimilation of immigrants and about possible responses to the restoration of white rule in the South in this period. This same issue of the rights and meaning of citizenship arose with the annexation of the Philippines: can a republic have colonial subjects?[64] Do all ideas of nation require a coherent national public? Does the identity of this public require a narrative identity, a shared story?

There are many ways of understanding the idea of America, some of which consciously attempt to deny the need for both a national public and a national public good. But this denial is also based on a narrative, one both familiar and popular. America has a liberal tradition, a huge land mass, plentiful natural resources, and a nonfeudal origin: ergo, our identity is preformed and de facto, not something to be articulated and contested. That is the "genius of American politics" (Boorstin, 1953). America is (or was or has the capacity to be) exempt from history as defined by the agonistic struggles of the nations and classes of Europe (or the Jewish nation in the Old Testament). Our national history is providential destiny in which fulfillment is the maximization of individual freedom—freedom defined as the absence of institutional restraint. Local restraints—cities, wives, churches, tight credit, intellectual tradition—do not count against this freedom and this destiny. Those duties can be evaded by changing locality, starting your own business, getting a new sidekick and a new self, dreaming new dreams, or redescribing one's reality. Although this narrative receives its most attractive guise in nineteenth-century imaginative literature,[65] it is associated with Jeffersonian and agrarian values as well, classically captured in Tocqueville's depiction of the restlessness, the "bootless chase" for happiness, that haunts the democratic individualist. In this narrative invisible hands are everywhere. If the narrative celebrates success, providence as the market is only giving everyone his due. If the narrative is used to mobilize anger, why then the invisible hands of providence must be restored to their timeless place by destroying the visible hands of "aristocratic" authority and duty and power. And if these bad hands are not visible, but life goes sour, then the evil manipulators must be in hiding. Once they are exposed and combated, the natural course of national destiny will reassert itself. As slaves, women, and native Americans pointed out, this narrative of boundless space and open possibilities was never quite as inclusive as it claimed. Nonetheless, to be in that narrative is to live "the American dream" without

64. Lasch, 1972, 70–79, shows why both the South and New England, as increasingly marginal regions of the country, opposed annexation for many of the same "racial" reasons that some imperialists favored it. Both regions feared the hegemonic implications of a national government undertaking such large and difficult responsibilities following the victory over Spain.

65. D. H. Lawrence's *Studies in Classical American Literature* is the first and classic study of this narrative.

the need for self-examination, personal development, or honorable subordination to others.

Periodically, this same narrative is simply turned inside out to become a story of an endless American nightmare. This narrative is also undemanding and popular because the need for considered judgments and difficult choices is equally avoided. This narrative also has a "people" or political community, that of the oppressed, but they have only a negative or reactive identity and no corporate agency to give them concrete historical location. This narrative, too, is dreamlike and abstract, expressing a hope for an alternative America that will someday be discovered. Signs and promises of its appearance break into history from time to time, but if they seek to endure by becoming institutions and practices, they quickly prove to be false prophecies.[66]

No narrative of American identity can altogether escape the "dream" (and perhaps "nightmare") elements of this narrative. This is so because American identity *is* constructed from American difference—difference from Europe, from the stories of "other nations." But other narratives of American identity, both in what they affirm and what they deny, anchor American uniqueness more in duty than in exemption, in struggle rather than escape, in temptation rather than innocence. Fulfillment is not a right or a condition, but a series of potentially tragic, sometimes ironic, and never fully realized projects. Knowing what these projects are and then undertaking them significantly alters the idea of national community and national destiny. Progressive narratives, whatever their individual differences, were within this latter structure. The narratives were set against what Progressives thought of as a facile and mindless optimism that simply eschewed responsibility or urged public indifference, usually under the name of protecting rights. This means that Progressive narratives contained national public agendas, projects, and causes seen as typological of past events, past projects, past causes. This history as call to duty was understood in the mode of the jeremiad, with generous measures of prophetic judgment and millennial hope served up together. But by keeping fulfillment at the end of or even outside of history—pace Fukuyama—a critical distance was established at least to the degree of requiring a deliberate and public discussion of the extent and bounds of the American people. This same requirement places issues of American national identity and purpose squarely in "contemporary history," requiring systematic social knowledge of uncompromising frankness.

---

66. This "dreamlike" quality of conceiving America is the theme of a review essay of two recent books on traditions of anti-Americanism at home and abroad (Bliven, 1992).

To that extent at least, the social scientist, the social evolutionist, and the social gospeler shared a narrative that denied at the start a certain kind of American uniqueness, one underwritten by isolation, innocence, and inertia. And to that extent, too, they implicitly forfeited a certain kind of American innocence and generosity, although that was not always clear to them. What was clear was that America was a nation acting in a world of nations, even as it received the nations of the world into its domain. In Progressive public doctrine, America was not to be viewed as either innocent or guilty but as just or unjust.

7

NATION & WORLD

We have all the elements of becoming a greater people, a mightier nation, and more endurable government than has ever held a place in the annals of time. The civilized countries of the old world will yet do homage to the wisdom and learning, the science and arts of our people; and the combined powers of all Europe shall bow before the majesty of our power.
—*American Republican*, 7 November 1844

Unlike most of their contemporaries, Progressive academics and intellectuals were "internationalists." They traveled and studied abroad, the journals and magazines they founded, edited, and wrote for routinely contained economic, political, and cultural news from abroad, and their critique of America and the resulting programs for reform were often constructed within a framework that compared European and American experience. Another source of internationalism was their special concern for immigration. Whether as economists concerned with industrial wage labor, as sociologists concerned with urbanization and assimilation, or as citizen-reformers concerned with municipal government, the Progressives, as students and residents of the industrial core region of the country, thought foreign immigration was an international issue because it raised for them the issues of how and on what terms new populations—literally, new "nations"—were to be integrated into the metropolitan country.

The primary source of Progressive internationalism, however, was nationalism itself. Because they were both proponents and builders of national institutions—called "parastates" in this study—Progressive reformers were acutely aware of resistance to those efforts. Reform at home meant both conflict and the need for conquest. Not unlike those who earlier created and staffed the national missionary institutions of the ecumenical religious establishment—the "parachurches" of the nineteenth century—Progressive reformers were out to conquer the nation, if not for Christ, then for social justice, brotherhood, and democracy. And just as this earlier crusade was seen as part of a larger plan of world redemption by America as the chosen nation, so the nationalism of the Progressives was an incipient internationalism with a decidedly militant—call it imperialist—edge. The spiritual link was the social gospel. The institutional link was from parachurch to parastate to the state itself, all acting in concert. The intellectual link was a philosophy of history that combined biblical typology, social evolution, and, in various measures, Hegelian thought and historical-economic materialism. The "concrete universal" in this philosophy of history was migration as founding, conquest, and expansion: from England to New England, to "West" as industrial core, to nation, to world.

The metaphor of migration was a protean one in Progressive conceptions of internationalism and America's role in the world. In earlier American usage, migration was the typological translation from Israel-Jerusalem to New England, as America–New Jerusalem. Progressive images of migration spoke more to its suggestion of the dynamism and power of expansion. The nations of the world streamed into America in ever-growing numbers.[1] American missionaries and salesmen and industrial goods increasingly covered the globe. The seat of empire migrated from Britain to America (and, in some readings, would find its capital in Chicago).[2] And, finally, there was the most important migration-as-expansion of all, that of consciousness, or "spirit" itself. This last idea was long voiced in the language of evangelical Christianity, in which the act of conversion was a rebirth into a new consciousness: grace enters into and transforms the body, animating it spontaneously to a higher way of life. When this language was combined with the social gospel, a collective spirit to achieve the kingdom on earth, the result became a vision of the American way of life as a civilizing and redemptive mission at home and abroad. As early as the mid-1870s one of the "new theologians" at Andover already voiced this connection when he said that "modern civilization is characterized by ideas derived from the gospel of the kingdom; the brotherhood of man and the fatherhood of God; philanthropy; the promise of human progress; the rights of man; the removal of oppression; the reign of justice and love displacing the reign of force" (Handy, 1984, 95).

1. Here, as in so many other areas, Chicago was an effective symbol. From a population of just over 500,000 in 1880, it doubled to more than 1 million in 1890 and doubled again by 1910. In 1900, more than a third of the population was foreign born and another 37 percent had foreign parents. Thirty-five different nationalities were listed in the census (Diner, 1975, 521).

2. As the "White City" of the World's Columbian Exposition of 1893–94, Chicago was already being heralded as the symbol of America's emergence in the world (Trachtenberg, 1982, 11–37 and 208–34).

Progressive academics discussed this idea of a shared consciousness in these same ethical terms, but the signs, locations, and expressions of this consciousness, while maintaining its "Christ ideal," was much more fully articulated in terms of knowledge, institutions, and power. To trace the various forms in which these ideas of migration and expansion were expressed is to review the primary ways in which Progressive intellectuals saw America in the world. This review also shows how their idea of nationalism was also an internationalism: America could no longer maintain its identity or fulfill itself without bringing the world into itself and projecting itself into the world. The most embracive expression of this migration of consciousness is in Simon Patten's economic interpretation of English moral philosophy. This may seem an odd place and an even odder way to locate American nationality in the world, but not if one sees Patten's scholarly enterprise as anticipation and preparation for fulfillment in American thought, American spirit, American power.

Religion has gradually divorced itself from asceticism, and utilitarianism from sensualism, until the two occupy the same field and have the same rules of conduct. [This union] has given a distinctive character to English civilization; on the one hand the local and peculiar have been subordinated to the general and national; on the other hand there has been a marked differentiation from foreign nations and standards. We are no longer cosmopolitans who wish to merge our civilization in that of the world. We think of ours as the civilization, and seek to impress our standards and ideals on others. There has never before been so large a body of people with practically the same standards and ideals. The unity is not merely one of language and tradition; it is motor as well as sensory. The unity of the race is thus not environmental but psychic (Patten, 1899, 366).

Across the range of Progressive writings this sense of America as a historic people finally prepared to assume its rightful place in the world was integrated into the genre of the jeremiad—America's historic destiny is America's covenant. Patten's formulation is framed in terms of a history of the incarnation of ideas or ideals in the past that has transformed religion "out of its historical and sensory settings, and made it like the national character." As such, "the unity and supremacy of the race [nation]" now rests on this "inbred" commitment, "a motor tendency that can find a new concrete expression in the Utopia the race is striving to realize." This destiny is an extension of the national covenant. The failure of its realization is a betrayal:

The success of these [religious and economic ideals and standards] means the success and supremacy of a race; their failure to meet the conditions of a world environment would mean that the race will disappear as other races have done under similar circumstances. Our progress and ascendancy depend on decisions that have already been made. Upon their correctness hangs the future welfare of the race (Patten, 1899, 368).

THE AMERICAN RACE AND
THE NATIONAL COVENANT

Almost all writings about America's role in the world in this period use the concept of "race." Indeed, the very concept of nationalism as developed in the nineteenth century presupposed some horizon of "people" that was usually expressed as "race." The historical method and its social-evolutionary philosophy not only stressed genealogy and destiny, but made nations, races, cultures, or peoples the primary subjects of its study. Political economy, with its focus on institutional development and the role of the state, rested on this same "racial" set of assumptions. Race, however, was used in many different ways in this period, both by Progressives and by their opponents. But, however used, the term and its family of meanings are indispensable if we are to understand the ways in which the Progressives created a public doctrine that linked national reform to international mission.

One of the more successful journalistic ventures in America at the turn of the century was Albert Shaw's *American Review of Reviews*. Shaw, one of the newly minted Ph.D.'s from Johns Hopkins and later president of the American Political Science Association, cofounded the monthly in 1891 and continued as its editor until 1937. By 1906 it had achieved a circulation of more than 200,000, the largest circulation in the world for a magazine not carrying fiction and, according to its advertising manager, having "the largest amount of advertising in any magazine in the world" (Mott, 1957a, 661). Progressive academics were well represented in its pages. In addition to Commons, Ely, Hadley, James, and Small, the *Review* published articles by university presidents David Starr Jordan of Stanford and E. Benjamin Andrews of Brown. Foreign affairs and foreign news were a distinctive feature of the *Review*. Each month, Shaw wrote a "Progress of the World" section that quickly reached thirty pages, stressing economic issues. As a "review of reviews," a large portion of the magazine's contents was devoted to the foreign press and periodicals, especially those of the British. Although the proportion of original articles, mostly devoted to domestic affairs, increased at the turn of the century, fully one-third of its pages were international.

What is noteworthy about this venture, aside from demonstrating the connection between internationalism and national reform, is that it did not begin in America, but in Great Britain. William Thomas Stead, a Gladstonian social reformer who earlier had edited the crusading *Pall Mall Gazette* for seven years, founded the *Review of Reviews* in 1890. Its purpose was made clear in the first issue:

> There exists at this moment no institution which even aspires to be to the English-speaking world what the Catholic Church in its prime was to the intelligence of Christendom. To call attention to the need for such an institution, to enlist the co-operation of all those who will work towards the creation of some such common centre . . . are the ultimate objects for which this review has been established. . . . Among all the agencies for the shaping of the future of the human race, none seems so potent now, and still more hereafter, than the English speaking man. Already he begins to dominate the world. The [British] Empire and [American] Republic comprise within their limits almost all the territory that remains empty for the overflow of the world. Their citizens, with all their faults, are leading the van of civilization.[3]

James Bryce, whom Shaw assisted in gathering materials for *The American Commonwealth*, brought Shaw and Stead together in England and suggested that Shaw undertake the American side of the project.[4] While Stead's side of the enterprise floundered, Shaw's prospered. Indeed, Stead came to America often and is noted in American letters for his best-selling *If Christ Came to Chicago* (1894), a journalistic account of more than four hundred pages on the social conditions of that city.[5] While suffused with condemnation and anger, its penultimate chapter is a tribute to Hull House[6] and ends with a prophecy. Chicago, reformed and redeemed, is on the verge of becoming America's capital city, having already achieved first rank as an ocean port and as the nation's transport, commercial, and financial center. Every reformer's dream has come true: prosperity, religious

3. Mott, 1957a, 657. On Stead and his relationship to British reform and American Progressive leadership, Stokes, 1983, 8–9; and Bliss, 1908, 1161. When Stead first joined the *Pall Mall Gazette* the editor was John Morley, the leading follower of John Stuart Mill.

4. Stokes, 1983, 7–8. There was also a *Review* in Australia founded a year after Shaw's.

5. Stead, 1964, 15, Harvey Wish, in the Introduction, calls the work an example of the "New Journalism." Stead was earlier hailed by Matthew Arnold as the inventor of this new genre of journalism because it combined human interest narratives and the cause of social reform.

6. In the prophetic chapter that follows, the most important offices of the city are mayor, school superintendent, chairman of the Civic Federation, president of Hull House, and chairman of the Church of Chicago (Stead, 1964, 417–18).

unity, housing cooperatives, popular education and culture, free medical care, and municipally owned utilities, stores, banks, gymnasiums, parks, pawn shops, and saloons (!), have made Chicago the model city. To crown its achievements, the city holds a great festival. The jewel in the crown of that festival is the arrival of the emperor of Germany who has come to see for himself "the ideal city of the world." He is on his way to City Hall to receive the freedom of the city from the mayor, Mrs. Potter Palmer (Stead, 1964, 428 and 397–427). Six years later Stead wrote another book titled *The Americanization of the World.*[7]

Patten's historical materialism, Stead's vision, and Shaw's success were not unrelated. Material and spiritual conquest, economic growth and social reform, and state and church all become harmonized as social knowledge and spiritual consciousness become one. One social gospel minister might emphasize charity as he lists the ways in which Christianity implants "regard for the personality of the weakest and poorest . . . the absolute duty of each member of the fortunate classes to raise up the unfortunate, . . . the prisoner, the stranger, the needy; . . . the obligation of a more equitable division of the profits of labour."[8] His colleague, participating in the same discourse and sharing the same ends, speaks of "Christianized Anglo-Saxon blood, with its love of liberty, its thrift, its intense and persistent energy and personal independence [as] the regnant force in this country. . . . God is using the Anglo-Saxon to conquer the world for Christ by dispossessing feeble races, and assimilating and molding others."[9]

Because the emphasis was always on what Lester Ward had earlier termed "psychic" factors, the exact correlative of "race" never found a stable referent. Sometimes it was expressed simply as "Protestantism" and included Germany (Handy, 1984, 105); at other times, it meant English speaking and included those of all "races" who inhabited English-speaking countries; at still other times, it may have referred to good American citizens, therefore including some Jews, blacks, and Catholics but excluding a major portion of white Anglo-Saxons who remained mired in individualism and greed. But the increasingly domi-

---

7. Based on a long-running series of articles in his *Review*, Stead's book assayed American power in the world in all its aspects, diplomatic-military, economic, religious, and intellectual. The book concludes with a long quotation from Gladstone, who seconds Stead's analysis and reflects his fears: "Will it make us, the children of the senior race, living together under his action, better or worse? Not what manner of producer, but what manner of man is the American of the future to be? How is the majestic figure, who is to become the largest and most powerful on the stage of the world's history, to make use of his power?" (Stead, 1901, 440).

8. Handy, 1984, 95, quoting from Charles Loring Brace in 1882.

9. Handy, 1984, 91, quoting from James H. King, 1887.

nant image was of America as "the race of races,"[10] a new people animated by a shared purpose. In the words of Edward Ross, "America is a psychic maelstrom that has sucked in and swallowed up hosts of aliens."[11]

But whatever its location, by the turn of the century the one constant feature, the "core" identity common to all specific readings, was the idea of America as covenant nation, the concentrated source of energy and power that would eventually determine the world's future. This constant was as true among the most cosmopolitan of American Progressives berating their fellow citizens for being so "behind" Europe in reform measures as it was for the most condescending of British Fabians making the mandatory visit to Hull House (Stokes, 1983, 10). Vida Scudder, perhaps the most Anglophile of the Progressive academics in this study, got the cause of this assumption exactly right. History as urbanization, immigration and industrialization had finally caught up with America. And, due to America's competitive individualism, the achievement of social justice would be that much more difficult. Scudder nonetheless concludes:

> If our conditions are in some respects even more complex than those of Europe, we have an immense advantage over her in the different foundations on which our national life is laid; in our assumption of social equality, and in the absence among us of solidified class feeling, *such as removes all possibility of unconsciousness* from social advance in the Old World. Ours not to create a tradition of freedom; ours only to maintain and apply a tradition, the chief glory of our inheritance (Scudder, 1898, 210, emphasis added).

For this intrepid fighter for the immigrant in the workshops of New England, this American "unconsciousness" is simply the tradition that says that our task "to realize spiritual democracy for the victims and outcasts of the Old World" in the New is "God-given," an indistinguishable part of American identity. This task and this spirit, migrating from the first Puritan settlements to the abolitionists, have

10. Although the origin of this term is unclear, it is used in *Review of Reviews* 25 (1902): 419, by an Italian journalist who then adds that America's triumph in the world "would only mean the triumph of our own best elements." Stead, 1902, 149–50, speaks of America as a giant crucible, "smelting . . . men of all nationalities into one dominant American type."

11. Ross, 1901, 85–86. He adds that a few thousand German university-trained Americans and Germans "have injected more German culture into our veins than all the (five million) immigrants that ever passed through Castle Garden."

''bequeathed to us purpose, strength, and hope for that impending test of our idealism.''[12] Lyman Abbott nicely summarized this psychic understanding when he contrasted the way in which ''the authority of the people is initiative and primary in America; it is derived and secondary in Europe.'' And because ''the people are trusted to govern themselves . . . the institutions, the history, the life of America, have been pervaded by the spirit, not merely of good will toward man, and of large hope for man, but also of faith in man. America has not always been conscious of the spirit which has possessed her . . . has not always consistently carried out the principles which she has professed.''[13]

SIGNS OF THE SPIRIT

The proof of a psychic unity or a common consciousness of America as democratic spirit in the world was often adduced from the sheer fact of expansion itself. The most obvious signs in the past were territorial expansion and the antislavery movement. The more recent sign was the victory over Spain. Both Abbott and Franklin Giddings, from whom Abbott borrowed many of his ideas, used the example of the annexation of the Philippines to show the primacy of democratic spirit over a conservative regard for traditional practices. ''We are a world power; we are likely to be a leader among the world-powers. We could not help ourselves if we would; we would not help ourselves if we could'' (Abbott, 1901, 266). The very reasons given by those opposed to the Spanish War were the refutation of their position. To indict Americans as ''jingoes, bullies, and sensation lovers . . . eager to engage in blood-letting'' was to say that ''it is a waste of breath to talk about what might have been'' had it not been. ''The truth that underlies the caricature is simply this: the American population of seventy million . . . is at this moment the most stupendous reservoir of seething energy to be found

12. Scudder, 1898, 211. The vehicle for this inheritance is our national literature. Gilman, 1898, 147–48: ''The signs of the times,'' can be read in this same way. She speaks of the American founding ''by sturdy races'' when ''men and women prayed together, worked together and fought together in comparative equality,'' which so ''strengthened, freed, emboldened, the human soul . . . that we have thrown off slavery, and with the same impulse have set in motion the long struggle toward securing woman's fuller equality.''

13. Abbott, 1901, 201 and 197; see also Giddings, 1900, 306. Croly, 1909, 266–67: ''The European nations are . . . not in a position to make their national ideals frankly and loyally democratic. . . . A European nation . . . cannot afford to become too complete a democracy all at once, because it would thereby be uprooting traditions upon which its national cohesion depends. . . . The American democracy can trust its interest to the national interest, because American national cohesion is dependent, not only upon certain forms of historical association, but upon fidelity to a democratic principle.''

on any continent" (Giddings, 1900, 271 and 273). To the charge that annexation overseas threatened our free institutions at home, both Abbott and
Giddings replied in the same way that Croly did regarding national democratic will versus the Constitution: the spirit must prevail over the law. As
in the case of American colonial status and American slavery, if "we have
not the form of government which fits us" for the task of bringing self-government to the world, "we should change the form of government" (Abbott, 1901, 276). Giddings, while granting that corruption might mar colonial administration, says that the increased responsibilities abroad and the
need "to respect the opinions, the manners, and the interests of other nations" would compel higher standards of administration than we have had
in the past (Giddings, 1900, 286–87). Even more, the war and the annexation had forced America to dispense with many illusions that had weakened its political institutions in the past. The first illusion was that our
monetary system and trade policies could be conducted as if they were only
issues of domestic and sectional politics. The second was that our national
welfare and prosperity and values could be advanced either in isolation or
apart from a more or less permanent cooperation with Great Britain.[14]

This second imperative, rapprochement with Britain, was itself taken as
a sign of American destiny and an expression of American nationalism.
Without going into the late-nineteenth-century politics of partisan attitudes toward Great Britain, the Republican hegemonic electoral victory at
the turn of the century occasioned a major shift toward cooperation with
Britain.[15] This shift was in part necessitated by the building of the Panama
Canal and by the fact that cooperation with Britain was a precondition for
entering the larger world of international trade agreements and naval arma-
ment pacts. In part, too, it reflected and paralleled shifts toward Britain that
were also taking place within church and ecumenical institutions and
among Progressive academics and intellectuals. The new edition of Bliss's
Encyclopedia of Social Reform (1908) was strong testimony to the existence of a sort of Anglo-American Progressive Internationale. Although
American contributors and information dominate, and other European
countries were generously represented, it was British reform history and
writings that set the contemporary stage and provided many of the contemporary reform contributions.[16]

14. Giddings, 1900, 279–82 and 288–89. Here the issue of the Panama Canal
loomed largest because of the preexisting Clayton-Bulwer Treaty (Perkins, 1968,
173–85).

15. Collin, 1985, Introduction, chaps. 6 and 7, and Epilogue; Perkins, 1968.

16. The most prominent contributors, listed on the frontispiece, are exclusively
American and British or from the British Empire and include Sidney Webb and two
members of Parliament. For Bliss's role in fostering Anglo-American reform ties,
Dombrowski, 1936, 96–107; Mann, 1955, 680.

The coming together of America and Britain at this time can be read as conservative (a circling of the ethnocultural wagons against the invasion of the "new immigration" into America) or even as reactionary, an exchange of republican innocence for the illicit joys of Old World empire.[17] Or, this same move might be read as the expression of American cultural insecurity and weakness requiring British sponsorship and example before Americans would undertake similar imperial ventures at home or abroad. The problem with both these readings is that those who were the primary movers both in rapprochement and in partnership were the same as those who led Progressive reforms, who most strongly urged and worked for assimilation of the new immigrants, and who were the most confident expositors of projecting the American way of life and democratic values into the world. Characteristically, both the South and genteel Boston were the centers of opposition to "imperialism," but their response was inseparable from their backwater status and their fear of being left even further behind in the new America.[18] Croly was simply stating nearly two decades of the facts of the matter when he declared in 1909 that one could not be taken seriously as a reformer at home unless he was an "imperialist" abroad. A conception of an embracive and national public good was inconceivable apart from powerful national institutions that upheld social justice and a national democratic culture at home and that defended the national interest abroad. Any other formulation was either illusion or hypocritical cover for class, sectional, or personal interest (Croly, 1909, 157, 255, and 272-314).

Whatever the reading one puts on resistance both to American expansionism and to increasing ties with Britain, Progressive intellectual and religious culture was becoming increasingly intertwined with that

17. In fact, the age of territorial expansion and overseas military conquest was rapidly closing, while that of trade and investment competition was becoming increasingly important. The main arenas of this latter competition were as much within the North American and European worlds as outside them (Collin, 1985, 1-14; Rosenberg, 1982, 14-62).

18. The way in which Giddings (1900, 269-70) addresses his New England audience in explaining and justifying American war and expansion at the turn of the century attests to this understanding. He tries to show why "the wisest men in the community" often waste their energies because they cling to worlds that have passed, giving their "conscientious convictions" an ultimate futility. In another context and less gently (247), he refers to "a healthy repugnance to certain nerveless types of 'mugwumpery.'" Another way to see this regional difference is by looking at the denominational sources, corporate organizational styles, and nationalist-imperialist rhetoric of the foreign missionary movements in this period. They were practically coterminous with the social gospel, and therefore increasingly removed from both New England and the South (Hutchison, 1987, 91-125; and Ernst, 1974, 1-35).

of Britain. Reading the pages of any of the new monthly magazines at the turn of the century would be proof enough. The success of Stead's book on Chicago and, earlier, Mrs. Humphrey Ward's *Robert Elsemere*, were preludes to an increasing transatlantic trade in reform values, personnel, and writings. Just as Toynbee Hall was a necessary stop for American reformers, so Hull House became the mandatory visit for the British. And just as American journals and magazines regularly carried news of British reform—especially at the municipal level—so British publications contained long summaries of American efforts.[19] The culmination of this interchange was represented by the founding of the *New Republic* in 1914. During its first year of publication, fully one-fourth of its signed contributors were British.[20] Church and missionary cooperation was also expanding at this time. The Methodist Episcopal Church, increasingly taking center stage in American Protestantism, voted in 1900 to display the American flag at its General Conference—and then narrowly defeated a proposal to fly the British flag alongside.[21] More substantively, the entrepreneurial and organizational genius of John R. Mott (1865–1955) symbolized both the energy of American nationalism abroad and its connection to Britain.

Mott, a native of New York State who had moved to Iowa, returned to his native state to attend Cornell in 1885. Inspired by the revivalist Dwight Moody at a summer camp, he became president of Cornell's YMCA and, within one year, turned it into the world's largest and most active student unit.[22] During the year following graduation he traveled more than forty thousand miles as an agent for the North American

19. As early as 1897, Leonard T. Hobhouse, the leading "new liberal" intellectual in Britain, wrote a summary of American Progressivism in his newly founded *Progressive Review*, and another in 1911 in *Contemporary Review*, one of the leading reform journals in England. For the relationship of American and British ideas, Kloppenberg, 1986, chap. 8; on personal relationships and cooperation, Stokes, 1983.

20. Steel, 1980, 68; see also Forcey, 1961, 228–31.

21. Handy, 1984, 110. On the increasingly powerful role of Methodism within liberal evangelical Protestantism in America, Stead, 1902, 264–66; and Ernst, 1974, 56–63 and 98–109.

22. The YMCA was founded in London in the 1840s and in North America in 1854. By the first decade of the twentieth century, three-quarters (2,339) of its paid staff, one-half (405,000) of its worldwide membership, and one-quarter (1,868) of its associations were North American. Annual expenditures for the North American unit in the year 1906–7 were more than $5 million, much of it in support of programs and associations overseas (Bliss, 1908, 1312). Following a worldwide trip in 1914, Oscar Brown, a professor at Vanderbilt, remarked only half jokingly that there were six global powers: "The British Empire, the Russian Empire, the Japanese Empire, the Chinese Republic, the American Republic, and the Young Men's Christian Association." This same overtaking of British resources was also evident in foreign missions generally (Hutchison, 1987, 91–95).

YMCA. His success led to an appointment as senior secretary of that organization: by 1895 membership of the American YMCA had doubled.

From then on Mott's career almost exactly paralleled that of successful corporate entrepreneurs at this time. His first step was merger. Having already founded the Student Volunteer Movement for Foreign Missions (SVM) at Cornell (their motto, "the evangelization of the world in this generation") he effectively integrated the SVM into the YMCA through summer conventions organized to recruit and support future foreign missionaries. Over the next thirty years this organization recruited and sent more than twenty thousand American missionaries abroad. In 1895, in cooperation with British student leaders, he organized and, for thirty years, headed the World Student Christian Federation, an American-led international holding company of the Christian student movement in all of its Protestant manifestations. In 1901 he was put in charge of foreign expansion of the YMCA, with special emphasis on Asia.[23] His success and power continued to grow.

As a sort of ambassador plenipotentiary of the Anglo-American mission to the world, he made more than 100 ocean crossings, organizing the ever-expanding network of secular and religious missionary activities and related ecumenical ventures. Although he had only an undergraduate degree, he was offered, but turned down, the positions of dean of the Yale Divinity School and president of Oberlin College. In 1911, Princeton awarded him an honorary doctor of laws as "a new Crusader bent on the Christian conquest of the world" (Handy, 1984, 119). During World War I, he organized 26,000 volunteers through the American YMCA to work with prisoners and refugees. Despite his international position, he accepted Wilson's appointment as a member of the Root mission to Russia in 1917 and attended the Versailles conference.[24] He declined Wilson's offer of the ambassadorship to China. After the war, he was honored by more than twenty countries in Europe and Asia for his organization of relief. Mott was called the "father" of the World Council of Churches, which was founded in 1946, the same year he received the Nobel Peace Prize (Handy, 1984, 112–20).

The career and success of Mott were paralleled on a lesser scale by

---

23. Handy, 1984, 112–15 and Mathews, 1934, chaps. 3–6. Rosenberg, 1982, 109–10, calls these initiatives a kind of international social gospel more than a distinctly Christian program. By 1910, of every 100 American and European missionaries serving abroad, about 30 were ordained men, 12 were nonmedical laymen, 4 were medical laymen or laywomen, and 55 were nonmedical laywomen (Hutchison, 1984, 99).

24. Mathews, 1934, 294–97, on postwar German student criticism of Mott for his diplomatic missions for the American government.

those of other Americans, notably Robert Elliott Speer, who headed the General Wartime Commission of Churches during the World War and then the Federal Council of Churches, from 1920 to 1924. Like Mott, he was not trained as a clergyman and, partly for that reason, was able to harness American religious energy to American national missionary and ecumenical organizations. This same combination conflated individual and social gospel and, more generally, Christianity and the American Way of Life. Until the Protestant split in the 1920s, the entire missionary effort blurred the line between proselytizing in behalf of Christianity and spreading American democratic civilization.[25] In this way, too, Progressive internationalism was an extension of Progressive nationalism. Symbolically expressed, the famous "Pittsburgh Survey"—that monument to the alliance of faith and social knowledge—was replicated in Peking, China, by the American YMCA. This same group, under a Carnegie Foundation grant, established the Institute of Pacific Relations, the dominant research center for American knowledge of Asia until destroyed by McCarthyism in the 1950s.[26]

"THE AMERICANIZATION OF THE WORLD"

The last important "migration"-as-expansion in this period was American business. Like the missionary effort, this expansion was a project of the industrial core and combined the selling of goods abroad with the export of a new way of life—a consumer economy based on high wages, lowering costs, and constant innovation. The Englishman William Stead wrote of the "Americanization of the World" as an event combining both matter and spirit, urging Britain to emulate America

25. Hutchison (1987, 102–24 and 138–45), writing well after the formal division between modernists and fundamentalists in the 1920s, discerns signs of this tension earlier between those who wanted to found churches of the converted, train a "native" clergy to convert more, and then leave and those who wanted a permanent American staff and an entire apparatus of educational and philanthropic institutions. The problem with the former model was that it would tend to transport American denominationalism abroad. The best example of the latter was the YMCA, which stressed education and social work, activities similar to later government aid programs.

26. Rosenberg, 1982, 109–11. On the relationship of the Pittsburgh Survey to Progressive academics and the social gospel, McClymer, 1980, Introduction and chaps. 1–3. On the later relationships between charity organization professionals, *Survey*, and the preparedness campaigns discussed below, see ibid., chap. 6.

and to join it as a junior partner.[27] From the end of the Civil War to the 1880s, Britain had been the leading long term capital investor in America, funding most of the early railroad system. Once America was firmly committed to the gold standard and capital could be amassed in sufficient amounts to fund great industrial mergers, America began to export both capital and organization. The dynamism of the American industrial and distributional economy was dramatic, not only rapidly outdistancing Britain, but clearly outperforming Germany as well.[28]

Although the reaction to America's dramatic growth in foreign trade and investment at the turn of the century was often based on exaggerated fears and naive projections, there was no denying that consolidation and rationalization in industry and transport was giving many American companies an extraordinary comparative advantage. A 1902 British report on competitiveness pointed out that the Steel Trust in America brought in ore by rail to its furnaces at one-sixth of a penny per ton mile compared to British costs of seven-eighths. American rail costs for heavy goods generally were less than one-half of Germany's and approaching one-quarter of Britain's. The railroad mileage controlled by the Standard Oil Trust exceeded the total railway mileage in the United Kingdom. Even more remarkable was the success resulting from linking cheap transport with mechanized agriculture, again a phenomenon of the American Midwest and West and not of New England or the South. By the turn of the century the United States was supplying the United Kingdom with over 50 percent of its salt pork, more than 70 percent of its live cattle and fresh beef, almost 89 percent of its bacon and ham, and 93 percent of its lard (26 *Review of Reviews* [1902]: 102, 213–14, and 41).

Albert Shaw's *American Review of Reviews* not only regularly republished this foreign economic understanding of America, it stressed this

27. This was a major editorial theme of the British *Review of Reviews*, culminating in a book of that title by Stead in 1901. This book praises the fact that America is forging all of the nationalities of the world "into one dominant American type . . . [creating] one uniform texture of American civilization" (Stead, 1902, 149).

28. While Great Britain's share of world industrial production fell from 32 percent in 1870 to 15 percent in 1906–10 and Germany's rose from 13 percent to 16 percent, America's went from 23 percent to 35 percent in that same period. The same shifts are reflected in per capita income. In 1870, Great Britain's was $972; Germany's, $535; and America's, $764. By 1913 the figures were, respectively, $1,491, $1,073, and $1,813. Figures from Chandler, 1990, 52. The Republican party platform of 1908, under the heading "equality of opportunity," took credit for this phenomenal growth. America now "owns one-fourth of the world's wealth and makes one-third of all modern manufactured products," it claimed, surpassing "England and all her colonies, and . . . France and Germany combined" (Johnson and Porter, 1975, 157).

same analysis in its excerpts from American monthlies and academic journals. The result was that America's economic and trade expansion was articulated and understood within the larger framework of America's domestic and world reform mission. Although *American Review of Reviews* was the major journalistic link, the material it reviewed was primarily supplied by American journals founded in the 1880s that became the expression and voice of Progressive public doctrine—*Outlook, Century, American Magazine, Arena, Cosmopolitan, Forum, McClure's,* and *Scribners.* Such was the demand for economic news and news analysis of the kind contained in Stead's journal that a competitor, *World's Work,* was founded in 1900 by Doubleday and an ex-editor of *Forum* and *Atlantic Monthly,* Walter Hines Page. Following the same format as the British and American *Review of Reviews,* it focused on economic news and issues at home and abroad. Firmly within the Progressive media network, it contained dozens of articles on successful reform efforts. In addition to articles and serialized books by prominent reformers such as Lyman Abbott, Gifford Pinchot, William McAdoo, Upton Sinclair (*The Jungle*), and Ray Stannard Baker (who became its managing editor in 1903), it carried Booker T. Washington's sequel to *Up from Slavery,* and occasional pieces by W. E. B. DuBois (Mott, 1957a, 773–88). Thus, what quickly became the nation's leading general organ for domestic and international developments in industry, technology, armaments, trade, and finance was also an important part of the reform press. And, as if to prove Stead's thesis of the Americanization of the world, Page's American original was copied two years later in Britain: Henry Norman, a Liberal party M.P., established *World's Work* for the British reader who "takes a serious interest in the forward movement of his own time and country." (26 *Review of Reviews* [supplement, 1902]: 637).

AT THE THRESHOLD OF TRIUMPH

The election campaign of 1912 was proof that Progressive public doctrine was victorious. All three major parties, in varying degrees and with differing emphasis, urged Progressive measures. Constitutional amendments mandating the direct election of senators and providing for a national income tax had passed Congress and were in the process of approval by the states. In all platforms, national responsibility for conservation, banking, trust regulation, and agricultural credit were declared. Although the Progressive party platform was by far the most extensive and coherent, both Democrats and Republicans urged new national domestic initiatives and accepted the new responsibilities of the nation in the world.[29]

By 1914, Herbert Croly confidently declared that Progressive ideas have "become the dominant formative influence in American public life" and that "the line of cleavage between progressives and non-progressives is fully as important as that between Democrats and Republicans" (Croly, 1914, 2). While unconvinced that Wilson's "New Freedom" was not a higher conservatism in disguise and therefore a series of dodges and evasions, Croly was confident that this new transparty dividing line would result in the increasing power of the progressive idea. Walter Weyl, Croly's colleague on the staff of the *New Republic*, declared in his *New Democracy* that same year the impending victory of "the new social spirit" and, like Croly, laid out a program of national legislation for that new spirit to instantiate.[30] In 1915 Benjamin De Witt wrote *The Progressive Movement* to make clear that Progressivism has "a universal character" in America and represents "the embodiment and expression of fundamental measures and principles of reform that have been advocated for many years by all political parties . . . for the past quarter of a century" (De Witt, 1915, vii). The purpose of his book was to consolidate the de facto victory by making articulate what those common purposes and policies were, what bound them together, and how they could be urged and defended in coherent ways. Much like Croly, he assumed that Progressive ideas and not party lines by then defined the important political divisions in America. De Witt goes further to say that Progressivism cuts across sectional and political-jurisdictional lines as well. In sum, Progressive institutions and public doctrine and not parties and constitutional courts now define American politics.[31]

Although almost all of the Progressive academics, intellectuals, and reform activists in this study rallied to support Theodore Roosevelt and

29. The Republican platform was decidedly less Progressive in 1912 than in 1904 and 1908, marked especially by their long section on the courts and the Constitution in 1912. The Democrats became more Progressive over that same period, courting northern industrial labor, accepting America's new international role, and urging more national responsibility in the economy.

30. Weyl, 1914, 156. Originally published in 1912, but revised and reissued in 1914. Weyl was one of Simon Patten's doctoral students at Wharton; his book, especially on social reform, reflects many of Patten's ideas.

31. De Witt, 1915, xi-xii. The table of contents neatly outlines the inner logic of his argument. Part 1 shows the power of Progressive ideas in each of five major party groupings; part 2 traces Progressive reforms in and by the national government, the state governments, and city governments.

the Progressive party in 1912,[32] they did so as adherents to a party against parties, as citizens who stood for ideas of common good that no party loyalty or advantage should compromise. Thus, by declaring that Progressivism was a spirit and purpose pervading all parties, all regions, and all jurisdictions, they were also declaring *themselves* as the authoritative articulators of its authoritative doctrines. Everyone else, though sharing in this common spirit, was partially captive of one or another particular manifestation of Progressivism, either by party loyalty, region, or jurisdiction. And because Progressivism manifested itself in different ways and in different measures within each institutional location, only those who could see the entire picture could articulate and maintain the guiding spirit.[33]

Progressivism in this essentialist sense and despite all of its particularity, nevertheless did have two—with the promise of a third—cosmopolitan locations and a clerisy in each: the professors in the new universities and professional schools and intellectuals writing for the nonpartisan national press.[34] And insofar as national universities and the national press produce, inspire, and mobilize a constant stream of good citizens who become politically active across the entire range of available locations, together they would represent the common spirit, the "public," America as a coherent nation. No matter what the obstacles and no matter what the temporary defeats, these Progressives thought they knew what the larger national good was. They knew that they and their allies were capable of distinguishing private interests

32. The most prominent was Jane Addams, who seconded his nomination and constituted a one-person national campaign apparatus, writing campaign articles for *Crisis, McClure's, Survey*, and *American Magazine*. With Florence Kelley, she also served on the committee that drafted the social and industrial planks (Davis, 1973, 185–93). Seligman was very active in the New York State party; Commons, Ely, and Ross were an integral part of Wisconsin Progressivism. Shaw often advised Roosevelt, and James contributed to his ideas on conservation (Ely, 1938, 277–79). Although Patten had advised Roosevelt as president and a host of his students— Walter Weyl, William Draper Lewis, Edward T. Devine, Frances Perkins—were active in the campaign, Patten himself remained loyal to the party of Lincoln and voted for Taft (Fox, 1967, 112).

33. This was in striking parallel to the self-image of modernist theologians and their parachurch institutions before the Civil War. They represented the universal and embracive, whereas "doctrinal" and "ritualistic" denominations and church members were the particulars who shared in but did not entirely embody the whole.

34. A third location waiting in the wings was the increasingly institutionalized office of president of the United States. Forcey (1961) nicely catches this presidential connection between the older Progressivism and the newer Liberalism in his study of the *New Republic*.

from public good, corrupt actions from uncorrupt actions, productive and moral ways of life from destructive and immoral ways of life. Like their clerical predecessors and colleagues, as keepers of the national covenant, they presumed to define American identity. They were also confident that more and more of their fellow citizens would become good citizens once they were emancipated from conditions that stood in the way: parochialism, habit, poverty, disease, illiteracy, and economic insecurity.

From the election of 1900 through America's entry into World War I there was hardly a moment when this vision and these hopes were not confirmed, both at home and abroad. No matter where one looked, Progressive reform ideas were taking hold. Direct democracy, government regulation of parties, new forms of city government and municipal functions, professionalization of public service, higher standards for public officials, coherent regulation of railroads, coordinated international trade policy and, most importantly, higher and enforced standards governing the relationship of business and government were the major structural reforms that accompanied significant improvements in governmental services and effectiveness. De Witt's book is a veritable catalogue of reform legislation at every level of government between 1900 and 1914, with confident assertions of how each of them might be perfected and completed in the future.[35]

The material basis for reform, what the political economists called "the social surplus," continued to grow at an astonishing rate even while industrial wages continued to be the highest in the world. Through combined governmental and private auspices, new forms of industrial relations were created, informed by reliable social statistics, new understandings of unit and labor costs, and new mechanisms of conciliation and arbitration. Spurred by exports, government-sponsored research, and continued processing and distributional efficiencies, productivity in the mechanized sectors of American agriculture also continued to increase at dramatic rates.

Given the success of the Progressives in setting the public agenda

35. De Witt, 1915, 193, 254, and 258, regarding woman suffrage (seven states, 1910-14), mothers' pensions (twenty states, 1908-13), minimum wage for women and girls (nine states, all in 1913); 269, regarding workmen's compensation laws (twenty-five states, no dates given); and 287 and 300, regarding municipal home rule and municipal charters. For reforms in the 1890s, Ely, 1903, 310-11, on state inheritance taxes (twenty-seven states; twenty-three between 1891-1901; 370-71 on compulsory school attendance (thirty-three states by 1901) and on child labor laws (twenty-five states by 1901). For the sudden burst of reforms in the period 1903-8, McCormick, 1986, 332-48, especially prohibiting corporate campaign contributions (twenty-two states) and mandating direct primary elections (thirty-one states). On "human conservation" reforms in the states, Weyl, 1914, 338-42.

and defining the public good, it seemed only a matter of time before the national government would complete its own work and that begun by the states and cities and voluntary groups. And given Wilson's labor support in the North and farm support in the West combined with Progressive party congressmen and senators, the stage seemed truly set for the final victory of reform in America. But when war broke out in Europe, the entire framework was altered. Demand for American agricultural and industrial goods climbed even faster. Indeed, such was the growth of prosperity and the consumer economy that, despite the wave of political and moral reforms, warnings were voiced about America being reenslaved by its very success.[36] Moreover, given the Progressive identity of American nationalism with internationalism and both with cooperation with Britain, a new world stage demanding a new drama quickly displaced the earlier domestic one. Writing in the period 1912–14, neither Weyl, nor De Witt, nor Croly paid the slightest attention to foreign policy in their books heralding the final triumph of Progressivism. Within two years, almost every discussion of domestic reform was framed in terms of its relationship to "preparedness" and the fulfillment of our world responsibilities.

WAR AS APOTHEOSIS

The preparedness campaign and war mobilization, 1915–18, are perhaps the most telling examples of public policy bearing the imprint of Progressive public doctrine as it was filtered through the prevailing structures of American political institutions. Despite the victory of Wilson and the Democratic party in Congress and, thus, of the periphery plus some of labor in the industrial core, Progressive leadership and industrial-core values immediately reasserted their primacy. Progressive academics, clergymen, journalists, and intellectuals were not only some of the earliest and most avid supporters of preparedness measures, they came to direct many of the leading parastate, parachurch, and governmental institutions that led the campaign for both preparedness and entry into the war. Their institutions, their journals, their magazines, and their organizational locales stood at the forefront in

36. And even after the war as well. Willard Price, editor of a Methodist publication, *World Outlook*, in December, 1918: "We must remember that for a long time the other nations fought for democracy while we made money out of the fight. Much of the wealth needed to wage this war for liberty and democracy has flowed into our pockets. The United States now stands war-bloated with a prosperity unequaled in the history of the nation or the world. We have not yet assumed our full share in the real sacrifice for democracy" (quoted in Ernst, 1974, 36).

mobilizing and leading the war effort. Rather than recount the ways in which Progressivism was quickly restructured to be coterminous with American preparedness or retell all the ways in which Progressive institutions were incorporated into that effort,[37] the more important story is that which examines these policies in light of Progressive public doctrine regarding citizenship, rights, and duties.

At the most general level, the preparedness and mobilization policies were undertaken with a marked absence of formal-legal governmental authority. Although the national government did use its coercive powers to crush opposition to the war and although the courts did liberally enforce the newly enacted Espionage Act and Selective Draft Law restraints on speech and association,[38] most of the sudden mobilization expansion of national authority rested, not on law at all, but on opinion; not on state power, but on parastate influence. Whereas this might be viewed as a kind of replay of Northern mobilization during the Civil War,[39] this time around there was no single and integrative parastate agency comparable to the Republican party and its auxiliary bodies but rather a huge and complex concert of journalistic, philanthropic, economic, religious, educational, and reform institutions that both legitimated and were legitimated by the national government preparing for war. The most dramatic result of this sudden expansion of national authority without comparable governmental growth was conscription. Almost the entire apparatus of the draft functioned outside of the official federal government: of the 192,000 workers involved in the administration of the draft, only 429 were salaried federal employees. A vast majority of the others were unpaid members of the more than 4,600 state and local boards.[40]

37. Vaughn, 1980, 36–37, on the role of Progressives in the Committee on Public Information; McClymer, 1980, chaps. 5 and 6 on professional social workers, Americanization, and the war; Kennedy, 1980, 33–44, on Progressives' shift toward war, and 45–61 on the role of Croly, Dewey and the universities generally in preparing the public for war; Wynn, 1986, 36–38 and 43–44, on support for the war by Progressive journalists, reformers and women's rights advocates; Thompson, 1987, 119–49, on the debate in the Progressive press over America's role in the world and intervention in the war; Schaffer, 1991, 90–95, on women reformers and the war, and 127–48 on the universities; and Ernst, 1974, 35–69, on the liberal evangelical churches and allied institutions in support of preparedness and war.

38. Chaffee, 1941; Peterson and Fite, 1957; Rabban, 1981 and 1983; and Weinstein, 1967.

39. Fredrickson, 1965; McKitrick, 1967; southern contrast, Bensel, 1990.

40. Wynn, 1986, 76–77. Given the propaganda for both preparedness and universal military service of these leading parastate institutions, success was never in doubt. The effect, nevertheless, was quite awesome. On 23 May 1917, Congress passed the Conscription Act; on 5 June, exactly two weeks later, nine and a half million men presented themselves to local draft boards (Gabriel, 1956, 389).

The ability of the national government to harness and direct the energies of the entire society with few laws and fewer officials also meant that the line between moral and legal coercion became blurred and the issue of rights against the government opaque. This pattern of power was exercised largely outside the law even as, in the words of Mary Follett, individuals end up "acting as the state in every smallest detail of life" (Follett, 1918, 138). Given the density, scale, and intrusiveness of this parastate voluntarism, success was assured from the start. The matrix of committees under George Creel's Committee on Public Information (CPI), the main propaganda arm of the government, read like a who's who of Progressive academics, intellectuals, journalists, and feminists. Its volunteer army of 150,000 people on twenty-one separate committees included the most prominent reform leaders of the day, from churches and divinity schools, journalism, universities, academic professional societies, women's organizations, labor, and the arts. Given its importance and its large immigrant population, Chicago was the main target and testing ground. There, more than 400 "four-minute men" gave more than 50,000 talks to a combined audience of 25 million at movie theater intermissions during the short course of the war.[41] Other wartime governmental organizations were equally dependent upon volunteers and volunteer institutions. Rather than resort to legally mandated and governmentally coerced food rationing, Herbert Hoover's Food Administration mobilized a largely female volunteer army of 750,000 directed by a paid general staff of only 1,400 to direct the entire system of price controls and publicity campaigns for food production and conservation (Wynn, 1986, 70). Even the Justice Department augmented its formal enforcement powers more through volunteers and informal coercion than through officials and laws. The American Protective League, 250,000 strong, became an unofficial arm of the government, investigating some 3 million cases of draft evasion and disloyalty and reporting to the Justice Department.[42]

Equally striking was the extraconstitutional and voluntarist nature of industrial mobilization and control. The War Industries Board (WIB), which directed the entire wartime industrial economy, *had no*

41. Wynn, 1986, 48–49 and 136–38, on the role of leaders of women's suffrage and women's organizations; and see Vaughn, 1908, 23–39, on the role of reformers, women, academics, and educators in the CPI. George Creel was one of the early supporters of the feminist movement, appearing with Max Eastman and Frances Perkins at one of the first mass meetings of feminists in New York, in 1914 (Cott, 1987, 38).

42. Wynn, 1986, 51. The Protective League soon proved an embarrassment and was opposed by Progressives because of its local-provincial values, its fear and distrust of foreign immigrants, and its heavy-handed (and often illegal) investigatory initiatives.

statutory basis whatsoever: President Wilson simply declared it into being and appointed its membership (Kelly, Harbison, and Belz, 1983, 452). Each state, through the voluntary cooperation of its governor, established parallel councils to coordinate industrial planning and controls. Combined, the WIB had national, state, and local planning councils with almost 200,000 members. The Board gave legal sanction to agreements within each industrial group on wages, hours, production quotas, and prices. The only exception to this "trusteeship" ideal was the railroads: they were formally nationalized, but continued to be managed by the same personnel. America suddenly had what functioned as a command economy with little evidence of formal commands and almost no official commanders.[43]

The blurring of unofficial and official power, the seamlessness between voluntarism and coercion, and the merging of private and public institutions were both pervasive and welcomed. We could keep our Constitution intact by generating power outside its official boundaries, power which matched or exceeded that of authoritarian and statist regimes in Europe.[44] Given opposition to the war and given the financial resources of the government, however, there were necessarily points of severe tension. One could be tried in the federal courts for criticizing the Red Cross. YMCA workers wore government uniforms. "Four-minute men" were given franking privileges. The national government subverted antiwar unions and secretly subsidized prowar ones. State and local prosecutors and vigilantes were merciless on the antiwar union organizers of the Industrial Workers of the World (IWW) (Peterson and Fite, 1957; Weinstein, 1967). Sometimes private organizations were

---

43. This experience and its influence on the National Recovery Administration during the New Deal has become the source of a huge scholarly enterprise to identify "corporatism" as the explanatory model for Progressivism generally. Hawley, 1978; Lustig, 1982; Sklar, 1988; Weinstein, 1968; and, through core-periphery analysis, Bensel, 1984. The overarching difficulty with much of this analysis for the period prior to World War I was the absence of a state with enough authority and coherence to pull it off and the presence of a very well mobilized Progressive constituency (not to speak of the Democratic party) to make sure it did not. The WIB lasted only two years, and the core of the corporatism of the NRA, the binding authority of private agreements, was quickly declared unconstitutional. The best antidote to the corporatist thesis, however, is to read the hopes of the German-trained American political economists writing in the 1880s onward: even to imagine an institutionalized corporatism without cartel courts and national incorporation laws and a central bank was, for them, sheer folly.

44. As a professor of English at the University of Illinois put it in a wartime publication, the German state is founded on "external control and 'inner freedom,' " whereas our polity, founded by our Puritan ancestors, is "external freedom and inner control . . . the check of individual responsibility which the good American's moral culture imposes upon his liberty" (from Vaughn, 1980, 46–47).

simply turned over wholesale to the government, as in the case of the Women's Land Army (250,000 full- or part-time workers) to the U.S. Department of Agriculture (USDA) and the *Ladies Home Journal* to whomever Wilson designated.[45]

Chautauqua Institution president Arthur Bestor was both very right and very wrong when he declared, "In a democracy like ours, steeped in a laissez faire individualism, [preparedness] necessitates a complete reorganization of our life."[46] He was right in the sense that there was now the very visible hand of the president and the entire national government directing the reorganization. He was wrong, however, to think that America was not already "reorganized" and quite prepared for national citizenship and the conscious pursuit of a common object. For over three decades, through the institutions and organizations of the industrial and urban core—including his own—a coherent and self-conscious national public had been created. Preparedness and mobilization only made suddenly visible America's incredible resources and resolve. This sudden appearance, and in alliance with a Democratic administration, the trusts, urban labor, and Great Britain, necessarily frightened and alienated some previously loyal adherents to that public—especially in small-town America. Nevertheless, the speed of response and the shortness of America's participation in the war blunted these forebodings. Indeed, for those more cosmopolitan Progressives in charge, the shortness of the war occasioned regret. Guy Stanton Ford, dean of the University of Minnesota's Graduate School and head of the Committee for Public Information's Division of Civic and Educational Publications, stated, "The Germans spoiled some perfectly good enterprises by ending the war when they did" (Vaughn, 1980, 59). He was certainly not alone; to many Progressive intellectuals the war was proof that America and Americans were capable of higher national service and selfless national citizenship.[47]

Progressive enthusiasm for and leadership of both official and unofficial

45. Wynn, 1986, 138; Mott, 1957a, 549. Herbert Hoover made his first public statement as food administrator through the *Journal*; Franklin Roosevelt, secretary of the navy, urged mothers to encourage their sons to enlist; and William Howard Taft, chair of the Red Cross Central Committee, edited the magazine's Red Cross Department. In addition, Queen Elizabeth of Belgium and President Wilson and other members of the executive branch (McAdoo, Baruch, Gerard) used its pages. *World's Work* and *Review of Reviews* saw explosive rises in circulation because they became major sources and conduits of preparedness and war information (Mott, 1957a, 773–88 and 657–64).

46. Vaughn, 1980, 127. Woodrow Wilson said: "It is not an army we must shape and train for war, it is a nation" (ibid., 4).

47. This was especially true among professional social workers and liberal evangelical churchmen (Ernst, 1974, 35–69; McClymer, 1980, 153–91).

wartime organizations was both natural and, in the circumstances, almost inevitable. (Forcey, 1961; Kennedy, 1980; Levy, 1985; Steel, 1980; Thompson, 1987, chaps. 2 and 3). In "state-building" language, they already possessed the ideology, the institutional resources, and the administrative capacity for these activities, including a quasi-monopoly on access to social knowledge and the organizational means for its dissemination. This was especially true of national journalists and editors, university administrators, leaders of the academic professions, ecumenical church leaders, and leaders of national women's organizations. Moreover, Progressives generally recognized in "preparedness" a model for the new citizenship and a testing ground for habits of public service (Ernst, 1974, 51–114; McClymer, 1980, 153–91; and Thompson, 1987, 127–41 and 168–77). Through the merging of public and private institutions of social reform and regulation, much of their reform agenda seemed suddenly in process of fulfillment: national woman suffrage, wages and hours legislation, national regulation of alcohol, Americanization programs for immigrants, recognition of responsible trade unionism, national economic planning, compilation of social and economic statistics, suppression of partisan politics, and the sudden prestige of professional expertise. For a short time, all areas of American life—even business—appeared to have become moralized by the common good. The agencies for this moralization were not laws, parties, or courts, but good citizens, with a little help from the government, voluntarily uniting to serve their country and the world.

WAR AS ATONEMENT

Although almost all of the Progressive academics and intellectuals in this study strongly supported America's new international role and its "civilizing mission" and were heartened by the civic virtue displayed in certain aspects of the preparedness campaigns, some were decidedly ambivalent about our formal entry into the war. Simon Patten and Edmund James were both decidedly unenthusiastic, Patten to such a degree that he was not reappointed at Wharton when he reached formal retirement age. James, as president of the University of Illinois, was put under very strong pressure to show more enthusiasm for preparedness and war, which he eventually did. Jane Addams, earlier one of America's most venerated and respected figures, came under vicious attack for her opposition to the war.[48] Dewey, initially quite supportive, looked with some horror at the patriotic excess that soon swept the country.[49]

48. Davis, 1973, 246–47. Until Secretary of War Newton Baker had it removed, her name was on a list of sixty-two persons considered especially dangerous by national military intelligence (252–53).

49. In his 1920 lectures in Japan, *Reconstruction in Philosophy*, he somewhat

Nevertheless, even these Progressives ended up doing their part. In 1918 James wrote a patriotic pamphlet, published as part of a series by his university, extolling American war activities and moral leadership. That same year Patten published a collection of his patriotic songs and had earlier written a series of proposals on wartime tax policies for *Annals*. Dewey wrote a "confidential report" in 1918 on the political loyalties and values of the Polish communities in America.[50] Even Jane Addams did her part: Herbert Hoover rescued her from popular wrath by making her an advocate of gardening and food conservation (Davis, 1973, 247; Vaughn, 1980, 129–30). Most others were more enthusiastic: Small, Gilman, Kelley, Commons, and Ely all wrote pamphlets in the period 1917–18 supportive of America's entry and its war aims. Both the *American Journal of Sociology* and *Annals*, which at least before Wilson's "War Message" to Congress on 2 April 1917 opened their pages to the opposition, were quickly enlisted. The *Review of Reviews* carried some anti-British articles and was almost banned in Canada until Albert Shaw was persuaded by Creel to omit offensive material (Vaughn, 1980, 225–26). Another factor, the age of these academics, also blunted their potential public roles regarding the war; almost all of them were nearing or just past sixty. Some of their students, however, from a combination of conviction, ambition, and professional expertise, played important wartime roles.[51]

Beyond these differences, however, was a deeper one: those who translated the social gospel or "Christian Sociology" directly into the Religion of America more quickly and enthusiastically reintroduced overt biblical images of atonement, suffering, and national salvation into their readings of American nationality and American patriotism. Patten and James were more distant from this reading of their own

---

obliquely summarized his own conclusion flowing from the war experience: "Pluralism is well ordained in present political practice and demands a modification of hierarchical and monistic theory. Every combination of human forces that adds its own contribution of value to life has for that reason its own unique and ultimate worth. It cannot be degraded into a means to glorify the State. One reason for the increased demoralization of war is that it forces the State into an abnormally supreme position" (Dewey, 1982, 196–97).

50. All sources, *National Union Catalogue*. Dewey's pro-interventionist arguments were written in the *New Republic* in opposition to Randolph Bourne, summarized in Thompson, 1987, 167–68. The Polish question episode in Dewey's life and the literature discussing it is summarized in Westbrook, 1991, 212–23.

51. Patten's students active in the war effort included Walter Weyl, William Draper Lewis, and Edward T. Devine; one of Small's was Frances Kellor; and two of Ely's were Guy Stanton Ford and Albert Shaw.

work, but the sociologists and, in a curious way, Dewey, were not.[52] The University of Chicago, in particular, seemed to be a center of this understanding, evidenced in Small's writings, in the pages of his *American Journal of Sociology (AJS)* and, especially, in the writings of its divinity school faculty.[53] In what must stand as one of the more striking expressions of the meaning of the Religion of America, Shailer Mathews, dean of the Divinity School, defended modernism and social gospel Christianity as ''a religion fit for democracy'' in his justification of our entry into the war.[54] Perhaps the best exponent of this view, however, was Lyman Abbott, editor of *Outlook* and longtime associate of Theodore Roosevelt. No writer at this time better captured and more effectively exploited this long-standing alliance in Progressive public doctrine.

Lyman Abbott edited the *Outlook* from its founding in 1881 until his death in 1923. It was one of the earliest reform journals, having its origins in Henry Ward Beecher's *Christian Union*. Although its most famous regular contributor was Theodore Roosevelt, other writers and re-

52. Compared to prominent (and younger) political scientists and historians, however, the sociologists could almost be accused of shirking. The CPI's Guy Stanton Ford created what he termed ''a war emergency national university,'' flooding the country and designated subgroups with pamphlets written by such prominent historians and political scientists as Carl Becker, Edward Corwin, Andrew McLaughlin, J. Franklin Jameson, Charles Beard, George Sabine, and Monroe Smith. The only academic in this study participating in Ford's enterprise was John R. Commons. Beard's colleague at Columbia and textbook coauthor, William C. Bagley, was editor-in-chief of the *National School Service*, published by CPI and sent twice monthly to every school in America. It urged national unity and patriotic sacrifice, inveighed against individualism, and associated the war effort with social and educational reform (Vaughn, 1980, chaps. 3, 5, and 6).

53. Small's ''Bonds of Nationality,'' discussed above in chapter 2, appeared in *AJS* in 1915, which also contained ''The Social Problem and the Present War,'' by Charles A. Ellwood, a prominent Christian Sociologist at the University of Missouri. Shailer Mathews, author of *The Social Teachings of Jesus, An Essay in Christian Sociology*, which first appeared as articles in the *AJS*, wrote a very influential book in 1918, *Patriotism and War*. Based on lectures that year at the University of North Carolina, it is a powerful defense of the interdependence of liberal Christianity and American patriotism to insure democratic values; it is also a ringing rebuke of dogmatic and ''church'' Christianity allied to authoritarianism, through regimes such as Germany's, and evident in the fact that conservative religious denominations in America were not sacralizing America's war crusade. Marsden, 1980, confirms the fact that religious liberals led church war mobilization and even accused religious conservatives of lacking patriotism.

54. Mathews, 1918, 121. His Chicago colleague, Edward Scribner Ames, codified this relationship of American democracy, post-Protestant religious modernism, and social science in *The New Orthodoxy*, published that same year. Ames (1925, vi) was quite explicit in the preface: ''This book seeks to present in simple terms a view of religion consistent with the mental habits of those trained in the sciences, in the professions, and in the expert direction of human affairs.''

formers who contributed were Jacob Riis, Booker T. Washington, and Frederick C. Howe.[55] Abbott's wartime book, *The Twentieth Century Crusade*, perfectly captures the marriage of church and nation in the gendered imagery that had always marked Progressive writings.[56] In Abbott's reading, this union is of the military courage of the son and the selfless moral nurture of the mother who sends him off to war. Their common bond is patriotism as atonement: American civic virtue is the willing sacrifice of national peace and comfort to redeem the sins of the world. Abbott's book consists of nine letters addressed to mothers about their sons. Except for Abbott himself (but in the persona of clergyman), middle-aged men as fathers are largely absent as either subjects or audience. The setting for the letters are "the three crosses" of Europe, "the cross of the unrepentant, bitter, wrathful brigand [Germany]; the cross of the repentant sinner [England and France]; and the cross of the men and women who are suffering for sins they never committed—for sins for which they have no responsibility." Though not without faults, America stands with the third cross, especially those Americans who are mothers and sons. "This book is written for those who are sharing in the great sacrifice in this world's Golgotha. Whether they recognize Jesus Christ as their leader or not, whether they are Roman Catholics or Protestants, believers or agnostics, Christians or Jews, they have taken up their cross and are following him; they are laying down their lives for their unknown kinsmen beyond the sea" (Abbott, 1918, ix, xi).

This image of American innocence and virtue is strengthened by one last prefatory note: no one "earns" repentance or "wins" forgiveness. Europe will be redeemed only by an inner transformation occasioned by witnessing the selfless acts of atonement represented by American mothers and American sons. This pair, representing the authentic nation, stands above the European conflict and between the unrepentant and the repentant thieves (even perhaps above the slightly tarnished middle-aged American male, the father-manager of the war effort in all his many roles and guises).

For all this sentimental overlay, the nine letters are a robust call to arms. Indeed, the civic virtue called for is much more demanding of courage than the easy virtues of democratic individualism practiced by the pattern American male—what Theodore Roosevelt had earlier de-

55. Mott, 1957, 422–35; and see above, chapter 1, note 12. Among the academics in this study, only Albion Small and Richard Ely wrote for Abbott's popular but pious weekly.

56. Kann, 1990, 46–81, argues that just beneath all of American liberal political discourse is a civic republicanism represented by young men as soldiers and women as teachers of morality and selflessness.

scribed as ''well to do hucksters . . . sunk in a scrambling commercial-ism'' (Giankos, 1966, 1: 52–53). The first letter recalls Lincoln and the Civil War and tells the mother that her son ''has joined the noble army of patriots.'' By the fifth letter he is contrasting the ''glory in tribula-tions'' to the sordid ends of personal happiness, quoting from Hermann Hagedorn's famous Phi Beta Kappa poem at Harvard. Those who say that America is ''a booth where doves are sold'' or ''a money-changer's cave'' are wrong: ''It is a vast cathedral . . . A church! Where in hushed fervor stand / The children of contending races, / Forgetting feud and fatherland—/ A hundred million lifted faces.''[57]

The distinctly political argument opens with the sixth letter, ''The Republic of God.'' Here, Abbott restates arguments now familiar in Progressive writings. Democracy is not a form of government, but a faith, a government by public opinion that underwrites the democratic character of all of American institutions: ''of religion, of industry and of education as well as in government; in a word it is human brother-hood.'' This democratic republic is founded on four corresponding lib-erties—religious, industrial, educational, and political—but ''these liberties are not only rights; they are also duties. We sometimes ought to forego our rights; we never ought to abandon our duties'' (Abbott, 1918, 64–65). The seventh letter reiterates the distinction between Is-rael and Rome by contrasting Lincoln and the present German Kaiser in their respective calls on God for victory. Lincoln-Wilson stand for the true union of reason and spirit—Hegel and Christianity,—because they know that America is to carry out God's design for the world only with the understanding that even defeat, unthinkable as it is, would serve a higher purpose that we must accept. In any event, ''Christ's Peace'' re-quires victory, whether over ''base appetites and passions'' within or injustice and criminality without. The concluding letters are trium-phal. Democracy and justice are winning in the world; America-as-Is-rael is leading the way against Germany-as-Rome. Recounting the prog-ress since his birth in 1835, Abbott concludes: ''He who believes that history is anything more than merely a series of accidental happenings, who believes that there is any continuity and coherence in history, who

57. Abbott, 1918, 52–54. Hermann Ludwig Gebhard Hagedorn (1882–1964) was a popular poet and author, having graduated from Harvard and taught in the English Department from 1909 to 1911 before striking off on his own as a writer. A Ger-man-American from a prominent New York mercantile family, he was lionized as a convert to full Americanism, forming a group called ''Vigilantes'' in 1916 to stimu-late patriotism among the young and writing an interventionist book, *Where Do You Stand?* in 1918. He became a close friend of Theodore Roosevelt's toward the end of his life, helped form the first presidential library at Harvard, and wrote many books on Roosevelt and other robust American figures.

believes in any ordered social evolution, should find it difficult to believe that this march of the century toward liberty will be halted" (Abbott, 1918, 99).

The final letter, "Coronation," addresses the problem of the reward for the mothers' brave sons "who have offered their lives, not merely for their country but for an unknown people, of a different land, a different language and often of a different religious faith." Here the Religion of the American Way overtakes more traditional biblical Christianity. Immortality is faith as such, "not a hope for the future [but] a present possession, . . . the consciousness that I am more than the body which I inhabit."[58]

THE ASHES OF VICTORY

America's crusade in Europe ended in quick victory—so quick that many of those who led were eager to turn that civic energy into new crusades at home and abroad. This was especially evident among labor leaders, professional educators, and social welfare professionals. The hopes of the two groups of professionals, however, were quickly dashed by demobilization and the withdrawal of the national government (and its funds) into its prewar constitutional boundaries. The hopes of labor were smashed by the end of the War Industries Board and the start of the Red Scare. Among those who led the parachurch organizations to war, however, optimism seemed more warranted. During the war unprecedented forms of cooperation were forged between government, journalism, philanthropy, parachurch organizations, and churches. In 1917 the YMCA sought to raise $35 million in contributions for its wartime work but received more than $50 million. Under Robert Speer, a General War-Time Commission of the Churches coordinated governmental support activities through Protestant, Catholic, and Jewish umbrella organizations. These groups, along with the YMCA, the American Library Association, and others, launched a massively advertised joint drive for funds in 1918 and succeeded in getting "the largest amount of money ever offered voluntarily in the history of the world"—$175 million.[59] It was as if America were one incredibly suc-

---

58. Abbott, 1918, 106 and 103. Douglas, 1988, 200–227, traces the origins of this "domestication of death" to the mid-nineteenth-century theologians such as Bushnell and Beecher and their female author-poet allies. This same treatment of atonement and immortality occurred in England. Abbott ends quoting a prayer by Gladstone, "For a Friend out of Sight" (Abbott, 1918, 109–10; see also Hilton, 1988, 340–72).

59. To put these amounts in perspective, the national budget in 1881 was $260 million and in the 1890s was in the $400 million range (Keller, 1977, 309).

cessful politico-religious revival meeting led by its most worthy citizens.

Protestant churchmen like Speer and Mott turned their immediate postwar energies to continuing the battle to redeem the world for American democracy. Their wartime successes and their organizational skills converged on a plan for a new national umbrella organization, the Interchurch World Movement, to carry on the cooperative ventures learned in wartime. In the words of one religious publication, "War drives for world freedom [were] passing into Christian drives for world redemption. . . . Christian churches mobilize when armies demobilize."[60] And mobilize they did. Plans were laid to raise $336 million over five years—$175 million in the first year alone—to fund church work of all types at home and abroad. Interchurch would be an American sponsored international parastate for the world conquest of poverty, disease, oppression, and injustice. Mott extolled the effort as "the greatest program undertaken by Christians since the days of the Apostles." Others seconded this claim, calling it "the greatest revival in history . . . a new epoch in the history of Christianity" (Ernst, 1974, 58–59). The organizing committee quickly began its work. By 1920, Interchurch had a full-time, paid staff of more than 2,600, renting office space in ten different buildings in New York City and incurring expenses that often exceeded $1 million a month (Ernst, 1974, 90–91). Even the Senate failure to ratify the treaty committing the United States to join the League of Nations did not dampen the enthusiasm of Interchurch:

> No matter how much our political leaders have failed us in this supreme hour of duty and honor, the Christian people of America still have a chance. The challenge comes to the church all the stronger because it is being refused by the state. How else shall we bear our humiliation before the world? America, which went into the war placarding her passion for service, her devotion to the good of all mankind, America, whose idealism was the strength of the armies of the Allies, the solace and hope of the crushed and bleeding nations throughout the world—America to fail them in the end (Ernst, 1974, 140)!

This was not to be Interchurch's only disappointment. In contrast to most individual Protestant congregations, that is, to its major constitu-

---

60. Ernst, 1974, 59. The image of America as redeemer nation at war was so deeply ingrained that one prominent church leader could ask, "Shall the Christian Church lag behind the state in its defense of Christian principles?" (138).

ency, the organizational structure, methods of operation, and local basis of support for Interchurch were urban, thoroughly modernist in theology, and cosmopolitan. Even its business supporters were overwhelmingly Progressive and reformist. Indicative of this spirit was the fact that Interchurch, like the Federal Council of Churches, combined social science and social gospel to address the major issues of the day.[61] When the great steel strike occurred in 1919 and while Interchurch was still only an organizing committee, its Industrial Relations Department immediately launched an investigation. Given its charter to help Christian America bring democracy to industry by "recognizing the essential partnership of capital and labor and the interdependence of social and industrial groups and their mutual obligations," the department issued a report clearly on the side of labor. And despite the rising popular hysteria directed against "radicals" such as the ex-IWW organizer and syndicalist William Z. Foster, the investigating Commission condemned not only the United States Steel Corporation but its allies in the press (Ernst, 1974, 128–30). Interchurch was soon accused of being "radical" by representatives of some of the more conservative religious bodies. The split between "liberal" and "conservative" Protestantism—implicit from the very start of the social gospel movement and even earlier in the new theology—was finally becoming articulate (Marsden, 1980; and Szasz, 1982, 68–83). In 1920, the editor of a Baptist religious publication, *Watchman-Examiner*, coined the term "fundamentalist" to designate those who insisted that all cooperation among Protestants must be founded on shared Christian beliefs before they can proclaim that message to the world. This is exactly what modernism, the social gospel, Christian Sociology, Interchurch, and the Religion of the American Way had always sought to avoid.[62] With this

61. Batten, 1911, 229–30, contains the Social Service Program of the Federal Council. It reads very much like the Progressive party platform planks on social and industrial justice. One of the early promotional efforts of Interchurch was to publish in 1920, *World Survey*, a two-volume compendium of statistics and descriptive materials covering each country of the world and documenting its literacy, health, education, the condition and status of women and children, and its religion. Its home survey section was a more detailed social, demographic, and economic description of America. In this sense, *World Survey* was a continuation of a genre begun by Lyman Beecher's *A Plea for the West* (1835) and Josiah Strong's *Our Country* (1885) (Ernst, 1974, 123).

62. Ironically, thirty-five years later, Will Herberg, 1983, 259, celebrated the result of this split as American liberal-pluralism. "Interchurch" became "interfaith": "Interfaith . . . is a religiously oriented civic co-operation of Protestants, Catholics, and Jews to bring about better mutual understanding and to promote enterprises and causes of common concern, despite all differences of 'faith.' The interfaith movement is not secularistic or indifferent but in its own way quite

declaration "Protestantism" suddenly collapsed as a coherent idea of America. Now it was only "liberal" Protestantism that served as the Religion of America, a religion that was as open to agnostics, Jews, and Catholics (in some ways more open) as it was to fundamentalists. Progressivism collapsed, too, because it suddenly lost most of its popular-populist base.

Interchurch was in fact an attempt to consolidate yet another quasi-official religious establishment in America, a parachurch above all churches and all particular doctrinal beliefs. In that sense, it was to be the most embracive and popular institutionalization of Progressive public doctrine, representing an ideal of national citizenship and service that stood above interest, creed, section, race, and status. Originally representing thirty denominations (60 percent of American Protestantism), it seemed bent on including not only all Protestant church members, but all other Americans as well. Secretary of State Lansing, Senator (soon President) Harding, Vice-President Marshall, House Speaker Gillett, Mrs. Woodrow Wilson, General Pershing, Treasury Secretary McAdoo, and Navy Secretary Daniels all publicly and actively promoted the Interchurch World Movement. Such were the dreams of its leaders that they stipulated that $40 million of its first year fund drive not be raised by and for the separate church denominations, but for Interchurch itself and *from those who go to no church at all!* Banks, corporations, labor unions, and, especially, the national press combined to ask all Americans "to do your share for a better America and a better world."[63]

Here, indeed, was a dream that expressed the very origins and spirit of Progressivism: a "church" without a creed except that of American democracy, a cosmopolitan ideal of membership that transcended and redeemed all American particularity, an identity that was as capacious as that of the whole world. But it all suddenly collapsed. Whereas the fund drive of the separate Protestant churches for their own use and growth was an overwhelming success, the campaign to fund the parachurch of the Religion of America was a disaster: not even 10 percent of

---

religious, for it is conceived as a joint enterprise . . . of the three religious communities dedicated to purposes of common interest felt to be worth while from the religious point of view. Interfaith is thus the highest expression of religious coexistence and cooperation within the American understanding of religion." More recently, Mooney (1990) and Hunter (1991) have urged this same grand coalition, but in order to excommunicate the fundamentalists from the reconstituted Religion of the American Way.

63. Ernst, 1974, 73–74. This, too, anticipates what was so celebrated as American liberal consensus during the Eisenhower presidency, what Herberg (1983, 260) termed "religiousness without religion."

the goal was raised. One after another the denominations that were the founders and major debt-holders of Interchurch—Methodists, Baptists, Presbyterians, Congregationalists, Disciples—quickly bailed out. Interchurch simply disappeared. And with that disappearance, both the term and the coherence of Progressivism also disappeared, to leave traces in what soon came to be called "liberalism." This liberalism, however, was lacking a good portion of American Protestantism, many of its institutional structures, and much of its national vision.

Suddenly, the entire axis of public doctrine and patterns of adherence to that doctrine seemed to shift.[64] What happened to the Progressive movement? Surely it was not suddenly relocated in the Democratic party and renamed "liberalism." In 1924 the Democratic nominee for president was John W. Davis, who later achieved fame as the lead attorney for maintaining de jure school segregation in the *Brown* case (Kelly, 1983, 608). Such was the divide in the core of the Progressive constituency and such was the resulting loss of a coherent public, that American historians quickly shifted from the question of what happened to the Progressive movement to a denial that there was such a movement at all.[65] Because it was thought that Progressivism had no future, historians soon decided that it had no coherent and authoritative past either. This is understandable given the association of Wilson and Progressivism and given the later victories of the New Deal. And because of these later victories historians were prone to read prevailing liberal-conservative divisions back into the Progressive Era. Thus, small-town evangelical Protestants become fundamentalists and conservative while urban, ethnic Catholics become liberal. German-Jewish Progressive Republicans are scorned for being misled into the trap of WASP assimilationism: the Red Scare and 1920s anti-Semitism is retroactive proof of their eighty-year-old error. Industrial policy and core prosperity from the 1880s onward was built on the exploitation of the South and the West, not by the savings, energies, and talent of industrial region capital and labor. So much revision; so much loss of memory.[66]

These convenient redescriptions legitimate the New Deal regime as

64. And just as suddenly, perfectly respectable Progressives were being accused of radicalism and un-Americanism. The Lusk Committee of the New York State Senate led the pack by seeking to discredit not only Jane Addams, who opposed the war, but Beard, Croly, Dewey, Ely, Florence Kelley, and Walter Rauschenbusch, all supporters of intervention, as well. Protestant seminaries, such as Union in New York City, and Progressive journals, such as *Survey,* came under the same ban (Mc-Clymer, 1980, 192–96).

65. Filene, 1970; Link, 1959; Rodgers, 1982. And see above, chapter 1.

66. A recent study of the extent and kinds of wealth in congressional districts, divided by region, shows that as early as the mid-1880s regional wealth disparities were already clearly established (James, 1992, 168).

liberal even as they extend full membership in the national community to regions and groups who were previously excluded or were offered only a kind of associate membership. This same redescription permitted liberal Protestant sons and daughters to take over where their evangelical fathers and mothers left off, even as Russian-Jewish sons and daughters could supplant German-Jewish "parents." In both instances, the cost of honoring the parents was partial denial of their parents' horizons. The alternative was to admit those horizons in order to reject them. These doctrinal and historiographical battles are now fought largely within the walls of universities, the conflicted twentieth-century churches of the Religion of America. The result has been a series of oscillations in memory and imagination regarding the traditions and theologies of American national identity. But the swing has been between a recognition designed for rejection (capitalist elites, racists, religious bigots) or a denial designed for reconciliation (we were all Progressives, we all had redeemable faults—except, of course, for those who became "conservatives," now defined as the ideological opponents of the New Deal and, later, the Great Society).

Now that enthusiastic defenders of New Deal liberalism as regime and as public doctrine are hardly to be found in the academy, we could do worse than seek to reappropriate some features of Progressive public doctrine that later liberal doctrine never understood or forgot. We might at least conclude that it was no small achievement to connect pride in one's country to mutual obligations and a national ideal of social justice.

CONCLUSION

Only recently has twentieth-century American liberalism come to understand that there is no necessary relationship between the expansion of the federal government and the extension of justice and freedom. Even the earlier move in liberal institutional identity away from executive and administrative power and toward the federal courts did not make this clear because the extension of rights was also their nationalization, and thus an expansion of the federal government. Although no reexamination of political and social theory written one hundred years ago will solve our present perplexities, I suggest that we can take some steps toward their clarification by reflecting on three separate and contradictory ways in which the Progressive vision *did* appear victorious. But because each of these apparent successes was at odds with itself and with one another, each success was also a subversion. The most obvious proof of this is the fact that we now have so many plausible but contradictory understandings of Progressivism. The more poignant proof is an intellectual legacy of liberalism that now perplexes more than it guides.

WILSONIAN PROGRESSIVISM

The first success-subversion was the victory of Wilson and the Democratic party under the auspices of a national legislative program bearing many Progressive marks. This populist-peripheral appropriation created a radical asymmetry between the production and use of political ideas—and worse, used ideas intended to be transformative largely to serve an ad hoc coalition of separate standing interests. Northern urban middle-class academics and intellectuals authored new public doctrines that undermined rights-based and laissez-faire values and laid the basis for more active governmental intervention. But many of the practical fruits of this theoretical victory at the national level were harvested by the South and the economic and cultural periphery. They did this by using the newly legitimated and expanded resources of the federal government to subsidize and preserve the values and ways of life that federalism and other rights-based constitutional values had previously protected. Until the business recession of 1913 and the beginning of war preparedness the national government under Wilson might well have itself become the equivalent of an ever-expanding patronage political party, using the productive resources of the industrial core to subsidize its peripheral clientele. This same contradiction can be put in party-political terms. The theoretical battles were fought and won by nationally oriented northern intellectuals and their urban, professional, middle-class followers, all with strong historic ties to the Republican party; most of the congressional support for what is considered a progressive agenda came from congressional Democrats in the South and Republicans from the Great Plains. This was true during both the Theodore Roosevelt and the Wilson presidencies (Buenker, 1978; Sanders, 1990; Sarasohn, 1989).

This party-political contradiction between "theory" and "practice" holds also in ethnocultural terms. Both the critique of the old regime and the legitimation of the emerging one was the product of the spiritual descendants of Puritanism and New England; many of the governmental policies and practices subsequently instituted were a creation of the South and other peripheral regions increasingly in alliance with immigrant and urban labor in the northern industrial cities. With the partial exception of some sectors of labor, no member of this coalition either represented or embodied new values, new ideas, new science, or new institutions. All were reactive against the new; all were seeking to defend older ways of life against the economic and cultural intrusions of the dynamic core. That the means necessary to protect sectional, local, and peripheral values (for example, the income tax, the federal reserve system) would themselves become engines of centralization and modernization was an open secret to Progressives but not known by the localized and disparate constituents of the legislators who voted for those reforms. They were told that their "rights" were being restored. The New Deal was an expanded version of this same story, albeit with sizable cosmopolitan, urban, and intellectual adjuncts, especially from the elite law schools.

MANAGERIAL PROGRESSIVISM

A second success-subversion of the Progressive vision was in the managerial and organizational revolution that was completed between World War I and the Great Depression. Its legitimacy derived not from the Constitution or political democracy and electoral victory, but from market success and the authority of expertise and professionalism. Although the institutional basis for this revolution was laid much earlier (national universities, professional associations, the modern business corporation, national retailing and advertising, government bureaucracy), the new institutions flourished as never before during this period even as the party-political system was being demobilized and as voter participation was falling to pre-Jacksonian-era levels. Whether one looks at university growth and the professionalization of academic disciplines, the rationalization of trade policy and business regulation, the reorganization of the federal bureaucracy, the growth of "welfare capitalism," or the position of women, the life-world of the urban professional middle class and the modern business corporation increasingly dominated the society and its culture in the 1920s. With the exception of large and powerful industrial unions—a legislative product of the New Deal—almost the entire apparatus of what later came to be called "the liberal establishment" was solidly in place by the beginning of the Great Depression. This establishment included those parts of the national government with greatly enhanced administrative capacity and a growing corps of talented people whose ends in life were inseparable from those of the state. With the exception of some firmly established labor unions (for example, railroads), however, this 1920s proto-establishment comprised a very different universe of people from those who constituted either Wilson's electoral coalition earlier or Franklin Roosevelt's, later.

This second success-subversion of Progressivism differed from the Wilsonian one in other important ways as well. Most important, it existed almost entirely outside the Constitution as that document was traditionally understood. *This is precisely what guaranteed its symmetry between theory and practice.* Now seen as the victory of Progressivism in the ideal of "corporate liberalism," its success seems firmly anchored on a single foundation uniting theory and practice, supporters and beneficiaries, culture and power. Organizationally and culturally, it represented the future. Constitutionally, however, it was a highly suspect world of illegitimate "private governments." But this did not matter, so this political culture held, because the Constitution, like its expression in the rights language of the courts, was archaic and largely irrelevant anyway.

Firmly anchored in the explanatory world of the Progressive political economists and sociologists, the success of the managerial and organizational revolution points to the ways in which the whole matrix of "modernizing" institutions and practices created in the three decades preceding World War I came to achieve dominance and legitimacy in the decades following. And such was the depth of this dominance that even the New Deal read as the "revenge of the periphery" left all of these institutions as strong at the end of its wave of reforms as they were at the beginning. Put differently, the "populist" or electoral side of national reform was resource-dependent on the productivity, wealth, and talents of the organizational-managerial side of national Progressivism. In Croly's prophetic terms, Jeffersonian ends were hostage to Hamiltonian means, both materially and intellectually. The problem was that constitutional legitimacy (that is, ideas of individual rights) belonged to the former while effective national resources were controlled by the latter. This explains, perhaps, the obsessive concern of the early Progressives with public opinion, with national consensus and community, with the need for a pervasive and nationalizing "Religion of America." Without that link, Progressivism would lack coherence; neither the Wilsonian nor the corporate-liberal side retained that link. Standing alone, neither was both democratic and national.

MODERN LIBERALISM AS
CONSTITUTIONAL PROGRESSIVISM

Modern liberalism can be read as the conflicted child of this Progressive couple, this marriage of two success-subversions. But if this is so, the first question to ask is whether the parents were ever legally married. The second is how they were able to produce such a viable offspring. The identity of each parent is constituted by the difference from the "other," making of their marriage some postmodernist parody, an internecine struggle for power. Wilsonian Progressivism in its party-legislative and sectionalist successes was rigidly constitutional in the old and juridical-rights sense. But so, too, was the legalism and rights-obsessions of the federal courts, which often subverted the governmental means required to restore what were putatively lost rights. Wilson, the Democratic party, and the Supreme Court spoke the same nineteenth-century political language.

In contrast, the managerial or "corporate liberal" parent consisted of large and national aggregations of power quite outside the accepted boundaries of the Constitution—thus the term "private governments" that came into use in the 1930s. Insofar as these institutions were powerful, governing de facto in crucial areas of American life, they could hardly justify this power under the rubric of the Constitution and Bill of Rights—the very ideas they so mercilessly attacked. This was and is also true in the case of academics and universities, journalists and the national media, and nationally organized professionals generally. Moreover, these people and institutions tend to be interrelated and interdependent, both in terms of professional values and specialized knowledge and in terms of national or cosmopolitan orientations. In a mirror image of the Wilsonian parent, their very success is also a subversion: so long as they are seen as willing agents and servitors to the older values of localism and democratic individualism (that is, social mobility, self-esteem, and economic growth) and appear willing to be used for those ends, they are accepted as constitutionally legitimate. When deep conflicts of value and interest arise, however, they immediately become "elitist" or "private governments." In older Jeffersonian terms, they are branded "monopolists" or "privileged orders." Their Jeffersonian tormentors, in turn, become dangerous populists led by demagogues who would destroy the fabric of modern society. Given this fate of Progressive public doctrine split in two, no matter its original and coherent vision, what philosophical integrity could its product—liberalism—possibly claim?

When intellectual and historical conundrums of this magnitude confront us our safest response is to repair to the many blessings of American uniqueness and American luck. I suggest, however, that there is a third success of the Progressive vision, one of sufficient power and persuasiveness to constitute some basis for this strange marriage and its offspring-legacy of liberalism. And, unlike those of the parents, each of whose philosophical and intellectual integrity subverted that of the other, the philosophical contradictions of this success were well hidden. Indeed, only recently has this third success been critically (philosophically) examined at all. I refer to the victory of the Progressive vision in the law schools and the elite bar in the 1920s and thereafter.

It is commonly said, and repeated here, that from World War I to the recent past there has been a dearth of interesting and sophisticated social and political theory produced in America. Indeed, to read the Progressive academics and intellectuals from the mid-1880s onward and to see the fruitful migration of their ideas into the wider public domain is to envy them their creativity, energy, and popular success. No matter the contradictory ways in which their ideas eventually played out, no group who came after was able to address public life in the language of social and political theory with comparable originality, force, and efficacy. Among the academics highlighted in this study, only Dewey was able to remain somewhat innovative during the period of intellectual drought of the 1920s and 1930s. But his energy was increasingly that of the outsider—one who even doubted that an American public existed, let alone one prepared to listen to an emancipatory and democratic message.[1]

1. Although Walter Lippmann might also be thought an exception, read in the light of earlier Progressives, most of his 1920s writings were modernist translations, especially emphasizing what I have termed the managerial or corporate-liberal side. See especially *Public Opinion*, published in 1922.

There is, however, a major exception to this familiar narrative. Foreshadowed by the legal writings of Oliver Wendell Holmes, Jr., and James Bradley Thayer at the turn of the century,[2] by the 1920s (and in marked contrast to the universities) the elite law schools were suddenly vibrant centers of social and political theory. That the framework for that theory was thoroughly Progressive and closely dependent upon social evolutionary theory, political economy, and sociology should not detract from the scale and scope of their intellectual achievement. The "constitutional" side of this story is familiar: a powerful attack on judicial activism and abstract rights was launched from within the law schools. Whether informed by the sociological jurisprudence of Roscoe Pound, by the developing field of administrative law defended by James Landis (both deans of Harvard Law School in the 1920s and 1930s), or by the treatise literature on corporations, property, and contracts, the doctrinal grounds for declaring legislative and administrative decisions unconstitutional on the basis of violations of individual rights were being systematically subverted in the major law schools. In the process of destruction legal theorists paradoxically constitutionalized and legalized Progressive public doctrine and public policies.

What is surprising when reading the legal literature of the 1920s and early 1930s is the belated but powerful effect the Progressive academic literature written at the turn of the century had on legal scholarship. To some extent, this new orientation was a natural by-product of the fact that law students in the national law schools increasingly had undergraduate degrees and that Progressive scholarship dominated collegiate instruction from the 1890s onward (Stevens, 1983, 73–111 and 172–204). But this orientation, though available, would not have been so enthusiastically employed without deep and fundamental problems within the law itself, problems caused by the nationalization of the economy and culture. In any event, the combined force of sociological jurisprudence and legal realism disconnected the authority of law from the rhetoric of constitutional rights in two senses: first, they sought to remove the courts from large areas of decision making in economic matters in favor of legislative delegations to administrators and therefore to the realm of administrative law. Second, the more technical doctrines that the courts and treatise writers shaped regarding corporations, contracts, and property had the effect of reading out older

---

2. Holmes's "Privilege, Malice and Intent" (1894) and "Path of Law" (1897) and Thayer's "The Origin and Scope of the American Doctrine of Constitutional Law" (1893) are the defining documents. See Horwitz, 1992, 33–167, for discussion of the relationship of these ideas to Progressivism.

individualistic and rights understandings[3] in favor of more impersonal and functional or "realist" understandings. The incorporation of these new understandings within a larger legitimating framework pointed naturally to Progressive academic writings. In this paradoxical way, then, Progressive academic and intellectual hostility to courts and lawyers received its ultimate vindication—but from within the legal profession itself and by the transformation of American constitutional and legal doctrine. Thus it was that New Deal liberalism, quite unlike Progressivism, was articulated and legitimated largely by lawyers.

This suggested explanation of the relationship of modern liberalism to older Progressivism is less a "solution" to the problem of philosophical coherence than a relocation and a call for further study. Symbolically stated, New Deal liberalism, as represented on the Supreme Court, embraced Justices Douglas and Black as well as Justices Stone and Frankfurter. Both sets were Progressive and liberal. Both were products and even producers of the new legal scholarship and served as agents of transition between Progressivism and the New Deal. Their agreement, both philosophically and in decision—on the role of government in the economy, on the importance of administrative autonomy and administrative law, and on the constitutionality of wide delegation of powers by legislators—was far reaching and substantial. Soon, however, deep disagreements surfaced with ironic results for the philosophical coherence of liberalism. It was as if the two Progressive parents cursed their juridical offspring with some massive genetic defect that surfaced only when coherent thought about rights and the rule of law was desperately required (Horwitz, 1992, 213-72).

It should appear obvious by now that it was the fate of both Progressive parents and their liberal child to be lacking an adequate national identity and therefore a sense of national democratic citizenship. It was precisely this feature that Progressivism had originally built into the foundations of its thought. The very features we now find repellent or dangerous—the stress on one people, a "Religion of America," a community of equals bound by mutual duties one to another—was lacking in both appropriations and its product. Wilsonian Progressivism was built on the Democratic party as a coalition of marginals whose unity was only defensive and reactive. They could act in common only on the illusion that their separate demands for privileges and subsidies were common rights against some single foe. Corporate or managerial liberalism implicitly saw national unity in what political scientists later

---

3. These developments are thoroughly summarized in Horwitz, 1992, 33-107 and 145-67.

termed a democracy of "elite consensus" or "the liberal establishment."[4] The emerging liberal legal culture of the 1920s also studiously read out any lingering traces of national citizenship or of America as a democratic faith community, opting instead for the virtues of "value-free" social science or, more dangerously, flirting with a sort of nihilistic deconstruction of all foundations.[5] And since post-Progressive social science forfeited most of its credit and all of its claims to be a normative source of national cohesion, it is no wonder that "taking rights seriously" made such a dramatic comeback in the 1960s. But this revival of rights comes in so many different guises and represents so many different substantive agendas that sorting out the new rights talk has itself become a major intellectual enterprise. More important, and here this study comes full circle, with the revival of rights talk came a revival of communitarian and civic republican history and theory. It is this latter body of writing that needs to be examined critically against the lost promise of Progressivism.

4. In Reagan-era retrospect, C. Wright Mills and William Domhoff can as easily be read as reactionaries as radicals. Such is the liberal legacy of Progressivism that, when populist winds blow, we can never be sure whether they come from the right or the left.

5. It is interesting to read legal realists like Jerome Frank (*Law and the Modern Mind*, 1930), Thurman Arnold (*Folklore of Capitalism*, 1937), and Robert Lee Hale ("Economics and Law," 1925) in light of the critical legal studies movement today. Both the legal realist and the critical legal studies writings are criticized as nihilistic in their attempt to delegitimate prevailing legal doctrines and practices. While there is some merit in this charge—Nietzsche seems to be appearing everywhere today—what is missed is the barely disguised faith, then and now, that when deconstruction ends, American virtue and innocence begin. Indeed, American "nihilism" often wears a friendlier face than its parent, the American jeremiad, and both are grounded in the assurance of a happy ending.

BIBLIOGRAPHY

Abbott, Lyman. 1901. *The Rights of Man*. Boston and New York: Houghton Mifflin.

————. 1918. *The Twentieth Century Crusade*. New York: Macmillan.

Adams, Ephraim Douglass. 1913. *The Power of Ideals in American History*. New Haven, Conn.: Yale University Press.

Adams, Henry Carter. 1898. *The Science of Finance*. New York: Holt.

————. 1954. (Orig. ed. 1887). *Relation of the State to Industrial Action and Economics and Jurisprudence*. Edited and with an introduction by Joseph Dorfman. New York: Columbia University Press.

Adams, John. 1851. *The Works of John Adams*. Vol. 10. Boston: Little, Brown.

Adams, John Quincy. 1831. *An Oration Addressed to the Citizens of the Town of Quincy*. Boston: Richardson, Lord and Holbrook.

————. 1839. *The Jubilee of the Constitution: A Discourse*. New York: Samuel Colman.

Addams, Jane. 1892. "Hull House, Chicago: An Effort toward Social Democracy." *Forum* 14 (October): 226–41.

————. 1902. (1964). *Democracy and Social Ethics*. Cambridge, Mass.: Harvard University Press.

————. 1910. *Twenty Years at Hull House*. New York: Macmillan.

Ames, Edward Scribner. 1918. *The New Orthodoxy*. Chicago: University of Chicago Press.

Anderson, Charles W. 1990. *Pragmatic Liberalism*. Chicago: University of Chicago Press.

Appleby, Joyce. 1992. *Liberalism and Republicanism in the Historical Imagination*. Cambridge, Mass.: Harvard University Press.

Baldwin, James Mark. 1906. (Orig. ed. 1897). *Social and Ethical Interpretations in Mental Development*. New York: Macmillan.

Barrow, Clyde W. 1988. "Charles A. Beard's Social Democracy: A Critique of the Populist-Progressive Style in American Political Thought." *Polity* 21: 253–76.

————. 1990. *Universities and the Capitalist State: Corporate Liberalism and the Reconstruction of American Higher Education*. Madison: University of Wisconsin Press.

————. 1992. "From Marx to Madison: The Seligman Connection in Charles Beard's Constitutional Theory." *Polity* 24: 379–97.

Batten, Samuel Zane. 1898. *The New Citizenship: Christian Character in its Biblical Ideals, Sources, and Relations*. Philadelphia: Union Press.

————. 1909. *The Christian State: The State, Democracy and Christianity*. Philadelphia: Griffith and Rowland Press.

_____. 1911. *The Social Task of Christianity: A Summons to the New Cru-sade.* New York: Fleming H. Revell.

Beard, Charles. 1908. "Review, J. Allen Smith, *Spirit of American Govern-ment.*" *Political Science Quarterly* 23: 136–37.

_____. 1912. "The Supreme Court—Usurper or Grantee?" *Political Science Quarterly* 27: 1–35.

_____. 1913. *An Economic Interpretation of the Constitution of the United States.* New York: Macmillan.

_____. 1915. *Economic Origins of Jeffersonian Democracy.* New York: Mac-millan.

_____. 1928. *The American Party Battle.* New York: Workers Education Bu-reau Press.

_____. 1928a. *American Government and Politics.* New York: Macmillan.

Beard, Charles, and Mary Beard. 1927. *The Rise of American Civilization.* Vol. 2. New York: Macmillan.

Becker, William H. 1982. *The Dynamics of Business-Government Relations: Industry and Exports 1893–1921.* Chicago: University of Chicago Press.

Beecher, Lyman. 1977. (Orig. ed. 1835). *A Plea for the West.* New York: Arno Press.

Belz, Herman. 1969. "The Constitution in the Gilded Age: The Beginnings of Constitutional Realism in American Scholarship." *American Journal of Le-gal History* 13: 110–25.

Bensel, Richard F. 1984. *Sectionalism and American Political Development, 1880–1980.* Madison: University of Wisconsin Press.

_____. 1990. *Yankee Leviathan: The Origins of Central State Authority in America.* New York: Cambridge University Press.

Benson, Lee. 1961. *The Concept of Jacksonian Democracy.* Princeton, N.J.: Princeton University Press.

Bercovitch, Sacvan. 1977. *The Puritan Origins of the American Self.* New Ha-ven, Conn.: Yale University Press.

_____. 1978. *The American Jeremiad.* Madison: University of Wisconsin Press.

Berk, Gerald. 1990. "Constituting Corporations and Markets: Railroads in Gilded Age Politics." In *Studies in American Political Development* 4, edited by K. Orren and S. Skowronek. New Haven, Conn.: Yale University Press.

Billington, Ray. 1964. *The Protestant Crusade, 1800–1860.* New York: Times Books.

Bledstein, Burton J. 1976. *The Culture of Professionalism: The Middle Class and the Development of Higher Education in America.* New York: Norton.

Bliss, William Dwight Porter, ed. 1897. *Encyclopedia of Social Reform.* New York: Funk and Wagnalls.

_____. 1908. *The New Encyclopedia of Social Reform.* New York: Funk and Wagnalls.

Bliven, Naomi. 1992. "My Country, 'Tis of Thee." *New Yorker,* June 8, 60–78.

Bloch, Ruth H. 1990. "Religion and Ideological Change in the American Revo-lution." In *Religion and American Politics from the Colonial Period to the 1980s,* edited by Mark A. Noll. New York: Oxford University Press.

Blodgett, Geoffrey. 1966. *Gentle Reformers: Massachusetts Democrats in the Cleveland Era.* Cambridge, Mass.: Harvard University Press.

Boorstin, Daniel. 1953. *The Genius of American Politics.* Chicago: University of Chicago Press.

Boyer, Paul. 1971. *"In His Steps*: A Reappraisal." *American Quarterly* 23.

———. 1978. *Urban Masses and Moral Order in America, 1820–1920*. Cambridge, Mass.: Harvard University Press.

Brandes, Stuart D. 1976. *American Welfare Capitalism, 1880–1940*. Chicago: University of Chicago Press.

Buenker, John D. 1978. *Urban Liberalism and Progressive Reform*. New York: Norton.

Burnham, Walter Dean. 1970. *Critical Elections and the Mainsprings of American Politics*. New York: Norton.

Chaffee, Zachariah, Jr. 1941. *Free Speech in the United States*. Cambridge, Mass.: Harvard University Press.

Chandler, Alfred. 1977. *The Visible Hand: The Managerial Revolution in American Business*. Cambridge, Mass.: Harvard University Press.

———. 1990. *Scale and Scope: The Dynamics of Industrial Capitalism*. Cambridge, Mass.: Harvard University Press.

Chandler, Alfred, and Louis Galambos. 1977. "The Development of Large-Scale Economic Enterprise in Modern America." In *Men and Organizations*, edited by Edwin J. Perkins. New York: Putnam.

Clark, John Bates. 1886. *The Philosophy of Wealth*. Boston: Ginn and Company.

———. 1887. "The Limits of Competition." *Political Science Quarterly* 2: 45–61.

———. 1899. *The Distribution of Wealth*. New York: Macmillan.

———. 1914. (Repr. 1973). *Social Justice without Socialism*. New York: Arno Press.

Clark, John Bates, and Franklin H. Giddings. 1888. (1973). *The Modern Distributive Process*. New York: Arno Press.

Clark, Norman H. 1976. *Deliver Us from Evil: An Interpretation of American Prohibition*. New York: Norton.

Clubb, Jerome E. 1978. "Party Coalitions in the Early Twentieth Century." In *Emerging Coalitions in American Politics*, edited by Seymour M. Lipset. San Francisco: Institute for Contemporary Studies.

Coats, A. W. 1968. "Henry Carter Adams: A Case Study in the Emergence of the Social Sciences in the United States, 1850–1900." *Journal of American Studies* 2: 179–99.

Cohen, Morris. 1928. "Property and Sovereignty." *Cornell Law Quarterly* 13: 8–30.

Collin, Richard H. 1985. *Theodore Roosevelt, Culture, Diplomacy, and Expansion*. Baton Rouge: Louisiana State University Press.

Commons, John R. 1894. (Repr. 1967). *Social Reform and the Church*. New York: Thomas Y. Crowell.

———. 1907. *Races and Immigrants in America*. Chautauqua, N.Y.: Chautauqua Press.

Commons, John R., and John B. Andrews. 1916. *Principles of Labor Legislation*. New York: Harper and Brothers.

Connolly, William. 1991. *Identity-Difference: Democratic Negotiations of Political Paradox*. Ithaca, N.Y.: Cornell University Press.

Cooley, Charles Horton. 1897. "Genius, Fame and the Comparison of Races." *Annals of the American Academy* 9: 317–58.

———. 1902. (Repr. 1956). *Human Nature and the Social Order*. Glencoe, Ill.: Free Press.

_____. 1909. (Repr. 1956). *Social Organization: A Study of the Larger Mind.* Glencoe, Ill.: Free Press.

Cooley, Thomas M. 1889. *Constitutional History of the United States as Seen in the Development of American Law.* New York: G. P. Putnam's Sons.

Cott, Nancy F. 1987. *The Grounding of Modern Feminism.* New Haven, Conn.: Yale University Press.

Croly, Herbert. 1909. (Repr. 1989). *The Promise of American Life.* Boston: Northeastern University Press.

_____. 1914. *Progressive Democracy.* New York: Macmillan.

_____. 1916. "The Effect on American Institutions of a Powerful Military and Naval Establishment." *Annals of the American Academy* 66: 157–72.

Crunden, Robert M. 1984. *Ministers of Reform: The Progressives' Achievement in American Civilization 1889–1920.* Urbana: University of Illinois Press.

Curtis, George Ticknor. 1903. (Orig. ed. 1889). *Constitutional History of the United States.* 2 vols. New York: Harper and Brothers.

Curtis, Susan. 1991. *A Consuming Faith: The Social Gospel and Modern American Culture.* Baltimore: Johns Hopkins University Press.

Danbom, David B. 1987. *"The World of Hope": Progressives and the Struggle for an Ethical Public Life.* Philadelphia: Temple University Press.

Davis, Allen F. 1973. *American Heroine: The Life and Legend of Jane Addams.* New York: Oxford University Press.

_____. 1984. (1967.) *Spearheads for Reform: The Social Settlements and the Progressive Movement, 1890–1914.* New Brunswick, N.J.: Rutgers University Press.

Dawley, Alan. 1991. *Struggles for Justice: Social Responsibility and the Liberal State.* Cambridge, Mass.: Harvard University Press.

Dewey, John. 1910. *The Influence of Darwin on Philosophy and Other Essays in Contemporary Thought.* New York: Henry Holt.

_____. 1916. *Democracy and Education.* New York: Macmillan.

_____. 1927. *The Public and Its Problems.* Chicago: Swallow Press.

_____. 1969. *The Early Works.* Vol. 1. Carbondale: Southern Illinois University Press.

_____. 1971. *The Early Works.* Vol. 4. Carbondale: Southern Illinois University Press.

_____. 1982. *The Middle Works.* Vol. 12. Carbondale: Southern Illinois University Press.

Dewey, John, and James Tufts. 1908. *Ethics.* New York: Henry Holt and Company.

De Witt, Benjamin Parke. 1915. *The Progressive Movement.* New York: Macmillan.

Diggins, John. 1984. *The Lost Soul of American Politics: Virtue, Self-Interest, and the Foundations of Liberalism.* Chicago: University of Chicago Press.

Diner, Steven J. 1980. *A City and Its Universities: Public Policy in Chicago, 1892–1919.* Chapel Hill: University of North Carolina Press.

Dombrowski, James. 1936. (Repr. 1966). *The Early Days of Christian Socialism in America.* New York: Octagon Books.

Dorfman, Joseph. 1966. (Orig. ed. 1934). *Thorstein Veblen and His America.* New York: Augustus Kelley.

_____. 1949. *The Economic Mind of American Civilization.* Vol. 3, 1865–1880. New York: Viking Press.

Douglas, Ann. 1988. (Orig. ed. 1977). *The Feminization of American Culture.* New York: Doubleday.

Douglas, Mary, and Steven Tipton, eds. 1982. *Religion and America: Spirituality in a Secular Age.* Boston: Beacon Press.

DuBois, W. E. B. 1897. *Conservation of Races.* Washington, D.C.: The Academy.

_____. 1898. "The Study of the Negro Problem." *Annals of the American Academy* 11: 1–23.

_____. 1901. "The Relation of Negroes and Whites in the South." *Annals of the American Academy* 18: 119–40.

Eisenach, Eldon. 1981. *Two Worlds of Liberalism; Religion and Politics in Hobbes, Locke, and Mill.* Chicago: University of Chicago Press.

_____. 1987. "Mill's *Autobiography* as Political Theory." *History of Political Thought* 8: 111–29.

_____. 1990. "The Reconstruction of American Political Thought in a Regime-Change Perspective." In *Studies in American Political Development* 4, edited by K. Orren and S. Skowronek. New Haven, Conn.: Yale University Press.

_____. 1990a. "Self Reform as Political Reform in the Writings of John Stuart Mill." *Utilitas* 1: 242–58.

Ellis, Richard. 1974. *The Jeffersonian Crisis: Courts and Politics in the Young Republic.* New York: Norton.

Ely, Richard T. 1880. *French and German Socialism in Modern Times.* New York: Harper and Brothers.

_____. 1884. *Recent American Socialism.* Baltimore: Johns Hopkins University Press.

_____. 1889. *The Social Aspects of Christianity.* New York: Thomas Y. Crowell.

_____. 1890. "A Programme for Labor Reform." *Century* 39: 938–51.

_____. 1893. (Repr. 1908.) *Outlines of Economics.* Chautauqua, N.Y.: Chautauqua Press.

_____. 1903. *Studies in the Evolution of Industrial Society.* Chautauqua, N.Y.: Chautauqua Press.

_____. 1915. "Progressivism, True and False—An Outline." *Review of Reviews* 51 (February): 209–11.

_____. 1938. *Ground under Our Feet.* New York: Macmillan.

Ely, Richard T., and George R. Wicker. 1904. *Elementary Principles of Economics.* New York: Macmillan.

Encyclopedia of the Social Sciences. 1930. "Cartels" (3: 234–43); "Trusts" (15: 111–22); "Income Tax" (7: 626–39).

Ernst, Eldon G. 1974. *Moment of Truth of Protestant America: Interchurch Campaigns Following World War I.* Missoula: University of Montana Press.

Everett, John R. 1946. *Religion in Economics: A Study of John Bates Clark, Richard T. Ely, and Simon N. Patten.* New York: King's Crown Press.

Fess, Simeon D. 1907. *The History of Political Theory and Party Organization in the United States.* Danville, N.Y.: World's Events Publishing.

Filene, Peter. 1970. "An Obituary for the 'Progressive Movement.'" *American Quarterly* 22:20–34.

Fine, Sidney. 1964. (Orig. ed. 1956). *Laissez-Faire and the General Welfare State.* Ann Arbor: University of Michigan Press.

Fitzpatrick, Ellen. 1990. *Endless Crusade: Women Social Scientists and Progressive Reform.* New York: Oxford University Press.

Follett, Mary Parker. 1934. (Orig. ed. 1918). *The New State*. London and New York: Longmans, Green.

Forcey, Charles. 1961. *Crossroads of Liberalism: Croly, Weyl, Lippman, and the Progressive Era*. New York: Oxford University Press.

Ford, Henry Jones. 1898. *The Rise and Growth of American Politics; A Sketch of Constitutional Development*. New York: Macmillan.

Formisano, Ronald . 1974. "Deferential-Participant Politics: The Early American Political Culture, 1789-1840." *American Political Science Review* 68: 473-87.

Foster, Charles I. 1960. *An Errand of Mercy: The Evangelical United Front, 1790-1837*. Chapel Hill: University of North Carolina Press.

Foster, James C. 1986. *The Ideology of Apolitical Politics: The Elite Lawyers' Response to the Legitimation Crisis in American Capitalism*. Millwood, N.Y.: Associated Faculty Press.

Fox, Daniel. 1967. *The Discovery of Abundance: Simon N. Patten and the Transformation of Social Theory*. Ithaca, N.Y.: Cornell University Press.

Fredrickson, George M. 1965. *The Inner Civil War: Northern Intellectuals and the Crisis of the Union*. New York: Harper and Row.

Freeden, Michael. 1978. *The New Liberalism: An Ideology of Social Reform*. Oxford: Oxford University Press.

Friedman, Lawrence M. 1985. *History of American Law*. New York: Simon and Schuster.

Furniss, Norman F. 1954. *The Fundamentalist Controversy, 1918-1931*. New Haven, Conn.: Yale University Press.

Gabriel, Ralph H. 1956. (Orig. ed. 1940). *The Course of American Democratic Thought*. New York: Roland Press.

Galambos, Louis. 1970. "The Emerging Organizational Synthesis in Modern American History." *Business History Review* 44: 279-90.

Galambos, Louis, and Joseph Pratt. 1988. *The Rise of the Corporate Commonwealth: U.S. Business and Public Policy in the Twentieth Century*. New York: Basic Books.

Galston, William A. 1989. "Civic Education in the Liberal State." In *Liberalism and the Moral Life*, edited by Nancy Rosenblum. Cambridge, Mass.: Harvard University Press.

————. 1991. *Liberal Purposes: Goods, Virtues, and Diversity in the Liberal State*. New York: Cambridge University Press.

Gaustad, Edwin Scott. 1962. *Historical Atlas of Religion in America*. New York: Harper and Row.

George, Henry, Jr. 1906. *The Menace of Privilege: A Study of the Dangers to the Republic from the Existence of a Favored Class*. New York: Macmillan.

Giankos, Perry E., and Albert Karson. 1966. *American Diplomacy and the Sense of National Destiny*. 2 vols. Vol. 1, *The Initial Thrust, 1885-1900*. Vol. 2, *In the World Arena, 1901-1918*. Belmont, Calif.: Wadsworth.

Giddings, Franklin H. 1896. *Principles of Sociology*. New York: Macmillan.

————. 1898. *Elements of Sociology*. New York: Macmillan.

————. 1900. (Repr. 1970). *Democracy and Empire*. Freeport, N.Y.: Books for Libraries Press.

————. 1904. "Sociological Questions." *Forum* 45: 245-55.

————. 1912. "The Quality of Civilization." *American Journal of Sociology* 17: 581-89.

————. 1916. "The Democracy of Universal Military Service." *Annals of the American Academy* 66: 173-80.

_____. 1974. (Orig. ed. 1924). *The Scientific Study of Human Society.* Chapel Hill: University of North Carolina Press.

Gienapp, William E. 1987. *The Origins of the Republican Party, 1852-1856.* New York: Oxford University Press.

Gilman, Charlotte Perkins. 1890. *A Clarion Call to Redeem the Race: The Burden of Mothers.* Mt. Lebanon, N.Y.: Shaker Press.

_____. 1898. *Women and Economics: A Study of the Economic Relation between Men and Women as a Factor in Social Evolution.* Boston: Small, Maynard.

_____. 1972. (Orig. ed. 1903). *The Home, Its Work and Influence.* Urbana: University of Illinois Press.

_____. 1904. *Human Work.* New York: McClure, Phillips.

_____. 1909. "How Home Conditions React upon the Family." *American Journal of Sociology* 14: 592-605.

_____. 1971. (Orig. ed. 1911). *The Man-Made World, or Our Androcentric Culture.* New York: Johnson Reprint.

Gladden, Washington. 1892. "The Problem of Poverty." *Century* 45: 245-56.

Glendon, Mary. 1991. *Rights Talk: The Impoverishment of Political Discourse.* New York: Free Press.

Gossett, Thomas F. 1963. *Race: The History of an Idea in America.* Dallas: Southern Methodist University Press.

Graham, Otis L., Jr. 1967. *An Encore for Reform: The Old Progressives and the New Deal.* New York: Oxford University Press.

Greene, Jack. 1984. "Suffrage." In *The Encyclopedia of American Political History.* New York: Scribner.

Greenstone, J. David. 1986. "Political Culture and American Political Development: Liberty, Union and Liberal BiPolarity." In *Studies in American Political Development* 1, edited by K. Orren and S. Skowronek. New Haven, Conn.: Yale University Press.

Grimes, Alan P. 1980. (Orig. ed. 1967). *The Puritan Ethic and Woman Suffrage.* Westport, Conn.: Greenwood Press.

Gutman, Amy. 1989. "Undemocratic Education." In *Liberalism and the Moral Life,* edited by Nancy Rosenblum. Cambridge, Mass.: Harvard University Press.

Gutman, Herbert G. 1976. *Work, Culture, and Society in Industrializing America.* New York: Alfred A. Knopf.

Hadley, Arthur Twining. 1885. *Railroad Transportation.* New York and London: G. P. Putnam's Sons.

_____. 1896. *Economics: An Account of the Relations between Private Property and Public Welfare.* New York and London: G. P. Putnam's Sons.

_____. 1901. *The Education of the American Citizen.* New York: Charles Scribner's Sons.

_____. 1903. *The Relations between Freedom and Responsibility in the Evolution of Democratic Government.* New Haven, Conn.: Yale University Press.

_____. 1925. *The Conflict between Liberty and Equality.* Boston and New York: Houghton Mifflin.

Hall, Kermit L. 1989. *The Magic Mirror: Law in American History.* New York: Oxford University Press.

Hall, Peter D. 1982. *The Organization of American Culture 1700-1900: Private Institutions, Elites and the Origins of American Nationality.* New York: New York University Press.

Handy, Robert T. 1984. *A Christian America: Protestant Hopes and Historical Realities.* 2d ed. New York: Oxford University Press.

————. 1990. "Protestant Theological Tensions and Political Styles in the Progressive Period." In *Religion and American Politics from the Colonial Period to the 1980s,* edited by Mark A. Noll. New York: Oxford University Press.

Hart, James Morgan. 1874. *German Universities: A Narrative of Personal Experiences.* New York: G. P. Putnam's Sons.

Hartz, Louis. 1948. *Economic Policy and Democratic Thought: Pennsylvania, 1776–1860.* Cambridge, Mass.: Harvard University Press.

————. 1955. *The Liberal Tradition in America.* New York: Harcourt, Brace and World.

Haskell, Thomas. 1977. *The Emergence of Professional Social Science: The American Social Science Association and the Nineteenth Century Crisis of Authority.* Urbana: University of Illinois Press.

Hawley, Ellis W. 1978. "The Discovery of a 'Corporate Liberalism.'" *Business History Review* 52: 309–20.

Heidenheimer, Arnold J. 1981. "Education and Social Security Entitlements in Europe and America." In *The Development of Welfare States in Europe and America,* edited by Peter Flora and Arnold J. Heidenheimer. New Brunswick, N.J.: Transaction Books.

Herberg, Will. 1983. (Orig. ed. 1955). *Protestant, Catholic, Jew.* Chicago: University of Chicago Press.

Herbst, Jurgen. 1959. "From Moral Philosophy to Sociology: Albion Woodbury Small." *Harvard Educational Review* 29: 227–44.

————. 1965. *The German Historical School in American Scholarship.* Ithaca, N.Y.: Cornell University Press.

Herron, George D. 1894. *The Christian Society.* Chicago: Fleming H. Revell.

Hilton, Boyd. 1988. *The Age of Atonement: The Influence of Evangelicalism on Social and Economic Thought, 1795–1865.* Oxford: Clarendon Press.

Hobhouse, Leonard T. 1899. "The Progressive Movement Abroad I: The United States." *Progressive Review* (January): 359–61.

————. 1911. "The New Spirit in America." *Contemporary Review* 100: 1–10.

Hofstadter, Richard. 1948. *The American Political Tradition and the Men Who Made It.* New York: Vintage Books.

————. 1955. *Age of Reform: From Bryan to FDR.* New York: Alfred A. Knopf.

————. 1962. *Anti-intellectualism in American Life.* New York: Vintage Books.

Hofstadter, Richard, and Wilson Smith, eds. 1961. *American Higher Education: A Documentary History.* Vols. 1 and 2. Chicago: University of Chicago Press.

Holmes, Stephen. 1989. "The Permanent Structure of Antiliberal Thought." In *Liberalism and the Moral Life,* edited by Nancy Rosenblum. Cambridge, Mass.: Harvard University Press.

Hopkins, Charles H. 1940. *The Rise of the Social Gospel in American Protestantism, 1865–1915.* New Haven, Conn.: Yale University Press.

Horwitz, Morton J. 1992. *The Transformation of American Law, 1870–1960: The Crisis of Legal Orthodoxy.* New York: Oxford University Press.

Howe, Daniel Walker. 1979. *The Political Culture of the American Whigs.* Chicago: University of Chicago Press.

————. 1990. "Religion and Politics in the Antebellum North." In *Religion and American Politics from the Colonial Period to the 1980s,* edited by Mark A. Noll. New York: Oxford University Press.

Hughes, Charles Evans. 1910. *Conditions of Progress in Democratic Government.* New Haven, Conn.: Yale University Press.

Hunter, James Davison. 1991. *Culture Wars: The Struggle to Define America.* New York: Basic Books.

Huntington, Samuel P. 1980. *American Politics: The Promise of Disharmony.* Cambridge, Mass.: Harvard University Press.

Hurst, Willard. 1956. *Law and the Conditions of Freedom in the Nineteenth-Century U.S.* Madison: University of Wisconsin Press.

Hutchison, William R. 1976. *The Modernist Impulse in American Protestantism.* New York: Oxford University Press.

———. 1987. *Errand to the World: American Protestant Thought and Foreign Missions.* Chicago: University of Chicago Press.

Jaenicke, Douglas W. 1986. "The Jacksonian Integration of Parties into the Constitutional System." *Political Science Quarterly* 101: 85–107.

James, Edmund J. 1886. "The State as an Economic Factor." *Science Economic Discussion.* New York: The Science Company.

———. 1895. "Bryce's 'American Commonwealth.'" *Annals of the American Academy* 7: 377–410.

———. 1899. "The Growth of Great Cities in Area and Population." *Annals of the American Academy* 13: 1–30.

James, Scott C. 1992. "A Party System Perspective on the Interstate Commerce Act of 1887: The Democracy, Electoral College Competition, and the Politics of Coalition Maintenance." In *Studies in American Political Development* 6, edited by K. Orren and S. Skowronek. New York: Cambridge University Press.

Jameson, John Franklin, ed. 1889. *Essays in the Constitutional History of the United States in the Formative Period, 1775–1789.* Boston: Houghton Mifflin.

Jandy, Edward Clarence. 1942. *Charles Horton Cooley: His Life and His Social Theory.* New York: Dryden Press.

Jensen, Richard J. 1971. *The Winning of the Mid-West: Social and Political Conflict, 1888–1896.* Chicago: University of Chicago Press.

Johnson, Diane. 1992. "Something for the Boys." *New York Review of Books,* 16 January, 16.

Johnson, Donald B., and Kirk H. Porter. 1975. *National Party Platforms, 1840–1972.* 5th ed. Urbana: University of Illinois Press.

Kann, Mark E. 1990. "Individualism, Civic Virtue, and Gender in America." *Studies in American Political Development* 4, edited by K. Orren and S. Skowronek. New Haven, Conn.: Yale University Press.

Kateb, George. 1989. "Democratic Individuality and the Meaning of Rights." In *Liberalism and the Moral Life,* edited by Nancy Rosenblum. Cambridge, Mass.: Harvard University Press.

Keith, John A. H., and William C. Bagley. 1920. *The Nation and the Schools.* New York: Macmillan.

Keller, Morton. 1977. *Affairs of State: Public Life in Late Nineteenth Century America.* Cambridge, Mass.: Harvard University Press.

———. 1980. "Anglo-American Politics, 1900–1930." *Comparative Studies in Society and History* 22: 458–77.

———. 1981. "The Pluralist State: American Economic Regulation in Comparative Perspective, 1900–1930." In *Regulation in Perspective: Historical Essays,* edited by Thomas K. McGraw. Cambridge, Mass.: Harvard University Press.

Kelley, Florence. 1905. *Some Ethical Gains through Legislation.* New York: Macmillan.

Kelley, Robert Lloyd. 1979. *The Cultural Pattern in American Politics: The First Century.* New York: Alfred A. Knopf.

Kelly, Alfred H., Winfred A. Harbison, and Herman Belz. 1983. *The American Constitution: Its Origin and Development.* 6th ed. New York: W. W. Norton.

Kennedy, David M. 1975. "Progressivism: An Overview." *Historian* 37: 453–68.

———. 1980. *Over Here: The First World War and American Society.* New York: Oxford University Press.

Kleppner, Paul. 1970. *The Cross of Culture: A Social Analysis of Midwestern Politics 1850–1900.* New York: Free Press.

———. 1978. "From Ethnoreligious Conflict to 'Social Harmony': Coalitional and Party Transformations in the 1890s." In *Emerging Coalitions in American Politics*, edited by Seymour M. Lipset. San Francisco: Institute for Contemporary Studies.

———. 1987. *Continuity and Change in Electoral Politics, 1893–1928.* Westport, Conn.: Greenwood Press.

Kloppenberg, James T. 1986. *Uncertain Victory: Social Democracy and Progressivism in European and American Thought.* New York: Oxford University Press.

Koistinen, Paul A. C. 1967. "The 'Industrial-Military Complex' in Historical Perspective: World War I." *Business History Review* 41: 378–403.

Kohl, Lawrence Frederick. 1989. *The Politics of Individualism: Parties and the American Character in the Jacksonian Era.* New York: Oxford University Press.

Kousser, J. Morgan. 1974. *The Shaping of Southern Politics: Suffrage Restriction and the Establishment of the One-Party South, 1880–1910.* New Haven, Conn.: Yale University Press.

Kraditor, Aileen. 1965. *The Idea of the Woman Suffrage Movement, 1890–1920.* New York: Columbia University Press.

Kramnick, Isaac. 1990. *Republicanism and Bourgeois Radicalism.* Ithaca, N.Y.: Cornell University Press.

Kuklick, Bruce. 1985. *Churchmen and Philosophers: From Jonathan Edwards to John Dewey.* New Haven, Conn.: Yale University Press.

Landis, James M. 1938. *The Administrative Process.* New Haven, Conn.: Yale University Press.

Lange, Lynda. 1991. "Rousseau and Modern Feminism." In *Feminist Interpretations and Political Theory*, edited by Mary Lyndon Shanley and Carole Pateman. University Park: Pennsylvania State University Press, 1991.

Lasch, Christopher. 1965. *The New Radicalism in America, 1889–1963.* New York: Vintage Books.

———. 1973. *The World of Nations.* New York: Alfred A. Knopf.

Letwin, Shirley Robin. 1965. *Pursuit of Certainty.* Cambridge: Cambridge University Press.

Letwin, William. 1965. *Law and Economic Policy in America: The Evolution of the Sherman Antitrust Act.* New York: Random House.

Levinson, Sanford. 1988. *Constitutional Faith.* Princeton, N.J.: Princeton University Press.

Levy, David W. 1985. *Herbert Croly of "The New Republic."* Princeton, N.J.: Princeton University Press.

Levy, Michael. 1988. *Political Thought in America.* Chicago: Dorsey Press.

Link, Arthur S. 1959. "What Happened to the Progressive Movement in the 1920s?" *American Historical Review* 64: 833–51.

Lippman, Walter. 1916. "What Program Shall the United States Stand For in International Relations?" *Annals of the American Academy* 66: 60–70.

———. 1961. *Drift and Mastery: An Attempt to Diagnose Our Current Unrest*. Englewood Cliffs, N.J.: Prentice-Hall.

Low, Seth. 1892. "The Government of Cities in the United States." *Century* 42: 730–36.

Lowi, Theodore. 1969. *The End of Liberalism*. New York: W. W. Norton.

Lustig, R. Jeffrey. 1982. *Corporate Liberalism: The Origins of Modern American Political Theory, 1890–1920*. Berkeley: University of California Press.

McClymer, John F. 1980. *War and Welfare: Social Engineering in America, 1890–1925*. Westport, Conn.: Greenwood Press.

McCorkle, Pope. 1984. "The Historian as Intellectual: Charles Beard and the Constitution Reconsidered." *American Journal of Legal History* 28: 314–63.

McCormick, Richard L. 1974. "Ethno-Cultural Interpretations of Nineteenth-Century American Voting Behavior." *Political Science Quarterly* 89: 351–77.

———. 1986. *The Party Period and Public Policy: American Politics from the Age of Jackson to the Progressive Era*. New York: Oxford University Press.

McCoy, Drew. 1980. *The Elusive Republic: Political Economy in Jeffersonian America*. Chapel Hill: University of North Carolina Press.

McCraw, Thomas K. 1984. *Prophets of Regulation*. Cambridge, Mass.: Harvard University Press.

McCurdy, Charles W. 1978. "American Law and the Marketing Structure of the Large Corporation." *Journal of Economic History* 38: 631–49.

Macedo, Stephen. 1990. *Liberal Virtues: Citizenship, Virtue, and Community in Liberal Constitutionalism*. Oxford: Clarendon Press.

McGerr, Michael E. 1986. *The Decline of Popular Politics: The American North, 1865–1928*. New York: Oxford University Press.

McKitrick, Eric L. 1967. "Party Politics and the Union and Confederate War Efforts." In *The American Party Systems*, edited by William N. Chambers and Walter D. Burnham. New York: Oxford University Press.

McPherson, James M. 1975. *The Abolitionist Legacy*. Princeton, N.J.: Princeton University Press.

Mann, Arthur. 1955. "British Social Thought and American Reformers of the Progressive Era." *Mississippi Valley Historical Review* 42: 672–92.

Marsden, George. 1980. *Fundamentalism and American Culture*. New York: Oxford University Press.

Mathews, Basil. 1934. *John R. Mott, World Citizen*. New York: Harper and Brothers.

Mathews, Lois Kimball. 1909. (Repr. 1962). *The Expansion of New England: The Spread of New England Settlement and Institutions to the Mississippi River, 1620–1865*. New York: Russell and Russell.

Mathews, Shailer. 1897. *The Social Teachings of Jesus: An Essay in Christian Sociology.* New York: Macmillan.

———. 1918. *Patriotism and Religion*. New York: Macmillan.

———. 1936. *New Faith for Old: An Autobiography.* New York: Macmillan.

Merriam, Charles Edward. 1903. (Repr. 1968). *A History of American Political Theories*. New York: Russell and Russell.

———. 1920. *American Political Ideas: Studies in the Development of American Political Thought, 1865–1917*. New York: Macmillan.

Mill, John Stuart. 1969. "Coleridge." In *Collected Works of John Stuart Mill.* Vol. 10, *Essays on Ethics, Religion, and Society,* edited by John M. Robson. Toronto: University of Toronto Press.

———. 1986. "Spirit of the Age." In *Collected Works of John Stuart Mill.* Vol. 22, *Newspaper Writings,* edited by Ann P. and John M. Robson. Toronto: University of Toronto Press.

Mill, John Stuart, and Harriet Taylor Mill. 1970. In *Essays on Sex Equality,* edited by Alice S. Rossi. Chicago: University of Chicago Press.

Miller, Perry. 1967. *Nature's Nation.* Cambridge, Mass.: Harvard University Press.

———, ed. 1962. *The Legal Mind in America.* Garden City, N.Y.: Doubleday.

Mills, C. Wright. 1951. *White Collar: The American Middle Classes.* New York: Oxford University Press.

———. 1964. *Sociology and Pragmatism.* New York: Paine Publishers.

Mooney, Christopher F. 1990. *Boundaries Dimly Perceived: Law, Religion, Education, and the Common Good.* Notre Dame, Ind.: University of Notre Dame Press.

Morey, William C. 1891. "The Genesis of a Written Constitution." *Annals of the American Academy* 1: 529–57.

Morgan, Edmund S. 1972. "Slavery and Freedom: The American Paradox." *Journal of American History* 59: 5–29.

Morgan, Kenneth O. 1976. "The Future at Work: Anglo-American Progressivism, 1870–1917." In *Contrast and Connection: Bicentennial Essays in Anglo-American History,* edited by H. C. Allen and Roger Thompson. Athens: Ohio University Press.

Mott, Frank Luther. 1957. *A History of American Magazines, 1850–1865.* Vol. 2. Cambridge, Mass.: Harvard University Press.

———. 1957a. *A History of American Magazines, 1865–1885.* Vol. 3. Cambridge, Mass.: Harvard University Press.

———. 1957b. *A History of American Magazines, 1885–1905.* Vol. 4. Cambridge, Mass.: Harvard University Press.

Nearing, Scott. 1925. *Educational Frontiers: A Book about Simon N. Patten and Other Teachers.* New York: T. Seltzer.

Nearing, Scott, and Nellie M. S. Nearing. 1917. (Orig. ed. 1912). *Women and Social Progress: A Discussion of the Biologic, Domestic, Industrial and Social Possibilities of American Women.* New York: Macmillan.

Ninkovich, Frank. 1986. "Theodore Roosevelt: Civilization as Ideology." *Diplomatic History* 9: 221–45.

Noble, David W. 1965. *Historians against History: The Frontier Thesis and the National Covenant in American Historical Writing since 1830.* Minneapolis: University of Minnesota Press.

Noll, Mark A., ed. 1990. *Religion and American Politics from the Colonial Period to the 1980s.* New York: Oxford University Press.

Norton, Anne. 1986. *Alternative Americas: A Reading of Antebellum Political Culture.* Chicago: University of Chicago Press.

Okin, Susan Moller. 1989. "Humanist Liberalism." In *Liberalism and the Moral Life,* edited by Nancy Rosenblum. Cambridge, Mass.: Harvard University Press.

Oleson, Alexandra, and John Voss, eds. 1979. *The Organization of Knowledge in Modern America.* Baltimore: Johns Hopkins University Press.

Outlook. 1909 and 1910. Reviews of *Promise of American Life* by Herbert Croly. 4 December 1909, 788–89 and 16 April 1910, 830–31.

Orloff, Ann Shola. 1988. "The Political Origins of America's Belated Welfare State." In *The Politics of Social Policy in the United States*, edited by Margaret Weir, Ann Shola Orloff, and Theda Skocpol. Princeton, N.J.: Princeton University Press.

Orloff, Ann Shola, and Theda Skocpol. 1984. "Why Not Equal Protection? Explaining the Politics of Public Social Spending in Britain, 1900–1911, and the United States, 1880s–1920." *American Sociological Review* 49: 726–50.

Parsons, Frank. 1904. *The City for the People*. Philadelphia: C. F. Taylor.

Patten, Simon N. 1886. "The Effect of the Consumption of Wealth on the Economic Welfare of Society." In Simon N. Patten, *Essays in Economic Theory*, edited by Rexford Tugwell. New York: Alfred A. Knopf, 1924.

———. 1889. "The Consumption of Wealth." *Political Economy and Public Law Series* No. 4. Philadelphia: Publications of the University of Pennsylvania.

———. 1889a. "Malthus and Ricardo." In Simon N. Patten, *Essays in Economic Theory*, edited by Rexford Tugwell. New York: Alfred A. Knopf, 1924.

———. 1890. "The Decay of Local Government in America." *Annals of the American Academy* 1: 26–42.

———. 1896. *The Theory of Social Forces*. Philadelphia: American Academy of Political and Social Science.

———. 1899. *The Development of English Thought: A Study in the Economic Interpretation of History*. New York: Macmillan.

———. 1902. "The Theory of Dynamic Economics." In Simon N. Patten, *Essays in Economic Theory*, edited by Rexford Tugwell. New York: Alfred A. Knopf, 1924.

———. 1902a. *The Theory of Prosperity*. New York: Macmillan.

———. 1903. *Heredity and Social Progress*. New York: Macmillan.

———. 1907. *The New Basis of Civilization*. New York: Macmillan.

———. 1908. "The Political Significance of Recent Economic Theories." In Simon N. Patten, *Essays in Economic Theory*, edited by Rexford Tugwell. New York: Alfred A. Knopf, 1924.

———. 1912. "The Reconstruction of Economic Theory." In Simon N. Patten, *Essays in Economic Theory*, edited by Rexford Tugwell. New York: Alfred A. Knopf, 1924.

———. 1916. "Taxation after the War." *Annals of the American Academy* 64: 210–14.

———. 1916a. "The Basis of National Security." *Annals of the American Academy* 66: 1–11.

———. 1924. *Essays in Economic Theory*. Ed. Rexford Tugwell. New York: Alfred A. Knopf.

Perkins, Bradford. 1968. *The Great Rapprochement: England and the United States, 1895–1914*. New York: Atheneum.

Perry, Michael J. 1988. *Morality, Politics, and Law*. New York: Oxford University Press.

Perry, Ralph Barton. 1935. *The Thought and Character of William James*. Vol. 2. Boston: Little, Brown.

Peterson, H. C., and Fite, G. C. 1957. *Opponents of War, 1917–1918*. Madison: University of Wisconsin Press.

Peterson, Merrill D., ed. 1966. *Democracy, Liberty, and Property: The State Constitutional Conventions of the 1820s*. Indianapolis: Bobbs-Merrill Company

Pisani, Donald. 1987. "Promotion and Regulation: Constitutionalism and the American Economy." *Journal of American History* 74: 740–68.

Pivar, David J. 1973. *Purity Crusade: Sexual Morality and Social Control, 1868–1900.* Westport, Conn.: Greenwood Press.

Quandt, Jean B. 1970. *From the Small Town to the Great Community: The Social Thought of Progressive Intellectuals.* New Brunswick, N.J.: Rutgers University Press.

Rabban, David M. 1981. "The First Amendment in Its Forgotten Years." *Yale Law Journal* 90: 514–95.

————. 1983. "The Emergence of Modern First Amendment Doctrine." *University of Chicago Law Review* 50: 1205–1355.

Rauschenbusch, Walter. 1914. *Christianity and the Social Crisis.* London: Macmillan.

————. 1945. (Orig. ed. 1917). *A Theology for the Social Gospel.* Nashville: Abingdon Press.

Rawls, John. 1985. "Justice as Fairness: Political, Not Metaphysical." *Philosophy and Public Affairs* 17: 223–48.

Remini, Robert Vincent. 1988. *The Legacy of Andrew Jackson: Essays on Democracy, Indian Removal, and Slavery.* Baton Rouge: Louisiana State University Press.

Ricci, David. 1984. *The Tragedy of Political Science: Politics, Scholarship, and Democracy.* New Haven, Conn.: Yale University Press.

Robertson, A. T. 1919. *The New Citizenship: The Christian Facing a New World Order.* Chicago: Fleming H. Revell.

Robinson, James Harvey. 1890. "The Original and Derived Features of the Constitution." *Annals of the American Academy* 1: 203–43.

Rodgers, Daniel T. 1982. "In Search of Progressivism." *Reviews in American History* 10: 113–32.

Root, Elihu. 1907. *The Citizen's Part in Government.* New Haven, Conn.: Yale University Press.

Rosenberg, Emily S. 1982. *Spreading the American Dream: American Economic and Cultural Expansion, 1890–1945.* New York: Hill and Wang.

Rosenblum, Nancy. 1987. *Another Liberalism.* Cambridge, Mass.: Harvard University Press.

————, ed. 1989. *Liberalism and the Moral Life.* Cambridge, Mass.: Harvard University Press.

————. 1989a. "Pluralism and Self-Defense." In *Liberalism and the Moral Life,* edited by Nancy Rosenblum. Cambridge, Mass.: Harvard University Press.

Ross, Dorothy. 1977. "Socialism and American Liberalism: Academic Social Thought in the 1890s." In *Perspectives in American History* 11, edited by Donald Fleming. Cambridge, Mass.: Harvard University Press.

————. 1979. "The Development of the Social Sciences in America, 1865–1920." In *The Organization of Knowledge in Modern America,* edited by Alexandra Oleson and John Voss. Baltimore: Johns Hopkins University Press.

————. 1990. *Origins of American Social Science.* New York: Cambridge University Press.

Ross, Edward Alsworth. 1901. "The Causes of Racial Superiority." *Annals of the American Academy* 18: 67–89.

————. 1905. *Foundations of Sociology.* New York: Macmillan.

———. 1907. *Sin and Society: An Analysis of Latter Day Iniquity.* Boston: Houghton Mifflin.

———. 1908. *Social Psychology.* New York: Macmillan.

———. 1914. *The Old World in the New: The Significance of Past and Present Immigration to the American People.* New York: Century Company.

———. 1918. *Social Control: A Survey of the Foundations of Order.* New York: Macmillan.

Samuels, Warren J. 1973. "The Economy as a System of Power and Its Legal Basis: The Legal Economics of Robert Lee Hale." *University of Miami Law Review* 27: 261–371.

Sandel, Michael J. 1984. "The Procedural Republic and the Unencumbered Self." *Political Theory* 12: 81–95.

Sanders, Elizabeth. 1982. "Business, Bureaucracy, and the Bourgeoisie: The New Deal Legacy." In *The Political Economy of Public Policy,* edited by Alan Stone and Edward Harpham. Beverly Hills, Calif.: Sage.

———. 1990. "Farmers and the State in the Progressive Era." In *Changes in the State,* edited by Edward S. Greenberg and Thomas F. Mayer. Beverley Hills, Calif.: Sage.

Sarasohn, David. 1989. *The Party of Reform: Democrats in the Progressive Era.* Jackson: University Press of Mississippi.

Schaffer, Ronald. 1991. *America in the Great War: The Rise of the War Welfare State.* New York: Oxford University Press.

Scheiber, Harry N. 1972. "Government and the Economy: Studies in the Commonwealth Policy in Nineteenth-century America." *Journal of Interdisciplinary History* 3: 135–51.

———. 1973. "Property Law, Expropriation and Resource Allocation by Government: The U.S., 1789–1910." *Journal of Economic History* 33: 232–51.

Schneider, Herbert W. 1946. *A History of American Philosophy.* New York: Columbia University Press.

Schwendinger, Herman, and Julia R. Schwendinger. 1974. *The Sociologists of the Chair: A Radical Analysis of the Formative Years of North American Sociology (1883–1922).* New York: Basic Books.

Scudder, Vida Dutton. 1898. *Social Ideals in English Letters.* Boston and New York: Houghton Mifflin.

Seidelman, Raymond. 1984. *Disenchanted Realists, Political Science and the American Crisis, 1884–1984.* Albany: State University of New York Press.

Seligman, Edwin R. A. 1887. "Railway Tariffs and the Interstate Commerce Law II." *Political Science Quarterly* 2: 396–413.

———. 1893. "Progressive Taxation." *Political Science Quarterly* 8: 220–51.

———. 1895. *Essays on Taxation.* New York: Macmillan.

———. 1905. *Principles of Economics.* Longmans, Green.

———. 1907. *The Economic Interpretation of History.* 2d ed., rev. New York: Columbia University Press.

Shanley, Mary Lyndon, and Carole Pateman, eds. 1991. *Feminist Interpretations and Political Theory.* University Park: Pennsylvania State University Press.

Shaw, Albert. 1895. *Municipal Government in Continental Europe.* New York: Macmillan.

———. 1895. *Municipal Government in Great Britain.* New York: Macmillan.

Shefter, Martin. 1978. "Party, Bureaucracy, and Political Change in the United States." *Political Parties: Development and Decay,* edited by Louis Maisel and Joseph Cooper. Beverly Hills, Calif.: Sage.

Sheldon, Garrett Ward. 1991. *The Political Philosophy of Thomas Jefferson.* Baltimore: Johns Hopkins University Press.

Shils, Edward. 1979. "The Order of Learning in the United States: The Ascendancy of the University." In *The Organization of Knowledge in Modern America, 1860–1920,* edited by Alexandra Oleson and John Voss. Baltimore: Johns Hopkins University Press.

Silbey, Joel H. 1991. *The American Political Nation, 1838–1893.* Stanford, Calif.: Stanford University Press.

Silva, Edward T., and Sheila A. Slaughter. 1984. *Serving Power: The Making of the Academic Social Science Expert.* Westport, Conn.: Greenwood Press.

Sklar, Martin J. 1988. *The Corporate Reconstruction of American Capitalism, 1890–1916.* Cambridge: Cambridge University Press.

Skocpol, Theda. 1983. "The Legacies of New Deal Liberalism." In *Liberalism Reconsidered,* edited by Douglas MacLean and Claudia Mills. Totowa, N.J.: Rowman and Allanheld.

———. 1992. *Protecting Soldiers and Mothers: The Political Origins of Social Policy in the United States.* Cambridge, Mass.: Harvard University Press.

Skowronek, Steven. 1982. *Building a New American State: The Expansion of National Administrative Capacities, 1877–1920.* New York: Cambridge University Press.

Sloane, William M. 1891. "Pensions and Socialism." *Century* 42: 179–88.

Small, Albion. 1895. "Private Business Is a Public Trust." *American Journal of Sociology* 1: 276–89.

———. 1895a. "The State and Semi-Public Corporations." *American Journal of Sociology* 1: 398–410.

———. 1905. *General Sociology.* Chicago: University of Chicago Press.

———. 1912. "Socialism in the Light of Social Science." *American Journal of Sociology* 17: 804–19.

———. 1913. *Between Eras: From Capitalism to Democracy.* Chicago: Victor W. Bruder.

———. 1914. "The Social Gradations of Capital." *American Journal of Sociology* 19: 721–52.

———. 1915. "The Bonds of Nationality." *American Journal of Sociology* 20: 629–83.

———. 1919. "The Church and Class Conflicts." *American Journal of Sociology* 24: 481–501.

Smally, E. V. 1882. "A Great Charity Reform." *Century* 2: 401–8.

Smith, James Allen. 1965. *The Spirit of American Government.* Cambridge, Mass.: Harvard University Press.

Soloman, Barbara. 1956. *Ancestors and Immigrants: A Changing New England Tradition.* Cambridge, Mass.: Harvard University Press.

Stead, William Thomas. 1902. *The Americanization of the World.* New York and London: H. Markley.

———. 1964. (Orig. ed. 1894). *If Christ Came to Chicago: A Plea for the Union of All Who Love in Service of All Who Suffer.* New York: Living Books.

Steel, Ronald. 1980. *Walter Lippman and the American Century.* Boston: Little, Brown.

Sterne, Simon. 1882. *Constitutional History and Political Development of the United States.* New York: Cassell, Petter, Galpin.

Stettner, Edward A. 1993. *Shaping Modern Liberalism: Herbert Croly and Progressive Thought.* Lawrence: University Press of Kansas.

Stevens, Robert. 1983. *Law School*. Chapel Hill: University of North Carolina Press.

Stevenson, Louise L. 1986. *Scholarly Means to Evangelical Ends: The New Haven Scholars and the Transformation of Higher Learning in America, 1830–1890*. Baltimore: Johns Hopkins University Press.

Stokes, Melvyn. 1983. "American Progressives and the European Left." *Journal of American Studies* 17: 5–28.

Story, Joseph. 1833. *Commentaries on the United States Constitution*. Boston: Little, Brown.

Stout, Harry S. 1990. "Rhetoric and Reality in the Early Republic: The Case of the Federalist Clergy." In *Religion and American Politics from the Colonial Period to the 1980s*, edited by Mark A. Noll. New York: Oxford University Press.

Strong, Josiah. 1893. *The New Era, or The Coming Kingdom*. New York: Baker & Taylor.

―――. 1963. (Orig. ed. 1885). *Our Country*. Cambridge, Mass.: Harvard University Press.

Szasz, Ferenc Morton. 1982. *The Divided Mind of Protestant America, 1880–1930*. University: University of Alabama Press.

Taft, William Howard. 1906. *Four Aspects of Civic Duty*. New Haven, Conn.: Yale University Press.

Tarbell, Ida. 1924. *In the Footsteps of the Lincolns*. New York: Harper and Brothers.

Taylor, Charles. 1985. *Human Agency and Language: Philosophical Papers I*. Cambridge: Cambridge University Press.

―――. 1989. "Cross Purposes: The Liberal-Communitarian Debate." In *Liberalism and the Moral Life*, edited by Nancy Rosenblum. Cambridge, Mass.: Harvard University Press.

Thelen, David Paul. 1972. *The New Citizenship: The Origins of Progressivism in Wisconsin, 1885–1890*. Columbia: University of Missouri Press.

Thompson, John A. 1987. *Reformers and War: American Progressive Publicists and the First World War*. New York: Cambridge University Press.

Thorpe, Francis N. 1970. (Orig. ed. 1901). *The Constitutional History of the American People, 1876–1895*. New York: Da Capo Press.

―――. 1902. "What Is a Constitutional History of the United States?" *Annals of the American Academy* 19: 95–101.

Tiedeman, Christopher. 1890. *The Unwritten Constitution of the United States*. New York: Putnam.

Timberlake, James. 1963. *Prohibition and the Progressive Movement*. Cambridge, Mass.: Harvard University Press.

Tocqueville, Alexis de. 1981. *Democracy in America*. New York: Random House.

Tomsich, John. 1971. *A Genteel Endeavor: American Culture and Politics in the Gilded Age*. Stanford, Calif.: Stanford University Press.

Trachtenberg, Alan. 1982. *The Incorporation of America: Culture and Society in the Gilded Age*. New York: Hill and Wang.

Trolander, Judith Ann. 1987. *Professional and Social Change: From the Settlement House to Neighborhood Centers, 1866 to the Present*. New York: Columbia University Press.

United States Bureau of the Census. 1975. *Historical Statistics of the United States, Colonial Times to 1970. Bicentennial Edition*. Washington, D.C.

Vaughn, Stephen. 1980. *Holding Fast the Inner Lines: Democracy, National-*

ism, and the Committee on Public Information. Chapel Hill: University of North Carolina Press.

Veysey, Lawrence. 1965. *The Emergence of the American University.* Chicago: University of Chicago Press.

Walker, Francis A. 1882. "The Growth of the United States." *Century* 24: 920–26.

Walters, Ronald G. 1977. *The Antislavery Appeal: American Abolitionism after 1830.* Baltimore: Johns Hopkins University Press.

Walzer, Michael. 1983. *Spheres of Justice: A Defense of Pluralism and Equality.* New York: Basic Books.

Ward, Harry F. 1919. *The New Social Order.* New York: Macmillan.

Watson, Harry L. 1992. "The Ambiguous Legacy of Jacksonian Democracy." In *Democrats and the American Ideal,* edited by Peter B. Kolver. Washington, D.C.: Center for National Policy Press.

Weinberg, Julius. 1972. *Edward Alsworth Ross and the Sociology of Progressivism.* Madison: State Historical Society of Wisconsin.

Weinstein, James. 1967. *The Decline of Socialism in America.* New York.

———. 1968. *The Corporate Ideal in the Liberal State: 1900–1918.* Boston: Beacon Press.

Westbrook, Robert B. 1991. *John Dewey and American Democracy.* Ithaca, N.Y.: Cornell University Press.

Weyl, Walter. 1914. *The New Democracy.* New York: Harper and Row.

White, Ronald, and Charles H. Hopkins, eds. 1976. *The Social Gospel: Religion and Reform in Changing America.* Philadelphia: Temple University Press.

Whitman, Walt. 1926. *Leaves of Grass.* Garden City: Doubleday.

Wiebe, Robert H. 1967. *The Search for Order, 1877–1920.* New York: Hill and Wang.

Wills, Garry. 1987. *Reagan's America: Innocents at Home.* Garden City, N.Y.: Doubleday.

Wilson, Major. 1967. "The Concept of Time and the Political Dialogue in the United States, 1828–48." *American Quarterly* 19: 619–44.

———. 1974. *Space, Time, and Freedom: The Quest for Nationality and the Irrepressible Conflict. 1815–1851.* Westport, Conn.: Greenwood Press.

Wilson, Woodrow. 1908. *Constitutional Government.* New York: Columbia University Press.

Wood, Gordon. 1987. "Interests and Disinterestedness in the Making of the Constitution." In *Beyond Confederation: Origins of the Constitution and American National Identity,* edited by Richard Beeman et al. Chapel Hill: University of North Carolina Press.

Woodruff, Clinton Rogers. 1909. "Municipal Review 1907–1908." *American Journal of Sociology* 14: 465–96.

Wuthnow, Robert. 1989. *The Struggle for America's Soul: Evangelicals, Liberals, and Secularism.* Grand Rapids, Mich.: W. B. Eerdmans.

———. 1990. "Quid Obscuram: The Changing Terrain of Church-State Relations." In *Religion and American Politics from the Colonial Period to the 1980s,* edited by Mark A. Noll. New York: Oxford University Press.

Wynn, Neil A. 1986. *From Progressivism to Prosperity: World War I and American Society.* New York: Holmes & Meier.

Zunz, Olivier. 1990. *Making America Corporate, 1870–1920.* Chicago: University of Chicago Press.

INDEX